SEARCH OF THE
PERFECT CODE
DISCOVERED

L. A. ESPRIUX

Search of the Perfect Code Discovered
Copyright © 2022 by L. A. Espriux

All rights reserved. No part of this publication may be reproduced, distributed, or transmitted in any form or by any means, including photocopying, recording, or other electronic or mechanical methods, without the prior written permission of the author, except in the case of brief quotations embodied in critical reviews and certain other non-commercial uses permitted by copyright law.

ISBN
978-1-957378-01-5 (Paperback)
978-1-957378-00-8 (eBook)

Table of Contents

Chapter 1   The Riddle of Mortality 1
Chapter 2   A Religious Conundrum 13
Chapter 3   The Culture of Death 40
Chapter 4   Hardware Code of Biology 57
Chapter 5   Wonder that is the Mind 75
Chapter 6   Coming of Age 92
Chapter 7   Seeds of Man 116
Chapter 8   Civilization 139
Chapter 9   Space Ship Earth 152
Chapter 10 From Paradise Lost to Darwinism 170
Chapter 11 Monsters and Supermen 184
Chapter 12 Aliens in Hollywood Hills 206
Chapter 13 Age of Maschinenmensch 224
Chapter 14 Sympathetic Vibrations Here and Beyond ... 238
Chapter 15 Stuff of Angels 259
Chapter 16 A Human Equation 286
Chapter 17 The Seven Mountains 309
Chapter 18 Knowledge of Everything 340
Chapter 19 Counting Among the Sheep 352

Preface:

This book is a presentation of possibilities based on a uniquely subjective experience. It is a feeble attempt to speculate on potentials less rational to conventional interpretation. It asks many questions. Do spirits exist, and if so, what are they? What is the nature of angels, if there are any? Who were a race of super beings described only vaguely in the Book of Genesis called the *Nephilim*? Where did they come from and where did they go? Were there beings in flying saucer machines circling the earth in the days before the flood of Noah, and are they still here now? Are the fabled Neanderthals a product of evolution or the DNA evidence of mortal decline? And was Pangaea the substance of the fabled continent of Atlantis? More importantly, what is the face of evil upon the earth? Is the instrument of fanatical religious ideology a manifestation of God or the Devil; and did the rise of the Third Reich of Nazi Germany forever change mortal consciousness by opening a portal of Pandora evil that continues to cultivate to this day?

There is history we can know, and history we can only speculate. What empirical science can ascribe to with any degree of certainty is barely the tip of the iceberg between *4500 to 8000* years ago. This history paints the portrait of ancient societal men, as sophisticated and human as our present homo sapient model. But the Holy Bible is not speculative in presentation of this historical past, nor has it been proven wrong. It states clearly where the first man came from and where that man stands today.

The world searches diligently for the perfect code of organization in the hope that it will provide valid parameters to the meaning of existence. In fact, this *God Particle* does exist, but not through the detectable elements of tangible time and space progression. When Jesus transfigured after the resurrection, he becomes the inspiration of both flesh and spirit, the perfected Adam to the regeneration of the sons of God. In this present moment all creation waits patiently together for that which is sewn in faith to appear. As stated in 1 Corinthians, Chapter 15, verses 35-38 (KJV):

> "But some man will say, How are the dead raised up? and with what body do they come? Thou fool, that which thou sow not quickened, except it die: And that which thou sow, thou sow not that body that shall be, but bare grain, it may chance of wheat, or of some other grain:"

Chapter 1
THE RIDDLE OF MORTALITY

Time is the only true constant. All things begin in time; as all things end in time. Time is an invisible string unraveling from what was to what will be, joined through a needle's eye of the fleeting now. We witness evidence of time through unchangeable events fading into a pattern comfortably called the past; and within these perceptible patterns, the logic of an imperceptible conclusion. Time exists before Einstein perceived it as a value of mathematical modeling to describe the relativity of the observable universe-- *but more on this later*. Time captures the imagination with possibilities, inspires the soul with eternal potential, and is the unalterable instrument of thermodynamic inevitability. And yet contained within this irresistible force: *the profound riddle of contradiction in being mortal.*

There is in all of us a face reflected from darkness. *What was before? What is now? What will be?* These are all questions that create the changing tapestry of our present being. The scientist and the layman look together into the immense expanse of a night sky: all intellect dwarfed by the magnitude of distant stars and galaxies that have twinkled little changed since the earliest scribbled records made by known civilization. I can remember clearly myself a child lying upon the hill behind our house as twilight descends into night, and thinking that I, too, am connected to the cold fiery enigma of these distant suns. In this moment I feel oneness with all creation, feel complicit to every man, woman, and child that has ever gazed into this wondrous constant reminder of fleeting mortality. And although I did not truly know the

Lord of my salvation then, I felt the embrace of a spirit greater than my imagination in present reflection.

The expanding universe has barely made a pulse since then; my awareness now vaster than ever I could have imagined. Through these eyes I have witnessed the several gifts of this present passage. Moments when I have embraced those most near, some still present, some vanished since a long time. And some with whom I have reasoned; and many that I have loved. I dare to imagine a myriad of souls passed along the way from then to the now. In the truest sense, I feel complicit to the dilemma of all living things, even the things that die daily for my fleshly survival. Even those multitudes of uncomely creatures that make the biological whole I call me. I do not speak as one enlightened or one who is religious, for these are natures with prescribed agenda. I speak only as a fellow sojourner given vision and a voice in season. If I were one without sin, then I would not need to speak at all. My prayer so simple now, summed up in these words taken from the Apostle Paul's letter to the Romans, Chapter 12, verses 1-3 (NKJV).

> *"I beseech you therefore, brethren, by the mercies of God, that you present your bodies a living sacrifice, holy, acceptable to God, which is your reasonable service. And do not be conformed to this world, but be transformed by the renewing of your mind, that you may prove what is that good and acceptable and perfect will of God. For I say, through the grace given to me, to everyone who is among you, not to think of himself more highly than he ought to think, but to think soberly, as God has dealt to each one a measure of faith."*

It takes a lifetime to unlearn the indoctrination of hate; to be cleansed of the capricious prescription of consensus. As with Paul, God has left a thorn in my flesh to keep me humble. For without the bearing of mortal presence, I should puff up and forget the mercy shown to me when I did not know the truest meaning of mercy. Perhaps, I am still here through continued remission just for this reason. I recently saw an exposition where people step and dance behind a large screen viewed by spectators, manifested as x-rayed skeletons: male or female, fat or thin, pretty or ugly, all faceless shadows without appearance. No gays, no straights, no religions, no pigment of skin, and no prestige--all human, and all the same without the self- indulgent veneer of being. I thought this is how God sees us. From the inside out, not as we appear to ourselves and to others. How much more simple the world might be if we were all able to see how common we truly are beneath the prejudice of our perceptive conditioning. I f all born blind, would there any longer be defined beauty or the face of ugliness? Would there still be murder for vanity's sake? Would there still be wars and the constant struggle for glittering riches? I think such a world as this unsustainable for the very reason of its utopia potential. Even then, some would choose to remain blind, while others pretend to see. *No–* I suppose that sin is not a factor of sight alone. Since the eye is the light of the body, then the question based more on perceptual indoctrination, than on physical evidence. Why are some men repentant, while others seek vengeance to the bitter end? There are those who embrace doctrines of belief to construct statues and conduct of behavior through vision of a better society. Some seek knowledge to the end of power; while others behold the mystery of presence with curious envy. There are those who build and those who destroy. But only a few that truly understand. And this comprehension not based on pure logic or product of academic learning alone.

    The recorded ministry of Christ during his manifestation in time lasted for only three years. During those thousand or so days many were healed of infirmities, but not all. Many heard the sermons in wilderness places, but not all. Many were relieved of demons, fed by miracles, or received the words of enlightenment of a better way to live. Many were forgiven of sin, escaping the Leviticus judgment of prescribed execution; and some rose alive from the dead. But not all living in Jewry in those days ever met, or even knew that the Messiah had visited planet earth. Not even all those that heard his words understood the true meaning of this only begotten Son of God. Nevertheless, multitudes from every culture, from every religion, and from every generation inspired to spiritual revival after the resurrection. The natural man receives nothing, except by provision; but the souls of the living a benediction beyond measure through the quickening of the Holy Spirit. In the Gospel of Luke, Chapter 17, verses 12-19 (KJV), Jesus heals ten lepers, but only one returns to give him glory.

> *"And as he entered into a certain village, there met him ten men that were lepers, which stood afar off: And they lifted up their voices, and said, Jesus, Master, have mercy on us. And when he saw them, he said unto them, Go show yourselves unto the priests. And it came to pass, that, as they went, they were cleansed. And one of them, when he saw that he was healed, turned back, and with a loud voice glorified God, And fell down on his face at his feet, giving him thanks: and he was a Samaritan. And Jesus answering said, Were there not ten cleansed? but where are the nine? There are not found that returned to give glory to God, save this stranger. And he said unto him, Arise, go thy way: thy faith hath made thee whole."*

Let me make it clear before I begin that I have no special knowledge of the intricate pattern weaving the destiny of this world, nor insight into scriptural meaning not already divined by the tireless labor of other men through the course of many accumulated lifetimes. No idea presented here is new. Indeed, the book I embrace, as God's living testament within the context of changing civilization, is beyond mortal interpretation. This book of collected text written through a span of centuries is but an abbreviation of generations touched by the Holy Spirit during process of thermodynamic progression. Words constructed of a living testament coinciding with progression of natural history to make evident the existence of an imperfect code corrupted by sin that we know as past and present. A code inscribed from beginning to end even before we are born. But in time divided by time a better code conceived of flesh and spirit to revive that which was lost from the beginning. This spirit, originating outside of diurnal time and space, subject to none of the laws defined through natural reason. This is a

Holy thing manifested in the beginning as a corrective measure to rewrite the matrix of a new heaven and earth: a code perfected in the manifestation of the resurrected Christ from the elemental condition of prevailing entropy. This new code inspired through revolution; not the product of evolution.

As an individual, all I do know with any certainty is that the undeniable power of the Holy Spirit first indwelled my mortal being nearly a half century ago. Never again will I perceive this world the same. I am a living testament of spirits in high places and the absolute power of God's Messiah, sent on a mission to save men's souls through humble submission. This miracle happened to me while I still served in the United States Marine Corps, less than a year after returning back from the Republic of Vietnam. Meritoriously promoted to Sergeant during my tour of duty I knew already where I belonged and could belong nowhere else. This clarity of being bitter recompense for successful achievement of a seemingly impossible mission: a position attained out of season. A position forced upon me that I had to diligently maintain by will of superhuman determination, both physical and psychological. Historically we were the first Marine Corps unit to redeploy stateside, taking every weapon, every tent pin, every nut and bolt with us. I will not go into details, only that under the circumstances the challenge almost insurmountable. I was still nineteen years old when promoted to Sergeant, with less than three years military service. I felt a sense of belonging in the Marine Corps. It had become my mother and my father, and the only future I could imagine. I became the man it expected of me, a man who knew the importance of order and self discipline. I cannot say that I loved the Corps, but it was as near to love as I knew at the time. But the spiritual toll far greater.

God had been calling me since a long time, only I could not hear the sound of his voice. But one Sunday afternoon I attend a choir in an Ocean Side Coffee house devoted to the needs of service men like myself. There were different groups sent by churches from districts of Southern California. The last group that sings produces a most beautiful chorus proclaiming the love of Jesus. I resist, but the music resonating more profound than I wished to acknowledge. After the recital, a lovely young lady obedient to the spirit comes and talks to me. After only a brief conversation, her clear blue eyes gaze deeply into my eyes.

"Here is the address of our church," she says, producing a piece of paper scribbled with an address. "It is located in the suburbs of Long Beach. I feel in the Spirit that the Lord calling you to join us."

Of course, I forget about this invitation, until another hangover Sunday morning, a piece of folded paper falls from my top locker shelf to my feet. It is the address of that church. On this bright California morning I decide to take a long drive north to a place I have never been. Nosing slowly through a maze of residential streets, I am unable to find this fabled place of worship. Then I hear singing beyond a grove of Weeping Willows, the same music I heard those many weeks earlier. Following the sound, I discover an abandoned school auditorium with a congregation of people inside. Upon entering I am immediately jolted by a force never felt before. There is no sense of religion here, but a presence as real as any previous experience. I have known Buddhist spirits, feeling their charisma in the dark shadow of Marble Mountain, a hollowed shrine jutting out of that ancient terrain of twisted jungle. Felt them near as they dance in the suffocating night air. But this presence nothing like that; rather it is as the magnitude of the morning sun consuming the illumination of a light bulb left on through the night.

Arriving only at the finish of this group's service, I silently bow my head and partition: "if this is God, please give me proof." Being a proud young man, I quickly seek the exit and would have been gone had that pretty young lady not intercepted me.

"I saw you come in," she says softly. "I am glad that you finally found your way here."

We talk. I meet her parents and am subsequently invited to their home for coffee and something to eat. The girl's name is Karen, a name written in heaven, a name that I will never forget. Karen convinces me to go on an afternoon horseback ride with her. I had little experience, so we end walking the horses instead. During this afternoon stroll, Karen speaks to my empty soul.

"Look at the sky, how blue. My God and your God made this for you and for me."

I look into the sky and it changes instantly into an infinite blue. Again she speaks.

"Look at the fields of grass covering the land, how green. My God and your God made this for you and for me."

I look at the grass and it changes emerald green, a living tapestry flowing into the distance.

She performs this magic for the trees and the birds, and all manner of creatures above and below. Things, I perhaps once saw as a child, but had faded since so many years into the grey of tainted experience. By the end of this stroll, I am emotionally speechless. We return to her family's home for an evening meal. Since the next day an official holiday of Washington's Birthday, I accept to stay overnight in the comfort of an extra room. I spend much of the next day in the backyard, contemplating the meaning of sky, the delicate design of things that grow, and the unsearchable pattern of lumbering insects riding invisible air currents.

Toward late afternoon we depart in separate cars to the home of some of their friends to share in a potluck dinner. From here I will jump on the Freeway and return to my Camp Pendleton base. In the course of a conversation with two young men about my age, a disagreement arises concerning the conduct of soldiers and the moral purpose of the Vietnam War. I instantly snap forward as a Sergeant prepared to consume these civilians, who dare to question my conduct in a war I did not personally choose to engage. A war of corporate greed that has taken so many of my generation and shattered the integrity of two nations--but at this time I am a young Marine Corps Sergeant--my conscience clear!

"A lot of men came back less than whole, or not at all just so you can sit here and question their conduct. So don't think you know anything about the war in Vietnam!"

I immediately see terror in their eyes. I have become a wild animal in a peaceful fold, and no longer know how to be anything else. It is time for me to return to the only true home I have in this world. As I edge toward the door, Karen enquires if I might come back again. In my heart I know already I never will. As I reach the threshold of escape, a veteran from another generation and another war intercepts me.

"Son, I would like to ask you a question before you go," he says intently.

"What would that be?"

"Do you know Jesus Christ the Savior of your immortal soul?"

After a moment of reflection, I answer factually that I do not know this Christ; nor do I believe in the presence of a God.

"I try not to be a hypocrite," I say sincerely. "I do believe that you people here in this room believe something, but I do not know what it is or how to believe it."

This man then begins to tell me of his experience as an American Bomber pilot during World War II. He had flown many successful missions, but shot down on the last run over Dresden. He and his injured copilot survive the crash. As they stumble through the burning city, he sees body parts of men, women, and children strewn like the heads, torsos, and limbs of broken dolls. For the first time, he realizes the destruction his bombs dropped upon the diver's places of mankind. He convinces himself that it had been necessary, but the carnage real all the same. He returns to his home, becomes a successful business mogul, but never can he escape that place in his mind. Then one morning decades later, he is invited by a friend to a Christian Businessmen's Breakfast, where he receives forgiveness in Christ and is *born again*.

"Just as God knew me, he knows you as well. It is not his desire that any should perish in sin. If you choose to pray with me now, and nothing happens, then you will depart this place and never see us again, nor we you. California is a very big place, the world beyond even greater. But if you find salvation to your soul in this moment, then you risk gaining the greatest gift of eternity."

"If your God will reveal to me that he is God, then I will serve this God all the days of my life."

These words seem to flow from the deepest part of my being, not rational, but more sincere than any I have ever spoken. I then submit to pray with this man. I sit in a chair, place my hands upon my thighs, and close my eyes. After a moment, I feel foolish, as my pride of self reasserts itself.

"I am a Marine Corps Sergeant!" I think to myself. "Here I am in a room of civilians, sitting like a child. To whom am I supposed to pray--to this man--to the ceiling?"

I determine to leave this place never to return. I will go back to my Marine Corps--the place I know--the only place where I truly feel at home!

This is the strange thing that happens next. I can feel my hands on my thighs, but I have lost all motor control to move them. My eyes are closed, but they will not open. I did not feel drugged; nor did I have any motive force. I suddenly begin to panic, thinking that maybe I have unsuspectingly fallen into the hands of a cult that mean to do me harm!

Then I am somewhere else. Somewhere I have always been and would always remain. It is the realm of a great outer darkness. Inhabiting this darkness a host of parasitical creatures, some attached to the corpse of my being, others waiting their turn to feed. It is not a terrifying place; nor is there any hope here. It is a place forever abandoned, inhabited by a host of indiscernible shadows. Suddenly the shearing of a flaming cross splits the darkness with the pure visage of a man upon it. Then a voice that speaks clearly.

"Place your eyes upon me."

In this moment I feel fearful and ashamed. As I begin to turn away from this blinding presence, I am aware of those parasitical creatures tightening the coils of their bondage. I stand at the fulcrum of a monumental decision. There is an almost pleasant familiarity to this place of outer darkness, like the pleasantness of a womb I have always known. Whereas, this burning apparition an altogether unknown quantum. Yet, I know in my soul the darkness to be *death everlasting*; this man on a burning cross *life everlasting*. I turn and look into his unwavering eyes and shout:

"Yes Lord!"

A shard of that cross shoots up into the void, circles down, and pierces through me, consuming my emptied soul in blinding light. From a distance I witness a physical body floating in limbo, stretched into infinity. Then I am aware of my spiritually revived soul refilling the corpse of that being like warm milk to overflowing. I am physically lying prostrate on the floor, where the man of sin has collapsed through spiritual aggression. Instantly I leap up from the grave of that former self, reborn alive, and begin praising God in the spirit. For the first time, I know my father in heaven. Know without any doubt the saving grace of his son sent to die on a cross for my sins, and know the abiding presence of the Holy Spirit. I leave this place a new person, delivered from the power of demonic influence.

The drive back to my base remains vague in my mind, as I am altogether elated in the spirit. That night I hesitate to sleep, fearing by morning it might all be gone, like so many other fleeting joys in life. But the next morning, it is still with me. I go out to my company of men and testify of the great gift of salvation provided by the God that has made the pleasant blades of grass and the inextricable blue of the sky. They surely think me mad. And by the standards of this world I was mad, and am mad still to this day. The next several days I begin to read a New Testament Bible given to me by my new brethren. It is not like reading a text, but as a confirming testament contained in the good news of salvation, bearing witness to my revived soul of life's greatest measure. Yes--I know this Jesus of the four Gospels! Know also his apostles, and the meaning of their many written letters. It has been scores of years since I last saw Karen and her family. We all attended church service for awhile, but in time scattered into the world through the leading of the Holy Spirit. I praise the Lord that one day I will be reunited with all my brothers and sisters.

However, this moment in time I must attend to a more temporal demand of logical discourse. I pray for the objective wisdom to openly examine the constructed pillars of worldly perception, which I believe to be influenced by a mind with an agenda older than genesis. I forewarn the reader that everything I have to say predicated on this undeniable personal spiritual event that has changed the directive of my life. A supernatural quantum originating from beyond the sensory definition of the world we think so evident. This is not a message to the religious, to the Clergy, or the Theologian. Nor is it intended to guide the sheep of the Lord through another way other than their spiritual calling. Christ has already fulfilled those convictions in good measure. I write this to the mind of an unbelieving world, as a challenge to challenge the basic foundation of academic interpretation.

In every legal or moral dispute, there are two sides to an argument. Each presents a judicious debate based on the facts. It is up to the jury to interpret those facts and deliver a verdict derived solely from the evidence. Because jurisprudence is a prevailing logic applied to prescribed institutional prejudices and beliefs, no position can represent an absolute standard of universal truth. All observed phenomenon is subject to interpretation and should remain free of bias. Through indulgence of distraction mankind has chosen complacency over engagement by eagerly allowing institutional positions to quantify human existence based on construction of incomplete models of extrapolation to define context, and meaning within that context. The prevailing consensus is to allocate responsibility of choice and determination to other entities more qualified of reason and moral directive. This is a perilous lack of engagement, considering that one's immortal soul in the balance. And, yes, there are those higher up--*but they are no gods; nor are they men!*

Modern science embodies the presence of trusted source in the minds of most. Successful in both applied and theoretical interpretation, science by simplest measure begins with the observation of the elemental building blocks that exist naturally. The dictionary definition of science is the systematic recording and experimentation to ascribe measure to existential conditions of constructed reality. Science is sometimes able to make predictions based on the accumulated history of observed patterns, thus giving birth to mechanical invention termed *technology*. It is by these technologies that man has excelled beyond environmental restraints, enhancing the way we live, the way we travel, and even the way we communicate. The utopia goal of technology is to compress time and space by meddling with complex machinery defining mortal existence. As appealing as this might appear on the surface, it ultimately assures a path leading toward mass destruction.

Through litany of many perceived accomplishments, science has little changed the position of man within context of the inhabited world, or provided more comprehension to the far distant universe, so clearly seen through time-lapsed photography. Science has yet to devise better principles of human equality by eradicating wars, curing pestilences, and feeding the masses of starving populations. Through measures of intervention science strives to save a few in the namesake of the many, while ensuring the extermination of the many for the sake of a few. Who might have predicted that un-harnessing the power of fossil fuels in the late 19th and early 20th century would jeopardize the entire ecosystem of planet earth by the middle of the 21 century? What mind can rationalize that by attempting to save everyone at any cost creates unsustainable population growth threatening future survival as a species? These questions raise an even more important quandary of reason: *Has science become an intellectual bridge redefining morality; and does it embody a supreme philosophical agreement elevated above all other challenge?*

When science proclaims itself to be a priesthood of infallible supposition and its accepted deductions based upon unquestionable precepts, it becomes a religion, open to scrutiny. And when any institution of examination becomes guided by zealous embrace, it also becomes the fertile ground for many deceiving spirits with a singular objective of collective deception.

I intend to present ideas of a terrestrial past and of a future extraordinary in interpretation, referencing both natural, as well as supernatural possibilities. It is not to say that this extrapolation of events exclusive to all other interpretations; nor is it meant to imply absolute conclusion when magnified under the lens escalating probability. Ultimately, it comes down to interpretation of the data and understanding the limited cipher of a predictable code corrupted by design within context of an invisible hyper reality. As science and technology continue to evolve through better optics of more precise observation, it approaches a frontier of meaning that only confirms what the Bible has been saying for more than five millennium: *God is a spirit and all things spiritually designed.*

So begins this Search of the Perfect Code Discovered.

Chapter 2
A RELIGIOUS CONUNDRUM

As we will begin to discover, personal identity remains the most rigid norm within societal context to ascribe meaningful purpose and behavioral predictability to the phenomenon of individual uniqueness. Within the systemic context of greater organization, each component rigidly defined through historical expectation. It is not difficult to imagine the enormous challenge of this task, considering the persistent birth and death rate around the globe. From the moment a baby is born, it is assigned gender, name, and a blueprint of future directive. Every sub category applies these same norms of physicality, as the immutable standard of being. This is particularly true of religious organizations burdened by congregational expectations, often stepping on the right side of political correctness, while adhering to doctrinal interpretations understood through the temporal lens of secular reasoning. This can only lead to violent aggression in the name of a righteous cause. It should be noted that individuals and institutions rarely subscribe unanimously to a norm of arbitrary prescription defining good and evil. Even though there has been address to the common thread of religious faith that inspires mortal men to submit to the voice of a higher calling, it is just as important to discern the source of that calling.

There is a grave difference between a spiritual revelation and religious belief. The first is a consuming fire that cannot be quenched; the latter, as the cold reflection of the moon lighting the way through dark places. Religion is a combination of logical association, emotional acceptance, and cultural politicized agreement to a conditional expression of community identification. Often based upon a handed-down testament of supernatural phenomenon, transferrable for awhile, but loses original virtue through political compromise of worldly process. This does not suggest religion an invalid expression, only the congregation as alive as the devotion of those engaged. Nor is religion a definition based solely on doctrine. But rather it is a conscious decision of the believer to accept certain interpretations of doctrine as a model of conduct *(or agreement with accepted moral values of what truth is and is not)*, thus embracing those doctrines as an outward expression, or by cultural infusion to construct a flawless theology. However, for a doctrine to retain integrity and not become ritualistic, it must survive the test of living generations. In other words it must be part of the growth of the individual and be fruitful of something tangibly better than present condition allows. By extension of similar reason, if it remains just a religious expression within a cultural or societal context, then it lacks vitality, becoming un-virtuous, hollow, and lacking a quality of ascendance. Enlightenment of doctrinal meaning replaced by ritualistic observance through enforcement of indoctrination: fear and intimidation the standards of blind obedience. One of the greatest dangers of any religious organization is something that might be termed *'the messiah syndrome'*, when a mortal man embodies a quality of charismatic leadership inspiring devotion to a specified religious conduct. This is particularly pronounced in the Muslim religion, starting with Mohammed and the many Mullah inspired Jihadist leaders since. Each arising from among the people with a strong agenda to sear the world of humanity with a holy brand of *Fatwa* sanctioned to enforce a new order here on earth. You also see this through the many reformations of Christian interpretation of doctrine leading to centuries of wars and division. We even witness this stubborn deterministic view of government control on the political horizon, as one philosophized manifesto attempts to impose its will upon that of another.

I remember as a child reading a story about six blind men sharing their interpretation of an elephant by touch alone. One man runs his fingers around the leg, describing the animal as a giant pillar. The second feels the length of the tail, saying it is like the twine of strong rope. The third man finds the steady trunk to be as the branch of a tree. The fourth man believes the circumference of the ear the likeness of a great fan. The fifth man certain the beast is a wall upon touching the unyielding belly. And the sixth blind man ascertains the beast to be made like a solid pipe upon feeling the smooth contour of the ivory tusk. A vehement disagreement ensues as to the true nature of an elephant, until a wise man comes along stating that they are all right, but none understand fully the comprehensive being of the animal in question. The moral of the story is analogist to the doctrines of spiritual enlightenment defining world religions and denominational agreements.

Forgetting for the moment that every tree has a root of genesis, all religions make reference to a non-material condition existing beyond the thermodynamic reality experienced through the living process. This is the place we come from at birth, and the place we go to when we die. Through material senses the body is made from identifiable elements of the earth and eventually returns to the inert condition of those elements. The animating life force *(defined as an electrometric energy field or as a breath of the divine)* also dissipates back to the source matrix. And this is where religion enters into the living equation. Religion serves as a polarized positional representation of a hyper-reality, which intersects the diurnal time progression of our terrestrial sojourn; and thus endures as a traditional reminder of a quickened spiritual influence into the affairs of men. As when God speaks audibly to Moses on Mount Sinai and engraves the Ten Commandments on tablets of stone, becoming an indelible testament of promise through mortal generations. Although the event not religious, it serves as a memorial of witness passed down to subsequent offspring. Over time this testimony becomes a ritual of vague appreciation, void of understanding, as evidenced by the self-righteous Pharisees in the days Jesus walks the earth in physical body. Before the birth of Moses, Egypt and the many surrounding principalities throughout Mesopotamia worship a variety of deities originating from supernatural entities of magnificent potential. Even the father of Abraham, the original patriarch of Jewish ancestry, was a maker of idols. Yet time and time again the potent God of the Bible deposes these flickering candles as a fiery sun consuming lesser lights.

The common denominator among all religions is an infusion between spiritual inspiration and a mortally contained element termed the living soul. It is this soul that hungers for more than flesh and blood existence can offer. It is this soul that seeks answers through moral guidance, or else becomes darkened with rebellion against the God of creation, exalting the flowering pride of humanity. This immortal part of us all remains trapped between the expanse of eternal heaven and temporal earth. This soul remains in awe to the enormity of things beyond comprehension, fluctuating between the eternal divine and the shadowy uncertainty of death, hovering always upon the horizon. We are warned from the perilous inception of our sojourn here, not all spirits are the same. Nor do all names raised above the altar profess the God of salvation. Since spirits abound, human discernment easily deceived by sensual elements that promise personal or tribal superiority through creature existence. This is a human interpretation defined through a mind of rebellion as old as creation. These are the doctrines of devils, blood thirsty deities with an agenda: to first enslave men's minds through rigid statues, and then to decimate the freewill of order and compassion that delineates mankind from all other beast of the earth. These creatures of fallen angelic apparitions seek continuously whom they may overshadow with pride and the promise of riches to the end of destruction. But we are also provided a means of discernment between spirits, a particularly poignant warning against the spirit of antichrist in the first epistle of John, Chapter 4, verses 1-3 *Berean Study Bible* (BSB).

> *"Beloved, do not believe every spirit, but test the spirits to see whether they are from God. For many false prophets have gone out into the world. By this you will know the Spirit of God: Every spirit that confesses that Jesus Christ has come in the flesh is from God, and every spirit that does not confess Jesus is not from God. This is the spirit of the antichrist, which you have heard is coming and which is already in the world at this time."*

Religion is only the beginning, a doorway through a bright passage of universal concept. It is like the differencing characteristics of our elephant perceived through blindness. Yes, all touch parts, and therefore all conclude to know the truth of the whole; yet as with the protagonist in the Book of Job, the acknowledgement of our creator only the beginning of true righteousness. Remembering that even the angels of hell know without any doubt God's supreme existence, we that believe should be most humble of our relative position in the scheme of unfolding events, accepting gladly the office of servitude for the benefit of our fellowman, declaring joyfully the majesty of our creation in worship of the creator. This is our only reasonable service, as those with eyes opened to see into the darkness to the end of a greater awakening.

It should be noted that there is very little difference between the definition of a religion and a philosophical discipline. Both retain the collective motivation of inspired multitudes, thus becoming the indoctrination of allegiance to political extremism. Through candidates of charismatic leadership the void of human dissatisfaction fulfilled with a tangible objective to somehow please God by the eradication of defined evil through mortal engagement. The flaw of every logic is the belief that some are better than others through birthright; or that some causes more righteous, therefore justifying the means to the end. It is easy to forget that the walls of Jericho fell by the will of God, not just by the faithful shout of many soldiers. This same observation applies throughout history of the Jewish people, as they are delivered time and time again by divine intervention, not by the strong arm of the sword alone. The apostles, who followed Christ, ultimately followed him to their death. Neither could they submit anymore to spirits of fear and persecution. They being profoundly liberated from the tyrannical forces overshadowing an unbelieving world inspired through evil communications.

The greatest danger in religion is that it becomes the holy institution of heavenly power upon earth. This does not mean that there are no holy sites. Only that what makes them holy found through the quickening of participation; not in actual terrestrial position. Jerusalem and Mecca are geographic locations on a continuum of colossal changing scale, but with fixed spiritual quantum intersecting time and space. The ancient city Jebus existed even before King David declares it Jerusalem, proclaiming it the future capital of Israel. It is the spiritual dwelling place of Melchizedek, King of Salem and priest of The Most High God, to whom Abraham bows, dividing to this Holy man ten percent of all his goods. It is where the man Jesus, crucified and raised victorious from the grave of thermodynamic reaction, lifted above heaven and earth as the only begotten son of our living God. This same Jesus will return, splitting the Mount of Olives to establish the foundation of a New Jerusalem.

This spiritual city is the stuff of prophecy, upon which rest the balances of judgment and angelic war: where past, present, and future coincide with the comprehension of measured existence and the incomprehensible notion of eternity. Within these walls of present dispensation breeds the greatest iniquity of all: *self-righteousness.* A self righteous man needs no correction and no better instruction. Nor can such a man be swayed from the certainty of his philosophy, because he has based his learning on the good works of others, also considered righteous. Well did Jesus say, in Chapter five of the Gospel of Mathew, a man's righteousness must exceed that of the Pharisees in order to enter into the kingdom of heaven. And again in Mathew, Chapter 15, verses 1-14 (KJV), Jesus admonishes the difference between laws based on understanding of men and the true righteousness found in God's commandments.

> *"Then came to Jesus scribes and Pharisees, which were of Jerusalem, saying, Why do thy disciples transgress the tradition of the elders? for they wash not their hands when they eat bread. But he answered and said unto them, Why do ye also transgress the commandment of God by your tradition? For God commanded, saying, Honour thy father and mother: and, He that curseth father or mother, let him die the death. But ye say, Whosoever shall say to his father or his mother, It is a gift, by whatsoever thou mightest be profited by me; And honour not his father or his mother,*

he shall be free. Thus have ye made the commandment of God of none effect by your tradition. Ye hypocrites, well did Esaias prophesy of you, saying, This people draweth nigh unto me with their mouth, and honoureth me with their lips; but their heart is far from me. But in vain they do worship me, teaching for doctrines the commandments of men. And he called the multitude, and said unto them, Hear, and understand: Not that which goeth into the mouth defileth a man; but that which cometh out of the mouth, this defileth a man. Then came his disciples, and said unto him, Knowest thou that the Pharisees were offended, after they heard this saying? But he answered and said, Every plant, which my heavenly Father hath not planted, shall be rooted up. Let them alone: they be blind leaders of the blind. And if the blind lead the blind, both shall fall into the ditch."

Where religion falls short, then living testimony prevails. For what good is an account, unless there remains also evidence of its verity? The book we know as the Holy Bible is not just the history of a people, but a testament of God's abiding presence to every living generation. The Jews are chosen as an undeniable witness of this God grounded in history. And from this testament given to a chosen people, comes the promise of a prophesied Messiah: *a Messiah chosen by God*; not by the careful logic of reason, or the complex web of plans within plans of mortal design and genetic engineering. History must run a course through time. But from the beginning to the end, Jesus Christ, the first and the last, the Alpha and Omega, the completion of a perfected code. This unique code made of flesh and spirit, designed by God even before the beginning of time and space. Since Christ is the completion of this perfect work, then why does religion strive to contain the body of spiritual value through the limitation of imperfect understanding? The Pharisee order that resisted the counsel of Christ had become a self-indulgent priesthood on earth daily interpreting laws and traditions passed down since days of Moses. But because of religious politics, they made themselves the enemies of God. Even Saul, later identified as the Apostle Paul after his conversion, boasted that he had been instructed from his youth in the teachings and righteous execution of the law. Until a faithful day when the prince of true righteousness appeared to him, unveiling this man's righteousness as filthy rags before the Lord of heaven, as recorded in The Book of Acts, Chapter 22, verses 3-8 (KJV).

> *"I am verily a man which am a Jew, born in Tarsus, a city in Cilicia, yet brought up in this city at the feet of Gamaliel, and taught according to the perfect manner of the law of the fathers, and was zealous toward God, as ye all are this day. And I persecuted this way unto the death, binding and delivering into prisons both men and women. As also the high priest doth bear me witness, and all the estate of the elders: from whom also I received letters unto the brethren, and went to Damascus, to bring them which were there bound unto Jerusalem, for to be punished. And it came to pass, that, as I made my journey, and was come nigh unto Damascus about noon, suddenly there shone from heaven a great light round about me. And I fell unto the ground, and heard a voice saying unto me, Saul, Saul, why persecutest thou me? And I answered, Who art thou, Lord? And he said unto me, I am Jesus of Nazareth, whom thou persecutest."*

The unbridled zeal of religion leads to varying degrees of sectarian violence through the lens of guided myopic definition. Ultimately religious interpretation of doctrine becomes the sword of execution to condemn sin in the world. But what is sin? The prodigal son said to his father that I have sinned against you and heaven and deserve only to be your servant. Yet, the father forgives him, providing his lost son, now found, with a royal robe and a feast of celebration. The woman brought to the feet of Jesus was caught in the act of adultery, yet Jesus forgives her and says go and sin no more. The Pharisees of Jesus' day were particularly keen on the definition of sin, yet Jesus calls them fools and hypocrites, not knowing their right from their left hand.

Sin existed before Jesus, and it continues to exist today. Not even ten righteous could be found in those great metropolises of Sodom and Gomorrah in the days of Abraham, because righteousness is not a natural quality, but rather a manifestation of heavenly grace. And if all saved by grace, then who mortal may judge another? After the day of Pentecost, those many filled with the tongues of unworldly inspiration, did not go about condemning the transgressions so evident in the world; but testified, as men drunk with too much wine, proclaiming the good news of personal revelation manifested through the resurrected Christ. Their supernatural joy imparted by the pouring out of the Holy Spirit evidenced a conviction of sin; and many who witness this revival repented on that day. They did not become architects of a better theocracy to replace the synagogues, or to promote a worldly authority greater than Roman to rule Israel and the present world. Rather, they proclaim throughout all earthly principalities the simple testament of the living Christ, him crucified, whom God raised from the dead. This man born in the likeness of flesh and blood is eternal witness of peace and reconciliation, providing a way of salvation to all nations of men, and freeing the yoke of religious servitude.

I think it is easy to forget the implication of grace, which is the essence of knowing Christ, and start thinking like self-righteous Pharisees. As Christians reborn through grace the testament of our mortal passing ought to be the joyful good news of our resurrected Lord and the wonderful hope unapparent through carnal existence. For the sin that appears in the world evidence of the infection, not the cause. And more disturbing, the sin that does not appear as sin, but is an abomination all the same. Condemnation only leads to separation; and separation to isolation. Christ forgave the sin of those who nailed his hands and feet to a wooden cross, *and condemned them not.* Ask first the question: *who is able to cast the first stone guiltless?*

God does not need the collective agreement of an institution to condemn sin. Sin is a condition of the flesh, not the evidence of good works by good men. While taking an urban sociology class at UCLA,

I remember reading about a unique study conducted by a renowned ethnologist, named John Calhoun, using rats. A controlled population was placed in a confined space and provided with sufficiency. The first several generations prospered well, performing normal mating activity and producing healthy offspring. But as the population grew into unsustainable numbers relative to the enclosure, a remarkable change in social behavior prevails. Males change more aggressive, exhibiting sexual deviant behavior, some becoming pathological stalkers prowling when other rats slept. Other males form member groups, hording the limited resources, and gang-raping the females. Some of these animals even resort to cannibalism. Infant mortality rises to an alarming statistic, as the females exhibit less maternal care toward their litter, many often dying before the end of their gestation period. This population explosion experiment, which Calhoun terms *"behavior sink"*, is a stark indicator of how stress and feelings of alienation play an important role in developmental psychology of the individual within a social context. Humans respond little differently when compacted within enclosed systems found in modern cities today.

Except that there is also a far greater spiritual toll with humans not discerned through experimentation. This a result of excess materialism and disproportionate value placed on the creature condition, fueled by two dimensional ideologies that enslave our minds from inception. This also might explain how and why people become radicalized to potent ideas, not based solely in existential concepts. The human soul hungers to be fed, easily drawn to any reflection like a moth to a distant flame. Philosophies may affect the wayward flight of a mind lacking conviction, but the unwavering power of God is a purging fire, renewing a man's mind and soul, as clearly stated by the Apostle Paul in 1 Corinthians, Chapter 4, verse 20 (KJV):

"For the kingdom of God is not in word, but in power."

God needs no clarification of his laws. They were first written in the human heart immutable from the beginning. The original Ten Commandments given to Moses on Mount Sinai inscribed in stone, already existed upon the tablets of men's souls, the shadow of something better with eternal potential. The amendments of Leviticus designed as a dynamic standard of social conduct to safeguard the integrity of a patriarchal linage to the future birth of the Messiah. But even then, God supplies a scapegoat of sacrifice once a year performed by the high priest, so that the continuing sins of individuals might be covered from irrevocable judgment.

Either, Jehovah supplements this clause of atonement by design, or it is a political instrument designed by men. If by men, then why consider God's plans of any influence in human affairs? But if by God, then his mercy seat must prevail. When Jesus walks the earth, the Scribes and Pharisees search the scriptures diligently to find a way to condemn this man as a sinner, without comprehending that they the ones blind to God's meaning and in need of atonement. Just as Christ submits without resistance to the cross for our redemption, then we should also willingly submit in love for the hope of our fellow man. If we are changed in the twinkling of an eye and swept up into the air-- *Praise the Lord!* But if we are to remain when there is no other light in the world, then greater ought our praises to our Lord in heaven, wishing not one sinner lost.

I think it is important not to confuse politics with Godly submission. The presence of modern day Israel is a material political state, not the spiritual kingdom of heaven to come. Nevertheless, it is the physical evidence that the spirit of God continues to strive with mankind. An abiding covenant of promise upon the earth, separated from humanism, and a symbol of divine prophesies fulfilled even in our time. But also this geographical location of mortal design is a miracle beyond earthly comprehension. To stand with the existence of Israel is to stand with God's chosen people. And to stand with the chosen of God is to stone upon the foundation of the coming Messiah. Not through the evidence of things seen, but in the certainty of future promise. For Christ has come, and will come again in time for the salvation of a chosen people through which the remnant of remaining mankind sanctified. This is a mystery sure to those born in Jesus Christ above all politics.

Once Christian men and women become politically inspired, they become the voice of opposing agenda. All conflict begins with ideas of right and wrong, escalates into words and provisions, and inevitably into armed aggression. Once open combat declared the memory of right and wrong become vague concepts, and in the end only the winner writes the history with blood of the fallen. As Christian soldiers, our warfare is not against flesh and blood, but against principalities in high places. Our victory here is not to the end of survival as last man standing, but to submit to the power of God's will for our lives. Unlike those in the world, we embrace the knowledge that this is only a passage, not our final destination. In this present moment, only the flesh can be killed, but we are alive already in the resurrection. Examine the powers that have been and now reside, and you will always find familial declarations of *"us and them"*. But this should not be the way of God's saints. God does not condemn men because of sin; it is sin that condemns men before God. Christ did not debate scripture with the lawyers and religious teachers; he was scripture. Since we are all born from the beginning in sin, then should we not be most happy of mankind to be made free from the yoke of sin? For if Israel is righteous in the flesh, then why must Messiah return? As the Apostle Paul writes in his letter to the body of believers in the Macedonian city of Philippi, Chapter 2, verses 5-18 (KJV):

> *"For let this mind be in you which was also in Christ Jesus; Who, being in the form of God, thought it not robbery to be equal with God: But made himself of no reputation, and took upon him the form of a servant, and was made in the likeness of men: And being found in fashion as a man, he humbled himself, and became obedient unto death, even the death of the cross. Wherefore God also hath highly exalted him, and given him a name which is above every name: That at the name of Jesus every knee should bow, of things in heaven, and things in earth, and things under the earth; And that every tongue should confess that Jesus Christ is Lord, to the glory of God the Father. Wherefore,*

my beloved, as ye have always obeyed, not as in my presence only, but now much more in my absence, work out your own salvation with fear and trembling. For it is God which works in you both to will and to do of his good pleasure. Do all things without murmurings and disputings: That ye may be blameless and harmless, the sons of God, without rebuke, in the midst of a crooked and perverse nation, among whom ye shine as lights in the world; Holding forth the word of life; that I may rejoice in the day of Christ, that I have not run in vain, neither labored in vain. Yea, and if I be offered upon the sacrifice and service of your faith, I joy, and rejoice with you all. For the same cause also do ye joy, and rejoice with me."

I have witnessed testimonies of devoted terrorist converted to a better way by the Holy Spirit. I have witnessed testimonies of murderers that find peace and forgiveness through the power of the Prince of Peace. The earth overflows with testimonies of men and women under the influence of Satan released by the authority and love found only in Jesus Christ, our resurrected Lord. These are not converted by the actions of good works or by religious consolation. They are, as *I am*, living testaments of a living God written in a moment of time by a finger infinite. However, it disheartens me when I see men and women rally in angry groups denouncing abortions or the emotional unity between two people of the same sex. They readily condemn, without addressing the real social and spiritual issues that breed these conditions. Many of the same denounce the radical reactions of Muslim groups expressing escalation of anger because of a caricature made of a dead prophet without physical aspect or visual comparison. Yet so easily provoked with like-minded emotions, as though God needs their political activism to make the world right-- as though their loud denunciations will change the times. Inspired with such strong convictions, I think their denominational fervor better expressed to provide support homes for young mothers and their children. Instead of Sunday congregations and lovely sermons to light the beacon of a righteous community, then perhaps also open-door facilities should be built to embrace the needs of a society blinded by excess and crippled by sin. For I doubt God needs many (*or even one*) worldly structure of worship to proclaim presence upon the earth, since his supreme holiness is everywhere, particularly in the humble hearts of the contrite. Since it is the nature of some of us to try and make the world a better place, then let us devote our efforts to change the things we can change, without condemnation and judgment, and leave the rest in God's capable hands.

Another example of dynamic testament comes several years after the resurrection through a religious leader named Saul, a devout Jew, also a free-born Roman citizen, authorized by the order of Pharisees to incarcerate and bring to judgment all who proclaim the resurrected Christ. But on the road to Damascus, the living Christ appears to this soldier of righteousness and reveals a profound correction to his zealous soul. After this supernatural encounter, Saul, a Sanhedrin Jew well studied in the law, becomes Paul sent, not to confound the wisdom of his own countrymen, but to challenge the worldly wisdom of the Gentiles. What better way to perplex the logic of wisdom? In the Book of Acts, Chapter 9, verses 1-18 (NKJV), the following commentary written:

> *"Then Saul, still breathing threats and murder against the disciples of the Lord, went to the high priest and asked letters from him to the synagogues of Damascus, so that if he found any who were of the Way, whether men or women, he might bring them bound to Jerusalem. As he journeyed he came near Damascus, and suddenly a light shone around him from heaven. Then he fell to the ground, and heard a voice saying to him, "Saul, Saul, why are you persecuting Me?" And he said, "Who are You, Lord?" Then the Lord said, "I am Jesus, whom you are persecuting. [a]It is hard for you to kick against the goads." So he, trembling and astonished, said, "Lord, what do You want me to do?" Then the Lord said to him, "Arise and go into the city, and you will be told what you must do." And the men*

who journeyed with him stood speechless, hearing a voice but seeing no one. Then Saul arose from the ground, and when his eyes were opened he saw no one. But they led him by the hand and brought him into Damascus. And he was three days without sight, and neither ate nor drank. Now there was a certain disciple at Damascus named Ananias; and to him the Lord said in a vision, "Ananias." And he said, "Here I am, Lord." So the Lord said to him, "Arise and go to the street called Straight, and inquire at the house of Judas for one called Saul of Tarsus, for behold, he is praying. And in a vision he has seen a man named Ananias coming in and putting his hand on him, so that he might receive his sight." Then Ananias answered, "Lord, I have heard from many about this man, how much[b] harm he has done to Your saints in Jerusalem. And here he has authority from the chief priests to bind all who call on Your name." But the Lord said to him, "Go, for he is a chosen vessel of Mine to bear My name before Gentiles, kings, and the children[c] of Israel. For I will show him how many things he must suffer for My name's sake." And Ananias went his way and entered the house; and laying his hands on him he said, "Brother Saul, the Lord[d] Jesus, who appeared to you on the road as you came, has sent me that you may receive your sight and be filled with the Holy Spirit." Immediately there fell from his eyes something like scales, and he received his sight at once; and he arose and was baptized."

What actually happens to the man Saul? The short answer, he is *born again*. After having a similar experience, I have come to realize over the years that the term *born again* does not mean the same for all persons. For some it is just another religious expression consolidated by an agreement of a shared alliance. I am witness to the miracle of Christ born flesh upon this earth. The congregation that first inspired me through charismatic revival begins through their offspring. These religious souls originally from different traditional denominations in Southern California, made one family by power of the Holy Spirit. It starts with perceived change in the behavior of their children that the parents cannot understand, only aware of growing resistance to the fundamental nature of religious upbringing. Being concerned for the strange behavior of their sons and daughters, these progenitors begin to attend the gatherings of informal pray meetings, hoping to uncover the contrary philosophy of some heretic sect. What they discover, instead, is the flowing living waters of spiritual salvation. One by one they are born again, not by worldly inspired wisdom or profound sermon, but by the pouring out of God's Holy Spirit as it was in the day of Pentecost. By the time I am drawn into this fold, they are a small congregation of less than fifty souls praising God in an abandoned school building tucked behind a grove of Weeping Willows within a suburb of Long Beach City California. There are neither rich, nor are there poor here, no academics, or hierarchy of prestige. They are as one body worshipping God in one spirit. I praise God that I became part of this living miracle, to know the power of the Holy Spirit the moment I am drawn into their midst. In time this congregation of believers, move first to the auditorium of an abandoned school house, and then to a rented church in *Forest Lawn Cemetery,* allowed to use the facility after the service of another congregational ceremony. My own father knows salvation here, only weeks prior to a fatal accident on the Pacific Coast highway. This is a remarkable testament of its own, as profound as my own miracle of when Jesus appears to my lost soul trapped in a darkness eternal, resurrecting me to life everlasting.

In time men of enterprise acquire positions of authority, as the congregation continues to expand, attracting the wealthier elite. Plans for the construction of a *super-church* with a school and Day Care Center designed around Christian values, soon occupies the minds and hearts of those dedicated to preaching the gospel. Projects of this magnitude cost money, which calls for the need of more tithing. Before long the emphasis begins to center around these worldly visions of economic enterprise. Soon popular political issues find their way into the pulpit, as greater interest placed upon values of affiliation. Standards of righteousness soon established to judge good and evil according to works of outward appearance. As this body of believers administer toward the needs of an earthly structure, the less spiritual the gold placed upon the altar. It is not my place to judge the intentions of these well-meaning souls; only in observation, it is contritely easy to be deceived by the Mammon of this world.

Just as the spirit disperses the early believers after Pentecost, nearly all these original believers dispersed like seeds from a pod, becoming sewn into many places determined by the Holy Spirit. I am such a seed, justified by God through Jesus Christ, with no certain destiny or place to call home upon this present earth. I am subject to judgment in this world, but my resurrection in the revelation of my Lord and savior, Jesus Christ, as certain as when first I believed. If I am made to be despised in my generation, then I pray it be to the glory of God, so that even one lost sheep might be found.

The greatest weapon of the enemy is to make the world think of Christianity as a competing new religion instructed since the past two thousand years to compare with the many other deities and philosophies of populated societies. Those truly born again are not indoctrinated into a new religion, but are the fiery embers of a living testament inspired through each generation, reaching into the firmaments of time and space. They are the sweet savor of praise unto God. Remembering that Jesus did not entreat men to submit to any law not already in existence, but becomes witness of how men ought to conduct themselves with one another. The famous Sermon on the Mount not instruction of how mankind ought to live; it is representation of different natures through submission. There is no mention of hierarch, political position, or greater earthly reward to the blessed. The blessing of the blessed is in doing God's will according to the calling of each. There are few men of greater religious prominence, than those Scribes and Pharisees living in Jerusalem in the days Jesus walks mortal upon the earth. Yet Jesus condemns them as fools and hypocrites. There are none that followed the precepts of the law more judiciously than those stewards of the Temple condemned as workers of iniquity. It is a fact that the son of a carpenter from Galilee represents the whole claim of their religious diligence, only they are unable to see it. Jesus provides this stern rebuke in the Gospel of Mathew, Chapter 5, verses 17-22 (NKJV):

> *"Do not think that I came to destroy the Law or the Prophets. I did not come to destroy but to fulfill. For assuredly, I say to you, till heaven and earth pass away, one[b] jot or one tittle will by no means pass from the law till all is fulfilled. Whoever therefore breaks one of the least of these commandments, and teaches men so, shall be called least in the kingdom of heaven; but whoever does and teaches them, he shall be called great in the kingdom of heaven. For I say to you, that unless your righteousness exceeds the righteousness of the scribes and Pharisees, you will by no means enter the kingdom of heaven. "You have heard that it was said to those[d] of old, 'You shall not murder, and whoever murders will be in danger of the judgment.' But I say to you that whoever is angry with his brother without a cause shall be in danger of the judgment. And whoever says to his brother, 'Raca!' shall be in danger of the council. But whoever says, You fool!' shall be in danger of hell fire."*

Except we have a mediator of promise as a guarantor of something far better than present condition allows, none can be saved. I wish to make it clear, that many of the opinions expressed here are my own based on present observation and I pray continually for the leading of the Holy Spirit. Ultimately the Lord will make a quick work of judgment, even without my consent or understanding. But make no mistake, the clock is ticking down; and there is nothing humanly possible to change the directional time flow. The salt in our lives is not the fruit of our good works only, but in the living testimony of our resurrected Lord. It is this power that convicts men of sin in the world to the end of salvation. Surely, I would not know the limitless victory in Christ today were it not for the boldness of many sent to preach to my lost soul. By the example shown to me in a season when my heart far from God, I maintain that love and grace ought to abound more abundantly. The name of Jesus Christ is the profound power that transcends all principalities and every stronghold of proud reason. If we are ourselves spared through acceptance; if our souls imparted with a revelation of grace; then should we not share that good report to all freely, as freely it is given? Nevertheless there are preachers of the gospel, and some made judges raised mightily against present evil. Of these I have no correction, for such are discerned by God in the time and season of their calling raised up for purpose of conviction. I pray only that I remember those in bonds, as though I share in their bondage, and those who are persecuted out of fear and ignorance. I pray that I look upon the least with abiding compassion, remembering always that I am the work of grace and not the many works of righteousness. Or else that I might forget that I, too, am born of flesh and blood after the similitude of Adam. May the love of Jesus Christ prevail over all reason, making straight the crooked way, providing hope to the hopeless, and giving security to those who hear his voice. To this I say amen!

So easily we deceive ourselves by thinking in terms of quantum value, becoming present day Scribes, easily discerning the evil in our brother's eye through the lens of our own righteousness, invariably perceiving good and evil as a sliding scale of forgiveness achievable through mortal comprehension. If the God of heaven and earth can animate dead stones to worship him, then this same God can surely preserve a living testimony in every generation: an illumination of compassion sent into the fortress of every darkness, as a beacon of hope to many lost souls that hear his voice. These messengers will stand justified in the last day.

However, the voice of a prophet is seldom recognized in his own country, or listened to by those most near. A faithless world might ask, from whence comes the horde of terrorism that strikes at the very heart of opulent society? It is a grave mistake to assume that the jaded vision of Camelot enough cake to feed the destitute poor of the world. By effectively removing the God of creation and his Messiah from the equation of present existence, humanity has bred the generations of discord and spiritual deficiency observed in the core of modern civilization. The multitudes of exclusion objectively reason the corundum of present conditions, which ultimately leads them into a future of servitude to an elite oligarchy blind to their needs. They have become the cry of the disenfranchised, a back lash against materialism fueled by zealous spirits of extremism. These armies of borderless occupation represent the collective grievances of the poor and the oppressed inspired through charismatic revelation of a future earthly kingdom ruled by a strict Caliph imposing a religious standard of blind obedience in the name of a divine vision. Such is the mind of deception: an order devoted to the promotion of tangible violence as the ultimate solution, a misguided doctrine of destruction with a purpose to annihilate every symbol of material organization, not designed after its own conception. Those that follow unwittingly, become the whip in the hand of Satan, hordes of consuming locust clearing away the chafe and sweeping clear the fallow land in preparation for the battleground of Armageddon.

Christians with knowledge of what it means to be Christian must stand neither on the left, nor on the right, or even politically in the center; but must walk upon the shifting earth, even as Christ walked, as an abiding living testament against the imaginings of this present world. They are the candlestick of hope and revival to all mankind for the remnant of salvation. Satan's kingdom is not divided, but is evidence of the earthly factions we clearly observe through a history of reorganization and at the malignant core of cohesive society. To fear Satan is to fear the chimera of death and destruction; the fear of the Lord is the recognition of salvation to our divinely inspired souls in the presence of physical calamity.

So what does it mean to fear the Lord? Fear is a mortal condition innately designed as mechanism of preservation in the face of imminent peril. We easily observe this action reaction formation in the animal kingdom between prey and predator. The rodent does not anticipate continuously the lurking presence of a hungry cat. Nor will every animal become the meal of another. All along the food chain, there exist autonomic reflex based on instinct of survival. But above this natural condition, there is a spiritual condition of determined order through faithful acceptance. And as we have already seen, there are existing forces of supernatural potential far more destructive than the preservation of physical life only. These ought to be recognized as the agents of entropic design of a directional universe fulfilling the consequential domino effect of sin and death within a prescribed context. They have no power other than the power given them from the beginning. But there exists a higher power, as far removed from this present earth, as heaven from hell. Only through faith in the one Christ, fashioned both man and God, the beginning heir of an eternal kingdom, not designed after the similitude of this present condition, can any be saved.

It should be further clarified that there have always been pluralistic gods historically considered terrifying influences demanding bloodlust and human carnage to satisfy an appetite for human suffering. Even to this day they continue to thrive on fear and statues of interpreted judgments executed through mortal dispensation. Although these fallen angels rule even now supreme over worldly principalities, they are lesser in force than the existing elements. In other words, they know their limits and are constrained by those limits. They know that only the God in heaven is able to bring rain in season and bountiful harvest to the inhabitants of the earth. They know only that this God was before the days of Noah, and is the living God of Abraham and of Moses. This is the only supreme potentate with the power to deliver, or to allow the angels of sin and destruction to follow their course of death and corruption upon the sons of men. Fallen Satan, as a hungry lion, roams continuously to snare whom he will. Without God's benevolent protection no flesh should be secured from his hungry jaws. Today we call the mischief of this devil an actuary of Murphy's Law, or the evidence of thermodynamic decline. Even the story of Job--about a man considered righteous in his generation--even this just man does not blame God after great loss and suffering, but bows down in humility before the visage of true righteousness, declaring the God of creation faithful in all his ways. It was not God that tormented this man in the flesh, but Satan by permission. Those that truly trust in God's benevolent nature have nothing to fear, but the children of rebellion have everything to fear. All living creatures are subject to death in this present world of sin, but greater is the promise of life everlasting to those that trust in the resurrected Messiah.

Just as our solar system and the cosmic position of planet earth exists precariously in a "Goldie Lock" zone, we too exist mortally by the abiding grace of our creator. The deliverance of the future Jewish people by the hand of Moses from Egypt, the deliverance from certain death in the wilderness, and the enduring testament of statues inscribed on stone tablets remembered from generation to generation. Through constant reminder, this promise of deliverance has endured through the millenniums by the diligent observance of days and events, thus providing consistency to the promise and to the fulfillment of all righteousness in the provision of Jesus Christ, God's only begotten son, as an eternal seal of resurrection to all those inspired through living faith. As it is written by a young shepherd boy named David in Psalms 111, verse 10, (KJV).

> *"The fear of the LORD is the beginning of wisdom: a good understanding have all they that do his commandments: his praise endureth for ever. Praise ye the LORD. Blessed is the man that feareth the LORD, that delighteth greatly in his commandments."*

Once again, this is not the heavy burden of a religion, but the living proclamation of a hope and a promise recompensed to the seed of the first man made of clay and in the image of the creator. This is the truth contained in a covenant of mercy and goodwill. Satan, disguised as religious obligation, manifests as a light of confusion to those who seek righteousness through mortal means.

Irrespective of the challenges of our gender, our physical capacity, our society, our language, or our religion, we are born individually, ultimately loved by our creator, and presented with the free gift of salvation to our immortal souls. Only it is up to us to accept or to reject this unconditional offer. It is not a contract with hidden clauses and concealed snares of oppression. It is a freedom immeasurable and a liberty beyond the imagination of present existence. I am less the example of righteousness in my generation; yet I am sent with an unfailing testament of personal salvation, proclaiming the righteous mercy of my God, and your God; my savior, and your savior. Refrain from judging the messenger, but consider well in your heart the message. Some choose to count among the sheep of this world for the sake of expedience; and others by the vision of a promised land to inherit. I would rather all allow the abiding presence of the Holy Spirit to inspire this brief measure of existence through the perfect love of our resurrected Lord. Jesus Christ a man that died on a wooden cross in a province of Rome more than two thousand years ago. But neither death, nor even hell could constrain this Messiah of divine providence, resurrected from the grave, whole and without sin, the first and the last code of eternal perfection. Mortal men strive through proud intellect to cultivate proselytes of a better and wiser progeny. However, in the Book of Mathew, Chapter 3, verse 9 (KJV), Jesus says to those standing by in judgment:

> *"And think not to say within yourselves, We have Abraham to our father: for I say unto you, that God is able of these stones to raise up children unto Abraham."*

In his many letters to the different Roman and Greek principalities, the apostle Paul addresses conditions specific to a particular *Polis*, each custom-written to the needs of that group. Paul speaks first to political conditions that exist within a specific community, as well as using references of allegory that a unique body of believers might relate to. Women excerpt powerful political influence within certain echelons of society, sometimes resorting to carnal reasoning based on pride and jealousies. Also there are the hierarchal structure embedded within these cultures, which greatly shapes the understanding and acceptance of those newly converted from remnants of dead religions devoted to meaningless rituals absent of power. Paul, therefore, instructs in terms that they could relate to, using identifiable examples. He is not teaching a prescribed hierarchy between men and women; nor does he send the same letter to all of the new believers in Christ throughout Asia to be included into a subset of doctrines for religious instruction. Paul knows well that the religion inflections that guided the Jewish people since the day of Moses the only true religious expression. The collective canon of twenty seven books, we know as the New Testament Bible, did not exist in its present abstract until almost two hundred years after Christ's resurrection. In fact, the only agreed upon commandments sent to all those early converts, who believed in the revelation of good news, pertained to four precepts of conscience, as clearly outlined by the early church leaders in the Book of Acts, Chapter 15, verses 19-31 (KJV).

> *"Wherefore my sentence is, that we trouble not them, which from among the Gentiles are turned to God: But that we write unto them, that they abstain from pollutions of idols, and from fornication, and from things strangled, and from blood. For Moses of old time hath in every city them that preach him, being read in the synagogues every sabbath day. Then pleased it the apostles and elders, with the whole church, to send chosen men of their own company to Antioch with Paul and Barnabas; namely, Judas surnamed Barsabas, and Silas, chief men among the brethren: And they wrote letters by them after this manner; The apostles and elders and brethren send greeting unto the brethren which are of the Gentiles in Antioch and Syria and Cilicia: Forasmuch as we have heard, that certain which went out from us have troubled you with words, subverting your souls, saying, Ye must be circumcised, and keep the law: to whom we gave no such commandment: It seemed good unto us, being assembled with one accord, to send chosen men unto you with our beloved Barnabas and Paul, Men that have hazarded their lives for the name of our Lord Jesus Christ. We have sent therefore Judas and Silas, who shall also tell you the same things by mouth. For it seemed good to the Holy Ghost, and to us, to lay upon you no greater burden than these necessary things; That ye abstain from meats offered to idols, and from blood, and from things strangled, and from fornication: from which if*

ye keep yourselves, ye shall do well. Fare ye well. So when they were dismissed, they came to Antioch: and when they had gathered the multitude together, they delivered the epistle: Which when they had read, they rejoiced for the consolation."

They rejoice not because of a better religious instruction, but because they are made free by the power of the resurrected Christ. As the Apostle Paul makes us continually aware, there were those even then constrained through the need for religious directive, which sought continuously to suppress the liberty of faith. And still today ordained preachers, and those who feel endowed with the responsibility of religious guidance, tend to espouse a theological interpretation that these combined letters teach a rigid definition of what a Christian life ought to be in all contexts, instructing a singular way to serve God. This exclusion doctrine is nowhere to be found in the teachings of Jesus Christ during his brief sojourn.

The original Ten Commandments designed as a clear directive to bring judgment upon a world turned to paganism. Laws revealed to a chosen people, written by the same finger that instilled these statues in the human heart from the beginning of creation. Laws not designed to oppress the population, as did the pagan gods, which brought upon mankind violent aggression, demanding cruel obedience by the bloody hands of their worshippers for fear of retribution. This first Testament provides to the flesh better instruction on the design of an embedded code. These statures revealed to the souls of men a visage of the creator that heaven and earth, reviving hope in mortal anticipation of a future Messiah to free all men from the yoke of sin and death, and ultimately from condemnation of entropy. The spiritual birth of a New Testament to fulfill the old, a better code to overwrite the first. This manifested in the death and resurrection of Jesus Christ, as affirmed by the Apostle Paul in his second letter to the Corinthians, Chapter 3, verses 1-18 *Berean Study Bible* (BSB).

"Are we beginning to commend ourselves again? Or do we need, like some people, letters of recommendation to you or from you? You yourselves are our letter, inscribed on our hearts, known and read by everyone. It is clear that you are a letter from Christ, the result of our ministry, written not with ink but with the Spirit of the living God, not on tablets of stone but on tablets of human hearts. Such confidence before God is ours through Christ. Not that we are competent in ourselves to claim that anything comes from us, but our competence comes from God. And He has qualified us as ministers of a new covenant, not of the letter but of the Spirit; for the letter kills, but the Spirit gives life. Now if the ministry of death, which was engraved in letters on stone, came with such glory that the Israelites could not gaze at the face of Moses because of its fleeting glory, will not the ministry of the Spirit be even more glorious? For if the ministry of condemnation was glorious, how much more glorious is the ministry of righteousness! Indeed, what was once glorious has no glory now in comparison to the glory that surpasses it. For if what was fading away came with glory, how much greater is the glory of that which endures! Therefore, since we have such a hope, we are very bold. We are not like Moses, who would put a veil over his face to keep the Israelites from gazing at the end of what was fading away. But their minds were closed. For to this day the same veil remains at the reading of the old covenant. It has not been lifted, because only in Christ can it be removed. And even to this day when Moses is read, a veil covers their hearts. But whenever anyone turns to the Lord, the veil is taken away. Now the Lord is the Spirit, and where the Spirit of the Lord is, there is freedom. And we, who with unveiled faces all reflect the glory of the Lord, are being transformed into His image with intensifying glory, which comes from the Lord, who is the Spirit."

All that profess goodness upon the earth should remember always the only commandments presented by God's begotten son are to love first the father, as he *first* loved us, and to cherish our fellow man, as we cherish our present dignity. Also consider that the greatest threat to the human soul is the coded DNA of our creature existence through rehearsed reasoning. Mankind is by nature xenophobic, hardwired to alienate anything that does not look and act as us or does not share our group affiliation. Mankind is naturally homophobic, because sexual bias represents a biological necessity for each generation to seed the earth and for specific population expansion. Mankind is naturally sexist, since the female of our species represents the foundation of cohesive society and the future resource of civilization. Mankind is naturally rebellious, quick to make war and destroy life. Too quick to judge and dispatch that which he does not understand. He is quicker still to establish a standard of good and evil based on a myopic understanding, defined through the presentation for a better future. Men with right wing agendas inadvertently become wolves in sheep clothing, desiring to maintain the flow of time progression in a rigid comprehension of what went before. Men too far left think the world is as it has always been, professing to be neither sheep nor wolves, yet oblivious to the fact that a society without restraint ultimately leads to anarchy. Both positions breed the conditions for Antichrist. Both ignorant of the true measure of mercy manifested in the birth, death, and resurrection of the Lord of Lords.

Chapter 3
THE CULTURE OF DEATH

Egypt that once great and ancient kingdom of the Nile revives to the consciousness of humankind the knowledge and fear of death. It also provides us with a glimpse into that perilous passage associated with apprehension of the underworld after this brief sojourn over. In the early half of the nineteenth century, the French linguist, Jean François Champollion, decrypted the meaning of the Rosetta stone, resurrecting a language composed in the *Book of the Dead*, as an instruction guide to what happens to the soul upon departure from the realm of this living.

The famous 5th century Greek historian, *Herodotus,* goes into great detail describing his observations of how Egyptian embalmers prepared the remains of the physical body for transition to the afterlife ruled by an incarnated God named *Osiris.* This precise and economically viable procedure made death a business of greater potential than any transaction conducted by the living. An enterprise that continues to flourish to this day, translating through many cultures and many histories. Economic issues aside, the remains of a person deceased evokes a range of emotions, often manifesting into feelings of obligation. Few people will stop on the roadside to collect the carcass of an animal killed by an automobile. Even fewer will bow their heads in respect for the cadaver they are about to consume during an evening meal. But when it comes to the death of a human body, the personal conflict between inescapable reality and impending fear of the unknown becomes irrefutable.

Much resource expended for the recovery of even one body trapped in an abysmal tomb, or scattered remains upon a battlefield. It could be inferred that society more devoted to the enshrinement of the dead, than the guaranteed surety of the living. We empty the chewed skeletal remains of our *roast beast* without conscience into the garbage pail, yet cringe at the thought of taking a shortcut through the local cemetery. Is human flesh therefore more sacred than the animals we eat or the many organisms nourished in season?

I remember from my childhood a great aunt, who died on my father's side of the family. Everyone goes to the funeral; all except me. I lay bedridden with a bad case of the mumps, cared for by a nurse hired to the occasion. It is the first time in my juvenile life that I hear the word *death*. What did it mean? Did the fact that I could not get out of bed mean that I am dying? It is not the death of this woman that inspired me, but the sudden realization of my own mortality. In honesty I did not even know the lady, nor have I ever gone to visit her graveside.

That day during the course of a feverous dream, I find myself between two wrestling giants: one blue and one pink. They say we rarely dream in color, but this indelible memory represents the vivid reminder of a personal exception. These two Cyclops are altogether hairless; their flesh pliable and suffocating, as they embrace, rolling over me time and time again. This escalating battle goes on all afternoon to my imminent peril. They seem oblivious to my presence, locked together in a desperate eternal struggle. I can only describe it as a mortal combat, a skirmish of immense consequence. Then they just turn and walk away in opposite directions. That night the fever breaks and I sleep. Never have I thought about that terrible battle again, until just now.

Much energetic construction and use of resources devoted to rituals of interment, which go back even as far as the prehistory customs of early Neanderthals. Recently discovered prehistoric *'grave fields'* contain the bones of once living beings believed to be the forefathers of modern man. A variety of artifacts that exemplify living achievements and worldly acquisitions (*for example a hunting prize or material adornment*) cherished by the departed.

This exaggerated reverence to the creature varies little in the analogs of many accumulating archeological discoveries, except for more or less elaborate window-dressing practiced by some cultures. The Mesopotamians often placed the bodies of the deceased into sealed jars, or lay them on their backs horizontally in wood or clay coffins. Some societies tend to express possessive attachment to their former lives by exacting cruel rituals dictating murder of those closest to the deceased; while other customs opt to choose the most simple and expedient means possible, as evidenced by the Viking pyres practiced by Nordic cultures. According to the ancient traditions of Greek ancestry, proper preparation and burial of the dead embrace prescribed etiquettes of respect. Once the *psyche,* or spirit, of the deceased person has left the body, then the remains are reverenced or disgraced in accordance to traditional judgment. It seems that all cultures and societies share this value to varying degrees with prescriptions of honor or dishonor to the remains of those past on, depending on the status of the dead individual. The most infamous example found in Homer's legend of Paris, whose headless body dragged around the walls of Troy for his bold insult of kidnapping the beautiful Helen, wife to king Menelaus. This despicable mutilation of a dead body marks the beginning of the end of the ten year Trojan War.

Nevertheless, we are most familiar with those Egyptian Pharaoh mummies sealed inside massive pyramid structures, entombed within elaborate coffins within coffins, which have made such an impression in early screen fiction, inspiring horrific tales of the walking dead returning to terrorize the living. For some reason this simulated idea of a life after death status appeals most to the western psyche. But it is by no means unique to history; nor is it the aspired summit of mortal imagination.

The dynastic rulers of ancient China often created intricately fashioned effigies to accompany them into the afterlife. Qin Shi Huang Di, the first emperor to unify the six warring states of the east under the banner of a singular kingdom, instructs an elaborate compliment to accompany him into the next world. Among his many ruling accomplishments is construction of China's first Great Wall, minting of a unified currency, as well as establishing a system of standardized weights and measurements. Without question the most enduring legacy of this ancient emperor, the uncovered remains of a terracotta army of more than 8000 life-size militiamen divided into platoons, along with a troop of entertainers to attend him beyond the end of his mortal existence on this earth. Each soldier provided uniquely individual features and armed according to rank. An entombment that occurs more than 200 years before the birth of Jesus Christ.

The fearless Celtics, the bloodthirsty Scythians, even the judiciously practical Romans-- all searching for a measure of afterlife through perverted notions of creature revival. Whether preserved by resins and the embalmed carcass entombed; whether cremated and the few pounds of ashes gathered into elegantly crafted urns; or the remains fed to carrion, fed to lions, or committed to the deep, rich or poor, male or female--every living generation acknowledges, and are undeniably a testament to the mortality of existence. In more than five thousand years of recorded history, there is only one man that rises from the grave in glorified form, no longer just mortal, no longer restrained by the elements of entropy, witnessed through the testament of many that saw and interacted with this person postmortem.

As callus as it may sound, death and attempts to prevent death, has greatly overshadowed the truer definition of what it means to be alive. Figuratively speaking, this is like the caterpillar refusing to slumber for fear of what it might become; or an expectant mother resisting the natural process of childbirth for fear of the pain. Although there have been many compositions about contrite souls of the damned returning to warn the living against the wages of sin and the judgment of damnation, no record that I can think of where an actual departed soul comes back and states that death, as an event, is a terrible occurrence. As long as neurons are transmitting, the transition in some cases may certainly be traumatic to the body. But is it really as gruesome an event as witnessed by the living observer?

I once touched a 12000 volt electrical medium tension voltage line, severely burned by the hot electricity, and then fall over 36 feet. The impact shatters my pelvis, breaking both hips and fracturing two vertebrae. On this day I die, aware of racing through a void of bright light, leaving the earth and life I knew far behind. Time and space become meaningless as I am drawn irresistibly to a final destination that I can only describe as the *Last Day of Judgment*. Then a voice from heaven shouts--*No!* Upon returning to normal acceleration, I am only vaguely aware of my broken body, detachedly conscious that it is in excruciating pain. Only my soul is now out of synchronization with present time, as though I am witnessing the event in the third person. This is not the first time I have come near to death of the flesh, but the first time I actually physically disconnect from diurnal time and space. This testament is true, as I continue in the temporal world of the living to this day by a grace not yet clear.

I am further reminded of a movie I saw recently called **127 Hours** based on an actual event. It is about a young man that becomes trapped in an isolated canyon with his arm pinned under a boulder. On the fifth day of his captivity, he makes the unthinkable decision to break the bone and cut off the dead appendage with a dull instrument. In my mind this takes courageous resolve and an enormous will to survive. Maybe this is an example of what animal existence all about, the instinctive determination to stay alive, no matter the cost. This is no doubt the underlying prognosis of xenophobia, material gluttony leading to elitism, and perhaps even the root cause of mass genocides. If only the animal matters, then all other considerations become irrelevant to the question of survival. What then is the significance of morality, integrity, or ethics?

The idea of suicide and assisted suicide is considered taboo in most societies. This is a subject that I wish to address cautiously, since physical death represents in the minds of many the final frontier of transition. While it is true that eternal longevity in the palm of no hand, this is not to say that everyone must continue to endure for the sake of moral prescription. I have witnessed many cases when individuals carefully calculated their suicides, only to survive by a miracle; while others obey judiciously all the insurance guidelines, exercise caution to the extreme, only to die because of some errant event beyond the peripheral of their observation. There have been cases when an individual avoids one kind of death, only to walk into the jaws of another. These facts do not secure permission to die or to live, only that it provides evidence that we are in less control of our destinies than we might think.

I believe wholeheartedly in miracles of healing, but not everyone sick or maimed are recipients of regeneration in their lifetime. Even though Lazarus raised whole from the grave, he still remains mortal and subject to thermodynamic processes destined not to continue in the flesh forever. Consider that when Christ walks the earth in physical presence, only a remnant of those in the city of Jerusalem and the surrounding principalities granted physical healing by his virtue; nor was global healing achieved by the hands of the spiritually charged apostles after the out-pouring of the Holy Spirit on the Day of Pentecost. Even to this day, we do not find evidence where every soul inside the most spirit-filled congregation all blessed with healing of the flesh. I have heard even men of God say that the reason for this is because of lack of faith. Nevertheless, the many letters and recorded accounts composing the New Testament Bible, states clearly that faith is not manifested in ourselves, but is a gift from God. Therefore, is it the will of God that only some be healed and others perish in vain? An explanation to this question provided in the Gospel of John, chapter 9, verses 2-3 (KJV).

> *"And his disciples asked him, saying, Teacher, who did sin, this man, or his parents, that he was born blind?" "Jesus answered, Neither has this man sinned, nor his parents: but that the works of God should be made manifest in him."*

Since a man cannot by self-determination bring good or evil to fruition, or to bring rain or a pleasant breeze, or even to add one hair white or dark to his head. How can this man judge the ways of almighty God, who has placed heaven and earth in a prescribed fashion as a small measure of designed purpose? I am convinced there is no power in this world, or the potential of many worlds presently unseen, capable of altering the manifestation of salvation presented in a time divided by time and in a season already clearly translated. A judge is an expert of laws and statues governing those under the law. But this assumes that a righteous standard is already in effect. The law that existed before grace is an exactitude of how to live as an individual in a community.

The sixth commandment given to Moses inscribed on stone tablets by the hand of God states, *Thy shall not kill.* Many religious scholars use this single commandment to condemn suicide regardless of the circumstances. These same scholars dismiss other commandments by suggestion that there are degrees of transgressions, or by rightly pointing out that Christ died on the cross as a sacrificial lamb to atone for deliberate transgression of the law. They should rather consider that God has not turned a blind eye on the many young people murdered in schools and social gatherings in America today because of epidemic gun violence; or those children condemned to live under medical supervision and destined to die early because of greedy food producers, valuing profit over the health of addicted populations. Nor has God abandoned the many thousands of innocent children which perish daily in desolate African countries and countries ravaged by war and famine. Do they think God blind to the many detrimental choices made by each one of us daily?

Another way of considering this question: Does the righteousness of some exceed that of others by better works presented through an unblemished life? And if even one man is capable to aspire to a condition of self-righteousness in the eyes of God, then what need have any in the sacrifice of Christ as a sin offering. In the book of Romans, Chapter 3, verses 10-12 (KJV) the Apostle Paul states:

> *"As it is written, There is none righteous, no, not one: there is none that understands, there is none that seeks after God. They are all gone out of the way, they are together become unprofitable; there is none that doeth good, no, not one."*

Jesus speaks even more plainly to the judiciously pure Pharisees concerning the attribute of sin:

> *"Whosoever hates his brother is a murderer: and ye know that no murderer hath eternal life abiding in him."*

These words spoken to make a point that a man might belief himself as a disciple of the law according to his own interpretation; but that God sees and judges the heart. For it is from the heart that good and evil seeds spring into life, thus making this world a better or worse place.

I remember seeing a very disturbing movie made in 1971 titled *Johnny Got His Gun*. Without going into much gruesome detail, this is a story about a young man horribly mutilated by an artillery blast, leaving him without limbs, destroying his eyes, teeth, and tongue, but his mind remains clearly intact. He keeps pounding his head on the pillow, until someone realizes it is Morse code. His first desire is to die, a demand refused on the position of morality. He is even denied the opportunity to be publicly displayed so that others might know the true horrors of war. Although this is a fictionalized account with very real survivors from the many wars that have occurred throughout history, it does raise some rather disturbing questions. Is life at any cost worth the price of suffering? And should that decision be universal to all and to all conditions? Most would agree that a terminally ill cancer patient should receive adequate quantifies of morphine, even if it poses the risk of a fatal overdose. This happened to my stepfather, who died peacefully in his bed, because a nurse administered an injection determined lethal for the patience's weakened condition. Along with a non-resuscitation order, my paternal guardian privately asked his doctor to make sure he did not experience the terrible pain associated with his particular type of disease. Actually, our family was happy that this loved one never had to experience the greater suffering of final stage cancer. Was the doctor guilty of premeditated murder, and was the patient accomplish to his own demise? Is a person alleviated of responsibility just because they choose death by cop-suicide, by smoking, using alcohol and drugs, or even by eating to death? Was even Christ guilty of premeditated suicide by not appealing to the mercy offered by Pontius Pilate, when Pilate states:

> *"Do you not know that I have power to release you or power to crucify you?"*

I realize that these are extreme examples, but personal life is an extreme condition. We tend to intellectualize for the sake of argument.

I am in no way denying the important difference of elevated principal, only that I believe such principal to be of a higher calling, not based on intellectual or political correctness. If God is able to raise-up the children of Abraham from inanimate stones, he is well capable of preserving his own at the appointed time.

History is laced with incidents of defiance even in the face of death. Many Rabbis take a more ambiguous position when it comes to suicide, suggesting that suicide is a better choice than humiliation and torture by an invader. Who can forget the fall of Masada, as detailed by Jewish historian Josephus, where nearly one thousand people killed themselves, rather than be taken prisoners by the Romans after the siege lasting nearly a year?

Nor should we ever forget the inspiring call at the Alamo overwhelmed by the indomitable Mexican army lead by General Santa Anna! One type of suicide becomes a call to glory, while another labeled as a coward's way out: one guiltless, the other a passage into eternal damnation. As with all matters concerning the rational of logic, the true answers remain within the abstraction of faith found in Romans, Chapter 14, verse 23 (KJV: *"for whatsoever is not of faith is sin."*

Just how deeply embedded is the taboo regarding the preservation of creature existence as God's highest priority? There is not a single world religion that does not take some position in reference to suicide. Catholic doctrine suggests that a person, who has successfully committed suicide because of psychological trauma produced by fear and perception of extreme hardship, are able to find forgiveness through post-mortem prayer. In the fourth century A.D., Bishop Augustine announced that several women, who had committed suicide to avoid rape, were forgiven in the sight of God because of the righteous indignation of their cause. This differs radically from many evangelical denominations, adhering to the doctrine that a person who commits such an act of self-murder is altogether damned: once dead, they can no longer repent and receive forgiveness. Of course, I suppose this assumes that such a person is unsaved, implying that if a person is saved by the blood of Christ, then why would they wish to leave this world? On the other hand, once we have seen beyond temporal existence and receive a glimpse of the eternal kingdom, then why should any of us wish to remain in the flesh longer than necessary? So many Christians get excited over the rapture, believing they will be extracted before the terrible events soon to come upon the earth, as detailed in the *Book of Revelation*. I, too, hope the rapture will come; but hope more that God will leave upon the earth in that terrible day a continuing witness to those abandoned of all hope. For if my Lord and Savior sacrificed his flesh for me, a sinner, then why should I wish not to be sacrificed for the hope of salvation of even one lost brother or sister, whom God loves? Instead to wish escape, perhaps we should remember the already quoted scripture that *"whatever is not of faith is sin"*. To lay down one's life for the salvation of even one soul is a gift of tremendous value. Rather, I think it better to pray for strength in the bosom of faith, than escape out of mortal fear. For if we love one another, as Christ loved us, we will find little room in our hearts for condemnation and loopholes of personal justification.

I read recently in the news that the Islamic general authority issued a *fatwa* against Muslims going to Mars on a one way journey, because it is considered suicide. Suicide is expressly forbidden in Islam. A trip without the possibility of ever returning considered an ultimate violation. Of course, this begs the question: how is it that extremist suicide bombers are encouraged through some interpretations, an act of self-sacrifice often resulting in the murder of innocent men, women, and children? Even though the Quran makes mention in a verse to not kill yourselves out of fear of Allah's judgment; yet, it seems that hatred against unbelievers and infidels trumps all other considerations, including suicide. In the many verses contained in this book, only one discourages suicide, while nearly two dozen rewards such an act when performed in the name of a *just cause* according to the words inspired through the one true prophet.

Hinduism, as with Jainism, sees taking one's life as a violent act resulting in the soul of that individual becoming a ghost and forced to walk the earth in a disembodied state. Whereas, a non-violent suicide, such as fasting to death (a practice reserved to old yogis void of desire or ambition), is considered acceptable. Also, an honorable death on the battlefield is considered a fortunate privilege.

Buddhism, it seems, is one of the few religions that does not altogether condemn the practice of suicide. It only states that there are negative connotations restricting the path toward enlightenment through reincarnation. Interestingly, Wiccans, a *neo-pagan* belief in witchcraft and nature gods, share this same philosophy that everyone gets a second, a third, or as many chances necessary to get it right regardless of how one lives or dies.

As we can see from these several examples, the creature existence seems bound to a collective belief inspired through individual consciousness. An innate code exists in all living matrixes with an innate awareness from the beginning that it is made eternal: a code corrupted by a curse of made mortal. This intricate code of many parts making the whole is integral evidence to the potential of immortality contrary to observation. Since all physicality has a beginning and an ending, the obsession with creature existence a logical absurdity within present context. Even what we think is us actually a composition of myriad thriving processes. Literally trillions of body cells, made up of even greater trillions of bacteria with coded design, die and are replaced in varying cycles throughout every individual's lifetime. Over a period of between 7 to 10 years nearly every cell in the body dies and will involuntarily renew, with only a few exceptions, mostly those surrounding the cerebral cortex. I hope to address these exceptions in more detail within context of a future discussion. The point being that today you are less the person you were ten years ago; even than the model of car that you are driving under an expired warranty. Meaning that the multitrillion cells composing your physical existence have died and been replaced by new ones, including your entire skeleton.

Of course, as I gaze into the mirror, I can attest to the fact that the process appears less than perfect, a process known as genetic programming, where failure of the software overrides the hardware design. Yes, we are programmed to grow old and die contrary to the way we are made. There are several theories surrounding our genetic clock and why this retro-failure occurs. Perhaps, this is a built-in failsafe to guarantee the balanced existence within temporal condition. Anything else would surely spell disaster, resulting in overpopulation, shortage of resources, and even cannibalism. The fact that we have an inherently eternal design in the hardware indicates a marvelous potential to the underlying architecture. Jesus Christ is living proof of this better hardware and software design.

The biology provides a blueprint for the matrix, the living soul a contained energy field, and finally a spiritual charge to lock the pattern into an eternal condition, not relational to present time and space. This trinity is essential to being, and without the completion of this cycle, the reaction contained in the first two conditions dissipate back into the base elements. The resurrected Christ represents the manifestation of a revived code transfiguring the old. This better code is the beginning of a new heaven and a new earth and worlds without end.

Presently the law of sin and death prevails. We hear almost daily in the news about a person of wealth and social statue, who inexplicably kills themselves. This is not supposed to happen. We can understand why a person burdened by some physical handicap, or by external pressures of survival might turn to suicide as a last measure of escape. But why someone who has everything the world can offer be depressed to the point of choosing self-annihilation? It is not substance that provides meaning and happiness in life, but the essence within context. Every urban community in the world gleams like a ripe apple in the sun, but rotten to the core with homelessness and poverty. Unwillingly, we are indoctrinated into a society ruled by principalities of division, becoming pawns of ideologies that inspire xenophobic hatred and rationalized fear. Human integrity overshadowed by the aloof arrogance of demagoguery in the blind pursuit of wealth and prosperity, resulting in crimes of acquisition and human despair. Even though an individual--or even a nation--chooses to live in isolation behind the walls of a fortress, the cries of those without cannot be muffled. Accept it or not, we are all connected like molecules of water in an ocean. This is both a legacy and a responsibility.

As an observation, it seems humanity devotes a great deal of attention to ethics of abstraction, but little to the equality of present need. We say the hungry of the world ought to be fed, but call proportionate distribution of resources irresponsible Socialism. We relish in luxuries promised by Capitalism, but groan at the idea of paying taxes that subsidize programs of inequity. Since when are the needs of humanity a platform of contention to be negotiated?

Though divided by politics, by culture, by historical integration, we are all human, and therefore brothers under the skin. If we truly love God, we will also love our fellowmen as ourselves, seeking always inroads of peace and shared prosperity: the true essence of humanity defined by the measure of human compassion. As Jesus warns in the Gospel of Mathew, Chapter 16, verses 26-27 (KJV):

> *"For what is a man profited, if he shall gain the whole world, and lose his own soul? or what shall a man give in exchange for his soul? For the Son of man shall come in the glory of his Father with his angels; and then he shall reward every man according to his works."*

We should not ignore the enormous meaning that even Jesus born in flesh as a Jewish man, walked the earth in Jewry, died and entombed according to Jewish custom. This is important to note, if we are to gain any real appreciation of our existence within context. His genetic birth, life, and death are the prophetic lessons, ultimately establishing the foundation of all things. All that is begotten and born must also die. But the true meaning of God's Messiah is not fixed in historical context only, nor is just about genetic code. This same Jesus, whom his brethren crucified without just cause, could not be contained to a grave of corruption; but is risen a regenerated being. He is the first of his kind, the matrix of a new and better archetype to both Jew and Gentile, and a jubilant inspiration to all mankind. Through this vital process of regeneration, this man made in the likeness of flesh no longer exists in locality of time and space. Jesus is the living archetype of new hardware exceeding the old. As stated specifically in 2 Corinthians, Chapter 5, verse 17 (KJV):

> *"Therefore if any man be in Christ, he is a new creature: old things are passed away; behold, all things are become new."*

The God of the Holy Bible represents a standard of absolute justice, as sure as the conditions regulating local time and space. It is literally the name *Jehovah*, the God of covenant first used in Genesis, Chapter 22, verses 2-14 (KJV), which ultimately spares the sacrificial blood of Isaac from his father's devout hand, presenting future analogy of God's only begotten son sacrificed for the sins of the world. It is interesting to note that within this same scripture the word "love" first appears in the Bible, when God instructs Abraham of the unthinkable surrender he must make.

> *"And he said, Take now thy son, thine only son Isaac, whom thou love, and get thee into the land of Moriah; and offer him there for a burnt offering upon one of the mountains which I will tell thee of. And Abraham rose up early in the morning, and saddled his ass, and took two of his young men with him, and Isaac his son, and clave the wood for the burnt offering, and rose up, and went unto the place of which God had told him. Then on the third day Abraham lifted up his eyes, and saw the place afar off. And Abraham said unto his young men, Abide ye here with the ass; and I and the lad will go yonder and worship, and come again to you. And Abraham took the wood of the burnt offering, and laid it upon Isaac his son; and he took the fire in his hand, and a knife; and they went both of them together. And Isaac spake unto Abraham his father, and said, My father: and he said, Here am I, my son. And he said, Behold the fire and the wood: but where is the lamb for a burnt offering? And Abraham said, My son, God will provide himself a lamb for a burnt offering: so they went both of them together. And they came to the place which God had told him of; and Abraham built an altar there, and laid the wood in order, and bound Isaac his son, and laid him on the altar upon the wood. And Abraham stretched forth his hand, and took the knife to slay his son. And the angel of the LORD called unto him out of heaven,*

and said, Abraham, Abraham: and he said, Here am I. And he said, Lay not thine hand upon the lad, neither do thou any thing unto him: for now I know that thou fearest God, seeing thou hast not withheld thy son, thine only son from me. And Abraham lifted up his eyes, and looked, and behold behind him a ram caught in a thicket by his horns: and Abraham went and took the ram, and offered him up for a burnt offering in the stead of his son. And Abraham called the name of that place Jehovahjireh: as it is said to this day, In the mount of the LORD it shall be seen. "

The second time the name of *Jehovah* appears is in Exodus, Chapter 6, verse 3 (KJV), as God reasons with Moses, his chosen deliverer

"And I appeared unto Abraham, unto Isaac, and unto Jacob, by the name of God Almighty, but by my name JEHOVAH was I not known to them."

It is the name *Jehovah* that forgives transgressions and delivers Israel time and time again from the hands of enemies determined against this people's destruction. By God *Jehovah* Christ the Lord conceived; and given a name above all names, *Yeshua*, redeemer of the Jewish people and all nations.

But not every soul who cry out in the name of God, worships the God of covenant. The history found in the pages of the Torah qualifies only one personage as the engineer of creation, emphasizing clearly that the God, *Jehovah*, is not found in the feeble elements of graven images, or in secret incantations, or cryptic meanings derived through devote ritual. Nor does this spirit dwell within the labyrinths of grand worldly structures hewn from the finest materials and made by the hands of the greatest craftsmen. Instead, we are warned that another power exist, given material reign in a season that is short, whose roots are clear and whose ambition for worship obsessive. For Satan is fallen, and even now roams the earth to the confusion and destruction of men. He sits upon a pinnacle of many thrones, ruling principalities through the command of angelic powers that have descended with him from a heavenly abode. Make no mistake there is a war going on here. A war of grand consequence divining the course and events we so candidly describe as reality and world history.

As contradictory as it may sound, fear, guilt, and religion zeal represents Satan's greatest strength over mankind. He knows the void in our souls and the need to fill it with worship. This wicked angel knows it is powerless against those who trust in the Lord of salvation. For during this mortal passing, we reside in shelters of protection against the elements. But when this mortal shall slip away as a spent garment, then we will be clothed in better than this. Therefore, what does it matter if this corruption is laid into a pit, fed to animals, or consumed in flame? The immutable truth: all born equal; all equal in the grave. What mortal truth more true than this? When the dead shall bury their dead, the living raised whole before a thrown of glory. As the Apostle Paul writes in 1 Corinthians, Chapter 15, verses 35-57 (KJV):

> *"But some man will say, How are the dead raised up? and with what body do they come? Thou fool, that which thou sowest is not quickened, except it die: And that which thou sow, thou sow not that body that shall be, but bare grain, it may chance of wheat, or of some other grain: But God gives it a body as it hath pleased him, and to every seed his own body. All flesh is not the same flesh: but there is one kind of flesh of men, another flesh of beasts, another of fishes, and another of birds. There are also celestial bodies, and bodies terrestrial: but the glory of the celestial is one, and the glory of the terrestrial is another. There is one glory of the sun, and another glory of the moon, and another glory of the stars: for one star differs from another star in glory. So also is the resurrection of the dead. It is sown in corruption; it is raised in incorruption: It is sown in dishonour; it is raised in glory: it is sown in weakness; it is raised in power: It is sown a natural body; it is raised a spiritual body. There is a natural body, and there is a spiritual body. And so it is written, The first man Adam was made a living soul; the last Adam was made a quickening spirit. Howbeit that*

was not first which is spiritual, but that which is natural; and afterward that which is spiritual. The first man is of the earth, earthy: the second man is the Lord from heaven. As is the earthy, such are they also that are earthy: and as is the heavenly, such are they also that are heavenly. And as we have borne the image of the earthy, we shall also bear the image of the heavenly. Now this I say, brethren, that flesh and blood cannot inherit the kingdom of God; neither doth corruption inherit incorruption. Behold, I shew you a mystery; We shall not all sleep, but we shall all be changed, In a moment, in the twinkling of an eye, at the last trump: for the trumpet shall sound, and the dead shall be raised incorruptible, and we shall be changed. For this corruptible must put on incorruption, and this mortal must put on immortality. So when this corruptible shall have put on incorruption, and this mortal shall have put on immortality, then shall be brought to pass the saying that is written, Death is swallowed up in victory. O death, where is thy sting? O grave, where is thy victory? The sting of death is sin; and the strength of sin is the law. But thanks be to God, which gives us the victory through our Lord Jesus Christ."

In the zenith of this shadow of passing, we behold evidence in every mortal generation a host of living witness of a far better resurrection. This is the only viable solution to the frustration of our temporal estate, based on a present code designed to fail. Even when this heaven and earth consumed in fervent heat and must pass away, a better code will ascend out of the ashes as God intended from the beginning. *Then will we know as even we are known.*

Chapter 4
HARDWARE CODE OF BIOLOGY

Have you ever stopped to ask yourself what is the meaning of biology? Dictionaries define biology as the study of life through the categorization of specific organisms, referencing phenomenon of physical structure, morphology of design within context of habitat, significance of community interaction, and specificity of reproductive sequence. The core all these driving forces instinctive, not intellectual. It is how kind perpetuates kind; this powerful code written into every gene of every living organism.

Being actively involved in raising a daughter, I observed few gender related differences in the energy level and freedom of participation, until this active pre-teenager had her first menstruation. It was a shock to us both. But after this biological event, we both became aware of some subtle changes, as the child body began to change into that of a woman. Nature imposes its own conditions, regardless of desired prescription. Through this mystery of metamorphosis, my daughter eventually grew-up, fell in love, and has born children. In the process, she and her mate became for a time one mind, devoted to the needs of their family. To such there can be no commandment, but an instinctive creature process fulfilled through nature. This is the truest definition of what it means to be male and female in the present world of conventional design. All things made to a purpose at an allotted time. This is just the way of organic existence. The instinctive code of every species populates itself. As King Solomon wisely states in Ecclesiastes, The Book of the Preacher, Chapter 3, verses 1-8 (KJV):

"To everything there is a season, and a time to every purpose under the heaven: A time to be born, and a time to die; a time to plant, and a time to pluck up that which is planted; A time to kill, and a time to heal; a time to break down, and a time to build up; A time to weep, and a time to laugh; a time to mourn, and a time to dance; A time to throw stones and a time to gather stones; A time to embrace and a time to shun embracing. A time to get, and a time to lose; a time to keep, and a time to cast away; A time to rend, and a time to sew; a time to keep silence, and a time to speak; A time to love, and a time to hate; a time of war, and a time of peace."

The Book of Genesis clearly states that in the beginning God created male and female of every species, imparting to each the natural ability to procreate and to fulfill the earth. The old adage: *put two Ferrets of opposite sex together and within six months you have a breeding colony.*

Regardless of one's philosophical or theological persuasion, this is an irrefutable fact of nature. Bring together a bunch of un-chaperoned teenagers, you can be sure the forces of human bonding diligently challenged. The natural joining of two human beings for the purpose of procreation breeds much more than just offspring, but litanies of romantic and tragic tales spanning the rise and fall of civilizations.

Who can ignore the tragic destiny of Paris because he loved the face that sunk a thousand ships? The consumptive beauty of Cleopatra--the burning lust of mighty Cesar--from what source ebbs these desires of possession of greater force than worldly estates? From what tangled source seep thoughts of darkness imagination to commit murder to one beloved, as witnessed in the Shakespearean tragedy of Othello? Are the many recorded historical events just examples of hormones out of control, or is it nebulous reflection of the human soul overshadowed by spiritual lust of a demigod? Is the attraction between a man and a woman the designed continuance of an earthly genesis, or just the chemical reaction of dopamine mixed with norepinephrine and serotonin, which can be simulated by a hand full of chocolate?

It is interesting to note, that before the revival of the Renaissance, our present notion of romantic love did not exist. Relationships based more on practical exchanges, than on love interest between two people. A father might agree to give his daughter in marriage to a relative stranger in exchange for physical property considered equitable to all. As was the case of Jacob, who served his kinsman, Laban, for fourteen years, having at the end two wives: the older daughter Leah, whom he did not love, and the younger daughter Rachel, whom he did love. In this example, it seems the definition of love more exclusive to the desire of the male, than of the female. History reveals the female psyche more complex to needs of being secure and feelings of being desired, which perhaps triggers a biological reproductive condition. This makes one wonder if what we call love nothing more than chemical reaction, then to what end serves the many expensive customs associated with love and marriage? Since beneath the social veneer, it all comes down to reproduction, why not simplify the process by making houses of reproduction and allow the state to take care of all the necessities of raising offspring? But obviously there is more to biological joining than just the successful passing of genes. Jesus mentions this mystery of entanglement in Mathew, Chapter 19, verses 2 - 9 KJV.

> *"And the Pharisees came to him, and asked him, Is it lawful for a man to put away his wife? tempting him. And he answered and said unto them, What did Moses command you? And they said, Moses suffered to write a bill of divorcement, and to put her away. And Jesus answered and said unto them, For the hardness of your heart he wrote you this precept. But from the beginning of the creation God made them male and female. For this cause shall a man leave his father and mother, and cleave to his wife; And they twain shall be one flesh: so then they are no more twain, but one flesh. What therefore God hath joined together, let not man put asunder."*

However, biology divides us as much as it drives us. A surviving percentage of fertile nature will copulate and conceive offspring, which usually implies sacrifice of individuality to accommodate this instinctive necessity. But in the moment, no one seems to mind. Depending on a couple's social expectations and the innate agreement of their programming, this change often accompanies a new demographic in a couple's individuality. No engaged parent will say that raising children is always a pleasurable experience; only that the responsibility of reward providing immeasurable meaning. Before in-vitro fertilization and surrogate parenting, most fertile couples had sex and produced offspring. This accomplished, either through accidental pregnancies or planned families. Many women died through the process. Nor do all children mature into adulthood. But through surviving genealogies, we can all trace a few branches of our family tree. This complex code combination only possible with consummation of genetic material exchanged between two biological donors of opposite sex.

Most people today, like those in the past, are not born with the fortune to live in luxury mansions with money trees growing in the backyard. People have always lived according to their means and in accordance to the constructed realities of their societies limited by the available commodities of the times. My mother's husband worked ten hours a day and was always tired. My mother a stay-at-home mom for most of my childhood engaged in maintaining our dwelling and raising four children. This was no comfort position, but a prerequisite of the times relative to the economy. We often ate beans and potatoes for dinner, and rarely went away on vacations. But my mom maintained our home and provided the necessary discipline. She would have preferred to get a paying job outside; however, realized that the constant duty of housework just as necessary. There is no glory being a servant to the needs of a family, but someone needs to do it. This does not make the person who submits to this careful responsibility any less valuable. These two earthly providers are forever my heroes, free- spirited individuals, who saw no dishonor in becoming a number on a social block. Nevertheless, there were often tensions between them as human beings, each sometimes resenting the position of the other. It is far easier for men to lose perspective because of pride and a false sense of perceived position of value in the greater scheme of things. This misjudgment can sometimes become fatal, as we often see in the headlines when an abusive partner is killed during an argument. In fact, the prisons are just as full of women as with men for various crimes. Although the reasons often different, both male and female genders have the capacity for heinous potential.

The definition of a wife is a 'helpmate', or one who compliments the needs of another. Adam, the first man, and Eve, the first woman, had no choice but to mate with each other. Interestingly, there is no place in the Bible that tells how or what kind of vows two people should exchange to consummate their union. There are several references in the Psalms, written by David, describing the love of youth and the respect engendered through bonding. But even David found it difficult to sustain the mystique of this *"romanticized"* vision throughout his adult years. Although there are many references in letters written to different congregations of early Christian groups concerning the mutual respect and behavior between husbands and wives, there is no specific doctrine instructing that two joined people must remain immutably bound together if their personal beliefs contrary, leading to contentious behavior. Jesus announces clealyr that two people, once consummated, become symbiotic in flesh, yet freed from this conventional pairing after death of the physical body and resurrection of the spiritual body, as presented in the Gospel of Mark, Chapter 12, verses 18-25 (KJV).

> *"Then come unto him the Sadducees, which say there is no resurrection; and they asked him, saying, Master, Moses wrote unto us, If a man's brother die, and leave his wife behind him, and leave no children, that his brother should take his wife, and raise up seed unto his brother. Now there were seven brethren: and the first took a wife, and dying left no seed. And the second took her, and died, neither left he any seed: and the third likewise. And the seven had her, and left no seed: last of all the woman died also. In the resurrection therefore, when they shall rise, whose wife*

shall she be of them? for the seven had her to wife. And Jesus answering said unto them, Do ye not therefore err, because ye know not the scriptures, neither the power of God? For when they shall rise from the dead, they neither marry, nor are given in marriage; but are as the angels which are in heaven."

Nevertheless, formal contracts of marriage are found throughout history and in every culture and in every religion, thus becoming an intricate part of social discourse. Marriage, therefore, is as much a legal instrument of society, as it is about two people intertwining into a complex physical alliance. Before puberty, girls and boys have a natural aversion to intimate contact with each other, which is perhaps a natural built-in mechanism to avoid complicated immature relationships. This suggests a protective state of nature, over-riding the prescription of nurture. Celebrity mothers should take this in consideration before dolling-up their little girls to look and act as miniature versions of entertainment icons.

Since population increase can only be achieved by physical union between two individuals of opposite sex, then history is a collage of inter-unions, variant to the conditions of present society. It seems obvious that Noah had only one wife by the time he entered into the Ark, as did his three sons. Abraham was joined to Sarah while still living in Err, presumably according to the arrangements of that particular society. Marriage is, and has always been, a personal agreement between two people with a common goal. Once this agreement made, then chemical changes take place to ensure an emotive physiological and psychological bonding, as a preparation to sire young into the world. All occurring naturally, and cannot be orchestrated solely by societal contract or moral obligation. It is a debatable possibility that this chemical inception, aptly termed *"first love"* happens only one time in a person's life. Although a man may have many wives and a woman many husbands, the miracle of this soul connection occurs uniquely. It does not always happen with the first person we marry, (as found in the example of Jacob and Rebecca), and to some it never happens at all because of ritualistic adherence.

This is not to say the model of marriage flawed, only that it as much a mystery as everything else we observe within reference to the basic code found in human nature.

Through the years, I have listened to many sermons concerning the place of Christian women in the church and how they should present themselves before God. No wonder that so many women turn to militant feminist ideologies, considering the continuous assault through every age just for being born female. Either raised on a pedestal of flawless being or dragged into the mud of sinful imagination, women have been subjugated and judiciously defined. We see this in every nation, in every culture, and in every religion. A condition of birth becoming a position in society subject to those considered ordained to higher stature. By nature of their gender, these people forbidden to make choices of pleasure, choices of education, and even denied choices concerning the use of their own bodies. My mother once shockingly confessed to me that she did not like the teachings of Paul because she believed he discriminated against women. I tried to convince her that much of what he actually meant taken out of context to construct a communal balance during the administration of an orderly assembly unique to a particular group. I wish my mother, as well as the reader, to consider that this man of God freely forfeited worldly position, denying himself worldly adoration, and spending his last days as a prisoner of Rome to the glory of the cross. This once educated and proudly successful man had learned through the obedience of his calling to submit to the Lord in all things. A quality he wished to share with all those whom he loved, and even those who rejected his spiritually inspired words. His message to believers within context of a matriarchal society, known as the Ephesians, Chapter 5, verses 2-33 (KJV), sent by letter as an instruction to remember Christ first, even above traditions and hierarchies of social politics. Not as an epistle of doctrinal design to formulate a blueprint for a future patriarchy, but as an example of true equality. How in all things the individual should strive for the Holy Spirit to move freely by setting aside hypocrisy and vain perceptions, which only leads to confusion. Paul knew that it is by conscious and willing submission of the outward nature that brings about peaceful assembly, allowing the spirit of love and unity to prevail above all other considerations.

"And walk in love, as Christ also hath loved us, and hath given himself for us an offering and a sacrifice to God for a sweet smelling savor. But fornication, and all uncleanness, or covetousness, let it not be once named among you, as becomes saints; Neither filthiness, nor foolish talking, nor jesting, which are not convenient: but rather giving of thanks. For this ye know, that no whoremonger, nor unclean person, nor covetous man, who is an idolater, hath any inheritance in the kingdom of Christ and of God. Let no man deceive you with vain words: for because of these things cometh the wrath of God upon the children of disobedience. Be not ye therefore partakers with them. For ye were sometimes darkness, but now are ye light in the Lord: walk as children of light: (For the fruit of the Spirit is in all goodness and righteousness and truth;) Proving what is acceptable unto the Lord. And have no fellowship with the unfruitful works of darkness, but rather reprove them. For it is a shame even to speak of those things which are done of them in secret. But all things that are reproved are made manifest by the light: for whatsoever doth make manifest is light. Wherefore he saith, Awake thou that sleeps, and arise from the dead, and Christ shall give thee light. See then that ye walk circumspectly, not as fools, but as wise, Redeeming the time, because the days are evil. Wherefore be ye not unwise, but understanding what the will of the Lord is. And be not drunk with wine, wherein is excess; but be filled with the Spirit; Speaking to yourselves in psalms and hymns and spiritual songs, singing and making melody in your heart to the Lord; Giving thanks always for all things unto God and the Father in the name of our Lord Jesus Christ; Submitting yourselves one to another in the fear of God. Wives, submit yourselves unto

your own husbands, as unto the Lord. For the husband is the head of the wife, even as Christ is the head of the church: and he is the savior of the body. Therefore as the church is subject unto Christ, so let the wives be to their own husbands in everything. Husbands, love your wives, even as Christ also loved the church, and gave himself for it; That he might sanctify and cleanse it with the washing of water by the word, That he might present it to himself a glorious church, not having spot, or wrinkle, or any such thing; but that it should be holy and without blemish. So ought men to love their wives as their own bodies. He that loves his wife loves himself. For no man ever yet hated his own flesh; but nourishes and cherishes it, even as the Lord the church: For we are members of his body, of his flesh, and of his bones. For this cause shall a man leave his father and mother, and shall be joined unto his wife, and they two shall be one flesh. This is a great mystery: but I speak concerning Christ and the church. Nevertheless let every one of you in particular so love his wife even as himself; and the wife see that she reverence her husband."

The key word here is *"submit"*. Submission is a choice, not a legal enforcement, and applies to all (to men, as well to women) the same. God's original Ten Commandments given to Moses on Mount Sinai are statues to both men and women. Later practical amendments added to accommodate sociological situations and inherent physiological differences.

Nevertheless, there exists in most societies of the world an often rigid division between role assignments based solely on gender perception, with females historically perceived as domestic property acquired for the primary purpose of reproduction. This schism can be traced far back into civilized history, implying that God made one gender naturally subservient to the other. Even though there are passages in the Bible that suggest this to be the case: the interpretation natural, not spiritually discerned. Without Adam, Eve would have been without meaning or purpose; without Eve, no future Adam possible. Through hormonal differences, one sex is biologically better adapted to certain applications of nurturing and physical endurance; but none exclusive to one gender only.

Men are from Mars and Women from Venus, a book written by the author John Gray in the early 1990s, further mythologized the difference between the sexes through urban examination of differences that are evident in contemporary society. Although I find this book of compelling interest, it addresses issues of division only contextually; without evaluating the societal institution as a whole. Mars is a mindset, just as Venus is a mindset. Both extremes accommodate an agreement of role order and institutionalized conditioning. Clinical studies reveal that the major differences between the two sexes are more an aspect of socialization, than genetics. In other words, conformity to expectation and peer identity encourages stereotypes and limitations. I have personally known some women with intimidating personalities, physically capable as any man. This does not necessarily make them *"butch"* or less feminine. They just realize their role identity differently. The same can be said for some men, who choose to embrace more their sensitive nature. Although traditional stereotypes appealing for demographic reasons, they are rarely consistent proponents in the real world. I think most will agree that the primary differences are biological. I do not mean this in terms of physical copulation only, but as the prevailing mechanism of procreation. Although biologically different, we are all anatomically the same. Nevertheless, there is a certain burden to the gender reality that cannot be understated. By a seemingly random association, a certain percentage of fetuses will be born male and a certain percentage female. This one factor becomes deterministic to many other factors. But the variant definition of masculinity and femininity measured on a scale less precise.

The fabled Amazonian female warriors, as divined by Homeric lore, may or may not have existed in ancient history. Yet, the female warriors on the Scythians steppes of what is today modern Russia, most definitely did exist. Archeological discoveries unearthed outside of the Russian outpost of *Pokrovka* confirm the remains of warrior women buried with their weapons, some with the bent arrowheads of the enemy still lodged in their corpses. These women were extraordinary in physical stature and apparently well honored as fallen soldiers. Nor are these female combatants unique in history. The women of Sparta defended the walls of their city against a violent bloody siege almost three hundred years after the resurrection of Christ. In ancient China a regiment of domestic women were trained by the infamous military general, Sun Tzu, as an example to the Emperor that all humans can be made into effective warriors regardless of gender or previous disposition. Even the Hebrew culture makes mention of female warriors capable of far more deadly engagement than mere manipulation of male counterparts. Living examples are Deborah, a military leader, as well as being a prophet, found in the Book of Judges; and the guerrilla assassin, Jael, who violently dispatched an enemy hostile to the early tribes of Israel. Today in modern Israel, the military is comprised of men and women, who serve on the frontlines together. This is true in other countries as well, including the United States, with men and women commanding equal positions in combat operations. When I was in the Marine Corps, women were less likely to be deployed into battlefield operations. And so are gone the days of pretense chivalry. On that faithful day of Armageddon, men and women will stand side by side against the Lord's Christ in a war of nations.

Other interesting facts in biology: a healthy adult human male will produce an average of 500,000,000 sperm during a single ejaculation, compared to the 400 fertile eggs that will remain by the time the female exits puberty. In fact, the female is born with all the eggs she will ever have in a lifetime, a significant number calculated to be in the millions, which dwindles over time. Out of this multitude contributed by the male, sometimes one (rarely more) will endure a hostile environment and impregnate a waiting fertile egg. Conditions must be absolutely right for this miracle of life to occur. Depending on the chromosome pairing, the sex of a child predetermined. The chemistry is simple enough, but other determining factors more complex. It seems that in light of contemporary understanding of physiology, this intricate organic spectrum has become a subject of much debate.

Have you ever considered the complex role of hormones on a developing fetus? Without hormones there could be no miracle of life: no fertile soil to plant seeds, no seeds to incubate, and no delicate recumbent combination to mix the XY and XX derivatives defining the human genotype. But this model is not always as precise as we may wish to believe. Recent research in endocrinology has revealed some rather starling, if not altogether disturbing, facts about differences that span between classic male and classic female gender types. For many years doctors have assigned genders at birth to babies born with unclear or undefined genitals. Most often the infant is assigned female (in cases where a descending scrotum is not detected) followed by surgical intervention. Many of these early patients matured dissatisfied with the appearance and function of their sexual organs. Some altogether abandon their assignment, calling themselves *inter-sexed*, and eventually choosing the gender most comfortable to their psyche. Some of these *inter-sexed* individuals have gone on to become vocal activist against the continued practice of birth assignments without the affected person's consent. These eunuchs of men reminds us of the imperfect doctrine contained in the standardized perception adhered to by the architects of fruitful nuclear society.

I wish to make a clear distinction that this is a physiological condition, and does not necessary apply to another gender contradiction, clinically identified as *transgender* and *transsexual* individuals: persons whose psychological perception does not agree with their gender role assignment or functioning physiology. This can lead many down a dangerous and painful road of radical surgical procedures, often with disappointing results. It is medically possible to change morphology, but not to change biology. There are far too many complex physiological, psychological, as well as sociologically nurturing aspects associated with this difficult perception. In light of present confusion in the world, I believe this shadowy path of deception unavoidable to some. Often the expectations unrealistic, many find themselves trapped between two worlds, unable to fully identify with one gender or the other; nor realize a defined fulfillment in their sojourn of flesh and blood. To consider this contradiction not real and valid to the person so afflicted would be a callused transgression of the facts. And to state that such a path not laden with landmines of deceit would be to say that none mortal are tempted. For only by the grace obtained through the uncensored sacrifice of Jesus Christ are any saved regardless of appearance or life choice.

There is a saying that all cats judged black in the dark. This is often the position of myopic society, clinging to definitions of structure. It is easier in the minds of many to gather all in the same snare of moral agreement, thus believing they are God's administrators of righteousness. I am glad that the Lord has opened my eyes to the possibility that he is able to make the unclean animal clean in his sight. This author stands hand in hand with those most easily judged in the hope that grace will abound, knowing that Christ died on a cross for the individual bound by sin, and not for any righteous collective. I pass daily into the revelation that God has power to make holy the sacrifice according to the measure of faith. And even that faith, not by mortal will, but given by the Lord, as stated in the letter to the Ephesians, Chapter 2, verses 8-9 (KJV):

> *"For by grace are ye saved through faith; and that not of yourselves: it is the gift of God: Not of works, lest any man should boast."*

Since all born in sin and all recipients of grace, then who should prevent even one lost sheep form being fed. I bear personal witness that if light not sent to penetrate the depth of every stronghold of darkness; then who so blinded might see? Because these most easily identifiable among the flourishing flock of healthy society, they are most easily condemned. But a reminder to those that would cast the first stone: they come from you. They are your brothers, your sisters, your children, and those you have known as friends. Are these more deserving of your derision, than the respect you give so easily to your esteemed neighbor about whom you know so little? Did Christ die less for their sin that appears, than for the sin more easily concealed? Did Christ rise from the dead for the sacrament of the religiously minded only? Indeed, God executes righteous judgment upon all things in due season. He also knows his own, providing a clear way of salvation, as the latter rain sent to cleanse the world of all uncleanness. As the scripture says, *"flesh and blood cannot inherit the kingdom of God."* Praise the Lord that his mercy poured upon all flesh without measure! All that I can agree to with any clarity is written in the letter of James, Chapter 4, verses 11-17 (KJV). The rest I lay upon the mercy seat of Christ's unfailing guarantee on that final Day of Judgment.

> *"Speak not evil one of another, brethren. He that speaks evil of his brother, and judges his brother, speaks evil of the law, and judges the law: but if thou judge the law, thou art not a doer of the law, but a judge. There is one lawgiver, who is able to save and to destroy: who art thou that judges another? Go to now, ye that say, To day or to morrow we will go into such a city, and continue there a year, and buy and sell, and get gain: Whereas ye know not what shall be on the morrow. For what is your life? It is even a vapor, that appears for a little time, and then vanishes away. For that ye ought to say, If the Lord will, we shall live, and do this, or that. But now ye rejoice in your boastings: all such rejoicing is evil. Therefore to him that knows to do good, and doeth it not, to him it is sin."*

I would like to clarify that transgender is not the same as homosexuality, nor can all homosexuals be labeled the same. The point I am making here is that the more we know and understand about the human condition, the more complicated when trying to ascribe a label of normative behavior. Many Bible believing Christians point to *Sodom and Gomorrah* as God's abhorrence toward homosexuality. But the portrait in the Bible of this wayward city is far more corrupt than sexual deviation only. Contextually, it represents a condition of violent rebellion and coordinated repression of mankind against mankind: a city not unlike the major cities of today, malignant with violence and perverse human behavior. Doubtless there were women in this city, mothers of children, and families not engaged in homosexual practices, all destroyed because of agreement within context of amoral violence polluting even to their offspring. If two hundred people (men, women, and children) all die in the crash of a jetliner, are we able to judge all as deserving of their fate? Yes, all these souls in Sodom and Gomorrah perished together *(even the innocent that had not yet sinned)*, with only reluctant *Lot* and his two daughters escaping alive. They survived not because of righteousness, but because God sent his angels to forcibly lead them out. Their salvation secured because they listened and obeyed by faith. Tragically Lot's wife turned to a pillar of salt, because she looked back with longing in her heart. This woman was not judged because of her sexual bias, but because she lamented in her heart that grand estate of material excess. A statement made by Jesus further clarifies the real reason why these twin cities were consumed. The judgment came not just because of immorality, but as a result of collective hubris, blind to the significance of their heavenly visitation.

In Mathew, Chapter 10, verses 13-15 (KJV), Jesus says to his apostles concerning the statues of judgment against those who reject the testimony of repentance unto salvation:

> *"And when ye come into an house, salute it. And if the house be worthy, let your peace come upon it: but if it be not worthy, let your peace return to you. And whosoever shall not receive you, nor hear your words, when ye depart out of that house or city, shake off the dust of your feet. Verily I say unto you, It shall be more tolerable for the land of Sodom and Gomorrah in the day of judgment, than for that city."*

Do not think that I am attempting to construct an argument of justification for or against any practice regarding fleshly participation. The point I am making is that we are all impure and all fall short of God's standard of righteousness. My observation is that many of my fellow Christian brothers and sisters expend far too much energy condemning sin. Sin is the evidence of mortal condition. In the days of Sodom and Gomorrah lived the Patriarch Abraham, the brother of Lot's father. Certainly, if there was one upon the earth capable of judging sin, it was this man, whose faith shined as righteousness before God. But what did this man do when confronted with the destruction of those cities? He appealed for mercy and forgiveness through futile supplication. There was no zealousness in this man's heart. He knew already that God's judgment just, but takes no pleasure in it. Nor does God ask Abraham for a consensus. Nevertheless, this man of God so grieved in his soul, that he makes an appeal of mercy for those living in these grand metropolises. In the Book of Genesis, Chapter 18, verses 20-33 (KJV), we find this discourse between Abraham and the Lord of judgment:

> *"And the LORD said, Because the cry of Sodom and Gomorrah is great, and because their sin is very grievous; I will go down now, and see whether they have done altogether according to the cry of it, which is come unto me; and if not, I will know. And the men turned their faces from thence, and went toward Sodom: but Abraham stood yet before the LORD. And Abraham drew near, and said, Wilt thou also destroy the righteous with the wicked? Peradventure there be fifty righteous within the city: wilt thou also destroy and not spare the place for the fifty righteous that are therein? That be far from thee to do after this manner, to slay the righteous with the wicked: and that the righteous should be as the wicked, that be far from thee: Shall not the Judge of all the earth do right? And the LORD said, If I find in Sodom fifty righteous within the city, then I will spare all the place for their sakes. And Abraham answered and said, Behold now, I have taken upon me to speak unto the Lord, which am but dust and ashes: Peradventure there shall lack five of the fifty righteous: wilt thou destroy all the city for lack of five? And he said, If I find there forty and five, I will not destroy it. And he spake unto him yet again, and said, Peradventure there shall be forty found there. And he said,*

> *I will not do it for forty's sake. And he said unto him, Oh let not the Lord be angry, and I will speak: Peradventure there shall thirty be found there. And he said, I will not do it, if I find thirty there. And he said, Behold now, I have taken upon me to speak unto the Lord: Peradventure there shall be twenty found there. And he said, I will not destroy it for twenty's sake. And he said, Oh let not the Lord be angry, and I will speak yet but this once: Peradventure ten shall be found there. And he said, I will not destroy it for ten's sake. And the LORD went his way, as soon as he had left communing with Abraham: and Abraham returned unto his place."*

Not even ten righteous might be found in those two great cities of the earth. This is a humbling prospect within context of spiritually defined mercy and judgment. God knew already not even ten righteous souls there, since he had not called any to righteousness in those worldly principalities. Even Abraham's nephew, Lot, is delivered by strong hands of angels, not because of righteousness attribute. If we, as present day Christians, have been reproved by the shedding of Christ's blood, then we should in humble submission be as ministers of light sharing the good news of salvation to all that might hear. Some may perchance turn from dark powers, receiving grace as once we received grace. God needs not our advocacy to judge the wickedness of this world. For salvation is by grace, not by righteousness, as we are reminded in Romans, Chapter 3, verses 9 - 28 (KJV).

> *"What then? are we better than they? No, in no wise: for we have before proved both Jews and Gentiles, that they are all under sin; As it is written, There is none righteous, no, not one: There is none that understandeth, there is none that seeketh after God. They are all gone out of the way, they are together become unprofitable; there is none that doeth good, no, not one. Their throat is an open sepulchre; with their tongues they have used deceit; the poison of asps*

is under their lips: Whose mouth is full of cursing and bitterness: Their feet are swift to shed blood: Destruction and misery are in their ways: And the way of peace have they not known: There is no fear of God before their eyes. Now we know that what things soever the law saith, it saith to them who are under the law: that every mouth may be stopped, and all the world may become guilty before God. Therefore by the deeds of the law there shall no flesh be justified in his sight: for by the law is the knowledge of sin. But now the righteousness of God without the law is manifested, being witnessed by the law and the prophets; Even the righteousness of God which is by faith of Jesus Christ unto all and upon all them that believe: for there is no difference: For all have sinned, and come short of the glory of God; Being justified freely by his grace through the redemption that is in Christ Jesus: Whom God hath set forth to be a propitiation through faith in his blood, to declare his righteousness for the remission of sins that are past, through the forbearance of God; To declare, I say, at this time his righteousness: that he might be just, and the justifier of him which believeth in Jesus. Where is boasting then? It is excluded. By what law? of works? Nay: but by the law of faith. Therefore we conclude that a man is justified by faith without the deeds of the law."

Biology, a code immutable, designed in present course to a conventional end. But this code, too, designed to fail. What glorious liberty when we open our eyes in the dawn of a new heaven and a new earth with our resurrected Christ shining as the sun: *former things passed away; all things made new.*

Chapter 5
WONDER THAT IS THE MIND

I have heard it said that the human mind is as vast and limitless as the reflected universe. However, it is important that we do not confuse the difference between what is synoptic chemical reaction of the brain, and a more complex manifestation comprising the combination of more profound synthesis. Socrates of ancient Greece considered the mind to be the seat of 'psyche', or the soul, a platonic elevation of self above the carnal condition. This idea revived during the classical resurrection of the Renaissance portrayed through Dante's Divine Comedy with Plato guiding this late medieval poet through labyrinths of the inferno. As a younger individual I felt the infatuation of this romantic journey through the underworld, sharing in Dante's desire to be united with his beloved Beatrice. After so many years, I still can visualize the wondrous magnitude of the *Paradiso,* as the poet and his beloved spiritually entwine with God in the tenth heaven. Of course this is a fictional account inspired through sub currents of intellectual elation.

The mind is defined as cognitive state, a conscious perceptive condition allowing for inductive, as well as intuitive discernment to visible and invisible conditions. However, the mind is also a product of the collective state, exceeding the sum of its parts. Consider the physical body a well organized machine consisting of many biological parts incorporated with a highly advanced sensory net calibrated within specific norms. It readily responds to stimuli by transmitting data along sophisticated pathways connected to the central nervous system, which transmits this information directly to the brain.

The brain receives these input variables from the physical senses wired into neuron receptors that continuously transmit telemetry concerning the ambient environment. Hot and cold become distinct values relative to the acclimate necessities of the body. The primary objective designed to promote comfort and survivability through a complex network of interactive signaling. The brain is the collaborating CPU, ever recording new information, and placing that information into storage. It is also an interpreter of spatial conditions based on this received telemetry, constantly sorting historical comparisons. The categorization of various light spectrums, devising color, depth of perception, and balanced orientation: all key to navigating the environment of physicality.

The brain also acts as a synaptic regulator to further evaluate information received from the body's automated sensory net by making intellectual comparisons, and is thus capable of circumventing the hardwire response of instinctual reaction. For example in certain emotive situations, such as the tragedy of a fire, the brain attempts to evaluate the situation to determine the best route of escape. This control mechanism can be enhanced through training exercises, successfully reinforced in military personnel to remain cognitively alert in combat situations. Hence, the conditioned choice between action-reaction flight or fight syndrome. Even something as mundane as a successful diet involves a regiment of exercise and restriction, which deny the body of a habitual sedentary lifestyle and excessive calorie intake proven to be unhealthy and counterproductive to a desired balance. However, the danger in this example is how easily the mind seduced by negative reinforcement through deception triggering a mechanism of physical addition.

The brain is responsible for even higher cognitive intelligence, such as the recollection of details in order to form a pattern of direction and progress, much like an interactive GPS establishing position based on rehearsed coordinates. Classic examples might be to recall the correct order of information for scoring well on a test, or remembering complex formulae isolated from context. It can make all the difference when navigating a mapped minefield, or making standardized math calculations used in practical plane geometry to construct a level foundation particular to architectural modeling. More remarkably, with the aid of other data processors, it can even determine atmospheric reentry variables when landing a spaceship on another planet, as has been successfully achieved on the moon or on the distant planet Mars. Most recently, a NASA probe launched in 2004 toward a spinning asteroid traveling nearly 55,000 kilometers per hour, landed successfully after a complex calculated trajectory of 10 years. These achievements represent the higher functions of mental reasoning most profoundly perceived through the clockwork design of local time and space used to calculate millions of light years in distant reaches of the universe presently unreachable. In some indeterminate way, it is the brain that triggers biological shutdown causing the secondary effects of aging and leading to cessation of the organism.

Most post-university students score well on oral and written test, which greatly improve their chances of aspiring into a professional field. There is even the revered *Mensa Society*, where individuals are awarded special honor by scoring exceptionally high (within the upper two percent over the general population) on intelligent quota test. Recent research into the phenomenon of Autistic children shows many to be high-functioning geniuses with remarkable potential, however lacking balance of perceptive reasoning and skills for social integration. Which raises the question: *is true genus a quantum of intelligence only?*

Rats are considered to have brains with cognitive potential very similar to human beings. Which I suppose makes sense when used in context of a sinking ship. Because of this unique characteristic (even more so when compared to dogs or other animals), rats are aggressively used to conduct intelligence learning test, like sending the animals through a maze, or reinforced conditioning through social behavioral technique. Nevertheless, no matter how well trained, a rat will not learn to tie shoelaces, dress in designer clothing, or drive a sports car, as endearingly portrayed by the lovable character *Stewart Little* in E.B. White's children classic by the same name. Rats are not humans.

At their highest potential, computers are mass data crunchers capable of immense mathematic model formulations that would dwarf legions of hypothetical minds. It is envisioned that one day artificial intelligence will replace thinking man, as though the sum of much input data to inspire the complexity of human behavior. *I Robot*, to one day suddenly open artificial eyes with sentient reflection of the universe. This raises another interesting question: *Is intelligence the core element of cognition or the cognitive evidence of a mind endowed with transcendent potential?*

But the final, and mostly overlooked, component of this mind is the animated charge of the human soul. This is the life force defining what it means to be alive. The body can be decimated, but as long as there is a cognitive connection to the brain awareness continues.

The brain can become comatose, but as long as neuron activity fires along the cerebrum halves, then there is life. Modern medicine has found ways to keep the body functioning by mechanical means long after brain functions have ceased. This is not life, but death in life. In such conditions, is the soul trapped? Is sensory perception the only evidence of a living being; or the few pounds of matter, labeled the brain, the throne of being? All that can be determined with any certainty is that awareness accounts for more than the just the sum of accumulated data.

There is a record of only one man, who died and was buried according to custom of mortal flesh and came back to life as mortal flesh. This man lay not in a deep coma. Was not preserved against the natural process of corruption, but pronounced by the living truly dead. This condition confirmed by all those who knew him. Why Jesus chose to reanimate this man remains a mystery of spiritual significance. Because in the course of time, this man named Lazarus would eventually die again, as is the destiny of all flesh. Yet his name remains immemorial, as one whom Jesus, the Christ, raises from finality of the grave. We read this account in the Gospel of John, Chapter 11, verses 11-44 (KJV):

> *"These things said he: and after that he saith unto them, Our friend Lazarus sleepeth; but I go, that I may awake him out of sleep. Then said his disciples, Lord, if he sleep, he shall do well. Howbeit Jesus spake of his death: but they thought that he had spoken of taking of rest in sleep. Then said Jesus unto them plainly, Lazarus is dead. And*

I am glad for your sakes that I was not there, to the intent ye may believe; nevertheless let us go unto him. Then said Thomas, which is called Didymus, unto his fellow disciples, Let us also go, that we may die with him. Then when Jesus came, he found that he had lain in the grave four days already. Now Bethany was nigh unto Jerusalem, about fifteen furlongs off: And many of the Jews came to Martha and Mary, to comfort them concerning their brother. Then Martha, as soon as she heard that Jesus was coming, went and met him: but Mary sat still in the house. Then said Martha unto Jesus, Lord, if thou hadst been here, my brother had not died. But I know, that even now, whatsoever thou wilt ask of God, God will give it thee. Jesus saith unto her, Thy brother shall rise again. Martha saith unto him, I know that he shall rise again in the resurrection at the last day. Jesus said unto her, I am the resurrection, and the life: he that believeth in me, though he were dead, yet shall he live: And whosoever liveth and believeth in me shall never die. Believest thou this? She saith unto him, Yea, Lord: I believe that thou art the Christ, the Son of God, which should come into the world. And when she had so said, she went her way, and called Mary her sister secretly, saying, The Master is come, and calleth for thee. As soon as she heard that, she arose quickly, and came unto him. Now Jesus was not yet come into the town, but was in that place where Martha met him. The Jews then which were with her in the house, and comforted her, when they saw Mary, that she rose up hastily and went out, followed her, saying, She goeth unto the grave to weep there. Then when Mary was come where Jesus was, and saw him, she fell down at his feet, saying unto him, Lord, if thou hadst been here, my brother had not died. When Jesus therefore saw her weeping, and the Jews also weeping which came with her, he groaned in the spirit, and was troubled. And said, Where have ye laid him? They said unto him, Lord, come and see. Jesus wept. Then said the Jews, Behold how he loved him! And some of them said, Could not this man, which opened the eyes of the blind, have caused that even this man should not have died? Jesus therefore again groaning in himself cometh to the grave. It was a cave, and a stone lay upon it. Jesus said, Take ye away the stone. Martha, the sister of him that was dead, saith unto him, Lord, by this time he stinketh: for he hath been dead four days. Jesus saith unto her, Said I not unto thee, that, if thou wouldest believe, thou shouldest see the glory of God? Then they took away the stone from the place where the dead was laid. And Jesus lifted up his eyes, and said, Father, I thank thee that thou hast heard me. And I knew that thou hearest me always: but because of the people which stand by I said it, that they may believe that thou hast sent me. And when he thus had spoken, he cried with a loud voice, Lazarus, come forth. And he that was dead came forth, bound hand and foot with grave clothes: and his face was bound about with a napkin. Jesus saith unto them, Loose him, and let him go."

The revival of Lazarus represents the first resurrection of a physical body in the truest sense. This mortal being, not only lived again after dead, but represents a complete reversal of thermodynamic disassociation. In other words, Lazarus did not only rise from the grave alive after many days, but the past of his being restored intact. This represents a complete reversal of entropy, an extraction of time within context of time. It would be like un-digesting the food I ate days before after consuming my meal today. The sheer magnitude of this miracle is staggering. This is the time differential mechanics of the first resurrection, as described in the Bible, practically demonstrating irrefutable evidence that future regeneration possible to flesh and blood. This is also why Jesus states plainly *"Lazarus is dead"*, so there could be no doubt of what is going to happen. Remember, the man Jesus is not yet crucified; nor the Lord's

Christ resurrected from the grave. This example provided as edification to those that believe by faith; and represents terror to those that scoff behind a veil of reason. This supernatural event, not only possible, but is imminent. As one whom God has spared once from the grave in my generation, I proclaim this first resurrection of the dead true, as stated in The Book of Revelation, Chapter 20, verses 11-15 (KJV).

> *"And I saw a great white throne, and him that sat on it, from whose face the earth and the heaven fled away; and there was found no place for them. And I saw the dead, small and great, stand before God; and the books were opened: and another book was opened, which is the book of life: and the dead were judged out of those things which were written in the books, according to their works. And the sea gave up the dead which were in it; and death and hell delivered up the dead which were in them: and they were judged every man according to their works. And the sea gave up the dead which were in it; and death and hell delivered up the dead which were in them: and they were judged every man according to their works. And death and hell were cast into the lake of fire. This is the second death. And whosoever was not found written in the book of life was cast into the lake of fire."*

This said, I propose that the mind is something else of much greater intrigue, existing without locality. Whereas, the brain is a hardwired input device, the mind the software code of a multidimensional probe that sorts and compares telemetry with the ability of innate extrapolation. It is the mind that imagines the singularity beginning and the collapsing end of the cosmos. The cerebral cortex did not alone hypothesize the structure of the subatomic universe, but by inquisitive observation of micro and macro processes giving birth to abstract organization defined by the mind. The mind is capable of embracing things invisible to make known the elemental state of this atomic universe. Without the mind existence would be meaningless, reality reduced down to anatomic response inspired by chemical reaction.

The dilemma of true science is to observe without speculation. Is it possible to accumulate data without inductive interpretation? The brain might say yes, but the mind insists on an anecdote of order. Human history is a compilation of stories with a beginning and an end. Thus the famous adage proclaiming being, as stated by the famous seventeenth century French philosopher René Descartes, "Cogito ergo sum!" (*I think, therefore I am.*) As judiciously as they may try, even the savants of scientific observation are never completely free of bias. But this is a subject for another discussion. Let it suffice to say that the mind is the evidence that a soul exists, and is the particle substance of eternal potential.

The body, brain, and mind work in seamless unison, discerning the worlds that appear and pentacles of understanding to reveal principalities that do not appear. It is this coalition that elevates man above all other creatures, a formulae of reason combined with a unique will to confront environmental obstacles. Potential challenge represents goal achievement relative to the degree of obstacle, thus weighed against perceived value or accomplishment. An example of this might be as simple as a child learning how to stack alphabet blocks to an obtainable height, eventually learning how to correctly spell words in the process. A more primitive situation are hunter-gatherers learning to direct a heard of massive bison off a cliff using only weapons of flint stone with the goal of harvesting the meat for food and the skins for protection against the elements. Even to split the first atom required many thousands of hours of chemistry equations and math calculations accumulated over several generations to achieve. Man may not sufficiently learn from his mistakes, but he certainly retains the memory of his victories. But with all this potential men still hunker in the shadows of limited reason like children fearing acceptance of the real world.

I have been blessed to observe more than one generation of young ones mature into adults. Without exception, there is a time during the developing process when they are rebellious for the sake of rebellion, thankless, and self-destructive. This restless arrogance seems as a retro code embedded into the program their software. In fairness, we all are born with it. Without it no one would ever leave their comfort zone and remain content to live as complacent drones within society, without ever venturing beyond imposed boundaries. While it is true that some cultures encourage conformity, history has shown this condition to be contrary to human nature. The metaphor of the young chick leaving the nest aptly applies in this case: *for through the envy of wings, the beginning of flight!* If it were not for this agitated desire to express a uniqueness of being, as defined by a generation, then society as a whole would quickly stagnate into irresponsible communism, as was the example of the Hippie movement in the United States during the drug revolution of the 1960s. However, I know parents of children still living at home, as full-fledged adults, who would strongly disagree with this premise. I suppose that these mothers and fathers should consider the warning of Proverbs, Chapter 22, verse 6 (KJV):

> "*Train up a child in the way he should go: and when he is old, he will not depart from it.*"

How easily this innate natural instinct corrupts into narcissistic self-adulation. There is a vast difference between the meaning of finding one's self and one becoming an egoist. Egoism manifests into defiance against what is not known, vehemently insisting that the little known is all one needs to know. Such insistence drowns out clarity of individual thought, imprinting institutional values, establishing unconditional statues of adherence. This, in turn, promotes a defined agenda rationalized by its own limitations. But do not just take my word on this. There has been legitimate research conducted in recent years suggesting that the new high-tech society is becoming dangerously depleted of human values. And even a book published on the subject conceived by two respected psychologist named Jean Twenge and W. Keith Campbell titled **The Narcissism Epidemic: Living in the Age of Entitlement. *They outline how the new media culture threatens to make the US into a*** nation of egomaniacs: beginning with the President and elected officials, and filtering down to popular media definition and control of information. These are pretty strong ideas to describe the recent

Cultural Revolution. Sound familiar? It should, since this phenomenon is not exclusive to the plugged-in generation of the 21st century. More than 2000 years ago, the Apostle Peter writes in 2 Peter, Chapter 2, verses 1-9 (KJV), concerning the self-willed arrogance of his day:

> *"But there were false prophets also among the people, even as there shall be false teachers among you, who privately shall bring in damnable heresies, even denying the Lord that bought them, and bring upon themselves swift destruction. And many shall follow their pernicious ways; by reason of whom the way of truth shall be evil spoken of. And through covetousness shall they with feigned words make merchandise of you: whose judgment now of a long time lingers not, and their damnation slumbers not. For if God spared not the angels that sinned, but cast them down to hell, and delivered them into chains of darkness, to be reserved unto judgment; And spared not the old world, but saved Noah the eighth person, a preacher of righteousness, bringing in the flood upon the world of the ungodly; And turning the cities of Sodom and Gomorrah into ashes condemned them with an overthrow, making them an ensample unto those that after should live ungodly; And delivered just Lot, vexed with the filthy conversation of the wicked: (For that righteous man dwelling among them, in seeing and hearing, vexed his righteous soul from day to day with their unlawful deeds;) The Lord knows how to deliver the godly out of temptations, and to reserve the unjust unto the day of judgment to be punished."*

A lot is condensed in these few lines, which might make many uncomfortable. We do not like to think about judgment, because judgment implies guilt. However, guilt is a subjective quantum within the context presented. The penalty of guilt applies only to those who deny judgment through impenitent action, denying the transgression, and thus rejecting absolution. There is no false accusation here, but rather a statement of an existing condition. This is not a condemnation of a specific act *(as many church religions like to qualify by their standards of righteousness)*. Rather, it condemns a mindset. For the *"angels that sinned"* is a quantified condition of unrepentant rebellion. These seraphic beings consider their perception of order to be the only definition, making an allegiance of choice to take the existing heavens by force. This violence is taking place even now on a timescale differential incompatible with perceived consciousness of present humanity. It is, therefore, imperceptible to temporal existence, just as the collapse of distant stars occurs in slow motion relative to our point of observation--*but not to our souls*! As I have already suggested, the human soul is *non-temporal*, and therefore absent of locality within a clockwork universe. This means that beginning and end, like biological existence, a conventional condition only. As long as this soul energy constrained within corporeal symbiotic relationship, the host still retains power of free will already forfeited by beings of greater stature. It is this essence denied; the substance of reason most influenced through a babbling of communication designed to restrain and corrupt. The brain has no choice, except to examine and categorize the incoming data; *but the mind is choice.*

New age religions preaching self-enlightenment within cosmic context are perhaps the most dangerous obstacles to discovering the true meaning of present passage. I have personally known many brilliant minds that collective embrace various techniques and disciplines applied through tantalizing teachings of meditative control. Either through chanting or energy channeling, the goal is to release one's self to universal higher power. I am not saying that such instruction altogether without value, only that it promotes a deceptive dimension of universal existence and cardinal positions within that universe. Elevation of the consciousness suggests personal mental control to enhance the potential of self-will, and thus engineering a better, more fulfilled life through techniques of psychology and faith training introduced through these practiced disciplines. Further suggesting that through harnessed techniques of decryption, a code within the physical universe can be broken, thus providing more profound understanding of mechanical processes.

A popular spiritual haven to many celebrities and successful business professionals is Christian Science, a belief that interprets the teachings of Christ as a technical manual on how to live and interact with others: love of God, love of self, and love of others, being the foundation elements. They further advocate that it is not God's will for anyone to become sick or to die, relying on scriptures of Christ's healings before the death and resurrection. They particularly draw upon examples of the apostles ordained with healing powers. However, what is so often neglected is that the major healing emphasized through those miracles is the transformation of the soul, the healing of the flesh being a secondary attribute. It is worthy to note that even Christian Science members become sick and eventually die. Although I think their perception of technique sound, many altogether miss the point, summed up in what Jesus says in the Gospel of John, Chapter 6, verse 26-27 (KJV):

> *"Jesus answered them and said, Verily, verily, I say unto you, Ye seek me, not because ye saw the miracles, but because ye did eat of the loaves, and were filled. Labour not for the meat which perishes, but for that meat which endures unto everlasting life, which the Son of man shall give unto you: for him hath God the Father sealed."*

Then there is Scientology, an intellectual religion designed to uncover latent extraterrestrial memories in the form of past lives lying dormant in the unconscious mind. L. Ron Hubbard, author of the famous book published in the middle of the twentieth century titled *Dianetics: The Modern Science of Mental Health*, established himself as the high priest of this controversial cult. The basic premise of this religion is that we are all eternal beings that have simply lost our way and are presently traversing the cosmos to awaken our deified selves. What makes this concept so tantalizing, is the support of many elements based on half truth. It rightly proposes a nature with immortal potential on a spiritual journey of many lifetimes with objective toward ultimate realization.

It accurately identifies extraterritorial beings referred to as *"thetans"*, or agents that exist on a higher level of existence with dedicated interest to guide us through entropic condition. But the major problem I have with this New Age Religion is it eliminates the supreme God of the universe as the source and sole creator of all things, *which is Satan's greatest lie.*

There are religious practices based on sun signs and love signs, on sympathetic vibrations; beliefs in the power of crystals, spiritual channeling, harmonic convergence, and the guiding influence of old souls. The list is endless to the many ways of human reason seeking a supernatural solution to the hunger in their souls: all promising a perfect code of encryption to mortal existence based on the architecture of a flawed model.

In reality many of these new age philosophies are not new at all, but flourish from occultist practices handed down since the earliest foundation of civilization. Transcendentalism, Idealism, Mesmerism, and various other soul-altering disciplines derived from eastern meditative instruction, transformed through western esoteric and occult beliefs. Modern Astrology is practiced by old and young alike, as well as various disciplines of magic, alchemy, and even Jewish Cabbalism.

The techniques of *"organism psychology"*, first introduced by the theorist Kurt Goldstein, is a discipline known to many as *Self-Actualization*. It stresses the supposition that creativity a driving force toward spiritual fulfillment. The most important aspect to this New Age philosophy is what he terms *"organismic"* existence. This later establishes the framework for psychologist Abraham Maslow's theoretical model known as the hierarchy of needs, creating a pyramid with basic survival at the base, and escalating to the peak of a *self-actualized* individual.

And who can forget the craze of the 1950s publication *The Power of Positive Thinking* written by the evangelical minister Vincent Peale. I am neither a critic, nor a supporter of the controversial content of this book, which provides to the reader a prescription of techniques designed to retrain the mind to a more positive outlook. Although his work widely received by public opinion, many critics (mostly psychology professionals, who consider many of Peale's concepts to be an affront to their occupation) condemn the publication for presenting to the layman potentially dangerous mind tools that should be executable only by a trained expert. Sounds to me a bit like the secret society of magic tricks shared only by magicians or the secret order of Masonry. One detractor even goes so far as to label Peale's life work as *"The Bible of American Auto-hypnotism"*.

Despite the many credentials of good meaning, all such practices share one common goal: to influence and deceive the soul by attempting to ground it within experience of the entropic universe. No doubt you must be thinking such statements as presented here nothing more menacing than fleeting doctrines of passing cults. But consider that these doctrines have managed to survive intact for many thousands of years. They continue to follow the divided paths of civilizations to converge into our present age of technology revitalized by inspiring new formulation made possible through cyber connection. Why do so many today seek the oracle meaning contained in the mysterious phenomenon known as *Maitreya's* lights? Why populated millions await the arrival of many false Christ? And why are there devout followers convinced that Lucifer is a wrongly accused angel of light soon to appear in physical form upon the earth?

We may, indeed, possess the potential of becoming gods, but are also made temporal for a reason. We are in fact the living meaning of the Holy Trinity: three separate entities with the potential of becoming one. We are born flesh with a capacity of reason and designed to live for a time to the end of disorganization. This corporeal existence provided a soul derived from transcendence to elemental state. This soul a quantum potential ripe for spiritual insemination to inspire being unto an eternal similitude. Hence, we are the living analogy of the son made flesh conceived by the father. Reanimation made possible by power of the Holy Spirit originating from beyond the entropic universe, and judged according to the servitude of our choices. There are many doors that lead into the several principalities of hell, but only submission into heaven.

A certain Pharisee named Nicodemus comes secretly to Jesus to enquire further the meaning of the Lord's teachings on resurrection. His instructed reason unable to reconcile the conflict of what his soul saying to him. How is it possible that this son of a carpenter can be so certain about the mysteries of God's will in resistance to his own religious counsel? This exchange recorded in the Gospel of John, Chapter 3, verses 1-21 (KJV).

> *"There was a man of the Pharisees, named Nicodemus, a ruler of the Jews: The same came to Jesus by night, and said unto him, Rabbi, we know that thou art a teacher come from God: for no man can do these miracles that thou doest, except God be with him. Jesus answered and said unto him, Verily, verily, I say unto thee, Except a man be born again, he cannot see the kingdom of God. Nicodemus saith unto him, How can a man be born when he is old? can he enter the second time into his mother's womb, and be born? Jesus answered, Verily, verily, I say unto thee, Except a man be born of water and of the Spirit, he cannot enter into the kingdom of God. That which is born of the flesh is flesh; and that which is born of the Spirit is spirit. Marvel not that I said unto thee, Ye must be born again. The wind bloweth where it listeth, and thou hearest the sound thereof, but canst not tell whence it cometh, and whither it goeth: so is every one that is born of the Spirit. Nicodemus answered and said unto him, How can these things be? Jesus answered and said unto him, Art thou a master of Israel, and knowest not these things? Verily, verily, I say unto thee, We speak that we do know, and testify that we have seen; and ye receive not our witness. If I have told you earthly things, and ye believe not, how shall ye believe, if I tell you of heavenly things? And no man hath ascended up to heaven, but he that came down from heaven, even the Son of man which is in heaven. And as Moses lifted up the serpent in the wilderness, even so must the Son of man be lifted up: That whosoever believeth in him should not perish, but have eternal life. For God so loved the world, that he gave his only begotten Son, that*

whosoever believeth in him should not perish, but have everlasting life. For God sent not his Son into the world to condemn the world; but that the world through him might be saved. He that believeth on him is not condemned: but he that believeth not is condemned already, because he hath not believed in the name of the only begotten Son of God. And this is the condemnation, that light is come into the world, and men loved darkness rather than light, because their deeds were evil. For every one that doeth evil hateth the light, neither cometh to the light, lest his deeds should be reproved. But he that doeth truth cometh to the light, that his deeds may be made manifest, that they are wrought in God."

So much easier to believe in tangible reason based on techniques of positive thinking; or application of cryptic meanings to unlock secrets of the universe. Of all things most difficult to embrace is divine grace without strings attached. So much attention dedicated to the definition of sin that the unconditional gift of salvation overlooked. The wonderful *"Good News"* of this gift overlooked by those most seeking righteousness. For whatever is not of faith *(the same faith by which the patriarch Abraham trusted in God)* is sin *(meaning a reward of the flesh)*. Only by the power of the Holy Spirit coursing through human flesh and human soul is it possible for the whole to be born again, resurrected from entopic design. This is the perfect code achieved through Christ's submission to the cross. As clearly stated in verses 2-3 (KJV) of the twelfth Chapter of the letter written by the Apostle Paul to the Romans,

> *"And be not conformed to this world: but be ye transformed by the renewing of your mind, that ye may prove what is that good, and acceptable, and perfect, will of God. For I say, through the grace given unto me, to every man that is among you, not to think of himself more highly than he ought to think; but to think soberly, according as God hath dealt to every man the measure of faith."*

It is just as possible that the man Jesus might have avoided crucifixion, and even an early death, simply by applying the faith that surely he knew. But greater the faith to submit to the destiny of a wooden cross placed upon a hill of destiny. There can be no meaning greater than this! This world has a course to follow, as certain as the gears and teeth of an automaton set into motion, designed for a specific purpose and to a predetermined climax. Nevertheless, we have hope in the mind of greater potential, through which our soul rejoices, a knowledge surpassing all understanding to the renewing of our mind. As the Apostle Paul again writes in a letter to the Philippians, Chapter 2, verses 4-11 (KJV):

> *"Look not every man on his own things, but every man also on the things of others. Let this mind be in you, which was also in Christ Jesus: Who, being in the form of God, thought it not robbery to be equal with God: But made himself of no reputation, and took upon him the form of a servant, and was made in the likeness of men: And being found in fashion as a man, he humbled himself, and became obedient unto death, even the death of the cross. Wherefore God also hath highly exalted him, and given him a name which is above every name: That at the name of Jesus every knee should bow, of things in heaven, and things in earth, and things under the earth; And that every tongue should confess that Jesus Christ is Lord, to the glory of God the Father."*

Chapter 6
COMING OF AGE

We live in an age overflowing with access to ideas, an age of mass communication, and an age rigid to a certainty of interpretation. The intention of this project is to examine the things we have learned and take for granted; but our understanding perhaps less conclusive. Mystery of the beyond has always been shrouded by the veil of infinite possibility restricted by intellectual boundaries of logic. It is more assuring to ascribe measured calculations to the immensity of time and space, than to huddle in awe beneath the canopy of an endless night sky. It is more comforting to identify the detailed function of living organs, than to ponder the animating force permeating the biology. And it is more assuring to create models to define the incomprehensible nature of random mechanics, than consider an intellect of intentional design.

To apply a secular term, *Symptomatology* is a branch of medicine which identifies the symptoms of an illness, but not necessarily discovering the source of the malignancy. To say society has become exceedingly sinful is an axiom simplistically obvious. With family divorce soaring disproportionately high since the latter half of the previous century, increasing gun violence in our schools committed against children by children, global environmental and economic distress, and political uncertainty matched by the proliferation of dreadnought weaponry--it is little wonder that a lack of faith prevails in our modern world! We embrace values of universal secularism in the name of a peace that cannot last. We have collectively surrendered our media communication networks to pornographic minds that seek to corrupt the flower of humanity into base conception. We forget the obvious fact that the aftermath of engagement by deploying weapons of mass destruction only guarantees destruction. To carpet bomb a roach infested building will only result in the annihilation of that habitat, not the deeper source of the invasion.

Present world leaders are aggressively engaged in trying to tackle the disturbing evidence of earth's changing climate believed to be the result of too much carbon emission. Although there is scientific data to support this present observation, the hydrostatic machinery of how our planet works is still being ignored. For many years, it has been a known fact that there is a direct correlation between the millions of hectares of disappearing rainforest in the southern and northern hemispheres and weather-making jet streams. I remember reading thirty years ago environmentalist sounding the alarm: a warning mostly ignored by prosperous energy producing western nations of the last century. Scientists embrace the empirical data of their science with unquestioned scrutiny, yet reject the Gaia theory (the belief that planet earth is a giant living organism) with extreme prejudice. If Gaia is alive, then might this presumption imply to the educated rational mind the existence of a living God of creation?

Even with all the new rhetoric to save the planet, we hear little about the importance of this vital geophysical circulation pump, and what is being done internationally to preserve these critical resources. It reminds me of a fire that burned in Greece for nearly a whole summer with ineffectual efforts to put it out. Only to be extinguished in a matter of hours by one thunderstorm of nature. Yes, carbon emissions are part of the problem, but the greater challenge is to better understand the machinery involved. As I have already explored in earlier chapters, the earth is still undergoing geological tectonic plate corrections. We see evidence of this in the North American mid-west that was once a submerged sea floor. This means that sea level and coastlines subject to change over time; and those many coveted multimillion dollar homes on the beach subject to future submergence. It seems that by acknowledging the obvious design in our planet and the natural hierarchy that exist everywhere we look, somehow threatens the self-proclaimed elevation of mortal comprehension within context.

As in all endeavors, the present coalition to save the world doomed to failure because of secular interpretation and solutions. It is like the corporate giant Monsanto, promising to feed the world's billions on a handful of non-producing grain, after rendering the bounty of earth's natural seeds infertile through genetic interference. Or the absence of spiritual guidance in the ranks of the United Nations forces to effectively solve the humanitarian crisis herding displaced populations as they flee across continents to escape war and famine. Unwittingly, the kings of the earth are being led to a time and place in future history to fulfill John's prophecy concerning the last days to come, as revealed in The Book of Revelation, Chapter 6, verses 5-8 (KJV):

> *"And when he had opened the third seal, I heard the third beast say, Come and see. And I beheld, and lo a black horse; and he that sat on him had a pair of balances in his hand. And I heard a voice in the midst of the four beasts say, A measure of wheat for a penny, and three measures of barley for a penny; and see thou hurt not the oil and the wine. And when he had opened the fourth seal, I heard the voice of the fourth beast say, Come and see. And I looked, and behold a pale horse: and his name that sat on him was Death, and Hell followed with him. And power was given unto them over the fourth part of the earth, to kill with sword, and with hunger, and with death, and with the beasts of the earth."*

Through human value, we strike most viciously at the symptom, without considering the precarious nature of our own exposed estate. The present grace showered upon own lives, evidence of a peaceful eddy given in season by our father in heaven. Why should we, therefore, stand dismayed by the visage of approaching darkness, as though we have been chosen to judge and condemn the earth by our own standard, separating what is good and what is evil? Are we better than they? More enlightened, the rags of our sin less soiled, our understanding of doctrine more precise, and thereby unlocking some encrypted mortal code to the end of an affiliated salvation? Can we judge better the wolf in sheep clothing or the sheep among the wolves just by the discernment of our senses; or by the reason of our minds shaped within the same pool polluted by sin?

Like it or not, our megalopolis societies have become analogy to Calhoun's micro-society of mice doomed to extinction. The only certainty any of us can know is the present living matrix, and even this fleeting reality based on a scheme of causality beginning with the first sentient man to gaze into the unknown with apprehension of what it all must mean. And still mankind labors under an illusion that he greater than his environment and superior to the elements consumed daily. Despite all his accumulated knowledge and despite the carnage of a xenophobic past, man still clings to the persistent idea that he is an evolving self-made god to live forever. This belief begins with Satan's first great lie to Adam and Eve in the Garden of Eden, as recorded in Genesis, Chapter 3, verses 1-7 (NKJV).

> *"Now the serpent was more cunning than any beast of the field which the LORD God had made. And he said to the woman, "Has God indeed said, 'You shall not eat of every tree of the garden'?" And the woman said to the serpent, "We may eat the fruit of the trees of the garden; but of the fruit of the tree which is in the midst of the garden, God has said, 'You shall not eat it, nor shall you touch it, lest you die.' "Then the serpent said to the woman, "You will not surely die. For God knows that in the day you eat of it your eyes will be opened, and you will be like God, knowing good and evil." So when the woman saw that the tree was good for food, that it was pleasant to the eyes, and a tree desirable to make one wise, she took of its fruit and ate. She also gave to her husband with her, and he ate. Then the eyes of both of them were opened, and they knew that they were naked; and they sewed fig leaves together and made themselves coverings."*

This same Satan has successfully perpetuated a second lie, even more consequential than the first. A lie so great that it threatens to undermine the very hope of salvation. I wish for the reader to consider that the genesis of what we call Christianity is not a religion-- not today, nor more than 2000 years ago. Those early souls that turn to Christ did so at their peril. They risk being ostracized by priest of the temple, representing God's eternal presence on earth. They risk being murdered by their own countrymen, who cling desperately to the traditions of idol worship. They risk being martyred as enemies of the state when the Emperor of Rome declares himself a deity demanding absolute worship. It is no religion that inspires these brave souls, but the power of the Holy Spirit. Even presently, there are those who suffer continued persecution and even death at the hands of those that gnash their teeth and are swift to violent retaliation against the word of spiritual salvation. Peter, a simple man of the sea, born a Jew and no doubt attended Temple on Sabbath, felt content to live out his days in the company of friends and family. This fisherman, along with eleven others like him, called to become disciples of a man from Galilee. These not a sect of holy men waiting in ascetic anticipation, but are tradesmen humble going about their daily affairs. The summons of Jesus not the allure of a business venture, or a call to arms; nor with incentive of wealth or promise of worldly position, but a simple command: *Come and follow me.* They respond to his call because he knows them already, and because God has prepared these men's hearts since the beginning with an uncomplicated faith that defies natural understanding. These men in effect leave the sanctity of the only religion they know to follow a living spirit quickened in temporal context.

The greatest flaw in humanity comes from a source outside of human nature. This retro- code of evil rebellion originates from a fallen principality we know only vaguely. Because we live within a construct of spatial geometry altered continuously through a kaleidoscope of changing light and shadow, we become conditionally blind to greater context. Subject to our senses, we cleave to the concept of a perceived reality, convinced that material and definition the greater value of fixed existence. Strip away the veneer of worldly apprehension, and what is the essence of humanity?

To quote a passage from the Book of Proverbs *"as a man thinks, so is he"*, but not necessarily before the Lord of true righteousness. Jesus appears to man as a man to reflect how exposed our appearance before God, naked of interpretation, and the flawed reason of worldly philosophy. In affect we are the manifestation of our thoughts, an action precipitating an equal reaction with predictable outcome. Jesus is also saying that as soon as we think to comprehend the meaning of the law, then we unconsciously create within ourselves a limited standard of the intent, thereby becoming judges and no longer participants. Only by being doers of the law by nature are we able to accede to the true intent. The only way to please God is to accept those instructions already written in our heart by faith, void of pride and worldly comprehension: faithful of the outcome; not convinced through the faith of our reason. Paul writes a letter on this point to the righteous Galatians, in Chapter 3, verses 6-15 (NKJV).

> *"Therefore He who supplies the Spirit to you and works miracles among you, does He do it by the works of the law, or by the hearing of faith?— just as Abraham "believed God, and it was accounted to him for righteousness." Therefore know that only those who are of faith are sons of Abraham. And the Scripture, foreseeing that God would justify the Gentiles by faith, preached the gospel to Abraham beforehand, saying, "In you all the nations shall be blessed." So then those who are of faith are blessed with believing Abraham. For as many as are of the works of the law are under the curse; for it is written, "Cursed is everyone who does not continue in all things which are written in the book of the law, to do them."But that no one is justified by the law in the sight of God is evident, for "the just shall live by faith." Yet the law is not of faith, but "the man who does them shall live by them." Christ has redeemed us from the curse of the law, having become a curse for us (for it is*

> written, *"Cursed is everyone who hangs on a tree"), that the blessing of Abraham might come upon the Gentiles in Christ Jesus, that we might receive the promise of the Spirit through faith."*

Pride and reason is primarily responsible for the present divisions witnessed through mortal history. It is the mortar and brick of constructed societies all over the world. There are some philosophies of societal leadership that are better conceived than others, but none sustainable because of greed and prideful avarice that accompanies the condition of limited being. We perceive these models of geopolitical archetypes through the lens of a term called Cultural Revolution.

Benjamin Franklin writes that "Democracy is two wolves and a lamb voting on what to have for lunch. Liberty is a well-armed lamb contesting the vote." But he adds that although it is the worst, it is still better than all those other forms of government that have tried and failed. As we know from history, monarchies lead invariably to revolt of discontented populations. Fascism rises as a pictorial dream to restore past glory, only to open the door through which dictators take control and mount an offensive of totalitarian world domination. Communism becomes paranoid and cumbersome to the point of being unsustainable. The example of free capitalism provides a promise of elite access to all participants, but ultimately leads to gluttony, to material excess, and to disproportionate distribution. Considering this the best of worldly organization, still it falls far short of utopia. And although democracy the preferred paradigm of social conduct, it is an ideal only, rarely equitable for all proponents through a measure of sustainability. One person's free speech becomes an assault on another person's perception of self worth; the prudent posterity of one individual becomes enslavement to debt of many. Without a spiritual connection, all earthly estates become instruments of harm in the hands of mankind's immortal enemy. However, as individuals, we have a personal choice, as stated by the apostle Paul in 1 Corinthians, Chapter 8, verses 9-13 (NIV).

> *"Be careful, however, that the exercise of your rights does not become a stumbling block to the weak. For if someone with a weak conscience sees you, with all your knowledge, eating in an idol's temple, won't that person be emboldened to eat what is sacrificed to idols? So this weak brother or sister, for whom Christ died, is destroyed by your knowledge. When you sin against them in this way and wound their weak conscience, you sin against Christ. Therefore, if what I eat causes my brother or sister to fall into sin, I will never eat meat again, so that I will not cause them to fall."*

I intentionally choose this scriptural interpretation, because it embodies the language most contemporary to present understanding. Consensus of worldly wisdom entices human imagination with a pledge of power over others and a false promise of becoming everlasting. I once met a young man on the Sunset Express, a transcontinental train that then travelled from Los Angeles to the southern east coast. Kind and unassuming, this charismatic individual claims to be a member of the *Rose Cross*. I had never heard of this society and feel intrigued to know more. He begins sharing with me a doctrine of profound brotherly love, with potential to transform the existing world of violence and division into a single-minded community. He further impresses upon me that there are prominent members present and past belonging to this secret society. He provides me a list of famous historical figures, who share discreet membership of the *Rose Cross*: names such as Benjamin Franklin, Abraham Lincoln, and Walt Disney. "We are stronger today than ever before," he says emphatically, his eyes glistening with the last glimmer of an Arizona desert sunset. "People you would never dream, occupying high positions in government, which control much of the world's wealth. There is an important meeting in Houston tomorrow. I am on my way there now. I know your spirit, and that you want to know all that is true. You are welcome to join me my brother."

As much as I am fascinated by this new information, I also feel spiritually apprehensive. Is this some Christian affiliation, as the name implies? How is it that I have never heard even a whisper about these followers of *Christ on a red cross*? I in turn share with him my own experience with the Holy Spirit a few years past. To my surprise, I am met with unexpected ideological resistance, as he implies the written Holy Bible only the first revelation of true knowledge. I admit that this makes me somewhat uncomfortable. Even though I still know little about his professed beliefs, I am certain in my spirit that the inspired history of the Bible a manifestation from God's Holy Spirit, unabbreviated and nothing lacking. We end by getting into a debate over the subject, until finally silence and sleep overcomes us both. A coach car is not the most comfortable passage when crossing a continent. I awake a few hours later to discover this young man's head in my lap sound asleep. I go to the observation car and sit under the myriad stars of a western sky until morning. I never see my unusual coach companion again.

It will be many years before I discover the true philosophy of this society of the *Red Cross*. They are properly called the *Order of Rosicrucian*, first conceived by a medieval German named Christian Rosenkreuz. Based on a theological doctrine of esoteric truths about metaphysical laws governing the universe resurrected from the ancient past, they adhere to a belief that only a select few worthy to acquire insight into the junction of the spiritual realm with the physical universe. This occult society makes claim that the treasure trove of their knowledge goes back to Alexandrian Gnosticism, conceived in the first century A.D. They also embrace Egyptian mysticism, acquiring purification through the teachings of Christianity. This suggests to them that all spiritual force contained within the natural universe stamped by a quantum signature that can be harnessed through the knowledge of proper equations.

I am personally convinced that these teachings are of the sect also known as the *Nicolaitans*, a corrupted religious philosophy, bringing heavenly forces down to earthly value. The belief that knowledge is power has always been Satan's lie to humanity. In the Book of Revelation, Chapter 2, verses 5-6 (NKJV), the returning Messiah Ben David admonishes the church of Ephesus with the following warning:

"Remember therefore from where you have fallen; repent and do the first works, or else I will come to you quickly

and remove your lampstand from its place—unless you repent. But this you have, that you hate the deeds of the Nicolaitans, which I also hate."

The hated deeds of the *Nicolaitans* represent the perverse idea that the power of the Holy Spirit just another random force to be humanly channeled for a purpose. I am here to testify that no such channeling possible. This world of carnal slumber may witness the eddy of change by those awakened, but the essence can never be sourced. Since the model of this code exists outside of time and space, it has no recognizable signature within present carnation. It is analogist to the wind, which has presence, but no discernable beginning or end. Just as the constant flow of time immutable, so is the Holy Spirit without physical locality. It cannot be apprehended, contained, bought, or sold. Those that try through temporal understanding to imitate this incomprehensible force are subject to judgment and destruction. Here I am reminded of a sorcerer name Simon, who though to purchase the gift of the Holy Spirit from Peter in the Book of Acts, Chapter 8, verses 9-23 (NKJV).

"But there was a certain man called Simon, who previously practiced sorcery in the city and astonished the people of Samaria, claiming that he was someone great, to whom they all gave heed, from the least to the greatest, saying, "This man is the great power of God." And they heeded him because he had astonished them with his [sorceries for a long time. But when they believed Philip as he preached the things concerning the kingdom of God and the name of Jesus Christ, both men and women were baptized. Then Simon himself also believed; and when he was baptized he continued with Philip, and was amazed, seeing the miracles and signs which were done. Now when the apostles who were at Jerusalem heard that Samaria had received the word of God, they sent Peter and John to them, who, when they had come down, prayed for them that they might receive the Holy Spirit. For as yet He had fallen

upon none of them. They had only been baptized in the name of the Lord Jesus. Then they laid hands on them, and they received the Holy Spirit. And when Simon saw that through the laying on of the apostles' hands the Holy Spirit was given, he offered them money, saying, "Give me this power also, that anyone on whom I lay hands may receive the Holy Spirit." But Peter said to him, "Your money perish with you, because you thought that the gift of God could be purchased with money! You have neither part nor portion in this matter, for your heart is not right in the sight of God.[22] Repent therefore of this your wickedness, and pray God if perhaps the thought of your heart may be forgiven you. For I see that you are poisoned by bitterness and bound by iniquity."

From the twisted roots of Rosicrucian philosophy sprouts another occult membership known as modern day Freemasons. This should not be confused with the original Masons, considered keepers of occult knowledge, dating as far back as the Babylonian Empire. Modern Freemasonry proclaims itself a morally pure fraternity devoted to preserving the integral meaning of God's kingdom on earth. The pervasive emblem of this congregation is the *All Seeing Eye*, a symbol of wisdom and guardianship. Like the Rosicrucian, Freemasons have a prestigious membership that includes remarkable historical figures such as the anti-Semitic Henry Ford, the obstinate opinionated author Mark Twain, and the stanchly conservative Winston Churchill. But these are only figureheads of an association far greater in scope than the average individual might imagine. The Freemasons point out that their knowledge of symbolism and spatial geometry inherited from the original Masons (*those masterful architects responsible for the construction the pyramids of ancient Egypt and the divinely measured physical structure of Solomon's Temple*). These architects of temporal reality dwell heavily on the structure of the universe that now appears, believing (like the *Rosicrucian*) perfection through metaphysical manipulation. This society lays claim to the secrets of power matrixes contained in strings of mathematical syntax that incorporate encrypted grand equations of design old as creation. What they do not say, and perhaps do not fully comprehend, is that all formulations derived through a temporal model, the equated values calculated on the principals of an entropic condition designed ultimately to fail. They ignore the greater meaning in the construction of Solomon's Temple. Although this measured structure manifested through coordinates of earthly equation, it is designed in the image of future construction, becoming the resurrected Christ in living spirit emanating from beyond conventional time and space. This evidence of spatial coordinates existing without physical locality and built upon a rock of everlasting. As with all occult institutions, this rebranded Rosicrucian philosophy claims to be a fractural religion ordained to shepherd the sheep of humanity into their vision of a new age of enlightenment. But really they are architects of dissolving foundations built upon a fallen estate. The scripture warns against such voices of deception in 1 Corinthians, Chapter 3, verses 10-23 (NKJV).

> *"According to the grace of God which was given to me, as a wise master builder I have laid the foundation, and another builds on it. But let each one take heed how he builds on it. For no other foundation can anyone lay than that which is laid, which is Jesus Christ. Now if anyone builds on this foundation with gold, silver, precious stones, wood, hay, straw, each one's work will become clear; for the Day will declare it, because it will be revealed by fire; and the fire will test each one's work, of what sort it is.[14] If anyone's work which he has built on it endures, he will receive a reward. If anyone's work is burned, he will suffer loss; but he himself will be saved, yet so as through fire. Do you not know that you are the temple of God and that the Spirit of God dwells in you? If anyone[b] defiles the temple of God, God will destroy him. For the temple of God is holy, which temple you are. Let no one deceive himself. If anyone among you seems to be wise in this age, let him become a fool that he may become wise.[19] For the wisdom*

> *of this world is foolishness with God. For it is written, "He catches the wise in their own craftiness"; and again, "The LORD knows the thoughts of the wise, that they are futile." Therefore let no one boast in men. For all things are yours: whether Paul or Apollos or Cephas, or the world or life or death, or things present or things to come—all are yours. And you are Christ's, and Christ is God's."*

The quest for pure knowledge, the fatal corundum of reason, is a snare to those most wise. Nor are members of these hidden societies of mystical interpretation alone in their search of the perfect code by imperfect means. Many philosophies, rich with logical interpretation, continue to flourish throughout the centuries of mortal reasoning. There are the Illuminati, a group claiming devotion solely to empirical evidence, neither publicly professing spiritual good or spiritual evil. There are as the stoic Sadducees mentioned in the gospels, believing neither in the existence of a soul or the resurrection. Although this cult an offshoot of the Freemasons, it has been refashioned as a New Age discipline promoting the idea of unity and toleration based upon material reality. Most visible in the music and entertainment industry of the present, this altruistic society wishes to dispel the idea of a loving God or an evil devil. Responsible for such disturbing plots as Rosemary's Baby and the futuristic doomsday scenarios of a soulless world slaughtering one another over vital resources, the architects of this philosophy have since many years systematically eroded the value of the human life and dignity. They also are creators of the anthropomorphized lovable Disney characters our children affectionately desire, further blurring the lines between what is good and what is evil. Their strongest infiltration is the music industry, creating a euphoric atmosphere of worldly presence, particularly appealing to candidates of the *Noveau Rich*, celebrities such as Beyonce, Rhinna, Bono, and the late Michael Jackson. By dismissing religion as superstition, this cult of elitism embraces with body and soul worldly fame and power in all its forms. It is this blinding influence most deceiving to those engaged. The allocation of excess in this present world comes at a heavy price. The true deception of this false code of abundant resources resides in the mind of worldly power. Whose power we see in Luke's account of how Satan tempts Jesus in the wilderness with promises of wealth and position, Chapter 4, verses 5-8 (NKJV).

> *"Then the devil, taking Him up on a high mountain, showed Him all the kingdoms of the world in a moment of time. And the devil said to Him, "All this authority I will give You, and their glory; for this has been delivered to me, and I give it to whomever I wish. Therefore, if You will worship before me, all will be Yours." And Jesus answered and said to him, "Get behind Me, Satan! For it is written, 'You shall worship the LORD your God, and Him only you shall serve.'"*

The most politically affiliated group of the occult in North America is the Yale University legendary Order of Skull and Bones, an Ivey League membership comprised of some of the most powerful elite in America's political arena. Some U.S. presidents, including William Taft, George Bush Senior (and Junior), are alleged participants of this invisible fraternity. Impressive lists of court judges and famous statesmen, all members of the secret society, have obtained high positions in government. Even the present Secretary of State, John Kerry, is reported to have an affiliation with the Skull and Bones, which shows that there is no political party immune to its influence. Like the Illuminati, the philosophical and theological roots of The Skull and Bones can be traced back to the occult practices of Masonry. Though seemingly harmless on the surface, this is an insidious organization that seduces brilliant young minds to serve and to obey a higher principal of defined values. Brotherhood and patriotism become the highest priority, synonymous with serving God and country--*but service to what God?*

When I become indoctrinated into the United States Marine Corps as a young man, I learn to support similar principals of discipline. I am not suggesting such patriotic devotion without merit; only that individual choice and free will become vague considerations in the face of collective embrace. A man must first learn to live by conscious choice, while considering skeptically the influence of the collective, regardless of how noble on the surface. My freedom to choose restored when I find the meaning of Christ through the Holy Spirit.

Because of the this early experience, I now better understand the difference between blind dedication to a greater good and the instrumentation of personal choice based on sound doctrine of spiritual instruction. It is easy to be appointed flag bearer of a respected society than to accept personal responsibility regardless of consequence. Satan's greatest victory over the human soul is to make murder appear as the only solution. It is the illusion of living inside a burning bubble and believing that the only resistance against the surrounding fire is more fire. This Darwinian interpretation of existence becomes all that is evil in the world. And those that interpret so become the butchers of mankind in the name of saving mankind. This sentimernt echoed through the ages, summed up in Proverbs 14, verse 12, (KJV).

> *"There is a way which seems right unto a man, but the end thereof are the ways of death."*

There are many other societies embellishing similar beliefs, all with roots that trace back to doctrines of enlightened reason and cryptic understanding. The *Biderberg Group*, a secret international coalition of the wealthy bankers and successful entrepreneurs dedicated to the intent of forcing upon the populations a New World government. This unified economic consortium believes that it is their calling to save the present world through a number of nefarious means, including close monitoring of the web of the world internet and the deployment of NATO forces to insure global control. Names like Bill Gates, Bill Clinton, Warren Buffet, and even prominent members of European nations, all share an affiliation of idealism. Even the G7 (formerly the G8 before the voting out of Russia) is believed to be a foundation bringing together the aspirations of these various occult doctrines to usher in the man of perdition, the reign of Antichrist. As with all secret societies, no one can know with any certainty the list of members or the scope of their activities. Although an intriguing subject, it is not my intention or desire to exploit the potential conspiracy theories that circulate throughout many echelons of present day subculture. The conspiracy theorist may be right, but their solutions flawed. For we all exist within the mind of this present world, *"seeing through a glass darkly"*.

There are other mysticisms just as spiritually distracting. Jewish Cabalism is an *Exegesis* approach to existence, within context of a finitely created universe abstractly related to eternal being. It attempts to weave a logical relationship to scriptural hidden meanings and human behavior. Convinced of a mystical connection between mortal presence and omnipotent ordinance, the practitioners of Cabala devote great energy, and weave complex scenarios, in an endeavor to establish an esoteric interpretation satisfactory to every context. Yet, it denies the greatest mystery of all time: *the plain meaning of the resurrected Christ*. Although fascinated by this cryptic preponderance of scripture and the meaning of life, I cannot help but think it little different than the examinations of the enlightened Illuminati. Since I consider it unlikely that the kingdom of heaven comprised of a members only club, then I cannot help but conjecture such vanity of reason to be counterproductive to God's most intimate testament to his most cherished creation. This God loved the world so much that he offers his only begotten son as a flesh and blood sacrifice for the sins of all, regardless of ethnicity, gender, or religion. Would such a God as this make the way of understanding buried in cryptic meaning? What testament can be made simpler in meaning than the birth, death, and resurrection of Jesus Christ? There are few men more skilled in the scripture than the Apostle Paul, a man with grand understanding of scripture and meaning given by the prophets. Nevertheless, after much reason and debate even this well educated Sanhedrin submits logical discourse to the simple testimony given him by the Holy Spirit in 1 Corinthians, Chapter 2, verses 1-5. (NKJV)

> *"And I, brethren, when I came to you, did not come with excellence of speech or of wisdom declaring to you the testimony of God. For I determined not to know anything among you except Jesus Christ and Him crucified. I was with you in weakness, in fear, and in much trembling.*

And my speech and my preaching were not with persuasive words of human wisdom, but in demonstration of the Spirit and of power, that your faith should not be in the wisdom of men but in the power of God."

Worldly wisdom receives its own reward, but not from God. The Torah is a compilation of less than 80,000 words copied from original scrolls, composing a remarkably accurate book (as to translation) just over an inch thick in standard print. Whereas, the Talmud (a collection of commentaries made by educated Rabbis over many centuries) is a book of more than 2,000,000 words comprising over 6000 pages to interpret and often redefine the meaning of the Torah. It is no wonder that Jesus condemns the Scribe and Pharisees of his days as fools and hypocrites, caring more for the praises of men than to do service unto God. No doubt the son of God knew well the meaning of scripture, yet speaks plainly, *"as one having authority"*. It is in human nature to make things complicated and to make carnal embrace to a mind of hierarchal meaning. It is easier through the reason of understanding to indulge intellectual theories than to hear the testament of one eye witness. Challenge of reason became Paul's greatest obstacle to conveying the simplistic nature contained in the gospel of salvation. These men trained through epicurean philosophy are always looking for something new to challenge the senses of intellectual curiosity, yet never considering the obvious as expressed in Acts, Chapter 17, verses 18-28 (NKJV).

"Then certain Epicurean and Stoic philosophers encountered him. And some said, "What does this babbler want to say?" Others said, "He seems to be a proclaimer of foreign gods," because he preached to them Jesus and the resurrection. And they took him and brought him to the[h] Areopagus, saying, "May we know what this new doctrine is of which you speak? For you are bringing some strange things to our ears. Therefore we want to know what these things mean." For all the Athenians and the foreigners who were there spent their time in nothing else but either to tell or to

hear some new thing. Then Paul stood in the midst of the Areopagus and said, "Men of Athens, I perceive that in all things you are very religious; for as I was passing through and considering the objects of your worship, I even found an altar with this inscription: TO THE UNKNOWN GOD. Therefore, the One whom you worship without knowing, Him I proclaim to you:[24] God, who made the world and everything in it, since He is Lord of heaven and earth, does not dwell in temples made with hands. Nor is He worshiped with men's hands, as though He needed anything, since He gives to all life, breath, and all things. And He has made from one blood every nation of men to dwell on all the face of the earth, and has determined their preappointed times and the boundaries of their dwellings, so that they should seek the Lord, in the hope that they might grope for Him and find Him, though He is not far from each one of us; for in Him we live and move and have our being, as also some of your own poets have said, 'For we are also His offspring.'"

The Jews in the days Christ walks the earth are of another persuasion in logic. They believe in the prophets killed by their fathers, but less in the prophecies. Some believe in the theory of resurrection, not in what it truly means. Some even hope that Messiah will come as their new Moses to deliver the children of Israel from Roman oppression. But few in Jewry hear the voice of fulfilled prophecy, or the abiding promise of resurrection, or that this man Jesus born with extraordinary spiritual presence sent of God. They have become so blinded by reason and in the ordnances of ordained priesthood that they think themselves judges above all humanity. They reason between each other that since God supreme then there must naturally be echelons of righteousness, placing them at the top. But Jesus says otherwise in the Gospel of Mathew, Chapter 18, verses 1-6 (NKJV), addressing a contention between his disciples.

> "At that time the disciples came to Jesus, saying, "Who then is greatest in the kingdom of heaven?" Then Jesus called a little child to Him, set him in the midst of them, and said, "Assuredly, I say to you, unless you are converted and become as little children, you will by no means enter the kingdom of heaven. Therefore whoever humbles himself as this little child is the greatest in the kingdom of heaven. Whoever receives one little child like this in My name receives Me. "But whoever causes one of these little ones who believe in Me to sin, it would be better for him if a millstone were hung around his neck, and he were drowned in the depth of the sea."

Since eye has not seen, nor has entered our imagination the things God has prepared for us in the resurrection, then why should we labor so through the perplexity of mortal reason? Should we attempt to bring the mysteries of heaven to earth for the sake of our limited perspective? The Bible states clearly that it is necessary Jesus be born into the world flesh from an eternal position to restore both heaven and earth. In the Gospel of John Chapter 1, verses 1-5 (KJV), we read concerning the genesis of the resurrected Christ.

> "In the beginning was the Word, and the Word was with God, and the Word was God. The same was in the beginning with God. All things were created through Him, and apart from Him not one thing was created that has been created. In him was life; and the life was the light of men. And the light shines in darkness; and the darkness comprehended it not."

Considering that Christ is God (*and with God*) since before the beginning of creation, then the mystery of his manifestation in time should be evident. The perfect code already written before the corrupted code conceived. A reboot of creation on the subatomic level predesigned to rearrange the molecular relationship between matter and energy bringing conclusion to entropy and the beginning of a new heaven and earth. This is a translation impossible to comprehend through present observation, but easy to understand by faith. Nevertheless, we have testimony of those who knew the man Jesus, and who commune with him again after the resurrection. They say he is the same, only changed. They claim he could eat, be touched, and yet vanish as a spirit. Yet, Jesus tells them plainly Luke, Chapter 24, verses 36-44 (NKJV) that he is not a ghost or spirit, but the archetype of a new man, as they too will be.

> *"Now as they said these things, Jesus Himself stood in the midst of them, and said to them, "Peace to you. But they were terrified and frightened, and supposed they had seen a spirit. And He said to them, "Why are you troubled? And why do doubts arise in your hearts? Behold My hands and My feet, that it is I Myself. Handle Me and see, for a spirit does not have flesh and bones as you see I have." When He had said this, He showed them His hands and His feet.[41] But while they still did not believe for joy, and marveled, He said to them, "Have you any food here?" So they gave Him a piece of a broiled fish and some honeycomb. And He took it and ate in their presence. Then He said to them, "These are the words which I spoke to you while I was still with you, that all things must be fulfilled which were written in the Law of Moses and the Prophets and the Psalms concerning Me." And He opened their understanding, that they might comprehend the Scriptures."*

This testimony abides still, lasting more than twenty centuries, experienced repeatedly from generation to generation alive through people like me, touched by the Holy Spirit and reborn through dynamic process. Being imperfect in every way I shout Hallelujah with the Apostles and with the angels that Jesus Christ is resurrected and more than capable finishing a perfect work.

The first verse of Genesis states plainly *"In the beginning God created the heaven and the earth."* This is the inspiration of spiritual and material existence. Both realms created equally, not one without the other. The material of a fallen state subject to time, the spiritual condition of our souls translated to angelic positions. Without the living soul of man, the angels incomplete; without spiritual birth, we as dead as the clay from whence we are made. Think of our living metabolic state analogist to our spiritual position in God's plan of eternity. The billions of micros that provide the unseen structure of our existence do not rebel against their function, but perform as they are designed. Since we are in the body of Christ, and Christ in God, then why should we refuse our station, as one who wishes to be in another position? If God has made me the foot, what benefit to the body if I willfully refuse, preferring instead to be the hand? To be even the least in the kingdom of heaven is far more perfect, than to be separated from the body, remembering that Satan's fall in defiance of his created glory.

"What is truth?" Pilot asked the accused man brought before his judgment seat. The question rhetorical, even cynical in response to a statement made by Jesus at the judgment seat, as presented in the Gospel of John, Chapter 18, verse 37 (KJV).

> *"To this end was I born, and for this cause came I into the world, that I should bear witness unto the truth. Every one that is of the truth hears my voice."*

Did Pilot hear the meaning in Jesus' words? The scripture does not definitively say, only that the *Roman Prefect* of Judea argues that he finds no fault worthy of the accusations, wishing to release the prisoner. However, this is not to be. Pontus Pilot realizes for perhaps the first time that he is as much snared in the politics of his position, as this man Jesus caught in the deadly web of a religious conspiracy. Sin is a world condition, the cogs and wheels of mechanical precision, a great cosmic clock wound-up and programmed to a finite hour. Sin is a rebellion beginning in the heart destined to run the gauntlet of fleshly corruption. No human righteousness greater than the consequence of sin; no discourse of reason master over the mind of evil inspired through rebellion. No guru able to transcend, no religion or philosophy profound to the design of a better code, than is already from the beginning.

There is one father above; one son sent into temporal time to restore that which was lost; and one spirit to unite the living soul born of clay to eternal position. All this accomplished even before Adam and Eve fled naked from the sight of God. God provides breadcrumbs to direct the souls of men through a confusing maze to the acceptable hour of salvation. To look is to see; to hear is to understand. Jesus first loves us that we might also know how to love the father, his promise made plain in the Gospel of John, Chapter 14, verses 1-7 (NKJV).

> *"Let not your heart be troubled; you believe in God, believe also in Me. In My Father's house are many mansions; if it were not so, I would have told you. I go to prepare a place for you. And if I go and prepare a place for you, I will come again and receive you to Myself; that where I am, there you may be also. And where I go you know, and the way you know." Thomas said to Him, "Lord, we do not know where You are going, and how can we know the way?" Jesus said to him, "I am the way, the truth, and the life. No one comes to the Father except through Me. "If you had known Me, you would have known My Father also; and from now on you know Him and have seen Him."*

The challenge to love one another is as great a personal test as I have endured since the hour of my salvation. At such an early age, I learned to be hard, to set my emotions aside, and be a fearless fighting machine in the service of country and committed to the *Semper Fidelis* of the Unites States Marine Corps. There was no question as to the requirements of my duty then. Physically and mentally prepared for any situation, be it war or peace, I knew my course in this world. Upon receiving the Holy Spirit, I realize a conflict I did not have before. A battle between the man of war and a new man born to peace; not conflict in being a soldier, but being a born again Christian in this worldly structured hierarchy. The Marine Corps had been my savior from a life of crime, my new home of acceptance, and a proud brotherhood of belonging, as great as any this world can offer. It saddens me greatly that I must no longer belong here. By inspiration of my new faith I step boldly into an unknown future knowing only the comfort of Jesus Christ my abiding comforter. Never has he left me in all these years. Part of me remains still that young marine; part of me an even stranger person that I have become today. Now I have come of age and what has been shared to me. I am one in Christ: past, present, and future. In these particularly troubling times, I have but one petition before God. I pray the Holy Spirit will strive unceasingly against the pride of self for the benefit of all I might touch and that touch me. Hoping always that love unfeigned may abound as pure as the love that first loved me.

In this present I also pray a sign of testimony given to the hearts of men made callus to the ways of this world. I pray for women changed to merchandise with only a reflection to keep them company, I pray for the children of this world born in shadows of fear and violence, remembering that smart bombs and military arsenals have no respect between the guilty and the innocent. I pray for those forgotten in distant lands subject to the wills of tyrants, whose blood runs etched along geographic borders drawn on a map. I pray for a world being drawn unknowingly to engage upon paths of swift destruction leading to the day of Armageddon. I pray for those destitute, those in bonds, those possessed by evil spirits, and those whose hearts have waxed dim in material excess. But most I pray that these words not written in vain to the end of vanity. To this end I add my voice to Paul's fist letter to the Corinthians, Chapter 2, verses 2-16 (NKJV).

> *"For I determined not to know anything among you except Jesus Christ and Him crucified. I was with you in weakness, in fear, and in much trembling. And my speech and my preaching were not with persuasive words of human wisdom, but in demonstration of the Spirit and of power, that your faith should not be in the wisdom of men but in the power of God.*

However, we speak wisdom among those who are mature, yet not the wisdom of this age, nor of the rulers of this age, who are coming to nothing. But we speak the wisdom of God in a mystery, the hidden wisdom which God ordained before the ages for our glory, which none of the rulers of this age knew; for had they known, they would not have crucified the Lord of glory. But as it is written: "Eye has not seen, nor ear heard, Nor have entered into the heart of man The things which God has prepared for those who love Him." But God has revealed them to us through His Spirit. For the Spirit searches all things, yes, the deep things of God. For what man knows the things of a man except the spirit of the man which is in him? Even so no one knows the things of God except the Spirit of God. Now we have received, not the spirit of the world, but the Spirit who is from God, that we might know the things that have been freely given to us by God. These things we also speak, not in words which man's wisdom teaches but which the Holy Spirit teaches, comparing spiritual things with spiritual. But the natural man does not receive the things of the Spirit of God, for they are foolishness to him; nor can he know them, because they are spiritually discerned. But he who is spiritual judges all things, yet he himself is rightly judged by no one. For "who has known the mind of the LORD that he may instruct Him?" But we have the mind of Christ."

Chapter 7
SEEDS OF MAN

In Genesis, Chapter 11, verses 4-9 (NKJV) we read:

> *"And they said, "Come, let us build ourselves a city, and a tower whose top is in the heavens; let us make a name for ourselves, lest we be scattered abroad over the face of the whole earth." But the LORD came down to see the city and the tower which the sons of men had built. And the LORD said, "Indeed the people are one and they all have one language, and this is what they begin to do; now nothing that they propose to do will be withheld from them. Come, let Us go down and there confuse their language, that they may not understand one another's speech." So the LORD scattered them abroad from there over the face of all the earth, and they ceased building the city. Therefore its name is called Babel, because there the LORD confused the language of all the earth; and from there the LORD scattered them abroad over the face of all the earth."*

Although we can only infer from the available abbreviated text the ultimate objective of this unified effort, the Tower of Babel remains a symbol of human achievement lost in history. Even a failed project on such a grand scale is an enduring testament of what the minds of men capable of. Would the completion of this endeavor have precipitated events leading to a premature final judgment? By the supernatural confounding of the language of communication I believe the earth of mankind reprieved from another final destruction? As tantalizing as the possibilities, we will never know for sure. But what we do know a far greater mystery.

Language is as much an acoustic phenomenon, as it is a transmission of sound patterns to form ideas. All unique languages are composed of intonations that denote an imprinted meaning within context of a group agreement. No one is born with a language. Language is acquired through a complex socialization process of auditory mimicry engaged by an infant, even before the development of visual depth perception. This transition, accompanied by patterns of association, trigger visual, tactile, as well as emotional receptors that reinforce a prescribed definition of reality and meaning. Through repeated reinforcement behavior, the brain equates communicative response algorithms with models of ideas. The left hemisphere of the brain communicates with the right hemisphere in a seeming dichotomous fashion. Each relays important information to finalize the agreement. It has been shown that the left hemisphere responsible for sound and syntax of a word; whereas, the right provides power and influence for emotional meaning. This processing homogenous to all languages, even to communications we do not think of as language. Subtle facial expressions, intonation of the words, and even the way we move our eyes, all convey a level of meaning clearly received by the listener. These qualities of non-verbal conveyance are not necessarily unique to any particular language. If I have unintentionally angered someone in China, I do not need to understand Chinese to pick up on the generated displeasure. By the same token, languages are transferable, meaning that anyone from another culture can be trained to understand and speak (*perhaps not always with the same emotional impact as a native*), but with competent transmission and comprehension.

Just as there are differing theories of how language began, a great deal of study into how these languages have evolved over time. A base mother tongue may give birth to differing dialects, which change over time by a process of external migrating influences. Some of these dialects so bastardized that they become unintelligible to the root language of origin. It is interesting that every language expands its vocabulary to define new things and new ideas. For example, aboriginal societies had no word for a chemical ballistic weapon, until they first saw a gun; and understood both its use and destructive potential. The description of a washing machine would have no meaning to someone, who has no basic experience with hydrostatic pressures. Nor would the concept of an extraterrestrial vehicle inspire anything but awe to a culture that had no word for spaceship. Although a seemingly minor consideration, it has been observed that different languages induces a different way of thinking. This may be a chemical reaction to the way sounds are translated and processed through the cerebral cortex.

The first and only historical record of mankind unified by language and committed to a singular objective, goes back to this obscure tale about the Babel Tower during the first millennium after the receding flood waters deposit Noah's Ark on the Steppes of the Ararat Mountains. There resounds no voice of dissention, since this grand edifice represents to the builders a refuge of protection against the possibility the waters might rise again to the peril of the human race. Learning through shared experience, this generation now trusts more in the ingenuity of their minds, than in an ambiguous God that spared their immediate ancestors. They have forgotten already the meaning in a giant wooden coffin that spared the genesis of man and the several animal species that have begun to repopulate the earth. They have forgotten that even the looming mountains covered by that irresistible deluge and all live beyond the Ark destroyed. Nor do they remember the sin that caused the destruction. By now they begin again to trust in the work of their hands and in the evidence of some vague technology incorporated in this spire reaching boldly heavenward. This ambitious project terminated when ability to communicate somehow impaired, thus ending the project.

Any mathematician will confirm that even simple equations must be consistent in model formulation. For example, modern Metric measurements, used by much of Europe, will not yield the same value as Standard measurements used in the United States, and Imperial measurements (yet another value) used in Britain. It is even unclear what constitutes a cubit, a unit of measurement often referred to in the Bible, and found in other historical legers with discrepant conversion agreement. Also, think for a moment how the mind processes auditory input within the environment. The slightest chemical change in this process, either by atmospheric density or biological processing, then the *phonemic* interpretation radically differs from one individual to another, making even basic communication of ideas challenging. But if several persons experience the same phenomenon, the result is splintered schism of communication, forcing individuals to form separate groups with independent coherence. This is not unlike the code of *cryptophasia*; whereby, twins develop between themselves a secret language complete with a lexicon of spoken and written syntax. Another example might be languages of an autonomous secret society, or an altogether artificially invented vocabulary, such as the idiosyncratic spoken *Klingon* language, a detailed *idioglossia* created for a nonexistent alien species. This factious race spawned from planet in another solar system, inspired by the 1960's network success of the television Star Trek series.

There is also a clinical condition known as APD (*Auditory Processing Disorder*), a systemic aberration of frequency disruption, which interferes with the brain's ability to process information through auditory distortion. The subject is well documented and should not be ignored within context of how the higher functions of the brain work. An analogy might be the way a sound perceived underwater, compared to the same decibel traveling through the less dense medium of air. There is a defined chemical response of the brain to the external stimuli of changing pressures associated with barometric and fluid dynamics on a grand scale. Communication is everything. Is it possible this might explain the confusion of communication described in the Bible? Could it not be coincidence that as earth's atmosphere settles over time, a subtle pressure accumulated in the inner ear, causing a distortion of auditory input, as well as a confused transmission of ideas? Perhaps this change occurs gradually over several decades, until finally the ambitious unified project of the Babel Tower becomes impossible to complete, and therefore abandoned. As condition worsen groups begin to splinter into communities, separating themselves from their now alien neighbors.

The great danger described here is not that men of this period might build a physical structure to the peril of heaven, but an apparatus designed by the use of formulas and mathematical equations preserved after the destruction of the first earth. The completion of this device would have only hastened man's final destruction. For surely there were technologies invented by the ancient *Nephilim,* the first superhuman offspring of fallen angels, which also survived through the DNA genesis of Noah and his wife, his three sons and their wives. It is worthy to note that these eight only are mentioned and no new children are yet conceived in the wake of this global destruction.

So there may actually be some empirical scientific evidence for the Tower of Babel mix up, and how independent languages evolved. An overture of peace in one language might be construed as a declaration of war in another. Also in a given society values for the same word may change over time. There is little agreement as to the meaning of a cubic within historical context. A Hebrew cubit might be calculated at seventeen and a half inches. An Egyptian cubit could be as much as three inches longer. Why in modern times metric calculations in one part of the world and standard measurements in another part? Returning to Einstein's clause of relativity, reality is from the point of view of the observer in space time. Even though both formulas yield the same solution, there will be discrepancies between the two methodologies. This actually happened in 1999, when a Mars Climate Orbiter lost by flying too deeply into the Martian atmosphere because of a math error in the reentry codes. A project of combined effort between two U.S. aerospace companies using different values resulted in a fatal error leading to the crash of the vehicle. JPL (Jet Propulsion Laboratory) located in Colorado, and California based NASA, shared critical data for the 416 million mile journey. One company uses measurements based on metric tons, while the other company standard foot-pounds in the flight correction thrusters. A minor discrepancy of communication results in failure of this expensive project.

We can see in this example the vital importance of communication agreement. Whatever might have been the ultimate purpose of the Tower of Babel, the magnitude change in transmission and comprehension of instruction calculations between the builders would have been insurmountable.

But even though the world now divided, God has not forgotten his first design for human kind. Out of the grandness of a new empire rising in the valley of Mesopotamia four hundred years later a man named Abraham, resident to a city called Err, is summoned in a dream to separate himself from earth's new citizenry. This man of faith will sire a nation, and from this nation will be born a Messiah reunite man in the collapsing midst of entropy. This promise described precisely by the Prophet Zachariah in Chapter 12, verse 10 (NKJV).

> *"And I will pour on the house of David and on the inhabitants of Jerusalem the Spirit of grace and supplication; then they will look on Me whom they pierced. Yes, they will mourn for Him as one mourns for his only son, and grieve for Him as one grieves for a firstborn."*

The state of modern day Israel is a military stronghold, armed to the teeth, surrounded by many nations of self-declared enemies. Some will point out that this is the way it has always been for this small country geographically no larger than the state of New Hampshire. But why is it historical significant in the history of empires? When both Abraham and his wife Sarah well passed child bearing age, they conceive Isaac, father of Jacob, who becomes the progenitor of the twelve patriarchs. These twelve men of sorted character sire the twelve Hebrew tribes that will be named the children of Israel. As yet, there is no consignment of laws and no religion.

But rather a contract based on promise to one man, whose father by all reports was a merchant of idols worshipped throughout Mesopotamia after the flood. Though there are many *Talmudic* fables of Abraham. Some portray his life as morally exemplary, others more human prone to vice. The *Torah* (the main book of Judaism) presents this man as one born mortal within mortal context; yet inspired by a revelation of faith through the Holy Spirit. Abraham is no Jew within this historical context, nor will he sire a family devoted to better understanding of some ancient doctrine. As were most men in his time, Abraham guided by oral translations passed down from before the flood. But like Noah, he believes the one God to be God, and obeys the directive of this God, departing from the secure diver's fortress built by a wicked generation devoted to the vain worship of many false gods. This faith not provided because of his own righteousness, but by the righteousness of faith that the God of creation his spoken to him providing instruction of a better promise inspired through his loins.

It is not until Moses leads the enslaved Israelites out of Egypt approximately 430 years later, that God speaks audibly out of the smoke surrounding Mount Sinai, imparting a living testament of his presence in temporal estate. This witness is a divine manifestation spoken to sinful mankind. The linage of this people has born testimony ever since, infusing into one body the legacy of a culture and a practice of worship. The Ark of the Covenant is for a time the only physical presence of God upon the earth, influencing hearts and minds of mortal men from generation to generation. This living testament later replaced by the Tabernacle of David, after the Ark pillaged by invaders. This second Ark continues to embody the symbol of faith that remains until the grandiose construction of Solomon's Temple. This first grand earthly structure razed to the ground after the conquest of Judah by Nebuchadnezzar, king of Babylon, which the scripture prophesizes as a king raised-up by God to correct his chosen people. Even Jesus warns his apostles to not look upon the grandeur of the second Temple that exists in his generation, for like the first, it, too, will be laid waste, *"not one stone left standing upon another"*. This happens after the future Roman emperor, Titus, (at the time a commanding general) orders the temple dismantled to reclaim the gold that had melted and seeped between the stones.

Today, there are serious plans to rebuild a third temple, which will serve to ignite an unprecedented conflict ultimately leading to final battle referred to as Armageddon. Israel and the world will realize the true cornerstone of the temple is the indwelling Holy Spirit of God's appointed Messiah, conceived since the beginning of creation: an eternal condition far more profound than any material structure or religious institution.

It is important to note that before the conception of Isaac with Sarah, the wife of his youth, Abraham sires his firstborn child by another woman living in his household named Hagar. This first son, christened Ishmael, will become the patriarch of peoples inhabiting the lands of present day Arabia. Ishmael represents the mind and obedience of the flesh; whereas, Isaac, the seed of promise. Even the elder son will ultimately receive blessing by the sanctification of the younger. Isaac's first offspring are Esau and Jacob, twin brothers, turbulently different, both appointed ambivalent destinies. These brothers have a falling out, as brothers often do, but will reconcile after the death of their father. Jacob, later named *Israel,* following struggler with an angel, basically means *"one who prevails with God"*. Israel becomes more than just a name, more than just a worldly principality. It is the mortal living testament to a world blinded by materialism of false gods. This continuing testament to all nations and to all tongues, not just the condition of an earthly heritage upon a geographical hill. Nor is it the evidence of just another government mightily armed, surrounded by enemies within and without. It is, rather, the promise and final hope of reconciliation through an incorruptible seed of God's chosen Christ.

We do not need to go far to hear the rumble of wars and rumors of war resonating around the globe in response to the radical insurgence of the Islamic State of Iraq and Syria, better known as ISIS. Up until a few years ago, the greatest threat to modern civilization was the spectral shadow of Al Qaeda. No one can deny the destructive potential of these fanaticized terrorist groups inspired by Jihad to restore the vision of the Mohammad Caliph. In my generation it was the blight of Communism that had to be stopped at the border of South East Asia. The nations say they will not get involved in the Middle East conflict, and yet are unwillingly drawn into the miry mud of an unwinnable opposition. The age old divisions between Israel and the kingdoms of Arabia have raged for millenniums, the holy city of Jerusalem being ground zero of the aggression. Since the beginning of the twentieth century there have been two World Wars deciding the topography of civilized society, the latter being more bloody than the first. These were wars of attrition and power alliances, with the objective of redefining a materialist structure with similar interpretive values. We continue to see this shifting of western demographics in our modern age. Even Russia, the great bear to the north, struggles to maintain a strategic foothold into the Baltic by annexing the Ukrainian port city of Crimean. Nor do I think this restless nation will stop there. China flexes its military muscle in the disputed areas off the coast of Japan and the Philippines in an intimidating show of superior force, all the while holding the leash of a dangerous North Korea. Even the United States and Canada engage with other nations in aerial bombardments against a primitive force in an unwinnable assault hoping to demoralize an enemy on the move, as a fire spreading across the Middle East. But this enemy is like no other seen in contemporary times, motivated by a burning moralistic ideology, not based on materialistic value, but instructed from a fire ignited more than thirteen centuries ago. This makes it, neither the better nor the worst of religious ideologies, but an instrument of consuming principal, driven as a horde of destruction flaming across the ancient lands of the Bible. This is a feudal call of blood for blood born from the wound of righteous defiance, with Islam the sword of ideology sharpened on two edges. It is a hatred based upon primitive jealousy, a *fatwa*, not inspired through logic, or strategy, or even upon material reward. It is as a chimera of nature dedicated to the destruction of Judaism, and all that is contrary to a cruel righteous standard prescribed by Allah, *God of the Moon*. The destructive force of this world religion is the unprecedented flow of populations, displaced by war and famine, fanning across safe borders like hordes of locust. The poisonous head of an unleashed javelin forged in scripted obedience to blind instruction of an indoctrinated hatred conceived by violent resolution against the Christ of God. It harnesses the fallen nature of this world to taunt arrogant civilization hastening its own destruction: the tares mingled with the wheat in the onslaught of humanitarian crisis. How does one effectively fight against a force of nature? How should another decide: *who should live and who should die*? Cries of the oppressed and ghettoized are not unfamiliar to history, only the present scale of inequity increasingly more horrific. What is the ultimate worldly solution to assimilate or cull the herds of human migration fleeing across continents, driven by forces unseen?

The escalating tensions sweeping the Middle East are as brush fires clearing the chafe of weaker elements. Looking back upon the chessboard of history, we see the ancient nations mentioned in the Bible, a collage of kingdoms rising and declining; but always remaining ghostly apparitions of their former greatness, as seeds in a dry earth waiting for rain to replenish the land. Names have changed, borders realigned, but the blessing upon Ishmael, Abraham's first paternal son, promising that he is to become father to a great nation of people: a promise that continues to flourish greatly to this day.

The beginning of the twentieth century provides renewed economic vitality to these fallowed lands after the initial discovery of oil in Persia. It quickly becomes apparent that not only Persia, but much of the Middle East contains this valuable energy resource. Soon, Saudi Arabia, Iraq, Syria, and Libya are gushing with the black gold to supply the needs of an oil-hungry world. Other countries follow the gravy train, making the Middle East a Mecca of the international financial markets. Military armament inevitable, as more aggressive elements begin campaigns to expand their borders. Though divided, most share a common interest in the obliteration of an ancient enemy resting as a rich jewel in the Land of Canaan.

Many are familiar with the history of how the Jews return to their homeland after the atrocities of Nazi Germany against ethnic Jews. It seems like a practical solution for the entire world at the time. No one wants to accept the flood of displaced refugees, nor is there much hope in the mind of many that these new settlers will survive for long. Forced from the beginning to learn how to protect themselves against an overwhelming Muslim population, they inspire from among their ranks a strong and dedicated military. Although outnumbered and surrounded by enemies, they retaliate time and time again victorious. Not only do they survive, they thrive, by making the desert bloom with irrigation techniques and the use of innovative technologies, which they eagerly share with the world. But this is not just a tale of personal survival and deterministic values. In fact, it is a world event altogether supernatural. God proclaims this remarkable resurrection by the prophet Ezekiel, Chapter 37, verses 1-6 (NIV) approximately 450 years before the birth of Jesus Christ.

> *"The hand of the LORD was on me, and he brought me out by the Spirit of the LORD and set me in the middle of a valley; it was full of bones. He led me back and forth among them, and I saw a great many bones on the floor of the valley, bones that were very dry. He asked me, "Son of man, can these bones live?" I said, "Sovereign LORD, you alone know." Then he said to me, "Prophesy to these bones and say to them, 'Dry bones, hear the word of the LORD! This is what the Sovereign LORD says to these bones: I will make breath enter you, and you will come to life. I will attach tendons to you and make flesh come upon you and cover you with skin; I will put breath in you, and you will come to life. Then you will know that I am the LORD.' "*

However, putting prophecy and ideology aside, it is a fact that since the middle half of the last century immigration around the globe has become an increasing strain on all nations as populations try to escape famines created by shifting jet streams, violent uncertainty created by escalating wars, and by economic disparity eroding the core of richer and poorer communities. Remembering that there are no demographics among survivors clinging to the hull of a sinking ship, perhaps a more objective approach needed to describe what is happening in the world today. What good is it to have a prosperous vineyard if those surrounding your borders are dying of starvation? There must be a better solution than the one presently divined.

When it comes to scriptural interpretation, even theologians and clergy fail to agree on the most fundamental arrangements. Were the two books of Isaiah written by the same person? Was the Apostle Peter ever actually in Rome, and was he crucified there at the same time of Paul's beheading by the Emperor Nero? Did Jesus somehow escape death and continue on to sire an earthly linage with Mary? Not to mention the myriad of denominational interpretations of even the most basic meaning. What is the status of women in the Episcopalian view? Can homosexuals go to heaven, and is there more than one hell reserved for sinners? There are as many Christian sects and interpretations of scriptural guidance, as there are inflections found in languages.

There should be no question unworthy of address regardless how much shrouded in mystery. Yet, the modern mind of secular reasoning prefers a quantified truth at the expense of inclusivity, than consider that the God of the Bible might exist contrary to worldly reason. Even many modern-day well-meaning Christians infected with censorship questioning from the pulpit the fundamental accuracy of Bible text under pressure of secular acceptance. These should be reminded that at the turn of the twentieth century many theologians doubted that the early Hebrews actually had contact with the Hittites, or that the early tribes had any intimate dealings with the Pharaohs of Egypt, as described in the Book of Exodus. Recent archeological discoveries have vindicated the Bible as a reliable geopolitical history book, expressing accurately the sociology, the etymology, and the epistemology of lost empires in contact with the early Hebrews over the past several millennia. So why should this remarkable text be limited to only the history of the past?

Prophecy is a subject embraced with much skepticism. Because prophecy based on visions outside of normal time and space, it intersects more than one prescribed reality. These messages most often conveyed by spiritual mediators identified as angelic translators. It is like a taller man describing to a shorter man what is over the horizon. Those engaged in the careful study of prophecy often conclude that prophecy found in the Bible reveals overlapping concentric patterns in the sand of time, each describing the future of local geopolitical events, while at the same time telescoping into a consequential distant future on a much magnified scale. As awareness of the world expands, the relative inclusion defined through global comprehension expands with it. This relevant cause and affect cycle becomes the self-fulfilled retribution of an unrepentant directive, more than an intervention of divine judgment. Prophecy is not the same as clairvoyance. Clairvoyance relies on information to project models of future probability; whereas, prophecy reflects events that have already happened in a space time continuum we statically term as the future. Remembering that the words contained in the scripture are of spiritual origin, and can only be understood through the spirit, prophecy becomes a source of anxiety to unbelievers, but comfort to true believers. Until fulfilled, prophecy has no logical validity, but is able to cause a soul to repent and turn away from the mass directive of the herd. This is why nations have an irresistible destiny, but individuals a way of escape through the spiritual intervention of Jesus Christ.

Worldly positions of present power have become so common place that we fail to appreciate the unique alignment of the domino effect that make the history we can trace to the present conditions we observe. Time is a constant flow forward. No deed can be undone, no decision reenacted, and nothing short of a miracle that can change the heart of a man when once committed. Not even Satan, with all his worldly power, can undo even the most modest temporal event. Lacking omnipotence, this fallen spirit is the very definition of entropy.

A little more than five hundred years ago, the proclaimed prophet of Islam receives instructions that it time for a campaign of forced unification of all people throughout the Arab lands and beyond. Israel is not even a principality then, the majority of Jews scattered far from Jerusalem. This establishes the first caliphate, a ruthless campaign to submit all to the yoke of Mohammed's vision of servitude to Allah, thus preparing the stage for a world religion controlled by judicious administration and blind obedience. Before the Koran, most Arabic people, either worship pagan idols or consider they are the children of the patriarchal linage going back to their patriarch, Abraham. The five books of Moses revered as the instruction of their worship. With the power of a sharpened sword, the Arab world unites into a singular mind and army called Islam, defiant against the God of Israel. Mohammed's teachings accomplish two major harms. First, it revives the ancient divisions between Jews and other Semitic people, erecting irreconcilable barriers. Second, it denounces the promise made to Abraham by inventing subtle interpretations with different meaning. But most damaging of all, it is a doctrine that deposes Jesus Christ as the Messiah and God's only conceived son. Like all religions, Muslims have become divided sects, each interpreting the meaning of the Koran differently. These teachings have created subdivisions, resulting in bloody massacres, not unlike the early Crusades and the later bloody wars between Catholic and Protestant.

The stage set in the day of Ezekiel, as it is today, in preparation for a battle to take place in the Levant of Jordan, which includes the borders of modern Israel. Following the revitalization of the Israeli nation, the prophet continues with a grime report against the northern kingdoms that will attack as described in Chapter 38, verses 1-23 (NIV).

"The word of the LORD came to me: "Son of man, set your face against Gog, of the land of Magog, the chief prince of Meshek and Tubal; prophesy against him and say: 'This is what the Sovereign LORD says: I am against you, Gog, chief prince of Meshek and Tubal. I will turn you around, put hooks in your jaws and bring you out with your whole army—your horses, your horsemen fully armed, and a great horde with large and small shields, all of them brandishing their swords. Persia, Cush and Put will be with them, all with shields and helmets, also Gomer with all its troops, and Beth Togarmah from the far north with all its troops—the many nations with you." 'Get ready; be prepared, you and all the hordes gathered about you, and take command of them. After many days you will be called to arms. In future years you will invade a land that has recovered from war, whose people were gathered from many nations to the mountains of Israel, which had long been desolate. They had been brought out from the nations, and now all of them live in safety. You and all your troops and the many nations with you will go up, advancing like a storm; you will be like a cloud covering the land." 'This is what the Sovereign LORD says: On that day thoughts will come into your mind and you will devise an evil scheme. You will say, "I will invade a land of unwalled villages; I will attack a peaceful and unsuspecting people—all of them living without walls and

without gates and bars. I will plunder and loot and turn my hand against the resettled ruins and the people gathered from the nations, rich in livestock and goods, living at the center of the land." Sheba and Dedan and the merchants of Tarshish and all her villages will say to you, "Have you come to plunder? Have you gathered your hordes to loot, to carry off silver and gold, to take away livestock and goods and to seize much plunder?" "Therefore, son of man, prophesy and say to Gog: 'This is what the Sovereign LORD says: In that day, when my people Israel are living in safety, will you not take notice of it? You will come from your place in the far north, you and many nations with you, all of them riding on horses, a great horde, a mighty army. You will advance against my people Israel like a cloud that covers the land. In days to come, Gog, I will bring you against my land, so that the nations may know me when I am proved holy through you before their eyes." 'This is what the Sovereign LORD says: You are the one I spoke of in former days by my servants the prophets of Israel. At that time they prophesied for years that I would bring you against them. This is what will happen in that day: When Gog attacks the land of Israel, my hot anger will be aroused, declares the Sovereign LORD. In my zeal and fiery wrath I declare that at that time there shall be a great earthquake in the land of Israel. The fish in the sea, the birds in the sky, the beasts of the field, every creature that moves along the ground, and all the people on the face of the earth will tremble at my presence. The mountains will be overturned, the cliffs will crumble and every wall will fall to the ground. I will summon a sword against Gog on all my mountains, declares the Sovereign LORD. Every man's sword will be against his brother. I will execute judgment on him with plague and bloodshed; I will pour down torrents of rain, hailstones and burning sulfur on him and on his troops and on the many nations with him. And so I will show my greatness and my holiness, and I will make myself known in the sight of many nations. Then they will know that I am the LORD.'"

Of course, this is nothing new to Bible scholars, who have meticulously pasted together the geopolitical meaning of these verses spoken by a prophet echoed through the violence of two and a half millennia. According to many experts these northern kingdoms are coalition forces forged between Iran and Russia, after the fire of the *Islamic State of Iraq and the Levant* has burned out. It is not my intent here to interpret scripture or predict future events. There are ample global experts versed in divining the times. I merely point out that the escalation of increasing instability centered in these lands, represent a return to the very cradle of civilization and cannot be ignored.

Clearly this is not the world of peace promised in our time. Rather, it is a world fragmented, escalating toward even greater violence and justifiable murder. An innate gene drenched in the irresistible flow of blood since the day of Cain, the first son of man, who slew his brother Abel out of jealous rage. This blood of man by the hand of man translated through the millenniums with hearts influenced by the very prince of rebellion. It is the false flesh and blood doctrine that by killing an opposition, then one may inherit the earth. Not only is this not true, but guarantees a future of carnage, often spanning generations.

Upon the mount of Hebron, God gives to Moses a ledger of *Ten Commandments* inscribed upon stone, with a special provision in the sixth statue, saying *"Thou shall not kill"*. Nevertheless, human history is sewn with the bones of murder weighed in the balance of personal gain, expansion of territorial borders, out of jealousies, and as a whim of power. The source of this violent aggression challenged in the Book of James, Chapter 4, verses 1-3 (KJV).

"From whence come wars and fightings among you? Come they not hence, even of your lusts that war in your members? Ye lust, and have not: ye kill, and desire to have, and cannot obtain: ye fight and war, yet ye have not, because

ye ask not. Ye ask, and receive not, because ye ask amiss, that ye may consume it upon your lusts."

I am not without compassion regarding the State of Israel's present dilemma. Once trained as a warrior, I wish to share with the reader how the will and the power of God revived me from certain death in flesh in 2003. A Muslim Arab family from Tunisia purchases the apartment building that had been my home for more than decade. They seem like nice people, accepting of my presence and unorthodox way of living. A disagreement arises concerning a permitted TV antenna installed on the roof since many years. I foolishly agreed to relocate the device in hope of maintaining peace. I inadvertently touch a 12000 volt medium tension electrical line, am electrocuted, and fall more than 36 feet to my death. But the Lord determines I not remain dead, and so revive only to spend the next six months hospitalized, recovering from severe second and third degree electrical burns, vertebra damage, and multiple bone fractures of both hips, as well as a shattered pelvis. Upon returning to my home, these people, whose culture I knew nothing about, turn viciously against me, desiring that I flee my home. After several verbal encounters, a young Muslim man stranger to the neighborhood, attacks me physically as I go to my car. Even though I am not fully recovered from my injuries, I sufficiently protect myself. However, I realize now that war declared; escalation inevitable. Determined not to abandon my home of many years, I find myself living under extreme stress for the next two years, anxious of the next terror attack. Often, I consider a preemptive strike as a measure of protection--*hurt the enemy before the enemy hurts you!* Yet, in my spirit such an act against the value of faith revealed to my delivered soul, or the measure of mercy shown to me when I was still lost in sin. I therefore determine to trust in the lord of my salvation, believing that to perish on earth in the name of righteousness, better than to lash out preemptively because of uncertainty. By now I know from experience that to trust in the power of the living God the greatest force against all other forces in the universe. Against sound advice from those most near me, I remain resolute, continuously on guard, as my injuries heal slowly. Then, in late fall of 2005, the long anticipated attack arrives. The owner of the building, a stocky gruff man stands outside in the yard. The heat to my dwelling, controlled by the landlord, turned off causing me personal discomfort. I go down and confront him, demanding he turn on the heat, which is his responsibility according to the law. He responds with an abusive remark saying that if I did not like the heating arrangement, then I could move elsewhere. This ill-conceived conversation quickly escalates into a heated exchange. His wife appears from the top of the stairs screaming something at me in Arabic and charges suddenly. The other man moves forward, as though he plans to intercept her, so I turn back. Then he does something altogether unexpected. He grabs my neck and performs a military take-down, forcing my spine down hard on his knee. This particular move is performed to paralyze and kill an opponent. Instinctively, I manage to twist just enough to thwart the deadly effectiveness of the maneuver. I then bring this beast down. By the time I am fully aware again, I have my self-declared enemy on the ground, his hysterical wife kicking my spine and pelvis, complicit of my fragile condition since the accident. Fortunately, neighbors end the violent altercation and police arrive. This uncivilized attack prompts the insurance company to settle my accident suit out of court with the added stipulation that I consider dropping the criminal assault charges against their clients. I had determined in my heart not to comply with this unreasonable request. These people had assaulted me more than once, and with murderous intent. They deserve to be punished! But on the morning of the legal hearing this mother and wife approaches me tearfully clutching her two children, pleading that I not to prosecute her and her husband. The spirit of compassion overshadows my desire for vengeance and in an instant I forgive. The husband is later deported because of an uncovered history linking him to a paramilitary group with ties to terrorism. I subsequently move to another apartment and have not heard from this family since. All that I know from this dark time is that my personal salvation secured by the invisible hand of God, and not by strength or agility of my flesh. Reminding me of the meaning contained in Mathew, Chapter 6, verse 14 (NIV).

> *"For if you forgive other people when they sin against you, your heavenly Father will also forgive you. But if you do not forgive others their sins, your Father will not forgive your sins."*

It is the nature of men to react out of fear and desire for vengeance. Easier it is to take up a sword against an enemy, than to strive for peaceful resolution. So unpredictable are the laurels of negotiation. Yet, as one, who has engaged in personal battle, I submit that to fail in the resistance of evil, only guarantees a cancerous condition. If the meek of this earth shall inherit, then they do so by an abiding strength, not solely sustained through the arm of flesh and bone. Nevertheless, I have also learned a measure of patience tempered in charity, believing that God more than able to deliver me from every adversity. Faith a far better defense than are the actions of any militant offensive. And this is exactly what God has demonstrated time and time again in the miraculous salvation of Israel against perils of nations, against calamity within, and against the coincidence of unpredictable elements.

It is difficult for even the most secular reasoning to ignore the obvious fact that the tiny nation of Israel continues to exist today against all logic. It is not the first time. In fact the people of unified Israel have been dispersed and reunified on three separate occasions through documented history. But even more astounding is that men we call prophets have foretold the demise and the reconstruction of the Holy Temple, as a physical marker in time and geographical space. I have no doubt in the strong political contingency dedicated to rebuild the final temple in modern Jerusalem. This will be accomplished with much bloody division, considering that the Al-Aqsa Muslim Mosque built on part of the Temple Mount. But even more tragic, such plans insure future violence of bloodshed as the world has never known. Nevertheless, I also believe this is what it will take to collectively turn the remnant of those surviving in Israel today, as well as Jews all over the world, to the embrace of the Messiah they have been taught to reject through religious obstinacy for nearly twenty-one centuries.

The truth is that no symbolic structure upon this present earth houses the spirit of almighty God, creator of the heavens and the earth. Once a place called Eden, where all principalities above and below created exclusively for possession of Adam and Eve. But that Eden removed and guarded by guarded by two armed fiery Cherubim, because of deception by guile of the serpent sent to test free will. First Eve is deceived by the voice of reason, and then Adam acts by natural choice. Theologians might argue that this is a constructed scenario allegorical of struggle between good and evil in the world today. I think it more. This agreement initializes a directional course creating a domino effect perceptible in present historical context. We are still this choice, and the choices we make daily based on the same dialectics. After expulsion from God's paradise, the earth and everything in it changes to something else, a haven for all manner of unclean spirits inspired to violence, all creation collapsing into entropy. Adam and Eve's first offspring turn to rivalry, ending with the murder of righteous Abel by the hand of Cain. Always it comes down to obedience by faith or rebellion by pride of reason. But Eden still exists prepared by the resurrected Messiah holding the keys to an eternity without beginning or end. He the Cherubim will allow passage.

So who is this Messiah really, and what are the conditions of his coming upon the earth of men? In the beginning the man named Adam is made perfect and with perfect DNA. He is formed in the image of God from elemental substance, made a living soul by the breath of his creator. From this subatomic DNA Eve also made that the two may be one in a realm of endless potential. These children of celestial inception designed to be the first fruit of creation made to populate in a way not provided to angelic positions created first. Then the fall from grace, allowing the sin and death of rebellion to corrupt that made perfect to run a course of entropy.

In every generation God preserves his original plan in one chain of perfect DNA so that Adam might live again. In other words the original code of perfection surviving through generations in the form of a recessive gene. This nucleotide protein sequence made from the chromosome chain of Adam's special DNA. This explains the often confusing geological list of generations from Adam to Noah, from Noah to David, and from David to Mary, the mother of Jesus. After Jesus there seems to be less emphasis placed on bloodline. The importance placed on the idea of bloodline today is just another tool in Satan's toolbox to blind minds corrupted by too much reason by reducing everything down to pride of an existential quantum. What little is known about DNA creates only part of the overall picture. Does the DNA of a mass murderer insure that his or her offspring doomed to follow the same path? If one man a coward does this mean his children will be cowards as well? Even children of those most noble rarely excel to the same degree of excellence. This suggests that what we know as DNA a combination of more than just genetic material composed of chromosome bindings. The evidence supports there exists a latent record of genealogical association not naturally identifiable; or can it be defined by classic markers of gene sequences of bloodline to denote superior or inferior cell architecture. This DNA record preserved through in an invisible matrix termed righteousness as found in Abraham when God makes a covenant with this man that his seed will be as the multitude of stars. This only made possible by the fulfilling prophecy of Christ's birth in Bethlehem delivered in the flesh by a young virgin preserving the original code made flesh.

But righteousness in flesh alone is not sufficient to be Messiah. For Jesus to be Christ he needs to be conceived by the direct insemination of God's Holy Spirit. This means the perfect DNA of Adam and the perfect supreme spirit of creation become one, making a new kind of man to supplant a present universe collapsing into entropy with a condition eternal. This is inconceivable to the organic structure presently conceived. But in fact it can be no other way, This better code preserved as an archetype to dwell in a prepared place also better, as promised by Jesus in John's Gospel, chapter 14, verses 1-6 (NIV).

> *"Do not let your hearts be troubled. You believe in God; believe also in me. My Father's house has many rooms; if that were not so, would I have told you that I am going there to prepare a place for you? And if I go and prepare a*

place for you, I will come back and take you to be with me that you also may be where I am. You know the way to the place where I am going." Thomas said to him, "Lord, we don't know where you are going, so how can we know the way?" Jesus answered, "I am the way and the truth and the life. No one comes to the Father except through me. If you really know me, you will know my Father as well. From now on, you do know him and have seen him."

In my spirit I feel a meaning even more profound. Because of mortal condition separating man from God, we are condemned to the idea and the fact of death. I think this analogist to a caterpillar dreading to become a butterfly. If we did not know death as an end we would not be apprehensive of its bearing. Because our cells die and renew daily without our conscious awareness, why should we think that systemic organic failure any different? If we rejoice when something born, much more would we rejoice when something dies having certainty death only the beginning of a better estate! This is not religious hope, but certainty by the promise of our resurrected Christ and from his own lips after passing through death.

In order to truly appreciate this profound promise of hope, one must return two thousand years into the past. While confined on the island of Roman controlled Patmos, six hundred years after Daniel, another divinely inspired prophet named John records future world history again. We do not know too much about this John, except that he is a man saved through the Holy Spirit and given a divine message to pass on to the seven churches of Asia concerning Christ's second coming. There is some debate if this the same John, one of Jesus' apostles, or another man by the same name. I think it makes little difference, considering that the same spirit inspires all born in Christ. Within context, the seven churches are expressions of faith placed as candlesticks in the world, each lighted by the quickening spirit of an angel. At this precise time in history, all converts to Christ are essentially converts to the inspired meaning of Judaism. What this means is that Jesus never preached any other religion or other spirit. He believes completely in the scriptures contained in the Torah, and knows by the faith of the Holy Spirit that his life and death represent the fulfillment of those scriptures. The seven churches are not temporal positions only; but rather, they are spiritual roots going back to the first souls that step off the Ark of New World promise in the days of Noah. There are seven individuals saved for the purpose of reseeding humankind, and one devout man of God. The Holy Spirit of God is not transferable to our spouses, to our children, or even to our fellow worshippers. To follow Christ is not just the practice of good works or learning scripture, but a submission to God's will. It is a gift from heaven, manifested to those that receive it. *But as history has shown, not all do.*

Chapter 8
CIVILIZATION

Ignoring for a moment the many theories of anthropological discussion on how cultures shaped by historical migration, let us try to examine objectively at what is culture and ethnicity. Culture is an expression of shared experience accumulated over a period of time; whereas ethnicity a genotype characteristic unique to a group of individuals. Although race can be a superficial marker denoting skin color, it is not an exclusive identifier. Many people of the orient share similar facial features, particularly notable by the shape of the eyes, and are generally smaller boned. Those born in Scandinavian countries are classically pale skinned, have light eyes, and are generally larger boned. The variant list of secondary attributes making up different human groups can be applied all around the globe within a degree of accuracy. Even though the DNA pool of combination varies, still the base code made up of the same chemical elements. In other words, all human, all made of the same stuff.

All evidence suggest that the seed of modern civilization begins a little over 5000 years ago in a geographical area stretching from the northern border of modern day Syria to the southern extreme of Iraq. Better known as the Mesopotamian Valley, this region sired generations of fully evolved hominids possessing instantaneous knowledge of complex tool production and advanced understanding of construction techniques with applicable comprehension of plane geometry. The time date also coincides closely to when *Noah's Ark* grounded upon the Ararat Mountains following the global deluge, as recorded in the *Torah*. Although versions of this diluvium catastrophe may be considered questionable history in the minds of many, since much of the record relies on Biblical text. Nevertheless, admissible archeological evidence based on secular interpretations validates the timetable of possible events, both topographically and historically.

While on the subject of historical incursions, I wish to further point out that there are some rather impressive anomalies smoldering in the ashes of past events, not easily dismissed in the arena of logical discourse. It seems that the more we know about the jumbled puzzle of the distant past, the less precisely all the pieces fit together. This raises some rather interesting possibilities once considered absurd within the boundaries of intellectual discussion.

Was the Ark of Noah real? Were the early Hebrews ever residents of Egypt; and if so, were they led away into the wilderness to cross the Red Sea by a man named Moses, as described in the Old Testament Bible? Through many centuries there have been multiple claims describing a structure existing on the slopes of Mount Ararat believed to be the resting place of Noah's Ark. Some eyewitnesses insist having seen a half submerged vessel resembling the biblical description protruding out of glacial ice. Other testaments assert that only the petrified outline of what could be remains of a man-made structure, closely matching the dimensions of the Ark. There have even been images from space capturing a rectangular object trapped an ice sheet contrary to natural formation. However, none are more tantalizing than the recent photographic records made by a Hong Kong based evangelical group, claiming that they have found, and even entered a wooden structure buried 13,000 feet above sea level. Is this proof of the fabled Ark still preserved after five millenniums near the summit of this high peak?

Nor does Noah's Ark stand alone as an unsolved mystery of past events involving biblical reference. Most of us have heard the story of how the Jewish religion begins. A man named Moses called by God to lead the enslaved Hebrews out of the land of Egypt and into the promised land of Canaan. Not only does this God bring ten plagues upon Pharaoh's kingdom (the last being the declaration that death of every firstborn, whose house not protected by the innocent blood of a Passover lamb); but this same God possessed with omnipotent power to part the waves of the Red Sea.

Such monumental events defy acceptance by the logical mind. Nevertheless, recent discoveries suggest there is more fact than fiction to these unlikely accounts. Modern satellite imagery has revealed a shallow underwater land bridge connecting the Egyptian province of Nuweiba to the western shore of Saudi Arabia, a distance of approximately two and a half miles. On each side of this submerged land bridge are deep trenches, making this location the only possible avenue, which also coincides with the biblical account. A few days journey North West is the mountain confirmed today as Sinai, where God establishes a covenant with 600,000 men, besides women and children, delivered on stone tablets written by his own hand.

Setting aside for a moment the magnitude of this witness, the physical evidence does not end here. Scattered along the bottom of this underwater ridge separating the ocean of Mediterranean and the Red Sea are preserved remains of Egyptian chariots, wheels and spokes, and even human bones of the warriors that braved the walls of water in pursuit of a people blamed for the inflicted plagues. Their judgment swift and without reprieve, as we read in the Book of Exodus, Chapter 14, verses 22-31 (NIV).

> *"Then the angel of God, who had been traveling in front of Israel's army, withdrew and went behind them. The pillar of cloud also moved from in front and stood behind them, coming between the armies of Egypt and Israel. Throughout the night the cloud brought darkness to the one side and light to the other side; so neither went near the other all night long. Then Moses stretched out his hand over the sea, and all that night the Lord drove the sea back with a strong east wind and turned it into dry land. The waters were divided, and the Israelites went through the sea on dry ground, with a wall of water on their right and on their left. The Egyptians pursued them, and all Pharaoh's horses and chariots and horsemen followed them into the sea. During the last watch of the night the Lord looked down from the pillar of fire and cloud at the Egyptian*

army and threw it into confusion. He jammed the wheels of their chariots so that they had difficulty driving. And the Egyptians said, "Let's get away from the Israelites! The Lord is fighting for them against Egypt." Then the Lord said to Moses, "Stretch out your hand over the sea so that the waters may flow back over the Egyptians and their chariots and horsemen." Moses stretched out his hand over the sea, and at daybreak the sea went back to its place. The Egyptians were fleeing toward it, and the Lord swept them into the sea. The water flowed back and covered the chariots and horsemen—the entire army of Pharaoh that had followed the Israelites into the sea. Not one of them survived. But the Israelites went through the sea on dry ground, with a wall of water on their right and on their left. That day the Lord saved Israel from the hands of the Egyptians, and Israel saw the Egyptians lying dead on the shore. And when the Israelites saw the mighty hand of the Lord displayed against the Egyptians, the people feared the Lord and put their trust in him and in Moses his servant."

Both these scenarios confirms the presence of a supernatural presence with enormous power and foresight: a being revealed to a chosen people, as potent witness against the many false principalities deceiving the societies of mankind since the day Noah and his family left the Ark to reseed mankind. Before Moses, the Hebrews knew only the patriarchal promise made to their father Abraham. But with Moses and his brother Aaron, the beginning of an earthly priesthood to represent living witness of almighty God manifested in temporal time.

Is human civilization a product of competing theocracies, evidenced by geopolitical assimilation spanning the millenniums? In ancient history, we find several polytheist religions sprouting into existence long before King David conquers *Jebus*, also known as the City of Zion, and gives it the name Jerusalem. David's son, King Solomon, makes it his capitol and builds the first temple, historically described as a magnificent structure unlike any other.

Long before this the rest of mankind has turned back to serving the fallen gods of a fallen world. But from where did these many deities come from; and what is the source of their inspiration? There is a distinct pattern of supernatural organization found at the fundamental core of every expression of worship. Beginning with the Sumerian Empire and later spreading into the Indus Valley, sits the henotheistic Siva, an entity exercising evil influence over the minds and souls of men. From the seat of this bloodthirsty devil spawns a host of other gods occupying high places in worldly positions.

In Sumerian cosmology there is no concept for heaven, but there is a very vivid hell mapped by distinct geography ruled by several unsavory deities with often competing agendas. Souls of the dead are cast in very similar circumstance, as found in the first book of a trilogy titled *The Inferno,* composed by the famous 14th century Italian Renaissance writer, Dante Alighieri. Here souls of the dead suffer without reprieve, whose physical existence extends into a cycle of never ending frustration. This, of course, makes sense within context of a consequential habitation collapsing into entropic solution, as depicted in the Bible to describe the fall of Satan and his belligerent army of angels. There is also an even more sinister inference within Sumerian religion that suggests extraterrestrial influence, or other worldly beings: entities denied the capacity to pass physically through a dimensional stream into present time and space. These technologically enhanced beings represent an altogether soulless condition, trapped in a kind of subspace seeking a portal of entry. Able to manifest periodically through sympathetic medium translation of micro energy filaments created from sources we cannot even begin to understand, they relentlessly seek entry into temporal condition by means of possession. Yet, Jesus saw them for what they are and understood how to deal with them. Summoning power to deliver those so afflicted, this son of God cast out demons into a habitation described as *outer darkness*. One of the more remarkable incidences is recorded in the Gospel of Mathew, Chapter 8, verses 28 - 34 (KJV) when Jesus castes out the *Legion*.

> *"And when he was come to the other side into the country of the Gergesenes, there met him two possessed with devils, coming out of the tombs, exceeding fierce, so that no man might pass by that way. And, behold, they cried out, saying, What have we to do with thee, Jesus, thou Son of God? art thou come hither to torment us before the time? And there was a good way off from them an herd of many swine feeding. So the devils besought him, saying, If thou cast us out, suffer us to go away into the herd of swine. And he said unto them, Go. And when they were come out, they went into the herd of swine: and, behold, the whole herd of swine ran violently down a steep place into the sea, and perished in the waters. And they that kept them fled, and went their ways into the city, and told everything, and what was befallen to the possessed of the devils. And, behold, the whole city came out to meet Jesus: and when they saw him, they besought him that he would depart out of their coasts."*

This first world submission to demonic presences often goes unnoticed, yet represents a thriving source feeding into the core of practically every sacred belief system found in today's modern world. For through these veins flows the very essence of the old knowledge, before the cataclysmic days of Noah.

We discover at the foundation of many primal cultures a hierarchal belief system called "animism". Animism is the anthropomorphic projection of cognitive spirit to bodies of water, to mountains, trees, animals, and even certain humans. It embodies the presence of a super consciousness that indwells physical substance for some constructed purpose. However, not all these possessions are benevolent, but often capable of indescribable violence and trickery for reasons already noted. Many North American native cultures have these beliefs embedded into the fabric of their tribal social history to such an extreme that everything living or dead becomes sacred through a hierarchy of being. By contest of measured challenges, the individual becomes part of a greater whole; and that greater whole subject to an even higher power, until reaching finally the pinnacle of being described ultimately as the *Great Spirit*. There is very little difference between this concept and the ultimate transcendence to Nirvana shared by Buddha and the Hindu religions of Asia. The problem with animism is that it quickly evolves into the worship of demigods, a condition by which the creature becomes greater than the creator, blind to the obvious limits of measured existence.

There are those practices based on philosophical logic by the use of meditative instruction to become spiritually in tune with universal energy. While promising to free the mind from the mundane concerns of everyday living, it can lead the practitioner into the consciousness of a simulated universe of designed thermodynamic inevitability. The hope of countless reincarnations again validates creature existence above all other potentials, while denying individuality of being. Without knowledge of the truest meaning of Nirvana, those engaged ultimately seek oblivion (or in terms thermodynamic reaction: to reach a state of absolute zero), while forfeiting the most unique potential of emerging creation. They are right to believe that all matter and energy an extension of God's being, yet lacking the appreciation that this same God has made man in his own image, as an equal to share his handiwork. First giving us a mind of comprehension and free choice, God has also provided to the sons of men a living soul, immortal, exceeding the limits of present being destined to inherit a condition excluded from the laws of entropy. Transgression of the first man makes all subject to the three laws of thermodynamic decline. This is to say that creation becomes subject to entropy, which is the prevailing condition of sin and death. Another way to express it is that when Lucifer fell because of hubris, mankind falls with this deceitful Seraph through choice. The ability to choose is also the potential of our salvation. A condition denied to the angels for reasons I will explore in a later chapter.

The universe that will be very different from the universe that is now. Jesus Christ is the first offspring of a new kind of man, resurrected from mortal elements to an eternal condition. He accomplishes this by making a choice to submit willingly and humbly to the design of God the father. He is the first corner stone of New Jerusalem after the elemental state transfigured to a better matrix. No one by worldly wisdom may instruct the ways of God, or to justify his actions according to myopic understanding. But we are recipients of promise, a promise made perpetual from the beginning. As the Apostle Paul humbly writes in his letter to the Corinthians, Chapter 2, verses 1-16 (NIV), making reference to the divinely inspired words of the prophet Isaiah:

> *"And so it was with me, brothers and sisters. When I came to you, I did not come with eloquence or human wisdom as I proclaimed to you the testimony about God. For I resolved to know nothing while I was with you except Jesus Christ and him crucified. I came to you in weakness with great fear and trembling. My message and my preaching were not with wise and persuasive words, but with a demonstration of the Spirit's power, so that your faith might not rest on human wisdom, but on God's power. We do, however, speak a message of wisdom among the mature, but not the wisdom of this age or of the rulers of this age, who are coming to nothing. No, we declare God's wisdom, a mystery that has been hidden and that God destined for our glory before time began. None of the rulers of this age understood it, for if they had, they would not have crucified the Lord of glory. However, as it is written: "What no eye has seen, what no ear has heard, and what no human mind has conceived-- the things God has prepared for those who love him—these are the things God has revealed to us by his Spirit.*
>
> *The Spirit searches all things, even the deep things of God. For who knows a person's thoughts except their own spirit within them? In the same way no one knows the thoughts of God except the Spirit of God. What we have received is not the spirit of the world, but the Spirit who is from God, so that we may understand what God has freely given us. This is what we speak, not in words taught us by human wisdom but in words taught by the Spirit,*

> *explaining spiritual realities with Spirit-taught words. The person without the Spirit does not accept the things that come from the Spirit of God but considers them foolishness, and cannot understand them because they are discerned only through the Spirit. The person with the Spirit makes judgments about all things, but such a person is not subject to merely human judgments, for, "Who has known the mind of the Lord so as to instruct him?" But we have the mind of Christ."*

New Age religions are particularly appealing to those seduced into believing that man is innately wise, capable of solving conditions of inequity and to quench the epidemic fires of violent escalations. They believe that it is within the reach of human progress to make the world a utopia through measures of mortal good decided by humanistic elitism. This popular philosophy fueled by the thirst for technological solutions to enormous contradictions to predictability. To these practitioners, the concept of present-being a moral interpretation of order in an apparently meaningless random universe. They embrace the premise through conscious means that it is possible to rationalize the design of God in the midst of a collapsing singularity. This perceived order based on logical interpretation through visions of enlightened individuals to construct a better socially balanced world. *Such is no prophet of God, but a deceiver deceived!* Action inspired through rational deduction ultimately channels into a quandary of disastrous eventuality.

Let us not forget the charismatic leadership of Jim Jones, responsible for the 1978 murder- suicide of more than 900 congregation members, including young children, of The People's Temple, as a show of defiant solidarity against what he called social injustice in the world. Nor is it alone as a cult following, snaring the thirsty souls of those looking to a worldly messiah for spiritual guidance. These false shepherds have altogether cast away the foundation rock of faith, choosing limited reason dressed in self-righteous fervor. Such become compelling examples of how easily many led astray by wolves adorned as sheep quick and ready to think for others. In 2 Peter, Chapter 2, verses 1-22

(NIV) a stern warning against such that would make merchandise of men's souls by intentional deception to lead the meek of this world astray in exchange for an hour of temporal glory.

> *"But there were also false prophets among the people, just as there will be false teachers among you. They will secretly introduce destructive heresies, even denying the sovereign Lord who bought them—bringing swift destruction on themselves. Many will follow their depraved conduct and will bring the way of truth into disrepute. In their greed these teachers will exploit you with fabricated stories. Their condemnation has long been hanging over them, and their destruction has not been sleeping. For if God did not spare angels when they sinned, but sent them to hell, putting them in chains of darkness to be held for judgment; if he did not spare the ancient world when he brought the flood on its ungodly people, but protected Noah, a preacher of righteousness, and seven others; if he condemned the cities of Sodom and Gomorrah by burning them to ashes, and made them an example of what is going to happen to the ungodly; and if he rescued Lot, a righteous man, who was distressed by the depraved conduct of the lawless (for that righteous man, living among them day after day, was tormented in his righteous soul by the lawless deeds he saw and heard)— if this is so, then the Lord knows how to rescue the godly from trials and to hold the unrighteous for punishment on the day of judgment. This is especially true of those who follow the corrupt desire of the flesh and despise authority. Bold and arrogant, they are not afraid to heap abuse on celestial beings; yet even angels, although they are stronger and more powerful, do not heap abuse on such beings when bringing judgment on them from the Lord. But these people blaspheme in matters they do not understand. They are like unreasoning animals, creatures of instinct, born only to be caught and destroyed, and like*

animals they too will perish. They will be paid back with harm for the harm they have done. Their idea of pleasure is to carouse in broad daylight. They are blots and blemishes, reveling in their pleasures while they feast with you. With eyes full of adultery, they never stop sinning; they seduce the unstable; they are experts in greed—an accursed brood!

They have left the straight way and wandered off to follow the way of Balaam son of Bezer, who loved the wages of wickedness. But he was rebuked for his wrongdoing by a donkey—an animal without speech—who spoke with a human voice and restrained the prophet's madness. These people are springs without water and mists driven by a storm. Blackest darkness is reserved for them. For they mouth empty, boastful words and, by appealing to the lustful desires of the flesh, they entice people who are just escaping from those who live in error. They promise them freedom, while they themselves are slaves of depravity—for "people are slaves to whatever has mastered them." If they have escaped the corruption of the world by knowing our Lord and Savior Jesus Christ and are again entangled in it and are overcome, they are worse off at the end than they were at the beginning. It would have been better for them not to have known the way of righteousness, than to have known it and then to turn their backs on the sacred command that was passed on to them. Of them the proverbs are true: "A dog returns to its vomit," and, "A sow that is washed returns to her wallowing in the mud."

These are strong words of condemnation, yet no less true today. For history has shown that from the vine of denominations claiming pure theology buds the fruits of cultism, ritualism, sectarianism, and moral terrorism authorized by justifiable consent. Examples of this, the material austerity imposed by modern Mennonites, the social contriteness of Mormons of Latter Day Saints, and the ritualistic austerity amounting to xenophobic excommunication practiced by sectarian Catholics and Jews. Let us not forget the fearful slaughter tactics practiced by Muslim extremist (even among themselves), or the stoic iron fist of communism-- each believing in interpretive validity of doctrinal truth given to a chosen enlightened flock. Nor does history paint a more pastoral picture of political harmony. From the Roman butcher of Christians and Jews in the name of the Emperor State, to the bloody Crusade battles fought in the name of a worldly church. Who can be so bold as to deny the extermination camps of Eastern Europe or the killing fields of South East Asia during the last century? These are only a few examples of progressive agents fertilizing the promised ground of civilization and cementing together bones of the collective elite. As 1 Corinthians, Chapter 15, verse 33 (KJV) states:

> *"Be not deceived: evil communications corrupt good manners."*

Yes, control of the masses very compelling in a world where the ideal of Social Darwinism prevails over the divine potential of humanity: a world where materialism outweighs the substance of compassionate value. The greater problem being that the line between faithfulness and spirit has become blurred. What remains is a distorted interpretation between what is right and what is wrong, between value and the true cost of inflated egotism. Soon all that remains of human division based on condemnation through mortal discernment executing without mercy the rigidly defined letter of the law: *an eye for an eye, and a tooth for a tooth.*

Although Christianity identified as a world religion, those reborn into the Holy Spirit know this not to be so. We know that the birth, the death, and the resurrection of Jesus Christ an event of historic significance, a testament profound meaning. It is not a philosophy or an order of conduct; it is transfiguration of the mortal to the immortal. This man historically known as Jesus had no earthly agenda. He did not come to stake out a missionary estate for some future society here on earth, but sent by the father to restore that which was lost. Nor was this

Jesus religiously or politically inspired according to the belief systems of the time. Christ did not come to change the statues and conditions, or to inspire a better conviction. He comes as a lamb of sacrifice and as a herald of good news sent to restore order in the midst elemental decay. The name of Jesus not inspired through earthly genealogy, but conceived in holiness to break the strong chains of darkness in the very heart of the enemy's camp. This accomplished not by dogma or declaration of religious war. Jesus never instructed his apostles to take up arms against the ruling Romans or sack the temples to replace the Tabernacle with a crucifix. Jesus makes it clear from the beginning that because he is sent by the father, that he and the father one. Also, Jesus states emphatically that no man can know the father except through him. This was not the hubris declaration of a man making himself God, but one inspired by absolute conviction. God's commandments are just dispensation since the fall of the Satan; the laws of this present estate immutable. Now the father and the son made one through transcendent mystery of the Holy Spirit. This is the mind and will of our father in heaven. Because the man Jesus chose in temporal course to submit willingly to physical death and humiliation, resurrection made possible to all creation. He alone is worthy, reproving once and for all the substance of weaker elements. This Jesus is final victory; the armed Messiah standing upon a cloud of glory to complete the final remission of entropy, consuming the lesser light of civilized enculturation. This is not a hope grounded in any worldly religion, nor in some better philosophy, but living New Testament of a better code overwriting the old.

Chapter 9
SPACE SHIP EARTH

All that we know through collective awareness is that we are begotten upon a world of unique character sustainable to a particular variety of thriving species. Just the right balance of atmospheric gases with just the right mixture and compression, life as we know it made possible. The temperature variances are calibrated within a specific norm to allow survivable habitation, and the hydrostatic circulation and proportion values of gas mixture favorable to a definition of habitability of life within a prescribed norm. But how much do we really know about the nature and genesis of the geo-sphere we call spaceship earth traversing through a void of cosmic space?

The geological phenomenon known as Pangaea concludes that earth was one great continent, which broke apart over billions of years to become the geophysics of the seven continents we know today. In fact it was not the first supercontinent, but the last of a cyclic pattern of previous supercontinents that subsequently collided and broke up. These include names like *Nuna* (also known as *Colombia*), *Rodinia*, followed by *Pannotia*, and finally *Pangaea*. Each fuse, disassemble and reassemble together by the process of accretion, expelling the shattered fragments of monolithic land-mass formations trailing over billions of years. But Pangaea is when all these coalesce into one giant cluster occupying the southern hemisphere. According to Uniformitarian interpretation this consolidated landmass began to split apart and move away through a process called *subduction*, opening large trenches to form new seas. Through many epochs of continental drift, modern science has concluded that with a little imagination and some creative manipulation it is easy to fit all the continents together like pieces of a great puzzle.

There is also extensive evidence of drowned micro-continents discovered all over the world. *Mauritia*, a micro-continent, off the coast of Africa, the *Campbell Plateau*, surrounding New Zealand, the famous *Beringia Strait* connecting Asia with North America during the last ice age; and finally, the less known *Hidden Landscape*, a submerged land mass of nearly 4000 miles supporting the Scottish coast.

Of course as many opposing researchers to the theory of uniform continental drift point out, this often ignores the submerged configuration of the continental shelves that can extend many nautical miles into the oceanic depths with geographical discrepancies, as well as legal claims relating to national sovereignty. This does not make the theory wrong, only the interpretation of observation subject to greater scrutiny. No one wishes to refute evidence indicating the persistent rising of mountain chains around earth's circumference, or the shearing forces of colliding massive tectonic plates resulting in devastating earthquakes. Nor can one ignore the contradictions found in the accumulated fossil records and glacial deposits on almost every continent, which further suggests that different animal species once part of a unified global community.

It is Alfred Wegener, who really sets the continents adrift at the beginning of the twentieth century. This remarkable individual perseveres in his augment for Pangaea against much opposition. His new theory eventually providing a new generation of uniformitarian science with what it needed to become an established authority. Now all the pieces aptly fit together in the minds of the *ancient earth* theorist. Before proceeding further, I wish to make a personal statement that I am not altogether opposed to the possibility that a supercontinent once existed. Only that I do not believe it to be the structure of logic design presented in the uniformitarian scenario. When the *"fountains of the deep"* broke open (as described in the Bible), then I believe the continents we know today are born: the subsequent appearance of a broken puzzle only coincidental. The fact that they are now moving directionally does not necessarily mean they have always been in this relative motion. Just as it takes miles to correct the motion of a massive ocean liner, the seismographic activity presently observed is the aftermath of what happens after the cataclysm of the flood. As with most creationists, it is not the possibility of the facts that are in dispute, but the interpretation of the meaning. Even more importantly, one must consider the initiative of the first cause. The consuming objective of modern science in recent years is to construct a global past absent of a creator. *No creator, no responsibility of sin: no sin, no consequence of personal accountability, and most disturbing, no God of creation.* This is Satan's persistent lie to mankind.

The most compelling evidence for the theory of ancient Pangaea is the discovery of similar fossil remains distributed on continents separated by many thousands of oceanic miles. Calculations related to continental drift in association with magnetic properties used as indicators to plot the direction and speed of today's continents, prove they are still moving away from each other. There is insistence that the match between glacial deposits found around the globe only proves the existence of a once *super continent*. Further to this are the very real records of escalating mountain chains and shearing plate-tectonic activity, being a cause of devastating earthquakes and monster tsunamis. However, just because chosen empirical facts support the deduction of one established interpretation, then why eliminate mountains of evidence just on the basis that they do not agree with the ancient earth hypothesis?

The end of the nineteenth century witnesses overall acceptance of Uniformitarian science based on the interpretation of geologist Charles Lyell in his book *The Principles of Geology*. Before this another theory called *Catastrophism* dominates the science of geology and archeology. The many categorized observations of Castastrophism science constructs evidence of a much younger planet plagued with unpredictable changes. It confirms that a global deluge did occur, as describe in Genesis, the first book of the Holy Bible, but this natural catastrophe having nothing to do with the hand of God or a god. Absent from these concepts of interpretation all notions of religious indoctrination, but based solely on volumes of accumulated research painfully excavated by respected individuals and societies trained in the sciences. Not all of these men possess interest in a creationist view, or even believers in divine possibility.

Then, as today, not all who disagreed with the uniformitarian principal non-scientist. An impressive example of this, the famous nineteenth century archeologist, Georges Cuvier, who strongly rejects the evolutionary claims in favor of what he terms *true science* by pointing out that present morphology is a condition of living organization; whereas, evolution speculative puzzle-making at best. Cuvier is more influenced by the concept of intellectual enlightenment born of the French Revolution, avoiding both religious and metaphysical arguments. Through *"stratigraphic"* records, he interprets that the earth underwent revolutions of natural catastrophes, occurring between relatively stable intervals. Based on accumulated data, he and many of his contemporaries, hypothesize the age of our planet to be millions of years, not billions of years. To this day, Cuvier's ideas have not been altogether discounted even among the most devout uniformitarian. Nevertheless, by present definitions, the findings of Cuvier considered as relic as the dinosaur bones aged within context of the surrounding stone. In other words, modern paleontology considers that the bones are evidence of a certain age based on the acceptance of a periodic table as the scale of reference. Therefore the age of the bones determines the age of the rock, and the age of the rock confirmed by the age of the bones. This paradoxical logic, the base of uniformitarian science, altogether dismisses the obvious evidence of a global catastrophic event. Rather it relies on instances of *thrust faults* and *reverse faults*, to describe why often older rock formations are found on top of newer rock. These are exceptions to the uniformitarian view, which describes a slow process of layered rock formations accumulated over vast periods of time. So if Cuvier's bones were to be uncovered a thousand years from now after a severe earthquake inverted the resting place of his grave into a much lower stratum, he would be dated perhaps a million, or even tens of millions of years into the distant past. This would no doubt cause the famed paleontologist of *Catastrophism* to chuckle victoriously. The baroque nineteenth century savant loved both the challenge and the prestige of being right in the face of intellectual debate.

We are able to perceive through the intellectual debris of the past several hundred years, the persistent pattern of chronologic discrepancy.

Through Uniformitarian interpretation of the raw data, the earth is billions of years old. The Catastrophist conclude the earth to be millions of years old using the same data. Whereas, Creationist base the age of the earth as being only thousands of years old, further supported by their interpretation of the scriptural record. Each theory remains consistent with the data, except for a conversion factor of ten to a power of one hundred for Creationist, ten to a power of one thousand for Catastrophist, and ten to a power of one hundred thousand for Uniformitarian formulation. Is it possible that all three of these theories are right and also are wrong?

Einstein's famous train travelling through a landscape is the best analogy to describe how observed phenomenon might yield three different conclusions. The train represents a constant based on assumed values relative to speed, distance, and time. Consider that there are three independent observers positioned at different perspectives of the event. Observer "A", we will call the Creationist, observer "B", the Catastrophist, and observer "C" the modern day Uniformitarian scientist. Using available evidence from observation and scriptural inference, observer "A" makes the determination that the train started at a defined beginning point travelling at "X" speed, thus arriving at a relative position by multiplying the speed times the distance to quantify the time of transit. The assumption here is that all variables have always been constant. Observer "B" may agree with the speed, but not with the distance traveled. Employing the same physical evidence used by observer "A", this observer insists that only the evidence matters, and rightly points out that the evidence is self-explanatory within context. They further postulate that the world is, and has always been an unsafe place to live. Although agreeing with the same principals, this group highly resistant to the idea of divine intervention. Observer "C" says, wait a minute, there is no starting point. The train has always been traveling at the same speed, therefore covering distances at elapsed intervals. This provides the intellectual agreement of an extremely old universe, with earth only an insignificant component mixed randomly into the whole, provided that one intellectually ignores the contradictions inherently contained with the vastness of the odds. By using complex extrapolation models, alongside other models based on similar assumptions, observer "C" altogether eliminates creative design from the picture. They obstinately insist that the elevation of a relative position the only one that guarantees a predictable future, thus securing the importance of their occupations, and enabling the validity of science as guiding force to the summit of mankind's eminent position in the greater scheme of things.

Since it is impossible to know the nature of infinite velocity, then there can be no accurate model of time and space dilation at the instant or even microns after the Big Bang singularity. When God separated the elements of matter and energy describing the days of creation, the calculation of day and night would have been based on a period between twilight of morning and twilight of evening relative to cosmic variation. It is unlikely the present twenty four hour of earth's rotation the same then as it is now. Time is a conceived model designed to describe entropic change, as observed from the aspect of a relative position within present context. This model makes possible an extrapolation of past and future possibilities based on present evidence. For all we know, a thousand years may have been equivalent to a day, as suggested in 2 Peter, Chapter 3, verses 5-9 (KJV).

> *"For this they willingly are ignorant of, that by the word of God the heavens were of old, and the earth standing out of the water and in the water: Whereby the world that then was, being overflowed with water, perished: But the heavens and the earth, which are now, by the same word are kept in store, reserved unto fire against the day of judgment and perdition of ungodly men. But, beloved, be not ignorant of this one thing, that one day is with the Lord as a thousand years, and a thousand years as one day. The Lord is not slack concerning his promise, as some men count slackness; but is longsuffering to us-ward, not willing that any should perish, but that all should come to repentance."*

Also, why is the *"old world"* before the flood mentioned within this context? To me, the reference suggests a discrepant time differential before and after the flood. Assuming that Adam and Eve are the two first humans created upon the earth, what was the nature of their existence? They are not first made as infants designed to mature and then grow up. They are made completely mature. They may easily have been in the Garden of Eden for many thousands of present-day earth years before being cast out. It is plausible the differential between light and darkness constructed on much grander scale. After being exiled from paradise, the entropic conditions of time prevails. The transition to mortal being would not have been immediate. I think there would have been a deceleration stage as cellular replication begins to fail. It seems reasonable to assume that since longevity decreased gradually, so, too, the planetary conditions change, becoming more erratic and less hospitable. All that we know with any degree of certainty is that plants and animals were all much larger, suggesting a condition of less gravity. Since there was less gravity, why not assume that each day also much longer. For all we know, the recorded years of Adam and his offspring could have been a factor ten times, or even a hundred times higher than the calculated years of present day earth. Even after the flood, when the days become shorter, the measurement of a day would remain still between sunrise and sunset.

There are many grand mechanics at work that make the consistent pattern of a solar day. Rotation speed and axis vectors would be affected by gravimetric influences, as subtle as a passing space body, or the absence of such a body. The Bible indicates existence of a unique atmospheric exchange process before the Flood of Noah, along with limited tidal action. Both suggestive that either there was no lunar body circling earth, or that it was much farther away than it is today. Even the two most local sibling planets, Mars and Venus, both have rotational characteristics relative to planet Earth's present rotation and tilt unique to these inner bodies of our solar system.

This has been verified to some degree in recent years, as we learn more about the space and matter around us. There is new evidence that the planet Mars once supported a biosphere with a liquid ocean. Just for a moment imagine through the lens of science fiction possibility that this other planet once inhabited by an ancient super race, mentioned in the Bible as the *Nephilim*. Because of a miscalculation of unknown technological experimentation, a third planet covered with gases, conceivably a distant moon of Saturn, caused to leave the trajectory of its orbital path and slip between the orbits of Mars and the planet Earth at perigee, dragging with it the body of a smaller moon. This lesser planetoid may have been snared in the gravitational spin of earth, becoming the scarred lunar body we take for granted today. While the larger mass, which we know as Venus in today's astronomy, may have settled into a synchronous orbit around the sun with a reverse rotation. The ensuing destruction may have ripped away more than seventy percent of the Martian atmosphere, as well as sizable landmasses; and resulted in disastrous upheavals on the planet Earth, as described in the Book of Genesis.

For those of you that think this possibility unthinkable consider there is a very real scientific formulation of how gravitons work in the arena of a non-static universe. The formula written as: *Force equals Gravity multiplied by the square of the ratio times two* or $F = G M1 \times M2 R2$. Meaning that every interstellar body, including the earth and its orbit around the sun, and even our solar system of planets in the Milky Way Galaxy, all occupy a symbiotic relationship relative to distance, mass, and attraction. A change in accelerated force, accompanied by an increase in velocity, equals to an increase attraction of gravity by another local body inverse to the square of the two.

Further ignoring the prescribed timetables constructed by the Uniformitarian geochronology, this and other astronomical modifications could perhaps have precipitated the impact of giant meteors believed to have struck the earth in the distant past, and thus severely altering terrestrial environmental conditions. The famous nickel-rich Sudbury Basin in Ontario, Canada, is considered one example of ground zero by many scientists agreeing to a catastrophic scenario that forever changes the face of the earth we inhabit today.

Consideration of this inconceivable event could help explain many of the mysteries of cosmic phenomenon recorded since the rebirth of civilization. It could also scientifically explain planetary disturbances responsible for the cataclysm of the great flood, as well as other historical observations difficult to reconcile logically. It may have taken thousands of years of cosmic corrections, as these planets settle into resonance to their new solar patterns. The shearing forces of gravitational interference stimulated by erratic orbits would cause each planet to lose energy, thus creating a slowing down effect, or even fluctuations in the axis. This could explain the incongruous entries found in many parts of the world describing an unusually long day. These include Babylonian text, Chinese scrolls, and also the discovered records of the Incas of Peru and the Aztecs of Mexico. Even the famous ancient Greek historian, Herodotus claims that he found in Egyptian achieves a recorded day twice the length of a normal rotation period. These could have been the aftermath of cosmic corrections through many centuries, coinciding with certain historical events. One of the most inspiring coincidences found in the Book of Joshua, Chapter 10, verse 13 (KJV), which describes an observation of the heavens apparently standing still.

> *"And the sun stood still, and the moon stayed, until the people had avenged themselves upon their enemies. Is not this written in the book of Jasher? So the sun stood still in the midst of heaven, and hasted not to go down about a whole day."*

Since this constructed fiction of events leading up to the flood only a possibility, I wish the reader to consider carefully that I believe that the historical event of a global deluge to be accurate, as described in the Book of Genesis. Also I have no doubt that the sun apparently stood still by the plea of Joshua. God is the time master responsible for the clockwork of the universe; therefore I think it valid to consider that from the instant of Satan's rebellion and Adam's deception, the cascade of events a pattern set immutable: the time scale changed, the earth scale changed, and man changed proportionately.

Considering what we do not know about miracles, maybe this is not so profound a theory as it may seem on the surface. Time and event is crucial to everything we divine from historical context, and just as crucial to predicting future events. If one knows where to look, gold will always be found, the fish always caught. Evidence of this providential certainty is exemplified in the Gospel of Mathew, Chapter 17, verses 24-27 (NIV).

> *"After Jesus and his disciples arrived in Capernaum, the collectors of the two-drachma temple tax came to Peter and asked, "Doesn't your teacher pay the temple tax?" "Yes, he does," he replied. When Peter came into the house, Jesus was the first to speak. "What do you think, Simon?" he asked. "From whom do the kings of the earth collect duty and taxes—from their own children or from others?" "From others," Peter answered. "Then the children are exempt," Jesus said to him. "But so that we may not cause offense, go to the lake and throw out your line. Take the first fish you catch; open its mouth and you will find a four-drachma coin. Take it and give it to them for my tax and yours."*

Jesus did not make a Roman shekel magically appear in the mouth of a fish. He knew it would be there; saw it through the lens of faith, spiritually aware of the father's omnipotent provision to every aspect of existence since the beginning. No doubt the minted coin slipped from someone's grasp, rolls across a wooden deck, and falls into the sea. A swimming fish gulps the shinning object into its mouth, unable to swallow or to eject the obstruction. This could have happened in the moment, or hours, or even days before Peter cast his hook into the water. Since the entire event all about perfect timing, then why should we be more amazed by other events on a much grander mechanical scale?

On a personal note, I observe a similar revelation of faith during an excavation job I organized for a girlfriend. I had hired several men to aid me in a project to landscape her backyard. I assign two men to dig around the roots of an insect infected tree so it could be knocked down. After hours of digging, the tree refuses to yield to their unified efforts. Somewhat agitated, I tell them to step aside. I then strike the base of the stubborn bark with the palms of my hands. With a sharp defiant crack, the tree falls. My two companions are awestruck. But it was not Herculean strength that brought down this resisting obstacle. It was all about timing, and just the right kinetic shear force. You might say that all conditions in the universe are perfectly aligned to accommodate the event. And somehow that precise instant I knew it.

One of the most interesting books I have had the pleasure to read on the subject of the flood history was written by John C. Whitcomb and Henry B. Morris titled The Genesis Flood: *The biblical record and its scientific implications*. During the first half of the twentieth century, many Bible believing *Creationist* were crumbling into silence behind the wall of unanimous consensus imposed by the scientific community, proclaiming uniformitarian ideology the only scientifically acceptable interpretation of earth's geologic history. Both Whitcomb and Morris, well versed in paleontology and geology, set out as a team to scientifically prove the validity of *catastrophism*, and how it fits the account described in Chapter 7, (verses 4-24 (KJV) and Chapter 8, verses 1- 19 *Berean Study Bible* (BSB) of the book of Genesis, which records in some geologic detail a dynamic global upheaval in earth's not so distant past, destroying all life, except for the life preserved in the Ark of Noah. And God said to Noah.

> *"But God remembered Noah and all the animals and livestock that were with him in the ark. And God sent a wind over the earth, and the waters began to subside. The springs of the deep and the floodgates of the heavens were closed, and the rain from the sky was restrained. The waters receded steadily from the earth, and after 150 days the waters had gone down. On the seventeenth day of the seventh month, the ark came to rest on the mountains of Ararat. And the waters continued to recede until the tenth month, and on the first day of the tenth month the tops of the mountains became visible. After forty days Noah opened the window he had made in the ark and sent out a raven. It kept flying back and forth until the waters had*

dried up from the earth. Then Noah sent out a dove to see if the waters had receded from the surface of the ground. But the dove found no place to rest her foot, and she returned to him in the ark, because the waters were still covering the surface of all the earth. So he reached out his hand and brought her back inside the ark. Noah waited seven more days and again sent out the dove from the ark. And behold, the dove returned to him in the evening with a freshly plucked olive leaf in her beak. So Noah knew that the waters had receded from the earth. And Noah waited seven more days and sent out the dove again, but this time she did not return to him. In Noah's six hundred and first year, on the first day of the first month, the waters had dried up from the earth. So Noah removed the covering from the ark and saw that the surface of the ground was dry. By the twenty-seventh day of the second month, the earth was fully dry. Then God said to Noah, "Come out of the ark, you and your wife, along with your sons and their wives. Bring out all the living creatures that are with you—birds, livestock, and everything that crawls upon the ground—so that they can spread out over the earth and be fruitful and multiply upon it." So Noah came out, along with his sons and his wife and his sons' wives. Every living creature, every creeping thing, and every bird—everything that moves upon the earth—came out of the ark, kind by kind."

This is by no means a disjointed Gilgamesh tale to explain some divine correction; rather a remarkably detailed human account recording a disaster of immense proportion and with terrifying consequence. The earth they knew gone, wiped-out by unimaginable geologic disturbances. This new earth, a hostile horizon of jagged high mountains and grand valley craters scooped out of a twisted landscape, exposed by the receding waters. Even the atmospheric radiation and the gravimetric forces different, meaning they would now age more quickly, become more subject to the elements. These few survivors had enormous challenge ahead: a challenge not only to seed the barren earth, but to preserve remnants of past knowledge.

Both Whitcomb and Morris agree that this no local deluge, as many pastors and practitioners had begun to believe based on the intellectual pressure of modern scientific investigation. The flood of the Bible was clearly global--predominantly because God said it within context of the preserved records--but also because the scientific data more supportive of a global flood, as described in the scriptures, than the interpretations presented by uniformitarian theory. Morris, being a respected hydraulic engineer, with a PHD from the University of Minnesota, applies his expertise to demonstrate that hydrodynamic selectivity responsible for fossil bearing strata of sedimentation layered during the flood and later subsidence of water levels. He goes on to attack the use of Carbon-14 dating as an invalid instrument beyond the measurable tolerance of a few thousand years, a highly contested verification factor not always supported by independent results. Anything beyond this time period pure speculation based on complex theories of cross-referencing with vast margins of error. The same applies to coral reef measurements, Petrified Forest samples, and radiometric dating of meteorite material. This all flies in the face of modern science, as well as the disciplined logical minds of many preferring a predictable future from a predictable past. Nevertheless, these exceptional theories prove that such evidence, institutionally accepted without question, contains elements of contradiction ultimately reconcilable either by faith in a theory or faith in a God. Because no matter how far one may digress into the distant past, sooner or later the question arises of which came first: the chicken or the egg?

Presence of an iridium layer assumes proof of the asteroid theory to further support the Uniformitarian timeline. However this is also consistent with extreme volcanic activity, surely present when the fountains of the deep erupted to the surface, releasing magma of iridium- laced ionized carbons created by the extreme pressures. The end result would be sedimentation deposits consistent with the heavier iridium, over-layered by lighter elements as the global flood waters subside. Uniformitarian science insist that stratification, as found along the walls of the Grand Canyon, obviously cut by a glacier during the last ice age, indisputable proof of a very old earth gradually changed over billions of years. Here again the data might yield a different possible interpretation. The recent volcanic eruption of Mount St-Helen's in Washington State has altogether redefined everything science thought to know about the time table of events. Within weeks after the eruption, the sudden outflow of sediments completely fill a valley adjacent to the new active volcano. Two years later a lake accumulated by melting snow fills the crater walls, until one wall breaks suddenly, spilling down the mountain. The ensuing flood tears through the soft sediment formed several months earlier, carving a deep canyon with defined horizontal sediment layers hundreds of feet deep into the surrounding terrain proving that catastrophic events can accomplish in months a phenomenon thought to take millions of years. Even the carbon debris forming the hardened rock cap produce an inaccurate radiometric reading, with an error of hundreds of thousands of years. But the most astounding observation is how quickly the area has rebounded ecologically. A little more than thirty years later a new forest has grown, with plant and animal life rebounding to levels prior to the cataclysmic blast. This is no surprise to creationists, who hold to scriptural evidence of life propagation on earth, as defined in the Holy Bible.

Surtsey is a volcanic island born off the coast of Iceland 130 meters below the ocean that rises to the surface in 1963. For four years the new landmass above sea level grows to a maximum size of 2.7 kilometers. Due to erosion by wind and wave agitation, it has since diminished to half this size, with a mean elevation of just over 152 meters. Since its inception Surtsey has become home to at least 69 plant species that have appeared on the island believed swept ashore by the wind. Several varieties of insect consisting of mites, springtails, and other egg laying arthropods have successfully colonized transported on pieces of driftwood. This has invited many types of birds to begin nesting, further enhancing the ecosystem. Lately more complex life such as earthworms, spiders, and beetles have appeared, meaning that Surtsey now has enough soil and life to support an evolving ecology. What is amazing about all of this is that from the time Surtsey was born to its present age, just over a half century has passed. According to Uniformitarian scientific theory, none of this should be possible in less than a few million years. So either there is a grand underestimation of evolution, or else it is simply in error.

Islands born and islands erased--there is nothing new under the sun. The real question is the time differential. Since the beginning of the twenty-first century, populated regions of the world are smashed by a slew of natural disasters of biblical proportion. Massive landslides bury an ancient village in China. Mountains in Pakistan and Russia slip away overnight burying thousand, and displacing thousands more, usually the result of an unexpected deluge. Sudden volcanic eruptions change landscapes around the world resulting in death and mass evacuations by those in its wake, particularly those most venerable in densely populated areas like the millions of Japanese living in the active shadow of the unpredictable *Sakurajima* volcano. Tropical storms flood low lying cities along the coast of the United States and Europe with devastating consequence, forcing the investment of millions to rebuild and a feeble launch of technologies to construct higher and better dykes in anticipation to even greater storm surges. But perhaps the most deadly of all forces are earthquakes powerful enough to bring down modern bridges, turn cities into rubble, and alter existing landscapes thought to be the steady architecture of hundreds of millions of years. And let us not forget the sired chimeras of shifting plate activity under the seas of the world, dredging up destructive tsunamis racing through the water at the speed of a jetliner. How can this generation not remember the bitter lash of the 2004 tsunami that decimated the shorelines of eleven countries along the Indian Ocean killing more than 150,000 people in a matter of hours?

These are insignificant compared to future scenarios devised by seismologist and those engaged in the study of earth and weather patterns. A 25 foot super tsunami predicted to strike the populated east coast of the United States and Western Europe with 3 to 5 hour advance warning, which will result in an unavoidable statistical fatality of 2 to 4 million souls. This does not take into account the tens of millions affected in the aftermath plagued by disease and disruption of vital resources to those that survive. The *Big One*, as it is colloquially called, referring to massive movement of the San Andreas Fault running along the costal state of California. Again millions of fatalities, total destruction of infrastructure, which will result in limited drinkable water and starvation. The famous Yellowstone Park located on one of the largest super volcanoes in North America, a massive caldera, like a seething teapot continuously on the verge of an eruption. It is predicted that when this monster access point in the earth's magma flow vents to the surface, the resulting explosion will release a poisonous dust cloud into the atmosphere covering a third of the earth worst than any nuclear winter. And these represent only the short list of potential disasters. It is not a question of *if*, but of *when*.

Through prophetic vision Jesus Christ sees the coincidence of events prepared to strike civilization in the end days before the rise of Antichrist into his grand entrance to power. He witnesses these cataclysms through the spirit inconsequential to the present. He sees the entropy of a universe that exist in present condition. Things that will surely be, not things that might be. In the Book of Mathew, Chapter 24, verses 7-8 (KJV), Jesus warns his apostles of a future time line to be fulfilled.

> *"For nation shall rise against nation, and kingdom against kingdom: and there shall be famines, and pestilences, and earthquakes, in divers places. All these are the beginning of sorrows."*

If a marble rolls across the living room floor, it might make a scratch in the leg of grandma's favorite antique table; but push a five ton bolder down a busy main street, the accumulated mass and inertial will inevitably result in major destruction. If this same boulder rolled down a vacant hill, then there will be no calculable harm. The real definition of disaster is habitation and population. One can see the frustration created by many possible interpretations of the available empirical observations. I personally fail to perceive the grand contention. Even if uniformitarian scientist, catastrophist, and creationist lack agreement, as to the conclusion of the evidence, the evidence remains the same. It is the same for the development of any logical structure: *everything possible in the absence of any absolute.*

There may be many who almost win the race, but only one who crosses first the finish line. Nevertheless, stubbornly the uniformitarian continue to hold on rigidly to the theory, more than to the consistency of facts. By definition true science is a discipline of deduction based on observation, without articulating the why or the how something exists. The process of scientific methodology is as follows. First make an hypothesis based on detached observation; then form a theory in collaboration with other similar patterns to accumulate measurable evidence in support of that theory; and finally to organize a principal of law that can be tested under laboratory conditions. Uniformitarian science, motivated by a crusade to embellish mortal reason as the pinnacle of evolutionary existence, seeks to remake the universe in the image of creature potential. Through academic acceptance it elevates the limited information verifiable to localized measurement and creates models of hypothesizes to rigidly define the universe of existence. In layman terms the theory of Uniformitarian science reads as this:

> *Energy and matter caused by a singularity of an unknown event. The earth forms by accident and life an even greater accident that kick starts evolution. Through this evolution Man crawls out of diluvium slime to become one of many beast of complex organization, but for some reason evolves wiser than all other beast, and therefore is a beast no longer.*

And this is what we are teaching our children around the globe. An evolutionary climb supported by inconclusive geologic evidence of ancient bones found in dated rock and disassociated fragments interpreted to fit the hypothesis. As the eloquent theory of Uniformitarian science becomes the focus of all data interpretation, it blindly dismisses all other possibilities. But adding to the confusion are complex formulas of model corrections used to make the ledger sheets add up. Even some of the most respected geophysics and professors of archeology silently break ranks in the face of many contradictions found present in hard accumulated evidence.

Whether the genotype of man a thousand, ten thousand, or millions of years there is always the question of the first cause. In other words how to define the excitation that inspires chemical sludge to morph into multi-celled integration, to develop air-breathing lungs for emergence upon dry land, and to eventually stand on two legs as bipedal homo erectus? Logically speaking this is like changing from a more durable model adapted to an environment covering two thirds of earth's surface to a condition less adaptable and with limited accessibility. Would not a creature with the ability to hibernate or a creature with less oxygen requirements be more suitable for long space explorations? And if it is just about brain size, then why are Sperm whales not calling all the shots?

Perhaps greater scrutiny should be applied to the true intent of the many deceptions presented through logical extrapolation and based on several unfounded principals. But science and theology do agree on one immutable fact: all organic structures (including human beings) are atomically made of the same gas and mineral elements that make the whole of our blue jewel of a planet. We and everything else here a composition of water and earth, as stated in The Book of Genesis, Chapter 2, verse 7 (KJV).

> *"And the LORD God formed man of the dust of the ground, and breathed into his nostrils the breath of life; and man became a living soul."*

What can be more explicitly grounded in present comprehension than this?

Chapter 10
FROM PARADISE LOST TO DARWINISM

Legends of lost utopia continue to haunt the pragmatic dissolution of world history like a shadow in the closet. But is this chimera better days of the past or dark reflection of an inevitable future? There exist many incongruous mysteries that continually undermine the Uniformitarian principal of ordered evolutionary progress in spite of eager attempts to compact world history into a predictable gradual process traversing inconceivable expanses of time absent of catastrophic event. As already examined this theory does not always yield consistent results to adequately describe the many contradictions found in geology and archeology. Nor as we will see here is it sufficient to answer basic questions of genesis? Was man once smarter than he is today? Was there once a technological civilization equal, or even superior to present understanding?

Though man dreams to go boldly where no man has gone before, he really has not gone very far with any permanent success. Yes, early colonial voyages added dimension to the world by connecting the continents. Accelerated modes of travel have greatly condensed global access; as ever advancing telecommunications continually makes everyone on the planet uncomfortably close. Nor am I belittling the many remarkable accomplishments of the last century. It is no small feat to plot a trajectory to the moon and back; or to design supersonic vehicles that crisscross the world daily, making every point on the globe accessible within hours. What I mean to say is that with all the innovation and exploration, so little has actually changed in the basic human genome through many thousands of years of recorded history. So what about the speculative history we do not know?

The abandoned lost city of Machu-Picchu perched high on the rising steppes of the Andes Mountains suggest that once this elevation less inhospitable than it is today. Many geologists theorize that there was a rapid change in tectonic activity taking place over a period of hundreds of years, rather than millions, pushing up the rock strata. The *Tiahuanacu* seaport, over two and a half miles above sea level (*by some estimates to be as much as 15,000 years old*) predates the flood of Noah. It presently rest high in the Bolivian mountains more than fifteen miles from the nearest body of water, the surrounding area populated with millions of fossilized seashells, indicating there was once a living ocean here. The *Bimini Mounds* near the Bahamas' is another example of architectural ingenuity from an ancient civilization built upon dry land before the Atlantic rolled over the face of this now submerged construction. Composed of flint-hard *micrite* (which in geological terms means that these large rectangular shaped stones were brought from somewhere else and placed here many thousands of years earlier), to form what appears to be the remains of an ancient highway approximately 300 feet wide and over sixteen hundred feet long. And perhaps one of the most baffling question that continues to plague modern architects is where did the geometry of the pyramids originate and what is the mystery of their design?

In more recent history, other anomalies uncovered even more puzzling. Tantalizing maps of uncharted Antarctica that were accurately drawn supposedly a millennium before an ice age covered the land in a tomb several miles deep. These sea charts reveal topography of a once known continent with vegetation and beaches. Another relic found in an old shipwreck revived from the silent deep holding within its decaying hull what appears to be a complex chronology machine resurrected from an even older civilization. Many such artifacts with inexplicable origins uncovered in very old strata depicting technological advancements not so different than the ones we take for granted today, Among these are batteries ingeniously designed for a specific use unearthed in strata dating many thousands of years before the first harnessing of electricity or the invention of the wheel.

We need not look too far back before realizing there are many unraveled threads suggesting lost civilizations from unknown origin based on more than just legend. Lost Atlantis looms in the murky depths of history in stubborn defiance of the notion that modern man represents the pinnacle of technological achievement. As a child I remember the acute inspiration felt upon reading for the first time Jules Verne's novel about the submarine Nautilus commanded by the enigmatic *Captain Nemo*. This adventure takes me *20,000 Leagues under the Sea* to explore a world unknown even to this day. But what captures most my imagination are the images of sunken Atlantis, ruins from an ancient metropolis abandoned in the silent depths of the sea.

Over seventy percent of our earth is covered by water, meaning there is a lot of subterranean area we do not know about hidden upon the planet we inhabit. Perhaps Atlantis is just legend; or perhaps it is the allegory of a past civilization retained through translation and genetic memory of an advanced civilization perished in a deluge. Whatever Atlantis was, it is today a disturbingly murky point of reference inspiring natural and supernatural investigation. Edgar Casey, a renowned Medium in the early twentieth century, devoted volumes of transcriptions to the prominence of this dead populace from the past; and even allowed himself possessed by a foreign agent. This entity speaks extensively about the last days before the destruction. It even goes so far as to make references about power helixes and weapons that dwarf even those of the greatest armed nations today.

But Atlantis is not just a place, but a concept. Submerged continents, lost worlds of civilization: all ancient knowledge hidden in the dust of time waiting to be revived by a curious hand--all woven into the very fabric of human imagination and wonder of the unknown. Much speculation has been devoted to how and why certain architectures from the ancient past align astronomically to stars and constellations. This reveals an understanding of the clock-work nature of local space in relative position to astronomical progression. It suggests masterful perception planetary positions and gravity mass somehow accomplished without the aid of today's massive computer hard-drives loaded with terabyte volumes of calculated data. What is the significance of *Stonehenge* or of the *Nasca Lines* (huge *"geoglyphs"* etched into the desert floor of Peru) discernable only from a respectable altitude? What is the magnetic relation between the *Bermuda Triangle* and the *Dragon's Triangle* aligned precisely through the center of the earth?

The ancients knew more about cosmic order than perhaps modern science is willing to admit. There are many other references to lost continents as well that further confuses the neatly organized uniformitarian evolutionary time table. Recent discovery of granite boulders scattered over the seafloor off the coast of South America provides more evidence of another lost continent. These rocks, much too heavy to be transported by glacial force, defy explanation for their presence. And what about the plentiful remains of scattered seashells and other crustaceans found on slopes in higher elevations?

In the Hindu *Mahabharata* text there are references to a celestial war between gods and demigods using formidable weapons, possessing aerodynamic vehicles piloted by humanoid beings. As a consequence of this conflict, or because of a domino effect (the text is unclear), a great flood ensues destroying all life, except for a man named Manu, who survives along with the plants and animals. Records of a global calamity involving universal flooding are found in many cultures all over the world. Despite all the physical and cultural facts against the uniformitarian concept, modern consensus embraces the *steady-state* theory of evolutionary progression above all other logic. Therefore, I wish to examine the premise of this conventional reason, as presented within context.

The true Holy Grail of scientific prestige since the time of Darwin is the tangible artifact of dinosaur bones. Since no one today should reasonably doubt the existence of dinosaurs, then only one real question remains: *how long ago did they live and why did they all perish?*

According to the periodic table, the last living dinosaur walked the earth 65 million years ago at the end of the Cretaceous Period, prior to large meteor impact that raises a dense dust cloud and plunges planet earth into a deepfreeze. This conclusion reached because the petrified bones of these beasts usually found in strata supportive of the uniformitarian theory of elapsed time, and the bones themselves providing confirmed evidence of the time slot. Therefore, it should be inconceivable that a living dinosaur could have existed since that time to present. Yet, there have been many contradictions that suggest major discrepancies to this theory.

One example, the well documented *Ta Prohm Temple* Hindu-Buddha monastery in South East Asia, depicting carvings of what strongly resembles a Stegosaurus. This particular dinosaur has only recently been categorized and reconstructed by archeologist, making it one of the rarer additions to the growing library of extinct creatures that once roamed the earth. What makes this of particular interest is that the *Kamer* civilization flourished between the 8th to the 11th century A.D., before succumbing to internal divisions and political decline. Nevertheless, one wonders where the artist acquired the model to represent this animal in such detail, including the distinctive horns along its spine. This fact alone leads many to think that the stone engravers, either heard of a very vivid firsthand account, or actually saw a living sample. This is not conclusive proof that this creature was alive and well a little over a thousand years ago, but does raise many questions.

Another piece of conflicting evidence to the ancient ancestry of extinct dinosaurs are the various *petroglyphs* discovered throughout regions of the Midwestern United States. In caves and on canyon rock walls are drawings of large reptiles identified as carnivorous dinosaurs cohabiting alongside modern hominids. Many of these drawings resemble the giant Apatosaurus, believed extinct for hundreds of millions of years before man stands erect on two legs. Fossils of these creatures have been found in areas around the Grand Canyon, indicating that they once roamed the region in plentiful numbers. Even paleontologist committed to the theory of a very old earth and dinosaurs going extinct long before human beings arrive on the scene admit to the contradictory implication of the evidence. Is it possible that the early *Anasazis* Indians, less than two thousand years ago, actually saw, and perhaps even hunted these earth-rumbling creatures?

Perhaps the most irrefutable evidence that bipedal hominids and dinosaurs once walked the earth together is found near Glen Rose, Texas. The well known *Paluxy River Ledge*, a limestone strata carbon dated to be 106 million years old, contains the fossilized footprints of dinosaurs and humans together. This could only have happened while the mud still soft enough to create a lasting cast. These petrified prints had to have been created within the same time period. Not separate steps spread over millions of years as maintained by the Periodic Table. This one piece of evidence (not unique to similar discoveries in other parts of the world) profoundly disturbs the anthropological evolutionary timeline embraced by uniformitarian science. No human (must less a bipedal hominid) could possibly be around nearly fifty million years before the great monsters of the Cretaceous Period went extinct. Adding to the discrepancy is a well preserved hand imprint as human as any today, suggesting that the hunters modern humans in pursuit of prey. To date no other plausible explanations provided by any department in the scientific community to cleverly refute the evidence.

The largest creature to ever walk the earth are the recently discovered bones of the *Dreadnoughtus*, a dinosaur believed to weight more than the accumulated weight of seven full- grown T-Rex placed on an opposite scale, and to be a third the size of a regulation football field. Just as a side note, if one considers the earth's gravity the same as it is today, this enormous herbivore would have moved like a sluggish ocean cruise liner, making it a slow-moving lawnmower clearing the way for smaller and more agile carnivorous creatures. However, it is more likely that this multi-ton creature would not have been able to move at all, collapsing under the irresistible gravity of its own mass density. The very existence of this enormous beast implies that the flood in Noah's time is not only catastrophic, but marks a major change in the overall mass of planet earth. A possible scenario already alluded to in a previous chapter.

Beyond the imaginative techniques of fossil reconstruction, there is little we can conclude about this oblique age of earth giants. However, I would like to remind the reader that there is one historical record of an aquatic dinosaur that is neither mythical, nor based on vague generalities achieved by paleontologist to restore the semblance of a dead animal. The 4th century BC *Book of Job* devotes an entire chapter describing in detail the nature and physical attributes of the terrifying creature we know today as a dinosaur, obviously alive and familiar during the author's writing of the text. Listen to the chilling vision of this monster of monsters as related in The Book of Job, Chapter 41, verses 1-34 (NKJV):

"Can you draw out Leviathan with a hook, Or snare his tongue with a line which you lower?

Can you put a reed through his nose, Or pierce his jaw with a hook? Will he make many supplications to you? Will he speak softly to you? Will he make a covenant with you? Will you take him as a servant forever? Will you play with him as with a bird, Or will you leash him for your maidens? Will your companions make a banquet of him? Will they apportion him among the merchants? Can you fill his skin with harpoons, Or his head with fishing spears? Lay your hand on him; Remember the battle— Never do it again! Indeed, any hope of overcoming him is false; Shall one not be overwhelmed at the sight of him? No one is so fierce that he would dare stir him up. Who then is able to stand against Me? Who has preceded Me, that I should pay him? Everything under heaven is Mine. I will not conceal his limbs, His mighty power, or his graceful proportions. Who can remove his outer coat? Who can approach him with a double bridle? Who can open the doors of his face, With his terrible teeth all around? His rows of scales are his pride, Shut up tightly as with a seal; One is so near another That no air can come between them; They are joined one to another, They stick together and cannot be parted. His sneezings flash forth light, And his eyes are like the eyelids of the morning. Out of his mouth go burning lights; Sparks of fire shoot out. Smoke goes out of his nostrils, As from a boiling pot and burning rushes. His breath kindles coals,

And a flame goes out of his mouth. Strength dwells in his neck, And sorrow dances before him. The folds of his flesh are joined together; They are firm on him and cannot be moved. His heart is as hard as stone, Even as hard as the lower millstone. When he raises himself up, the mighty are afraid; Because of his crashings they are beside themselves. Though the sword reaches him, it cannot avail; Nor does spear, dart, or javelin. He regards iron as straw, And bronze as rotten wood. The arrow cannot make him flee; Slingstones become like stubble to him. Darts are regarded as straw; He laughs at the threat of javelins. His undersides are like sharp potsherds; He spreads pointed marks in the mire. He makes the deep boil like a pot; He makes the sea like a pot of ointment. He leaves a shining wake behind him; One would think the deep had white hair. On earth there is nothing like him, Which is made without fear. He beholds every high thing; He is king over all the children of pride."

Scale away the religious overtones and you are left with a giant creature endowed with an impenetrable armored hide, silvery reptilian eyes, and a huge head surrounded by sharp teeth. These certainly are not creatures for recreational hunting, but a collective challenge to any party sent out to try and contain a dangerous predator that strays too near to human settlement. I once met a hunter, who for a living tracked the enormous Polar Bears in Northern Alaska. He agrees that such a monster, as described in the Book of Job, would be like tracking a dangerous creature the size of a school bus.

Although many Creationists suggest that these huge reptiles included in the inventory of the Ark, I personally disagree. First of all, many of these creatures were oviparous, reproducing by egg-laying, as do most reptiles today. Sea turtles bury their eggs on beaches, which do not hatch for two months. Whereas, Alligator Snapping Turtles can take up to five months to hatch without the mother's constant attention. Chameleon lizards might not hatch for a year. Therefore it seems plausible that many dinosaur eggs might have survived the deluge buried in the earth or inside of caves in the same way the great mammals of the deep survived. There is so little really known about these cold-blooded creatures. What was their gestation period? Were some able to hibernate for long periods of time, like the present day Southern Africa Lungfish that can breathe both air and water, known to lay dormant inside a mud coffin for as long as four years? Even the contemporary Crocodile, able to slow down its metabolism so low that it can lie in a shallow for up to two years without eating, and then snap to life suddenly with deadly consequence.

Though the abundance of dinosaurs greatly diminished after the flood, their resilience could possibly have continued for thousands of postdiluvian years. This suggest some truth to the mythology of *dragons*, the nightmare legends of sea monsters, and many other encounters filling volumes in the pages of antiquity. This might also explain much of a history we know so little about by connecting the spaces between many dots of facts and legends. These becoming the monsters slain by hero quests, and may continue still as lake-dwelling silhouettes etched against a night horizon.

But it is not just dinosaurs creating a disturbing trend of disagreement even among Uniformitarian scientist, but also the genesis and evolution of man himself. Before dawn of the nineteenth century, all men are basically considered equally created outside ordinance of social dominance. Despite the practice of exploitation and colonial slavery spanning hundreds of year, there existed in the past cross-cultural acceptance that all men everywhere possessed with equal intellectual ability if provided with the same privilege and education. Then in the late nineteenth century Social Darwinism changes this by scientifically justifying a belief that some men superior and more qualified to rule based on a premise of genetic superiority. No longer is man product of the creator, but evidence of a successful multispecies that has evolved out of different primeval pools. This naturally implies that some more fit than others decided by many deterministic factors. All sorts of intellectual markers established to measure the cranial capacity and aristocratic dominance acquired through linage. There are even those that apply doctrinal interpretation of scriptures from the Bible to justify inequality and abuse of human dignity. A cruel example is the slave trade of African people removed from their homelands and bartered around the world. It should be reminded that many of these directly descended from the Nubian Empire that flourished in cultural richness while much of Europe still barbarians living in tents. Nevertheless, based on this new Theory of Origin, institutional science has strived ever since to organize a quantum model composed of genetic markers using collected DNA samples. This data collection made in the guise to better understand viral contagions with ultimate goal of one day curing death through DNA manipulation. The inevitable realization is a dark corridor of discrimination based on the false assumption that the present model of man inferior and that scientific research the lordship of a superior future race.

The attempt to tie up all the looses strings of human evolution theory has proven a great empirical challenge. Unlike dinosaur bones, the fossil record of man remains most sparse. It is rare to find a complete skull, and rarer still to find enough bone fragments to construct a complete skeleton. Most of these are vague, as to origin, many not even confirmed through consensus to be primates even remotely related to modern Homo sapiens. I also find it a little distrustful that the same technique of *strata-bone-dating* used to confirm much older specimens, particularly since there is so much controversy involving the many discrepancies these theories inherit from parent techniques.

It is particularly curious that dinosaurs seemed to have evolved in a little over 165 million years (according to the fossil record) without too much change; whereas, the first appearance of a hominid emerges 65 million years after the last of these monsters have gone extinct. This new hominid species seems to acquire an advanced IQ in a relatively short period of time. Obviously, the genus of man did not evolve from these dominate reptilian species. Is this because the magic genie of evolution suddenly becomes more exemplary, thus allowing greater complexity of brain chemistry? Within 6 to 7 million years these forefathers of man crawl out of a pool of primeval slime, form vertebrae, and manage to survive many clandestine sequences of metamorphosis. By first rising up on four legs and then standing erect on two, these intrepid survivors develop useful appendages with brilliant capacity to construct tools. Then one day this new species gazes collectively up at the stars with sudden apprehension of awareness deprived of all other species.

Modern science would have us believe that this mysterious phenomenon occurred over long periods of time, with spontaneous leaps forward through the transition of missing links. Further, that we should accept this logical hypothesis by faith, since the past hundred or so years of dedicated anthropological research has failed to produce even one missing link. It is sort of like saying *Natural Selection* sometimes gets hooked on steroids, making a sink or swim scenario imperative. Only this profound evolutionary leap forward is too brief to leave behind sufficient evidence. Either because of rapid change in climate, alteration in the prey-predator balance, or some other undefined external condition, normal evolution falls dormant into a consciousness of compressed quantum necessary to insure survival of the species. As an analogy, I get the mental image of many generations of humanoid beings sent to an alien planet perishing in a cloud of methane gas, while a few gasp weakly, as their lungs magically adapt to breathe poison, instead of oxygenated air. But the real change seems to have happened in the last *150 to 200* thousand years. This is when the fossil record tells us that modern man really begins to emerge above his primate ancestry. *Wow--that is an evolutionary leap!* In this *miraculously* short span of time, a brilliant awakening of cognition. And somewhere in the mix, after the ascension of an elusive missing link, a completely evolved enigma emerges. *Neanderthal* man, believed to be the genetic donor of us all, becomes the famous poster child to support the modern theory of evolution.

This is basically the tale of Darwinian science, wrapped-up in a neat package, and tied together with a brightly colored bow of logic to indoctrinate present and future generations in the guise of education. Even Plato, the master of reasonable discourse might pose the question: Does this sound more credible than the account given in the Holy Bible about omniscient God, creating everything to a purpose, fully realized from the beginning? Genesis, Chapter 1, verses 25-28 (KJV) says:

"And God made the beasts of the earth after their kind, and the cattle after their kind, and everything that creeps on the ground after its kind; and God saw that it was good. And God said, Let us make man in our image, after our likeness: and let them have dominion over the fish of the sea, and over the fowl of the air, and over the cattle, and over all the earth, and over every creeping thing that creeps upon the earth. So God created man in his own image, in the image of God created he him; male and female created he them. And God blessed them, and God said unto them, Be fruitful, and multiply, and replenish the earth, and subdue it: and have dominion over the fish of the sea, and over the fowl of the air, and over every living thing that moves upon the earth."

The day Noah and his family sealed into the Ark, also preserved are the animal genres containing archetypal DNA information necessary to replenish the earth with kind after a kind. Messenger RNA, codified as (*mRNA*), kicks-in as an automatic messenger transcriber to necessitate real-time stimulation to metabolic response through a process of natural selectivity. This built-in mechanism manufactures successive gene transcription sequences inherent to all earth-bound creatures designed to help a host organism adapt to ecological changes. To suggest otherwise is to deny the clear evidence. All animals, including humans, have within them this latent code of modification reactive to environment stimuli. Although the phenomenon more obvious in animals of shorter life spans, it can easily be speculated that even the Wooly Mammoth not always adapted to a cold weather climate.

Since this process of adaptability inherent to all complex organisms, it should be little surprise that there exist many identifiable secondary features found in humans indigenous to different regions on the earth. This no doubt lends explanation to the varying types of humans we physically observe today. In hotter climates skin pigmentation darkens to better filter solar radiation and insulate against heat. This physiological alteration may have occurred to varying degrees around the globe as men migrated together in tribal groups. Changing gravity and atmospheric pressures may have stimulated RNA coding to modify the DNA archetype for specific challenges of adaptation. As these pressures equalize, then more homogenous comparisons become the new norms, differing only slightly in these secondary characteristic development.

This is by far a more acceptable possibility than to hypothesis that disorganized matter formed into complex chains of proteins evolving into coded strands of complex DNA. Not only is this contrary to entropic observation, but it defies the reality of our integrated condition. We are each a collective of many billions of organic life forms integrated into an interdependent agreement beneficial to the whole. This is analogist to my experience as a child after getting my first fish tank. Of course, I supply it with all the colorful fish I want, but soon realize it necessary to acquire several less comely creatures, such as bottom-feeders and snails, to maintain a balance to the aquatic environment. Were these creatures any less valuable than the colorful fish that filled my eyes?

God has created each after its kind so says the Bible. What does this mean really? Zoology is the bioscience devoted to studying different animal species, past and present, making up the ecosystem of planet earth. This inventory of species well documented through legends of categories and subcategories painstakingly entered in *Linnaeus's Table of the Animal kingdom*. The research finding of this field of study removes the supposition of cross-species fertilization predicted by Darwinian evolutionary probability. It confirms that all animal species distinctly defined by groups with *genus-type* restrictions that are genetically and physiologically incompatible. Although wolves and dogs enough alike to mate and produce offspring; dogs and cats cannot be crossbred to fertilize another kind of animal. The same is true for all other classifications in nature, including different species of plants, unless artificially inseminated. In fact, this rigid barrier extends across every living thing, from microorganisms, to birds of the air, and to creatures of the deep. Even gorillas and chimpanzees will not mate, even if an opposite sexed pair retained in close confinement for the duration of their lifespan. Only animals with higher reasoning of imagination might dare to cross-copulate with another species. Only through forced application of DNA manipulation to achieve deterministic goals are true monsters of malignancy made. Even viruses and bacteria respond to the same restrictions of genome isolation that prevents hybrid types from evolving. This is not the same as mutation, which is a process of a specific genome type adapting to new conditions. Unless manipulated by a foreign intelligence, SARS and E-Coli lack protein compatibility to merge and integrate into a strand of contagion possessing properties of both, or even to become something altogether different.

Science has now become the devil in the works by meddling with architecture it fundamentally knows little about. Nor is this the first time in world history the gene pool corrupted by forces outside of natural design. From the beginning fallen Satan has a plan to rewrite God's designed code by sowing seeds of deception going back to when the serpent says to Eve "you *will know and be as God*". This betrayal expressed in the Book of Genesis, Chapter 3, verses 1 - 4 (NKV).

> *"Now the serpent was more cunning than any beast of the field which the LORD God had made. And he said to the woman, "Has God indeed said, 'You shall not eat of every tree of the garden'?" And the woman said to the serpent, "We may eat the fruit of the trees of the garden; but of the fruit of the tree which is in the midst of the garden, God has said, 'You shall not eat it, nor shall you touch it, lest you die.' "Then the serpent said to the woman, "You will not surely die. For God knows that in the day you eat of it your eyes will be opened, and you will be like God, knowing good and evil."*

Chapter 11
MONSTERS AND SUPERMEN

I remember as a child being terrified by late night horror films about monsters that destroy the world of civilization; or worse those evil creatures on missions to harvest the souls of innocence. I often hid my head under a sheet, the hairs on my body raised electrified, aware that another presence the room with me manifested through a portal of imagination made real by this flickering black and white box. I little understood at the time how truly near these presences. Only, at the time I did not realize how real these chimeras.

The child I had privilege to raise, to love, and to think of as my own apprehensively watched the same kinds of thrillers with similar reaction. Often she would rush into the bedroom screaming and bury beneath the covers of father and mother feeling safe. As a parent, you become the monster slayer, forcing the undead back into their coffins, and the destroyer of alien invasion forces for the future salvation of human kind. Those of you, who have children know the kind of warfare I am referring to. Usually, this involves just turning the channel. But there are times, the monsters more real than the contrivance of imagination. These are usually manifestations of the flesh, becoming the evil of sinister headlines in the morning news reporting the abduction of a child, molestation, or worse. So where do these real monsters come from?

There are latent patterns translated from generation to generation manifesting into images glimpsed between light and shadow: not altogether of this world; not altogether unreal. These phantom shapes appear terrifyingly grotesque, or wear a mask pleasingly sensual.

Although an infant can see only the distance of a few inches, this new being has infallible perceptiveness capable of divining the deceptive elements between the cracks in accepted reality. In other words, they see what we no longer see: the spirits of the air, demonic forces, like the seeds of tares sewn in the wind. But these young ones are protected by the faith of their innocence with souls incorruptible. This protection does not last, because of sin in the world. Monster movies are only paths of cookie crumbs into the spectacular halls of Satan's luminescent kingdom. A reflection only-- a darkness made darkest when the light of the world gone. In fact we cannot imagine a world without light, or the delicate balance of every aspect of nature providing the temperate conditions agreeable to biological existence. It is a simple matter of mental creativity to imagine a silicone life form with a respiratory system designed to inhale a combination of Argon and Ammonia. However, the realization of an anatomic structure necessary for this exchange almost inconceivable on the level of molecular processing.

There is much discussion about the importance of DNA, as the inimitable source code hardwired into all living things. The main topic revolving around the subject of how it can be used, changed, or manipulated. But still it remains enigmatic as to origin or purpose of design. As already graphically illustrated by the *Linnaeus's Table of the Animal kingdom,* DNA strictly determines a species by transcribing by encoded genetic messages on strands of amino acid to make proteins necessary for building cells. Fish, reptile, birds, animals, insects, and plants--all have DNA instructions unique to the species. Even if species share a common genus of similar characteristics, such as monkeys and gorillas, they are worlds apart on the nuclear level. Although apes and modern man share a similar genus of hominid characteristics, they are not considered related, except in the rare anthropological associations with missing links. However, one thing that is certain, there is presently no research on the technology horizon predicting dynamic creation of even a single strand of DNA.

It seems that, like the creation of matter and energy, an unknown event precipitates measured conditions to inspire the myriad of life as we know it. The source of this sudden propagation categorized as just another cosmic accident without explanation. As far as I know, there are only three scenarios for life on earth: either man evolved from innate material by the abstract influence of an unnamed first cause, life seeded here by an advanced alien race, whose genesis also unknown, or God created man whole and complete from the beginning, as described in the first book of the Holy Bible. Ignoring the obvious dilemma of too many unknown factors, only one of these choices is provided in text form with an explanation of the why, the how, and the force responsible. A statement profound beyond meaning; nor can the fact of existence be more clearly stated. Found in the first of the five books given to Moses, Genesis, Chapter 1, verses 11-31 (NIV):

> *"In the beginning God created the heavens and the earth. Now the earth was formless and empty, darkness was over the surface of the deep, and the Spirit of God was hovering over the waters. And God said, "Let there be light," and there was light. God saw that the light was good, and he separated the light from the darkness. God called the light "day," and the darkness he called "night." And there was evening, and there was morning—the first day.*
>
> *And God said, "Let there be a vault between the waters to separate water from water." So God made the vault and separated the water under the vault from the water above it. And it was so. God called the vault "sky." And there was evening, and there was morning—the second day.*
>
> *And God said, "Let the water under the sky be gathered to one place, and let dry ground appear." And it was so. God called the dry ground "land," and the gathered waters he called "seas." And God saw that it was good. Then God said, "Let the land produce vegetation: seed- bearing plants and trees on the land that bear fruit with seed in it, according to their various kinds." And it was so. The land produced vegetation: plants bearing seed according to their*

kinds and trees bearing fruit with seed in it according to their kinds. And God saw that it was good. And there was evening, and there was morning—the third day. And God said, "Let there be lights in the vault of the sky to separate the day from the night, and let them serve as signs to mark sacred times, and days and years, and let them be lights in the vault of the sky to give light on the earth." And it was so. God made two great lights—the greater light to govern the day and the lesser light to govern the night. He also made the stars. God set them in the vault of the sky to give light on the earth, **to** *govern the day and the night, and to separate light from darkness. And God saw that it was good. And there was evening, and there was morning— the fourth day. And God said, "Let the water teem with living creatures, and let birds fly above the earth across the vault of the sky." So God created the great creatures of the sea and every living thing with which the water teems and that moves about in it, according to their kinds, and every winged bird according to its kind. And God saw that it was good. God blessed them and said, "Be fruitful and increase in number and fill the water in the seas, and let the birds increase on the earth." And there was evening, and there was morning—the fifth day. And God said, "Let the land produce living creatures according to their kinds: the livestock, the creatures that move along the ground, and the wild animals, each according to its kind." And it was so. God made the wild animals according to their kinds, the livestock according to their kinds, and all the creatures that move along the ground according to their kinds. And God saw that it was good.*

Then God said, "Let us make mankind in our image, in our likeness, so that they may rule over the fish in the sea and the birds in the sky, over the livestock and all the wild animals, and over all the creatures that move along the

> ground." So God created mankind in his own image, in the image of God he created them; male and female he created them. God blessed them and said to them, "Be fruitful and increase in number; fill the earth and subdue it. Rule over the fish in the sea and the birds in the sky and over every living creature that moves on the ground." Then God said, "I give you every seed-bearing plant on the face of the whole earth and every tree that has fruit with seed in it. They will be yours for food. And to all the beasts of the earth and all the birds in the sky and all the creatures that move along the ground—everything that has the breath of life in it—I give every green plant for food." And it was so. God saw all that he had made, and it was very good. And there was evening, and there was morning—the sixth day."

The problem with this presentation is that it does not fit in with the constructed models of model predictability. As already addressed in previous arguments, the accumulated evidence must agree with theoretical assumptions based on a consensus of logical agreement. Any evidence to the contrary dismissed as myth and fable. In my mind this kind of reasoning equivalent to creating an arbitrary model of reality and only including the data that fits the agreements of assumption. I think the real universe much more immensely designed than this.

Most present day interstellar observes agree that cosmology started with a singularity termed the *Big Bang*. By applying an arbitration of time progression formulation of earth's relative position in the vastness of stars and galaxies racing into the past, it is estimated that the age of the universe approximately 13.8 billion earth years. This does not take into account a value termed infinite velocity present at the beginning, or how to explain the absence of sufficient energy and matter, which should be present. The real question on the minds of all: *What happened at the instance of this singularity birth; and do present values of time and measurement reliably describe what we can see?* But more importantly, *what about the stuff we do not see?* As research into quantum mechanics moves from theoretical to applied laboratory test results, the quantified

Quarks and Flavors of subatomic analysis begins to paint a different picture from the Uniformitarian model. Since I have already addressed many of these pillars of assumptions in earlier chapters, I will strive to remain focused on the present challenge of defining the genus of man within context of anthropological history.

Legends and myths permeate the root of every world culture, injecting the lost past with veins of exotic possibilities. Embedded within these tales, an entourage of unusual beings that once walked the earth; their existence further supported by archeological discovery. A twenty three foot skeleton of a man found beside a river in Valance, France, in the year 1456 A.D. during the reign of Richard of York at the end of the bloody 100 year war between France and England. In 1577 A.D. a nineteen and a half foot human skeleton discovered under an uprooted tree in the Canton of Lucerne. Another human skeleton unearthed near a castle of Chaumont, France in 1613 A.D. In 1833 soldiers of the new America accidentally dig up the skeleton of a twelve foot man surrounded by carved shells and Stone Age weapons. In this case the jaw of the deceased documented to have double rows of upper and lower teeth, further substantiating local legends of Piute Indians about a tribe of ancient red-haired giants they refer to as Si-Te- Cahs, described as a cannibalistic fearless warrior clan living in Nevada. Giants, it seems, have been around for as long as our ancestral memory. There are even suggestions men of giant statue responsible for the building of the more profound architectures found on our planet originating from a time older than the oldest civilization in post diluvium history. Throughout regions of South America impressive structures with hewn rocks of staggering size, the weight too heavy even for the largest modern crane of today. The grand monoliths of Stonehenge, jutting out of the landscape of Wiltshire, England, believed to predate even the Druids. People from around the world gather within the circle of these enigmatic stones during the summer solstice to marvel at the present day astrological significance of the architecture.

Serious speculation attributes the building of the great pyramids of Egypt to the combined efforts of giants, who with the aid of technology, erect the precisely hewn stone blocks that have defied the erosion of time. These mighty men and their deeds are recorded everywhere on the face of the earth, and found even in the depths of the seas, as already mentioned earlier in reference to the mystery of the *Bimini Mounds* off the Bahamas shoals.

Some less moderate theologians believe that Nimrod was in fact a giant. This son of Cush, Noah's great grandson sired by his second son Ham, described as a man of extraordinary stature unchallenged in his generation. The early Bible describes Nimrod as a mighty hunter before the Lord. Those versed in Hebrew interpret this to mean that this mortal giant stood "defiant" against the God responsible for scattering the survivors of the flood from unified Babylon. Nimrod aspires into a warlord of cruel reputation. His main legacy is the worship of the god Ashur, giving birth of the Assyrian Empire from the plains of Babylon, to the lush Euphrates valley spreading into the rich delta of the Nile. What little is known about this tyrant paints a portrait of a rebellious nature and insatiable hunger for conquest.

From this appetite for dominance rises the earthly glory inspired through violent aggression driving the many ancient empires that follow. If we examine carefully anthropology records unearthed daily, it becomes abundantly clear that present day geopolitical contour and demographics have roots that can be traced back to this finite point in time. The Bible also confers that the fruit of every tree springs forth from the root. In Genesis, Chapter 10, verses 1- 32 (NIV) we get a glimpse of this early genealogy that will set the momentum to seed the rise and fall of future civilization.

> *"This is the account of Shem, Ham and Japheth, Noah's sons, who themselves had sons after the flood. The Japhethites The sons of Japheth: Gomer, Magog, Madai, Javan, Tubal, Meshek and Tiras. The sons of Gomer: Ashkenaz, Riphath and Togarmah. The sons of Javan: Elishah, Tarshish, the Kittites and the Rodanites. (From these the maritime peoples spread out into their territories by their clans within their nations, each with its own language.) The Hamites The sons of Ham: Cush, Egypt,*

Put and Canaan. The sons of Cush: Seba, Havilah, Sabtah, Raamah and Sabteka. The sons of Raamah: Sheba and Dedan. Cush was the father of Nimrod, who became a mighty warrior on the earth. He was a mighty hunter before the LORD; that is why it is said, "Like Nimrod, a mighty hunter before the LORD." The first centers of his kingdom were Babylon, Uruk, Akkad and Kalneh, in Shinar. From that land he went to Assyria, where he built Nineveh, Rehoboth Ir, Calah and Resen, which is between Nineveh and Calah— which is the great city. Egypt was the father of the Ludites, Anamites, Lehabites, Naphtuhites, Pathrusites, Kasluhites (from whom the Philistines came) and Caphtorites. Canaan was the father of Sidon his firstborn, and of the Hittites, Jebusites, Amorites, Girgashites, Hivites, Arkites, Sinites, Arvadites, Zemarites and Hamathites. Later the Canaanite clans scattered and the borders of Canaan reached from Sidon toward Gerar as far as Gaza, and then toward Sodom, Gomorrah, Admah and Zeboyim, as far as Lasha. These are the sons of Ham by their clans and languages, in their territories and nations. The Semites Sons were also born to Shem, whose older brother was Japheth; Shem was the ancestor of all the sons of Eber. The sons of Shem: Elam, Ashur, Arphaxad, Lud and Aram. The sons of Aram: Uz, Hul, Gether and Meshek. Arphaxad was the father of Shelah, and Shelah the father of Eber. Two sons were born to Eber: One was named Peleg, because in his time the earth was divided; his brother was named Joktan. Joktan was the father of Almodad, Sheleph, Hazarmaveth, Jerah, Hadoram, Uzal, Diklah, Obal, Abimael, Sheba, Ophir, Havilah and Jobab. All these were sons of Joktan. The region where they lived stretched from Mesha toward Sephar, in the eastern hill country. These are the sons of Shem by their clans and languages, in their territories and nations. These are the clans of Noah's sons, according to

> *their lines of descent, within their nations. From these the nations spread out over the earth after the flood."*

This is rather an impressive detailed genealogy that could not be better organized had the record been researched by the popular modern day *Ancestry.com*. But as for the man named Nimrod, one can only speculate as to his true stature and nature. Much evidence survives suggesting Nimrod's human linage sews the seeds of philosophies and religious perceptions of grand empires that continue to echo into our 21st century world. There are few scholars in disagreement with the premise that modern civilization begins in Mesopotamia, along with basic theologies of god worship. But are all these gods equal; and do they just represent mankind's psychological need to create a deity? Or are these gods sourced from conditions and experience more existential?

Many ancient texts, and particularly the written Torah, make reference to an age of gods and demigods even older than this. An age when Seraph creatures visit the earth of mankind and devise techniques to synthesize and inseminate a new kind of DNA, producing a breed of human corrupt and monstrous from the original design. This mechanically living being defined somewhere between animal and human. These offspring become known as the *Nephilim*.

Unlike their progenitors, the *Nephilim* are able to produced children through direct copulation. They and their children become the supermen of folklore and a technologically advanced race forming the foundation of legend. They are the fabled dragon's teeth seeded into the gene pool of every culture. Even though latent, the host survivors that step off Noah's Ark retain the code of original corruption in their DNA after the old world destruction.

Let us stop and think about this definition describing the concept of a *superman* within context of present day society. A superman is a being that resembles a human, but endowed with abilities exceeding the standard definition of what it means to be human. We are immediately inspired with the vision of a person capable of lifting locomotives and leaping over tall buildings with a single bound. This superman would be stronger, smarter, and more adaptable to various conditions. A superman would not need special environment suits, protective gear, nor have necessity for diplomacy. Such beings would stand unchallenged, except by resistance of another being endowed with equal abilities. But would such a human really be human in the conventional sense?

As already postulated the seat of consciousness is the human soul. B*ut what is the nature of a soul inspired by spirits of rebellion?* Now deprived of choice, these children of devils become the condition of sin. They represent something unnatural to God's perfect creation and are condemned from the moment of their conception. Perhaps these are the souls of purgatory referenced in almost every religion. Entities conditionally exiled in outer darkness, a place existing between the temporal condition of earth and the entropic finality of hell. But where do children of the *Nephilim* appear in context of contemporary human history?

We might find at least some of these answers in the bosom of Classical Homeric Greece. Here the idyllic pictorial beginning of western civilization and birthplace of the Greek gods of antiquity. It is said that before Olympus, Titans walked the earth, terrible creatures ruthlessly destructive. The issue of these grand progenitors born with more anthropomorphic passions nearer to the mortal condition of humanity, than the altogether ruthless nature of their fathers. According to legend, the children of these first gods live on Mount Olympus, a place, both physical and non-corporeal. These Olympian gods capable of transporting by will or by apparatus to other locations; and are able to change matter and rearrange energy. They can shape-shift with the goal to impregnate a fertile human female. Sometimes these encounters are brutal rapes; sometimes by beguile of pretense. Very often these lustful acts result in conception of a hybrid child. The offspring children do not make Olympus their home, but are *"earthbound"*. Nevertheless, their legacies outshine even the gods. Names like Hercules, Achilles, and Perseus ring loudly the accolades of Greek reverence of great deeds; whereas, the gods Zeus, Poseidon, and Hermes are only references of irresistible force executed by irrevocable decree. These children of the gods are in fact mortal men, but possessed with extraordinary ability. This makes them worthy of respect and valor in the eyes of their peers.

Men may kneel in awe to gods, but only men of exceptional character and mortal identity worthy of true devotion. A reverence that continues to this day by our love of modern day gladiators in sports arenas and irresistible attraction to pop stardom. It is in human nature to choose a strong role model for positions of tribute and authority.

Because of unconscious awareness within each of us that there is potential of a better man than presently perceived, mankind longs pensively to be revived from latent decline. One might also call this *"the Christ code"*, or an embedded archetype of what man originally meant to be. It is this better DNA capable of saving by rewriting the old corrupted a quantum value based on entopic collapse. Innately, we look intuitively for a Messiah: one chosen from our midst to save mankind by defeating death and injustice.

Another way of thinking about this is to consider the practical application of electromagnetic resistance. All matter and energy within the conceivable universe retains a quantum signature unique, which can only be comparable to other states. Scientific principles of strong and weak forces attempt to reconstruct this model of potential. In fact our entire perception of reality based on this flawed principal, as we are taught to believe that greater the power the more perfect the code. The mind of secular reasoning embraces this lie as proof of logical design, elevating the present quantifiable genius of man into a race of immortals. In desperate attempt to disannul intent of created design, the mind of this world attempts to redefine existence from within the bubble of a collapsing universe. Although the code may potentially be perfect; the existing model flawed, requiring fundamental revision. This reminds me of the famous line in Milton's Paradise Lost, when Satan defiantly proclaims *"It is better to rule in hell, than to serve in heaven!"*

In historical context of primordial history there is much speculation about the genetic difference of Neanderthal man compared to those believed to be his ancestors and descendents. Namely us zoologically classified as the glorified fruit of this genetic first. Some think this enigma to be an evolutionary oddity produced by external manipulation. Not everyone, including Theologians, agree that Neanderthal man an inferior prototype of what man has become. The biblical account states emphatically that all air breathing flesh upon the face of the world perished. Nowhere does it make reference to any hybrid humans walking the earth after Noah and his family stepped upon dry land to reclaim the earth. It seems unlikely that God would hide this oversight from Abraham's seed even to this day. It is more likely that the little we know about these beings of different genetic character represents a more durable and intellectually diverse human. Not wishing for the moment to digress into an argument of retro- DNA and modern gene-splicing techniques resulting in hybrid species, I would like to point out that there is no suggestive evidence that these early prototypes malevolent; or that they tried to subdue the local population to establish themselves as ruling tyrants. As far as investigative research can determine, these giants were relatively peaceful in nature, perhaps even bringing a wiser and more creative enlightenment to hominid ancestry. Also, we have no idea how a living body might change during the aging of almost a thousand years. Remembering that Noah is already 600 earth years old when he began building the arch, and lives another 350 years after the flood. No doubt his three sons inherit the same characteristics of longevity. The wives carry the genes of the rest of mankind, including those of the genetically enhanced *Nephilim*.

According to the Genesis genealogy, Shem, Noah's first born lives to be over 600 years. Perhaps as a result of environmental modification, successive future generations begin to live shorter lives naturally. These survivors and their offspring, would gradual adapt to altered gravity conditions and to the damaging effects of changed radiation spectrums. Increased exposure to ultraviolent light and oxidation of the atmosphere begins to take a fatal toll. As life expectancy shortens mental agility begins to decline. By the time the patriarch Abraham obeys the faithful call of God in a dream, nearly a half millennium has passed. Abraham lives only to be one hundred and seventy-five years. A little over 400 centuries later, Moses, Israel's deliver from Egypt, dies at a hundred and twenty years. And the natural human life spans have decreased ever since. You might say that surviving man found himself on an alien world much different than the one that existed before the cataclysm. But what is the scientific explanation?

Recent strides in the field of microbiology have provided some discreet insight into molecular cohesion of cellular building block construction. Since DNA is the signature of all living things, from microbes to more complex organisms, containing the mitochondria machinery to build the genetic material necessary for cell management, it represents the unique blueprint of all living entities. However, it is messenger RNA *(the code transmitter)* that insures the integrity of gene transcription by building protein chains out of amino acids. It is also the transcriber of memory chemically infused for short term storage and latent patterns passed on through hereditary genes. Any first year student of biology will agree to this well studied process. However, there is some disagreement as to the vital role this process plays constructing the end product. Not only is RNA the code-master, but also an architect, infused with the ability to revise the plan of the original instructions. Whereas, *DNA* is the topographic map of design, *RNA* the actual responder to real time reconstruction. This is also why viruses use single-strand RNA, and not DNA, to invade an organism through a process called *reverse-transcriptase* to become potent retrovirus, such as Ebola, Hepatitis C, and Aids. It is only because of the presence of this retro DNA organizer that successive offspring capable of adaptive survival. This raises the question: is RNA really a retro gene, or a more resilient chemically reactive code to supervise the integrity of a surviving species?

First we must understand a little better how this process works. At first glance RNA is as a mirror image of DNA, but in one dimension only: a reflection of reverse engineering coded as single-stranded RNA, then translated into a more complex chemical code on only one side of double-stranded DNA to genome into cell reproduction with either beneficial or destructive consequence. There is ongoing research that suggests this process, known as RNA editing, responsible for the innovation of natural selection of a spices to undergo physical change in response to a less hospitable environment. A known example is the ability of canines to adapt to colder climates with decreased abundance of food, thus requiring morphology of hair follicle, longer fangs, and even increase in body size. A better example is a recent study demonstrating the chemical process by which Octopus' adapt to extreme water temperature changes from tropical to arctic conditions. Through a reaction of RNA editing of protein chains along *ion channels* responsible for the animal's physiological adaptive transition, cellular morphology occurs, making it adaptive to radically different environments. This proves conclusively for the first time that natural selection is a built-in response, and thus providing insight into the complex role of proteins stored in RNA coding triggered by altered environmental conditions in an attempt to compensate through biological editing of species. There is much academic acceptance that differences in chromosome morphology found among humans living in different regions of the world evidence of Natural Selection. These subtle instructions affecting skin pigmentation and other physiological adaptations observed in different regions of the earth. This design integrated into the genome to ensure survival through changing conditions.

New studies are underway by pharmacology giants around the world to edit RNA as a measure to control viral infections. This novel approach holds exciting promise to the vision of an antiseptic world absent of disease. The inherent danger is the incumbent morphology response to instructions not provided by organic nature. In other words, the premise of scientific evaluation is that man is a sequence of evolutionary change from lower to higher function, inherently flawed, and in need of further correction. Drug producers no longer content just to treat system failure, but are determined to redefine biology. Ignoring the architectural design of the host organism within context powerful chemical agents produced to alter overall body function. This is proven to lead into chemical dependency even on the most basic autonomic delivery systems like heart rhythm and blood flow. Although a goal of slightly increased longevity achieved at great expense, it also ensures a weakened gene pool. Future manipulation of Messenger RNA relies on the same premise that a correctable mistake exists in nature. To circumvent the embedded mechanics of this little understood code instructor creates a concern of even greater risk. Venturing into this unexplored territory with the goal to extend life may very well lead to the downfall of civilization as we know it heralding in even worse disaster. It should begin to become obvious that the base interpretation of data formation as critical as the actual data used to create a model. As noble as man may be in through present consent, he is not made to live forever in present format. This is a built-in failsafe monitoring all organic and inorganic structures within thermodynamic context.

The future of RNA editing is an avenue evoking extreme concerns in even those most dedicated to existential values. The question arises if it should be done at all, and if so with what precaution. In nature this process usually happens gradually to ensure the ultimate goal of species survival. There are examples where radical changes accomplished within the lifespan of a single or can happen in a few generations. There are many forces monitoring the process with delicate scrutiny. It is just the nature of things.

I suppose you are wondering what all this has to do with post diluvium man, and *the world that was then.* No one knows with any certainty the nature or physical characteristics of these first Homo sapiens. I speculate that Neanderthal man more near to the perfected image of the creator than men are today: men of superior strength and wisdom able to adapt to a world of much different character. These first humans were given authority even over the great dinosaurs. Using a colloquial science fiction comparison, they would have been as fearless and determined as *Klingons* on steroids. (*For those unversed in star lore, Klingons are a ruthless warrior clan of testosterone-driven characters in the Hollywood Star Trek saga*).

After the expulsion of Adam and Eve from the domain of Eden, the seed of man flourishes upon the face of a world framed into a finite matrix of an entropic universe. Cain becomes the prodigal son of jealousy and murder. Abel the blood foundation of Satan's *first estate* bridging a temporal alliance through the flesh in an attempt to further pollute the immeasurable potential contained in the living souls of humankind. Men of this beginning age larger, stronger, and intellectually superior, meaning they are able to access more than the six percent or so limit of brain activity observed in modern humans. Only a few in the beginning, they quickly begin to subdue the untamed earth by force. As their numbers increase, they learn to work together, building safe havens, teaching their children and their children's children the ways of rebellion and death. These children of men start to trust more in the works of their hands than in the mighty hand that has established the universe for their present dominion.

Nevertheless, a few remain faithful, their hearts prostrate toward the future kingdom of God and to the glory of the creator, recognizing their creation in an image potentially higher than the angels. Their faith resting not in the might of their weaker flesh, but in an unseen promise of a better estate prepared for them through the victory of a coming Messiah. Being not high-minded dreamers of some better place, they embrace the challenge of flesh and blood toil, submitting in humility to the moment, waiting patiently for God to restore the potential of original creation.

Still Satan is not content with just the fall of humanity into mortal misery, but desires self-worship and the absolute corruption of man's immortal soul. This angel of sin and those that follow him know that designed within the human seed an invaluable pearl of eternal life.

Therefore they abandon their heavenly habitation to indwell human host willing to receive them. They begin dissecting and studying these men of the earth to gain better understanding of the mechanical design. Through genetic manipulation and medical intervention, these immense beings construct compatible avatar bodies for themselves in order to copulate with human females, thus corrupting the gene pool in an attempt to prevent the Messiah from ever being conceived. From these unholy unions are born the *Nephilim*, tyrannical creatures bent upon conquest and destruction. They are giants in the literal sense, but also brilliant in devising technologies to ensure their absolute dominance. So wicked are these offspring of angels that in time they begin to war among themselves, carving up the earth into borders of dominion, and even extending their violence into the heavens. The dominos soon all aligned, now only a matter of time before inevitable destruction.

Noah is a righteous man (a man whose faith remains uncorrupted) and hears God's commandment to build an ark specifically of golfer wood, with precise instructions of dimensions and how to seal the seams against leakage. It is interesting to note, that under certain conditions of radical expansion and contraction as a result of pressure changes, a dowelled wooden vessel would be more resilient than a riveted vessel constructed of steel today. The unknown density and strength of this fabled wood less important than the workmanship and prescribed design. In Chapter 6 of Genesis, verses1-22 (NIV) God provides Noah with terms of a new covenant to spare him and his wife, his three sons and their wives, and the future promise of animal kind.

> *"When human beings began to increase in number on the earth and daughters were born to them, the sons of God saw that the daughters of humans were beautiful, and they married any of them they chose. Then the LORD said, "My Spirit will not contend with humans forever, for they are mortal ; their days will be a hundred and twenty years." The Nephilim were on the earth in those days—and also afterward—when the sons of God went to the daughters of humans and had children by them. They were the heroes of old, men of renown. The LORD saw how great the wickedness of the human race had become on the earth, and that every inclination of the thoughts of the human heart was only evil all the time. The LORD regretted that he had made human beings on the earth, and his heart was deeply troubled. So the LORD said, "I will wipe from the face of the earth the human race I have created—and with them the animals, the birds and the creatures that move along the ground—for I regret that I have made them." But Noah found favor in the eyes of the LORD. This is the account of Noah and his family. Noah was a righteous man, blameless among the people of his time, and he walked faithfully with God.*
>
> *Noah had three sons: Shem, Ham and Japheth. Now the earth was corrupt in God's sight and was full of violence.*

God saw how corrupt the earth had become, for all the people on earth had corrupted their ways. So God said to Noah, "I am going to put an end to all people, for the earth is filled with violence because of them. I am surely going to destroy both them and the earth. So make yourself an ark of cypress wood; make rooms in it and coat it with pitch inside and out.

This is how you are to build it: The ark is to be three hundred cubits long, fifty cubits wide and thirty cubits high. Make a roof for it, leaving below the roof an opening one cubit high all around. Put a door in the side of the ark and make lower, middle and upper decks. I am going to bring floodwaters on the earth to destroy all life under the heavens, every creature that has the breath of life in it. Everything on earth will perish. But I will establish my covenant with you, and you will enter the ark—you and your sons and your wife and your sons' wives with you.

You are to bring into the ark two of all living creatures, male and female, to keep them alive with you. Two of every kind of bird, of every kind of animal and of every kind of creature that moves along the ground will come to you to be kept alive. You are to take every kind of food that is to be eaten and store it away as food for you and for them." Noah did everything just as God commanded him."

"All that God Commanded him, so did he." In simple terms, the man Noah obeys God's instructions in spite of the wondrous technological achievements he no doubt witnessed in his generation since exiting the womb. He remembers and trusts more the God, who created heaven and earth and Adam and Eve in his own image, than the many arrogant gods that roam the world like raging lions. If the story of Noah's ark were not so engrained into our social consciousness, it would be profound beyond any measure. But because the minds of modern reason conditioned to

a myopic secular understanding, we dismiss this extraordinary account as a fairy tale to entertain small children.

We know from the Biblical record what happens to Noah and his family, and the successful reseeding of the earth. We are also told that the rest of humankind, along with all the air breathing animals, perished. But were all the *Nephilim* destroyed as well? Being the offspring of angelic creatures, then surely Satan's plan for these hybrid souls not concluded. When Jesus walked the earth, he encounters many demons, which originate from a dimensional realm referred to as *an outer darkness*. This is not the hell of the Hebrew *Geneah*, or the burning lake of everlasting fire. Nor is this the transpiring kingdom of Lucifer established upon the seven worldly estates of temporal entropy. Rather, this is the habitation of old souls inter-spatially trapped, seeking migration into the living presence. These demons are the spirits of the air, as referenced in the Bible, the steadfast will of their rebellious progenitors (though absent of flesh), yet endowed with a physical essence to invade and to possess. We have the natural tendency to anthropomorphize, or to make human and endow with human emotions, these ancient *men of renown*. Yet, this is contrary to our social unconscious revived through legends and perceived myths of an incomprehensible history of bloodlust. In every ancient text that makes direct reference to these creatures, they are neither human nor beast, representing a hybrid race of tyrants conquering and laying destruction in their path. They require absolute worship and sacrifice of human blood. Those who follow their rule become as demigods possessed of the same spirits of evil. However, it is logical to assume that the offspring of these *Nephilim* had offspring of their own, as already outlined, further polluting the human gene pool. Since the sins of the father pass down to the children, these offspring of the *Nephilim* are the most probable producers of technologies to reach beyond the confinement of earth and into the cosmos. Not with the intent to abandon earth, but in an attempt to mimic creation in the hope of altering the entropic countdown. They are the inventors of lighter than air travel and inter-dimensional vehicles capable of bending time and space. Their ultimate corrupting objective: to make compatible the human DNA code for medium possession by angelic principalities. In other words, to terra-form the human soul so that Lucifer might be born of flesh and of spirit and become the false Christ to a sinful humanity.

Nevertheless, as grand as the unfolding universe, they fail to change the cascade of causality that began the moment of Adam's deception. With the help of their progenitors, they succeed in unlocking mysteries contained in the molecular bond of subatomic matter by channeling entropic energy through a helix matrix grander than any conceived of today. As these experiments escalate, this race of super intelligence seeks ways to reshape local space on the subatomic level. This inevitably results in an atomic cascade that will redefine the curvature of time progression, changing the plane position of planet earth in relation to its central gravity field and neighboring planetoids. But not all these super beings perish; rather many become inter-dimensionally trapped in a layer that we might call subspace. Here time and consequence unfold on a grander scale than experienced on the temporal plane of local time progressive.

These trapped beings are capable of manifesting for brief periods in chronological time through the soul energy of a willing living host. In this state, they are the demons and minions of angelic dispensation, which the present consciousness perceives as contained ghost, living monsters, and alien creatures. For as long as the host is alive, they can instigate great evil upon the world by destroying all in their path and by spreading across the globe like consuming locust. These are the blood thirsty warlords and tyrants, the murders and the torturers of mankind against mankind, and charismatic ideologies descending as pestilence upon peaceful coexistence. Demons are forces of potential: some more powerful; others less so. As I have already mentioned in an earlier chapter, religions that overtly recognize demonic influence agree that there are demons of alliance that can produce a terrestrial condition of wealth and power to individual prosperity, until challenged by a demon of greater force.

Through a process called exorcism demon possession can be broken even without the conscious consent of the infected host. On several occasions, Jesus commands demons to vacate possessed individuals, which they do with deliberate protest. Some demons are too powerful to be exorcised by word only, but require prayer and fasting on the part of the exorcist, as noted by Jesus to his disciples after they fail to cast out a certain type of spirit. Presumably, these exorcised spirits return to their habitation of outer darkness reserved unto the *Day of Judgment*. But unlike their progenitors, they retain knowledge of flesh existence and subtly crafty. This makes their presence particularly appealing to those in tuned to their habitation. It also makes them comprehensive of human value and human aspiration. Since they once reached toward the heavens in anticipation of changing the clockwork organization of a universe spinning toward entropy preordained by the first Adam's fall. Even these may retain some hope in the resurrection of the second Adam made perfect.

Because these souls are damned, they can only be reprieved through special permission, as when the legion of demons appealed to Jesus to allow them to migrate into the herd of swine, rather than to be immediately exiled into outer darkness. This act of leniency by the Lord is mysterious. Why allow these evil beings a place to further destruction? Were not the swine, though born as unclean animals, also creations of God? And where did these entities migrate to after the herd of swine chocked to death in the sea? These are questions better addressed by versed theologians. Nevertheless, it implies that there exists a dispensation even to these arrant consciousnesses that might seek a place of mercy.

I personally do not know what God has ordained for all creation. Only that it is my firm belief that all things possible in the resurrection. I once communicated with a soul trapped in a corridor of darkness and locked in symbiotic bondage to a demonic spirit. A sense of timelessness to this place, as that place I was before being freed by power of the Holy Spirit. I am at the mouth of an abyss I once inhabited and reason with a chained chimera to repent in the name of Jesus Christ. In this moment, I feel powerless, and yet faithful to the Christ in me. This moment I think of a scripture from the Book of Mathew, Chapter 18, verse 18 (KJV) where Jesus says:

> *"Truly I say to you, whatever you bind on earth shall have been bound in heaven; and whatever you loose on earth shall have been loosed in heaven."*

It seems strange to have compassion for a demon, yet in this timeless expanse divided by time, I am sent to intercede on behalf of a living soul inextricable bound. It is my belief that God allowed me into that dominion of darkness, the Holy Spirit restraining the powers there, so that I might pray for the extrication of this demonic possession. This implies to me that capacity of choice still resides in spiritual symbiosis confined in a place of neither time nor space. Not even the immutable dominion of hell greater than the vision of hope manifested through God's Messiah, Prince over every principality. I continue to pray for this soul even now, believing the resurrection possible even to the minions trapped in darkness reserved unto the *Day of Final Judgment*.

The scriptures declare that it is expedient for Christ, our Lord, to first descend into hell and preach the gospel, then ascend to a position of completion in God's holy trinity. In the first book of Peter, Chapter 3, verses 18-22 (KJV) we read:

> *"For Christ also hath once suffered for sins, the just for the unjust, that he might bring us to God, being put to death in the flesh, but quickened by the Spirit: By which also he went and preached unto the spirits in prison; Which sometime were disobedient, when once the longsuffering of God waited in the days of Noah, while the ark was a preparing, wherein few, that is, eight souls were saved by water. The like figure whereunto even baptism doth also now save us (not the putting away of the filth of the flesh, but the answer of a good conscience toward God,) by the resurrection of Jesus Christ: Who is gone into heaven, and is on the right hand of God; angels and authorities and powers being made subject unto him."*

Chapter 12
ALIENS IN HOLLYWOOD HILLS

The greatest barrier to understanding the meaningful text contained in the book known as the Holy Bible is the clockwork compression organized through logical discourse. In other words, man stubbornly designs the nature of time and space to fit the limits of his imagination, rather than to imagine the unimaginable. Even though these collected manuscripts contain coherent chronological record of events, it is so easily dismissed by the secular mind. Not because it is disjointed, or because of abject disagreement with the accumulated evidence, but because it conflicts with the definition of probability imposed by a reason of limited perception.

Rational science agrees that something happened in the not so distant cosmic past *(by temporal calculation about 13 billion years ago)* resulting in an acceleration of space time expansion. Through logical extrapolation models created to describe the aftermath of chaos. But try for a moment to imagine from outside the conditions when the universe begins. There is no infraction of time, nor coalescence of elemental patterns. Now imagine beginning of time as elastic, expanding and contracting without spatial dimension or locality at intervals of infinite velocity. Suddenly a day becomes a thousand years and a thousand years a day. From this non-linear perspective an expanding singularity appears creating an illusion of time and space as observed from any given point inside the bubble.

In this scenario, the earth a much different place, radically dissimilar in terms of geology and atmospheric pressures, perhaps not even the same on a molecular level. It is further logical to assume that the cataclysm precipitating the global changes of Noah's time may have caused a fracture in elemental time and space, causing a convergence of temporal reality. If this is the case, then it is possible that subspace portals opened; thus allowing a directional constant of time flow. But in the same instant the fabric of local space radically altered, creating dimensional folds with different frequency signatures, fundamentally changing reality.

Such a phenomenon would act like the panes in a glass enclosure with mirrors positioned at refracting angles, thus creating the illusion of linear existence. It is significant to consider that from this position of perception dictates every conclusion we collectively experience as real, thus making historical reference hypothetical. Science labels present cosmic position as the *"Goldie Lock Zone"* of existence, precisely balanced conditions allowing life as we know it.

To any consciousness existing in vortexes outside of this controlled interval, then the concept of time and space radically altered. To these trapped entities, the elapse of time compressed into moments, with intermittent glimpses into the slower progression of mortal event spanning many generations. For them time and space is rhetorical; history only intervals of manifestation and their influence in human affairs only fleeting. They continuously seek locality in physical form. But what are these entities and from where to they come?

The Biblical description of the *Nephilim* and their offspring are beings endowed with superior strength, as well as enhanced calculable reasoning; whose very existence poses an existential threat to the old earth and surrounding space. They become the embodied force of rebellion against God and his creation, exercising diabolical experimentation to change the imposed law of entropy. These children of devils are not content to remain bound within the confinement of earth's atmosphere and devise technologies of space travel to explore the delicately balanced cosmological clock. In doing so they will ignite the catalyst that nearly destroys everything. Although I am not an active advocate for the Book of Enoch for reasons of unverifiable source evidence, I nevertheless find the text compelling when referencing the known facts about the *Nephilim*. The following cryptic passage found in Chapters 18 and 19:

"And beyond these mountains is a place, the edge of the great earth; there the heavens come to an end. And I saw a great chasm among pillars of heavenly fire. And I saw in it pillars of fire descending; and they were immeasurable toward the depth and toward the height. And Uriel said to me, "There stand the angels who mingled with the women. And their spirits—having assumed many forms—bring destruction on men and lead them astray to sacrifice to demons as to gods until the day of the great judgment, in which they will be judged with finality. And the wives of the transgressing angels will become sirens." Beyond this chasm I saw a place where there was neither firmament of heaven above, nor firmly founded earth beneath it. Neither was there water on it, nor bird; but the place was desolate and fearful. There I saw seven stars like great burning mountains. To me, when I inquired about them, the angel said, "This place is the end of heaven and earth; this has become a prison for the stars and the hosts of heaven. The stars that are rolling over in the fire, these are they that transgressed the command of the Lord in the beginning of their rising, for they did not come out in their appointed times. And he was angry with them and bound them until the time of the consummation of their sins—ten thousand years." I, Enoch, alone saw the visions, the extremities of all things. And no one among humans has seen as I saw."

Wherever these *Nephilim* presently reside is a continuum incompatible with present value of time and space. They are neither flesh, nor are they spirit, inter-dimensionally trapped in a region of subspace the Bible refers to as an *outer darkness*. For this reason, they seek a living host to indwell, in order to reenter into temporal existence. Through this condition of shared consciousness, the evil soul obtains cognition within context of measured time. However, for the deception to be effective, there must contain a discourse of reason, a recognizable context with identifiable markers of defined logic.

Christ's earthly ministry brings more than salvation to a world restrained in sin. It manifests as light into consciousness, inspiring discernment of unconscious forces all around us. The spirit of Christ reveals shadowy strongholds and true source of demonic possession, as even these ancient creatures subject to his command. The interspaced principalities of their dark lords intersecting time and distance inconceivable through natural reason become inconsequential to the magnitude of a new emerging heavenly kingdom.

Men no longer trapped in the snare of their destiny, to live and to die according to a fixed chronology of fleshly events. In the name of God's Messiah, mortal beings now possess power even over dominions ruled by monarchs of darkness in high places. Before Jesus walks the earth as a man, demonic forces rule with an iron fist of fear and oppression, now made powerless by the name of God's only begotten son. In Luke, Chapter 10, verses 16-20 (KJV) Jesus sends many of his followers out into the world to testify of this dramatic change in the spiritual balance.

> *"He that hears you hears me; and he that despises you despises me; and he that despises me despises him that sent me. And the seventy returned again with joy, saying, Lord, even the devils are subject unto us through thy name. And he said unto them, I beheld Satan as lightning fall from heaven. Behold, I give unto you power to tread on serpents and scorpions, and over all the power of the enemy: and nothing shall by any means hurt you. Notwithstanding in this rejoice not, that the spirits are subject unto you; but rather rejoice, because your names are written in heaven."*

A dramatic spiritual shift happens again after the end of the Second World War. Nazi Germany revived new technologies from occult relics believed significant throughout recorded history. There are persistent rumors that Hitler personally sent agents to precise locations for purposes of recovering certain artifacts believed essential to the success of the *New Reich*. Perhaps this was a delusional belief by a group of men suffering from severe psychosis; but more likely the rational engineering of ancient minds, as old as the foundations of the world. In just a few short years, Germany goes from a modest industrial country to a technological giant in possessing of innovative war machinery. The destructively advanced armaments on the battlefield insignificant compared to other apparatus' in varying stages of development. By the end of the war, plans are already well advanced to develop a nuclear arsenal, as well as stable energy matrixes capable of negating gravitational influence. Even prototype flying saucer designs recovered by the victorious western alliance forces; and many other superior inventions spirited away to secret areas for further analysis. Interestingly the Third Reich's is obsessed with genetic engineering of human and animal DNA. The significance of these facts cannot be underemphasized, as evidenced by the many horrific experiments conducted upon European Jews in the many Concentration Camps. Why this obsession and why specifically the Jews?

There are many unsupported theories, based on secret intelligence, of the possibility that a small armada of Nazi scientist and engineers escape to secret bases beneath the miles of ice covering Antarctica. It is further speculated that this is the source of many UFO sightings in recent history since the end of that grand global conflict. But the mystery does not end here.

The persistent phenomenon of UFO reports has become common in recent years, representing, either an epidemic of hysteria, or else a pandemic of an imminent and systematic invasion. I am not suggesting that *"they"* are here, but that *"they"* have always been here. The real question being: *what are they really?* There are, in fact, so many UFO sightings around the world daily that little more than a passing reference made on the evening report. The presence of digital handheld devices usually uploads images of unexplainable lights in the sky onto a social media platform long before a news team has opportunity to verify the information. So let us examine first at the nature and history of *Ufology*.

Ufologists are people who study reports, sightings, and physical evidence related to unidentified flying objects. Through the years volumes of records have been amassed by individuals and professional teams in the hope of either dismissing the events as episodic hysteria, or in an attempt to better understand their nature. Records of unexplainable UFO observances go back more than 2000 years, each described with a flavor relevant to the time context. The ancient Romans often ascribe them with military potential, calling these ephemeral sightings as "*ships in the air*", coinciding with omens of good and evil. Later, during the Middle East wars over possession of the Holy City of Jerusalem, celestial incursions referred to as *angelic forces* in full battle gear. Even as recent as World War II *Foo Fighters* commonly reported and occasionally photographed by battle-weary Bomber crews. Still to this present day these fast moving metallic balls and saucers of light have not been logically explained away. Improved networks of sophisticated radar stations on the ground, as well as famous astronauts in space, bear witness that something else is out there that defies normal laws of gravitation and acceleration. It would be easy to devote an entire book to this fascinating singular subject. Yet, I believe this to be counterproductive within context. Let it suffice that the UFO phenomenon more than a linage of crackpot activist motivated by the misguided hopes in an alien potential.

Objectively, there seems to be more than one type of extraterrestrial vehicle involved in the many described sightings. Or better put, more than a singular type of manifestation. We must remember that our atmosphere is a gaseous environment with a layered stratosphere. Anything that disturbs this firmament through penetration creates an observable trail. Saucer or spherical shaped objects most often appear as balls of light with maneuverability aspects impossible within conventional time and space and possessing ability to vanish just as portentously. These are the evidence of manifestation, but not the actual vehicle. Another type seems to incorporate both physical and metaphysical potential. Here there is a physical craft involved, capable of remaining dimensionally suspended between temporal and non-temporal locality within context of conventional time and space. These are the traditional aliens and apparatus' of physical transition. In other words, this is an insertion technique of the *"demons of the air"* into the temporal plane we presently know as reality. The space between manifestations occurs within context of human existence over a period of generations; but to them the simultaneous elapse of only moments.

Then there is the physical craft, technologically constructed to transition into temporal reality. These are the first wave of infiltration made possible by the melding of Nazi science and the occult. This is the inception point of trans-human worship deceptively embedded in the foundation of our modern world of technological advancement and paving the way for a far more sophisticated invasion with little resistance. Make no mistake-- *world consciousness is being conditioned to embrace these demons as their collective saviors!* Since the beginning of the new twenty-first century, strange configurations of lights in the night sky have provoked several theories, as to their meaning and origin. Commonly referred to as *Maitreya's Star*, these well documented and repeated patterns of UFO appearances possess a portentous significance to those who are followers of the occult. Stemming from the philosophy of Buddhism of a hierarchical transcendence to the eventual incarnation of the Sanat Kumara, or *The Lord of the World*, the sign of Maitreya is the most persistent manifestation to be documented in recent history. These sightings are often associated with the apparitions labeled as a *"Christ"* manifested upon every continent. These false Christ are believed by new age religious groups to be the messengers of Lucifer sent to prepare the world for his descent into mortal existence. Interestingly, these devoted worshippers know this fallen angel by name, convinced that he is also the same antichrist referenced in the Book of Revelation. Only that their version of future events radically differs from the scriptural warning. Instead of being the nemesis of God, Lucifer is a misunderstood savior of mankind, likened to the story of Prometheus, desires only good for the children of his special interest. To his committed followers, he is not the devil, but a victim of God's jealousy. However, it is important to note that this premise based on a static perception of existence, as defined through an uniformitarian assumption void of entropic meaning. These alien creatures will have as much in common with humanity, as farmers with their prize livestock. To fallen Satan and the angels that fell with him the human collective only a means to an end. The true objective is first to deceive and then corrupt God's most valued creation. Perhaps, this Lucifer will possess some mortal apprehensiveness in the beginning, but once this mortal dies and he becomes transcendent, then he will manifest as the tyrannical soulless beast that he truly is, as revealed in *The Book of Revelation*, Chapter 13 verses 5-18 (NIV).

> *"The beast was given a mouth to utter proud words and blasphemies and to exercise its authority for forty-two months. It opened its mouth to blaspheme God, and to slander his name and his dwelling place and those who live in heaven. It was given power to wage war against God's holy people and to conquer them. And it was given authority over every tribe, people, language and nation. All inhabitants of the earth will worship the beast—all whose names have not been written in the Lamb's book of life, the Lamb who was slain from the creation of the world. Whoever has ears, let them hear. "If anyone is to go into captivity, into captivity they will go. If anyone is to be killed with the sword, with the sword they will be killed." This calls for patient endurance and faithfulness on the part of God's people. Then I saw a second beast, coming out of the earth. It had two horns like a lamb, but it spoke like a dragon. It exercised all the authority of the first beast on its behalf, and made the earth and its inhabitants worship the first beast, whose fatal wound had been healed. And it performed great signs, even causing fire to come down from heaven to the earth in full view of the people. Because of the signs it was given power to perform on behalf of the first beast, it deceived the inhabitants of the earth. It ordered them to set up an image in honor of the beast who was wounded by the sword and yet lived. The second beast was given power to give breath to the image of the first beast, so that the image could speak and cause all who refused to worship the image to be killed. It also forced all people, great and small, rich and poor, free and slave, to receive a mark on their right hands or on their foreheads, so that*

> they could not buy or sell unless they had the mark, which is the name of the beast or the number of its name. This calls for wisdom. Let the person who has insight calculate the number of the beast, for it is the number of a man. That number is 666."

It is Hollywood in the early 1950s that first romanticizes the smooth seamless exterior of flying saucer design, speculating that other worldly beings of benevolent character have built and inhabit them, not much different than us. Yes, some of them might be bad, like the emotional mixture found among human beings; but there are others that might even be better than human, ushering in a new age of technological advancement.

The questions in everyone's mind then became: *are they real, and are they extraterrestrial?* It is only after the movie ET that unworldly creatures obtained a cute fuzzy appeal, now familiar to nearly everyone engaged in film entertainment pastime. Something not so fuzzy and cute are the many testimonies of people claiming they have been physically abducted by strange alien beings and taken to what they can only describe as a medical facility inside a spaceship equipped with terrifyingly unusual surgical instruments. These beings have human-like attributes, but with most inhuman features. The experience is portrayed as being in a waking dream, a kind of sleep paralysis, being aware of the event, yet powerless to resist. Sometimes these abductions take place while the person is in bed (without the knowledge of their spouse) and returned before morning. This sounds very similar to the accounts of demonic possession. Consider that demons of the air are all around us, constantly searching for a willing host to receive them. Their first assault is to find a familiar avenue through the imagination or a vice of desire. And once they know you, they never stop trying to find you again, unless prevented by a greater force.

I personally have had experiences such as this, feeling the presence of something powerful and oppressive. At these times I call upon the name of Jesus Christ and the presence leaves. It is interesting to note that of the hundreds of alien encounters documented through many years of researcher a consistent pattern emerges. All evidence from supported testimony of the abductees suggests it is possible to stop an abduction experience just by calling upon the name of Jesus. It seems unlikely from personal experience that this coincidental. It suggest that these extraterrestrials less alien to our human culture than we might believe. It is also important to mention that nearly always the primary interest of these beings is in the reproductive organs. Cattle livestock and other animals have been found mutilated, sometimes with their internal organs surgically removed. This sounds uncomfortably familiar when one looks into the meaning of ancient texts that claim to chronicle the events of a pre-history past, also alluded to in the Book of Genesis of the Holy Bible.

Again in the *Book of Enoch*, Chapter 7, there is a reference that the *Nephilim* children *"began to sin against birds, and beast, and reptiles, and fish, and to devour one another's flesh, and drink the blood.* There is at least one among many unreferenced accounts claiming to be from the lost *Book of Jasher* (a supposed contemporary of Enoch) a passage which states *"After the fallen angels went into the daughters of men, the sons of men taught the mixture of animals of one species with another in order to provoke the Lord."*

The worship of supermen has returned upon planet earth, as modern man altogether forgets its long linage of nightmare monsters. Also forgotten, the horror of what this world like before the testimony of brotherly love and a concept of grace prevailed. With each passing generation nations around the globe embrace materialism as the highest potential of existence, while multitudes perish from famine, disease bred of poverty, and displacement caused by escalating wars. While elevated institutions speak of peace and justice, behind the scene they make merchandise of everyone and everything. Good and evil redefined through humanistic values, measured out to the masses as a quantum, rather than the true meaning of compassionate nature. Through the embrace of philosophies to prolong life (measured by the cost of life) mankind has guaranteed a future ruled by demonic forces. Fear of the devil has become a byline; the name of God vain and impotent. Oscar night in Hollywood engages greater interest of creature reverence, than the starving multitudes around the world displaced by war and drought. All forgotten until the next year, and all made irreverent in the shadow of a golden idol.

The allure of *Trans-humanism* has made men spiritually blind to the greater value of being, by denying the greater potential contained in the meaning of a living soul. In an attempt to expand the universe, intellectual reasoning has reduced human existence to a cosmic accident, fearfully clinging to a myopic view of reality no matter how absurd. Although the New Age leaders of this world claim enlightenment, they embrace demigods of invention, worshipping the heroes they have made superior in the face of growing uncertainty.

In recent years Hollywood directors have even turned their imagination to rewrite the meaning contained in the Holy Bible, creating action blockbusters to satisfy a desire for hero- worship inspired through the appetite of a multicultural audience. Consensus of ratings, demanding creative license of blasphemy, mixed with new age secularism has intentionally diminished the motive intervention of the living creator in the course of human events. The man Noah recently depicted as a wild-eyed fanatic driven by human doubt and paranoia. His faith in God depicted as scenes of Shakespearean madness interpreted through a psychosis of comprehension. Perhaps there is some merit to this portrayal; only that by the end, God is written into the scenario merely as an impersonal elevated force of nature. In still another prominent film, the audiences presented with a conflict of two wills. Moses and Pharaoh, romanticized as arch-nemesis, locked in a human struggle of good and evil, based on what they think is best for the survival of their cultures. Two alpha-males leading their armed masses into violent conflict with deterministic fervor, a struggle between two minds of obstinate character, each dedicated to personal conviction. Both arrogantly prideful, portrayed as mortally grounded men lacking the character of true spiritual submission. Again God represented as a cultural element constructed by religion persuasion and intellectual guidance inspired through secular reasoning.

In these analogist scenarios, the history of Israel portrayed as a self-made principality, armed to the teeth, and morally superior, established by military might and instructed by a linage of proud sages. The word Zion has become a battle cry to arms, more than the divinely preserved hill of the holy city of Jerusalem, where Jesus wept because of the hardness of their hearts. In a time of prescription, Messiah must return, whose foot will split the mountains, and whose glory will shine as the sun. This day of salvation will come from the God of heaven to subdue all worldly resistance, delivering Israel as God always has done since the first promise made to Abraham. On this notable day the warlord lust for blood and revenge will be stopped at the source, a power no force on earth, or beyond earth, can resist.

There is another element of media persuasion just as disturbing, and with even greater influence. Personal computer systems are more common than the number of people capable of riding a bicycle. This should be of no surprise, considering the health epidemic ravaging developed societies related to sedentary lifestyles and poor eating habits. But the greater harm of these devices is their ability to control the way we think and ultimately shape what we believe. A well meaning generation has grown up in the shadow of this technology. They are now the thinkers and media engineers of social platforms influential to definitions of political correctness. Because of trolls and pariah bullying, internet giants, such as Google and Facebook, have been forced to imbed in their popular software new detection algorithms; even if it means the crippling end of free speech and independent thinking. And no one seems to notice or express conscious awareness of what this means to the future exercise of free will. The true danger being that this is only the first step toward a metamorphosis into a new consensus of thought and behavior, based on these soulless algorithmic instructions. It is not so difficult to imagine a worldly collective conditioned by peer acceptance and technological directive. A future generation prepared to embrace the artificial visage of hybrid humanity, bearing the promise of an antiseptic trans-humanist society. The world I speak of will have outgrown the idealism of a God: a world, where Christ reduced to mere mortal being with a traceable dynastic linage; and the hope of salvation, a fairytale only.

The even greater danger is secular humanism's embrace of the living God of creation, as a reactive stimulant of an evolutionary force. I can testify with certainty that this is a lie made by the father of lies. God does not throw cosmic dice to prove which species is stronger, which will prove more enlightened, and which will succeed through better genetic pruning. This is and has always been Satan's game. The scriptures of the Bible are inspired by a medium termed the Holy Spirit to provide instructions to the living soul embedded in each one of us. It is an abiding witness signifying that there is much more to reality than the things we think to see.

According to the census records made in the days of Rome's first emperor, Augustus, the grand nephew of Julius Cesar, a man named Jesus, son of Joseph and Mary, born mortal upon the earth in the Jewish province of Bethlehem. From the first word of beginning to the last word of end, every syllable testifies of Messiah to come. This Son of God and Son of Man, the perfect code embodying human salvation is to arrive upon the Temple Mound as deliverer of the Jewish people. It is incomprehensible to religious leaders of the time to believe that this Jesus could be God's chosen. How can one born mortal and counted among sinners of infirmity possibly be the Messiah named by the prophets? According to scriptures Jesus returns to Nazareth in the power of the Holy Spirit after being tempted of the Devil in a wilderness for forty days. Here begins his short ministry upon the earth lasting just three years. This historical testament evidence of not only temporal incursion, but transcendent to every principality everywhere, as recorded in Luke's Gospel, Chapter 4, verses 16-20 (KJV).

> *"And he came to Nazareth, where he had been brought up: and, as his custom was, he went into the synagogue on the Sabbath day, and stood up for to read. And there was delivered unto him the book of the prophet Esaias. And when he had opened the book, he found the place where it was written, The Spirit of the Lord is upon me, because he hath anointed me to preach the gospel to the poor; he hath sent me to heal the brokenhearted, to preach deliverance to*

the captives, and recovering of sight to the blind, to set at liberty them that are bruised, To preach the acceptable year of the Lord. And he closed the book, and he gave it again to the minister, and sat down. And the eyes of all them that were in the synagogue were fastened on him."

Even in the shadow of this grand empire, men of religious understanding sought patiently the heavens for one to deliver them from the weaker forces of worldly power with the might of an irresistible hand. Only they look for the *Messiah Ben David*, the King of Kings, promised by God through the prophets to subdue the earth and restore the house of spiritual Israel and the Holy Temple. They look for the formulae to fit the existing mix; yet ignore the clear prophecy of *Messiah Ben Joseph*, who must first appear to restore all things. What exactly could this mean?

For something to be restored, it must first be something lost that is valued. Mankind represents God's stolen possession. Because Lucifer created initially a most wondrous Morning Star, this beautiful angel grows jealous of God's most endeared creation, a man created in the image of the creator. This jealousy changed malignant; and Lucifer changed to fallen Satan. Instantly war declared in heaven with the soul of the first man Adam in the balance. By free will this Adam chooses to be subdued by pride of the flesh, therefore becoming weak through sin. Through battles of heavenly aggression the first man and woman exiled from the garden of paradise. But God preserves in wisdom a perfect code in the midst of chaos. This is the meaning in the *Messiah Ben Joseph* that comes first to restore that which is lost, both Jew and Gentile. Then will come again *Messiah Ben David* with power and the Holy Angels to pause entropy for a thousand years before final erasure.

Jesus Christ is not an afterthought, but a code made perfect before the singularity of beginning. In scientific terms this second coming a spatial interlace of time dilation, marking the finality of present temporal existence, and emergence of a new heaven and new earth revised on the sub-molecular level with Christ shining as the sun. However, by the same token the spirit of antichrist must first run the course of entropy. This is the man of Satan realized into mortal existence. A man born of this world, embodying the elevated thoughts of worldly wisdom, embellished through material concept of flawed human value. A man destined to proclaim himself the crowning center of creation. In other words, this man of perdition will fulfill that empty place in the arrogance of men's souls with Satan's original doctrine of pride and rebellion. The hour of this beast will last for only a short season, already fallen into the carefully prepared snare of his own design.

But there is another story of mankind's destiny providing hope beyond entropic design. By recognizing and submitting to the will of the true source of all power, the man Jesus becomes the source code of a creation rewriting the old. A potential originating outside of perceived time and space, Jesus becomes Christ by submitting willingly to the will of the Father. The singular evidence of this perfect DNA conceived by the Holy Spirit, made worthy by sifting of generations, preserving a living sacrifice for my sins and the sins of humanity. In the book of the prophet Isaiah, Chapter 53, verses 3-12 (KJV) this profound reference stated with indisputable clarity.

> *"He is despised and rejected of men; a man of sorrows, and acquainted with grief: and we hid as it were our faces from him; he was despised, and we esteemed him not. Surely he hath borne our griefs, and carried our sorrows: yet we did esteem him stricken, smitten of God, and afflicted. But he was wounded for our transgressions, he was bruised for our iniquities: the chastisement of our peace was upon him; and with his stripes we are healed. All we like sheep have gone astray; we have turned everyone to his own way; and the LORD hath laid on him the iniquity of us all. He was oppressed, and he was afflicted, yet he opened not his mouth: he is brought as a lamb to the slaughter, and as a sheep before her shearers is dumb, so he openeth not his mouth. He was taken from prison and from judgment: and who shall declare his generation? for he was cut off out of the land of the living: for the transgression of my people*

was he stricken. And they made his grave with the wicked and with a rich man in his death, although he had done no violence, and there was no deceit in his mouth. Yet it pleased the LORD to bruise him; he hath put him to grief: when thou shalt make his soul an offering for sin, he shall see his seed, he shall prolong his days, and the pleasure of the LORD shall prosper in his hand. As a result of the anguish of His soul, He will see it and be satisfied; By His knowledge the Righteous One, My Servant, will justify the many, As He will bear their iniquities. Therefore will I divide him a portion with the great, and he shall divide the spoil with the strong; because he hath poured out his soul unto death: and he was numbered with the transgressors; and he bare the sin of many, and made intercession for the transgressors."

The man Jesus did not need to feel empowered; he is power, able to command the very angels. This is an extraordinary dynamic of faith altogether transcendent to reason. Those who knew the man Jesus in life did not immediately recognize him after the transfiguration. He appears to them changed in a glorified way: flesh, but no longer flesh; spiritual, but something more than spirit. This new kind of man able to materialize and dematerialize, passing between the atoms of constructed matter, no longer restrained to the temporal clockwork mechanics of conventional reality. A better DNA now perfect, purged of sin and death, no longer mixed in an earthly linage of corruption passed down to the children of men from the time of the mighty *Nephilim*.

Christ does not overcome the world by worldly device, by positive thinking, or by a Hollywood billboard. He needs no military, no earthly alliance, and no consensus to be validates. He is word made flesh spoken from the beginning. The Father and the Holy Spirit bearing witness that this is Messiah sent into the world so that which was lost in the beginning might be saved.

In this present, we each have power within us to choose: either to live in conflict one against the other, as did the *Nephilim*; or to live in peace, as brethren and fellow sojourners, waiting patiently upon the day of the Lord. Although the world has a certain destiny, we that are born again in Jesus Christ are not of this world. A promise guaranteed by one that has gone before, as stated plainly in the Gospel of John, Chapter 17, verses 6- 19 (NIV).

> *"I have revealed you to those whom you gave me out of the world. They were yours; you gave them to me and they have obeyed your word. Now they know that everything you have given me comes from you. For I gave them the words you gave me and they accepted them. They knew with certainty that I came from you, and they believed that you sent me. I pray for them. I am not praying for the world, but for those you have given me, for they are yours. All I have is yours, and all you have is mine. And glory has come to me through them. I will remain in the world no longer, but they are still in the world, and I am coming to you. Holy Father, protect them by the power of your name, the name you gave me, so that they may be one as we are one. While I was with them, I protected them and kept them safe by c that name you gave me. None has been lost except the one doomed to destruction so that Scripture would be fulfilled. "I am coming to you now, but I say these things while I am still in the world, so that they may have the full measure of my joy within them. I have given them your word and the world has hated them, for they are not of the world any more than I am of the world. My prayer is not that you take them out of the world but that you protect them from the evil one. They are not of the world, even as I am not of it. Sanctify them by the truth; your word is truth. As you sent me into the world, I have sent them into the world. For them I sanctify myself, that they too may be truly sanctified."*

The age of the *Nephilim* will surely be fulfilled, returning upon planet earth with dazzling apprehension that a new era has begun. They will come as they have come before, bringing with them terror and swift destruction. Rather they arrive in shiny spaceships or as apparitions of blinding light, they will awaken the genetics of trans-humanism dormant in the sons of men. As it was in the beginning, so will it be again. This will usher the world into the approaching days of antichrist.

Chapter 13
AGE OF MASCHINENMENSCH

A few years ago, I saw an interesting movie called *Metropolis* directed by Fritz Lang during the silent film era of the early 20th Century. It is basically an allegory about the soulless nature of industrialization and the negative consequence to humanity. The story begins in a futuristic city of an urban division representing the material superstructure inhabited by the wealthy elite, contrasted against the steamy underground environment of the workers that maintain the machinery. *Freder*, son of an industrial tycoon, is in love with an empathetic female character name *Maria*, who represents a medium between the two diverse realities. This sets the stage whereby a corrupt version of Maria, impersonated by a riotous robot lacking any virtue called the *Maschinenmensch*, (literally meaning *'human machine')*, made by the bitter inventor, *Rotwang*, to destroy mankind's hope in a nurturing nature. Without going into the metaphoric meaning of this remarkable film, I will simply point out that it summarizes the essential meaning of *Trans-humanism,* (more than human), which so captivates the science and science fiction culture of modern robotics, thus inspiring new frontiers of research into the application of technology.

Trans-humanism, a term originally meant to convey a state superior to mortal infirmity, by identifying the human condition as flawed. Robotics is a techno-science dedicated to the philosophy of improvement for the immediate and future hope of the mankind. In its most benevolent definition, it is the betterment of the human race, bringing sustaining resources to the destitute of this planet with the goal to modernize retro cultures by bringing a revitalized consensus of awareness. It promises the blossoming of deserts, united peaceful exploration into the vastness of galactic discovery, and equal opportunity, without threat of aggression. It is the utopist vision of men one day emerging as gods. However, to reach these goals a few inalienable alterations become necessary--for one thing, mortality!

This reminds me of the quandary of a group of four characters in another 1982 Science Fiction thriller named Blade Runner, starring Harrison Ford, who plays a cop of the future commissioned to hunt down and *shutdown* malfunctioning droids. These four physically superior replicated super human beings (*a type of test-tube hybrid clones*) hijack a space ship and return to earth in search of their creator. The object is to find a cure for mortality, which in their particular case is a five year failsafe that triggers a retrograde physiological cascade resulting in termination. As a consequence to their rebellion, all are tracked by Ford and decommissioned. The last of the four, a military leader played by *Rutger Hauer*, murders his maker in a psychotic rage upon discovering that there is no way to reverse the failsafe sequence. Nevertheless, in the last hours of his existence, he also discovers the true meaning of what it means to live. Rich with metaphor, this film constructs a hypothetical warning against meddling too deeply into hyper genetics to create a soulless future of patented codes packaged inside artificial bodies. Such is the glimmer of technology: the sterile promise of an antiseptic future, where life is but a switch of one upgrade model to a sleeker, better, and more efficient design constructed on an assembly line.

As a child I was fascinated by the idea of a Dick Tracey watch with two-way visual communication, considered by me an impossible technology of the future. Today, not only is this dream past its prime, but ever newer innovations astound the imagination. Smart homes connected through a network of computer systems allowing many controls through a cell phone the size of a baseball trading card. Automobiles programmed to auto-park and even drive themselves by connecting to a GPS signal sent from outer space. Supersonic jet propellant vehicles able to penetrate the stratosphere as a commercial joy ride for those with enough money. And men and women living extended periods in constructed orbiting facilities nearly 300 miles above the highest elevation on planet earth. Who can deny the wonders of modern invention? And is there a more sinister element forewarned in the scenarios presented in the pages of many Science Fiction accounts of a future controlled by machines?

It seems this is not the first time mankind has ventured so near the stars. Remnants of ancient texts referencing a time even before recorded history, we find mention of flying craft with an aerodynamic profile matching the requirements for extraterrestrial maneuvering. Grand terrestrial symbols, identifiable only at a respectful altitude attainable by a propulsion driven air machine, further bare witness that these crafts existed. Unearthed designs of power helixes, dating back thousands of years, have no apparent explanation as to their use or meaning within context. Strange manmade devices, described as batteries, found in sediments predating known civilizations not even in possession of an artificial light source. Intricately fabricated machines, dating back before the time of Marco Polo's expeditions into the mysterious lands of the Far East, resurrected from the drowned bellies of much older shipwrecks. These many unsolved contradictions of mapped history make even the most casual archeologist question the theory of primitive apes climbing toward the glory of our modern future on the predictable steps of a steady state universe. Are these evidences from a destroyed forgotten past, warning us of potential folly of allowing technology to outrace the caution of human wisdom?

The Old Testament *Book of Obadiah*, Chapter 1, verses 3-4 (KJV) makes this disturbing prophetic warning,

"The pride of thine heart hath deceived thee, thou that dwellest in the clefts of the rock, whose habitation is high; that saith in his heart, Who shall bring me down to the ground? Though thou exalt thyself as the eagle, and though thou set thy nest among the stars, thence will I bring thee down, saith the LORD. ."

When all other reason fails, modern man looks to the heavens for salvation (*not in the hope of discovering God*); rather, hoping that some superior extraterrestrial civilization will arrive upon our planet in the nick of time and provide the ultimate solution. Meanwhile there is consuming effort to revise the anthropomorphic dilemma of present thermodynamic condition. If the only way to save humanity is to destroy the inherent weakness of being human; then better this than extinction.

The glitter of technology never ceases to inspire hope of something better and more enduring than biological existence. Within perspective, every technical step forward toward higher productivity entails the loss of something. It has always been the pound of flesh grinded beneath the turning wheels of progress. Modern society's infatuation with handheld chatting devices, and other compressed-wave mediums, continually expands into twilight dimensions of communication. We chat, blog, and tweet with additive vigilance, tirelessly dedicated to algorithmic responses, as we form virtual relationships with cyber affection and vicious jealousies. We have more *friends* in our list of favorites, than we can possibly remember. We call those, whom we do not know, our *following;* while reserving the omnipotent power to delete someone with a single click. While mimicking human behavior, we are slowing being absorbed into a mega consciousness, resulting in a waning connection with what it means to be a human community. We are encouraged toward continuous distraction, while at the same time instructed not to think independently for ourselves. Lavished with high-speed *Wi-Fi connections* everywhere we go, it is easier to indulge in missed TV shows, on-line gaming, or mindlessly texting volumes of community commentaries through social networking, than to reflect on what is really going on in the world. Because of increasing fear of radicalism, the epidemic of identity theft and identity fraud has become primary in everyone's mind. A new wave of technology born with pretense to protect the individual, but is insidiously designed to destroy the personal confidence of individuality. This new layer of protection called *Biometrics* guarantees the sacrifice of privacy and the freedom of liberty appreciated by western civilization for more than a century. Though in its infancy, biometric technology promises a new age of identity protection and ease of access to all your banking and commerce needs. By inserting a small microchip under the skin, your child's location is never farther away than your cell phone, and your specific health condition instantly retrieved by a medical professional. Because of the proliferation of cameras equipped with facial recognition software nearly everywhere we go, there is no hiding of the guilty or the innocent from investigative scrutiny of censure. Like it or not, biometrics, with ever increasingly sophisticated hardware and software development is here, and will not go away even with the absence of threat. There will come a day when that computer device or cell phone in your hand will become your personal snitch wired into an implanted chip that will determine your every movement and activity. It may even control the way you think through algorithmic stimulation of brainwave communication. Sounds a bit too Orwellian? Then consider this passage from the Book of Revelation, Chapter 13, verses 15-18 (KJV), written by an Apostle named John exiled to the island of Roman Patmos more than twenty centuries ago describing the power of the antichrist in a future age.

> *"And he had power to give life unto the image of the beast, that the image of the beast should both speak, and cause that as many as would not worship the image of the beast should be killed. And he causes all, both small and great, rich and poor, free and bond, to receive a mark in their right hand, or in their foreheads: And that no man might buy or sell, save he that had the mark, or the name of the beast, or the number of his name. Here is wisdom. Let him that hath understanding count the number of the beast: for it is the number of a man; and his number is Six hundred threescore and six."*

Interestingly an advanced computer memory core system developed by CDR/NCR in the early nineteen seventies uses the binary numbers of 6-60-66 (*pronounced 666*) for instruction stacks of barcode identification software universal to every computer. Beginning with simple 8 bit instruction, the early computer systems quickly evolved into 16 bit code, exponentially increasing ever since to 32 bit, 64 bit, 128 bit, and so on. But all these revolutionary multiprocessors continue to use the basic core memory platform of *0110, 0110, 0110,* which translates into the binary of *666*. This is biometrics at its worst, latently designed to be a tool of censorship to control and enslave mankind into the snare of a principality designed upon entropic consequence with an endgame of Armageddon. I will later extrapolate further on the contextual meaning of this inevitable cascade event.

Since 1973, when the first successful genetically modified bacteria became a tangible reality, science has pursued this line of research with or without government approval. The commercial acceptance of insulin producing bacteria ten years later opens the door to a host of sustainable food and medical products through a process called *point manipulation (adding or subtracting DNA nucleotides genes to achieve some desired goal)* This alteration of *DNA* sequencing makes possible a myriad of creatures only imagined in the grim tales of mythology. Goats combined with spider *DNA* to produce silk used in the production of military armor; the injection of salmon *DNA* into produce, resulting into cold resistant crops; and even a type of household pet named the *glofish* that actually glows in the dark by extracting a florescent protein by extracting it jellyfish and inserting the protein into the embryo of a species of *zebra fish*. The resulting mutations promise countless benefits to feed growing world populations with the potential to eliminate disease and death. Already special gene experiments are being conducted to enhance man on the nuclear level, thus redefining the standard definition of a perfect being. But many prominent detractors suggest otherwise, keeping alive the ethical debate with diminished agreement. As the famous geneticist, David Suzuki once said, *"Is a genetically altered tomato still a tomato on the nuclear level?"*

Even technologies that promise better and longer life have undercurrents with less than altruistic benefit. Designer drugs, termed as *biologic,* manufactured in living micro-organic systems by using recumbent *DNA* technology to chemically synthesize a specifically defined chemical structure. This research increasingly provides new promise with decreased side effects common to traditional medicines. However, these new generation compounds are closely guarded with secret patents tired up in much red tape and legislative protectionism. In an extreme scenario, the user of such a medication maintains a dependant functionality, and even life, by investing in these very expensive drugs. Thus redefining the motto: *Life at any cost*! Biopharmaceuticals have opened wide the door to renewed controversy surrounding the ethical practice of transgenic experiments (*combining one or more genotypes to make a prototype for purposes of cloning*), which are only the beginning of laboratory miracles to rise out of test tubes in the not so distant future.

    Hybrid cloning and genetically modified products are only infant steps toward a future of unspecified design. Transfer of technology between machine and living organisms already glimmers in the market place, paving the way into hell on earth. We know that when predator populations reduced, then the inhabiting fauna populate to unsupported numbers. We know already what happens when any given ecology becomes affected by chemical influence: ponds subject to pesticide and other run-off solvents, breeding monstrous tadpoles with two heads and three eyes, fish vital to the food chain too poisonous to eat, and water not even fit for agriculture after extensive microbiological filtration. We know that within any conceivable distance from our jewel of existence are conditions uninhabitable without artificial means. And that even the plentiful oceans covering our earth conceal unexplored regions as mysterious and unobtainable as travel to the nearest star. Yet we continue to solicit the idea that artificial is better than organic, and that the computer in the palm of our hand more sophisticated than the consciousness of imagination. Like it or not, our minds are already being terra-formed to believe in a technological savior. We think we are training computers to be more like humans with cognitive intuition, but actually computer interaction is training our minds (*our very soul!*) to think more along algorithmic probability of equations.

    But what if you could lose an arm in an accident and later make a visit to the nearest medical center and have a new arm made cell by cell, layer by layer, and ready to be attached the next business day? *3-D* printing technology makes this exaggerated scenario a possibility. Already, *3-D* printers have been used to create living skin cells and some body parts with the precision guidance of fast error redundant computer technology. The goal is to eventually produce fresh rejection-free organs, such as hearts, livers, and even kidneys for transplant.

Presently, the greatest challenge remains how to replicate the many thousands of intertwining blood vessels only microns thick necessary to sustain the healthy function of these vital body parts. As grand as these predictions sound, would such advancements be available to everyone, or just to the lords with adequate resources?

Man or superman, a dilemma that has tortured the human psychic since earliest preponderance of mortal imagination. What if we could somehow undo mortality, become stronger than the elements that plague our daily existence and live uncounted days indestructible to pestilence and to harm? There is a sense that we are already on the threshold of a brave new future with bold promise. Trans-humanism has revolutionized the medical industry with better robotic prosthesis', organ replacements, and even precision laser-sculpted and laser printed plasticized parts to substitute for lost bone structure. It is a wave to future potential intersecting the mundane of everyday living, changing even the way we think about existence. These technological miracles free the imagination from the ravages of time and decay, opening a door into future utopia populated with bionic men and women inhabiting a society where death and debilitation an uncommon event. A society devoted to cryonic preservation of human tissues and brain function; where seamless virtual reality chambers make for added dimension; where gene manipulation resulting in more efficient units, as simple as going to the pharmacy. And where replaceable bodies is an almost guarantee of eternal longevity. What man would not give anything for perpetual vitality; or any woman for everlasting beauty?

The present human condition is a cycle of realization, revitalization, propagation, and decimation. But trans-humanism promises an end to this irrefutable cycle of being: frailty of flesh and blood to be replaced by robotics, normal genetics substituted by replicated designer templates with predictable results, and human reason substituted by artificial intelligence. Future man reborn in the image of *Maschinenmensch!* But what might be the drawbacks of such a human, if it would still be human at all? This is the true stuff of science fiction. A man made without the burden of a conscience and void of an eternal substance fleetingly glimpsed as the soul.

Shelley's Frankenstein monster made from dead body parts and animated by an electrical charge is perhaps the most infamous creation of all time. This creature knows only pain and misery, as it roams the world outcast from the living, yet unable to die. Though embodied with power and indestructibility, this 19th century monster knows no peace, no vision beyond present existence. Is this the future we want for ourselves and our future offspring? As computer technology becomes more optically advanced and the peripherals more sophisticated, then many believe it only a matter of time until a *Frankenstein* rises from the operating table made piece by piece. As computer technology becomes more optically advanced and the printers themselves more sophisticated, then many believe it only a matter of time until a glorified *Frankenstein* rises from the operating table made piece by piece.

Regenerative medicine is only a first step into the bionic horizon. Even though bio-printing holds great promise for general repair and maintenance, it goes nowhere near as durable as a fully synthetic model incorporating systematic design. Because anatomic existence is perceived as a flaw of inherent weakness, an evolutionary characteristic in need of correction, then science strives forward to the day when present biology equated with ameba existence. An age of machines created in the image of machines, better, stronger, and immortal.

The first prototype of a *nanite* existed as a software code to identify and repair program consistency. It is not until many years later the concept applied to bio-mechanical reactive substances labeled *"machines"*. The scientific value for a nano is approximately one billionth of a meter (or twenty-five namites to cross the width of a single human hair), meaning that it would take 1 nano, measuring 1 billionth of a meter, to make the molecular diameter of ten atoms. *While–that is pretty small!* But for these *nano-motors* to be practical they need to also be self- replicating. Though presently not as small as scientist predict possible within the next 25 years, the early stage models based more on toxic chemical reaction. It is hoped that by incorporating ultrasonic waves for propulsion and magnetic forces for maneuverable navigation, a brave new future awaits the future awakening of these microscopic entities. Nevertheless, even *nano- motors,* as conceptualized today, fit the definition with intriguing potential, especially useful to future medical application. Although far short of the Borg *Nano-Probes*, as imagined in the Star Trek Sci-Fi series, it still qualifies by definition as a semiconductor life form. In other words it exists as a contained unit with an independent propulsion system with a programmed directive.

Later generations have proven more successful in terms of practical use, incorporated with enhanced types of power supplies. Already there are designs for synthetic DNA to independently combine along predictable parameters to produce a *nano-machine* capable of making other *nano-machines*. A recent innovation in circuitry design allows non-silicon wires and other nanostructures to combine with silicon, opening doors to a new generation of electronic and photonic devices thought impossible just a few decades ago. These futuristic pioneers promise fulfillment to the trans-humanist dreams of one day stepping foot on other distant planets without fear of the unknown. Uploading consciousness into a new body made of composite circuitry, as simple as logging into the nearest server.

The present vision is that eventually these microscopic mechanical robots, driven by photonic energy, will join together to make more complex machines, ultimately replacing the weaker elements of biological infestation. These superhuman bodies literally made with nerves of steel, performing task far more productive than anything dreamed possible by even the most savant dreamer. In other words, the complete eradication of biology by technology: an apocalyptic day when human consciousness and machine meld into one. And this again is not the first time this dream realized.

Again in the Book of Enoch we find this chilling account of when fallen angels mated with women breeding a super-race of giants. These giants sire offspring termed the *Nephilim*, as recorded in Chapter 7:

> *"And they conceived from them and bore to them great giants. And the giants begot Nephilim, and to the Nephilim were born Elioud. And they were growing in accordance with their greatness. They were devouring the labor of all the sons of men, and men were not able to supply them.*

And the giants began to kill men and to devour them. And they began to sin against the birds and beasts and creeping things and the fish, and to devour one another's flesh. And they drank the blood. Then the earth brought accusation against the lawless ones."

There may be an even more ominous potential to humanistic pursuit of immortality. It may be that these microscopic *nanites* will spawn into legions of tormentors unleashed against mankind, instead of promised salvation. But even in the most benign definition drug medication should not be a substitute because of bad life choices or as a mechanism of prolongation to ward off the inevitable at any cost. There comes a time when even the beloved family pet must be allowed to die. This is not a heartless assessment, but humane in the most human acceptance possible. The point I am trying to make in context of history is that transition as important part of genesis as being here. Data bases are only models of reality, but not the myriad whole of reality. I have unwavering belief that we remain for however long the Lord determines, and not all for the same reasons. The God I know and serve retains count of every hair on my head and even the millions of skin follicles that perish in a day. But in a quantum universe conceived by the blinded mind of this world all become numbers in a lottery machine. Those numbers allowed continued living by a pharmacy prescription. One day soon mankind may find itself trapped in a constructed web of *Big Pharma* deciding who lives and who dies.

What man would wish to live beyond his days to the peril of his own children? It is certain that the endgame objective of concentrated global research has little to do with altruistic prosperity for all humanity. Millions will ultimately perish for the less than one percent with enough resources, and who out of fear worship longevity of life above all else. In a mechanical world designed in the image of artificial *DNA*, divers masses will inevitable become the targeted enemy and most likely a food source for those that wish to live forever in Satan's fallen principality: a place where human emotions and human biology labeled expendable encumbrances to a perfect value of organized utopia. The *Holy Bible* calls this the age of *Antichrist*, a deliverance of God's greatest creation into the evil imagination of a soulless being with a reason of strong deception, and for whom destruction certain. The *Book of Revelation*, Chapter 9, verses 6-11 (KJV) speaks of unusual creatures one day to appear, which very well may be a swarm of perfected *nanites* glimpsed under the lens of an electron microscope.

> *"And in those days shall men seek death, and shall not find it; and shall desire to die, and death shall flee from them. And the shapes of the locusts were like unto horses prepared unto battle; and on their heads were as it were crowns like gold, and their faces were as the faces of men. And they had hair as the hair of women, and their teeth were as the teeth of lions. And they had breastplates, as it were breastplates of iron; and the sound of their wings was as the sound of chariots of many horses running to battle. And they had tails like unto scorpions, and there were stings in their tails: and their power was to hurt men five months. And they had a king over them, which is the angel of the bottomless pit, whose name in the Hebrew tongue is Abaddon, but in the Greek tongue hath his name Apollyon."*

Another disturbing consideration to all this is that as the age of artificial intelligence and robot bodies approaches reality, then it brings into question the position organics will occupy in such a world. If anything threatens human extinction more, then it is an age where computers communicate exclusively with computers and in a language compatible only through algorithmic comprehension. Also, algorithm is just another type of code encryption constructed through frequency. As already presented even distance quasars and black holes emit energy signatures that translate into dialectic patterns converted to acoustic values. Since demonic principalities exist within the sensory illusion of vast space, it is reasonable to assume that computers will eventually bridge the fixed barrier between their dominion and our world experienced in temporal condition. Already they communicate ideas and ways of thinking, only we are too entertained in the moment to notice. Soon society will even forget what it means to be really human through homogenized indoctrination. These communications spiritual in nature, but not spoken unto God. The interaction with these many lying spirits is nothing new. Those born in the spirit of Christ speak and hear in the spirit, able to discern the bedlam of deception, even as the Apostle writes warning to the Ephesians in Chapter 6, verses 11-12.

"Put on the whole armour of God, that ye may be able to stand against the wiles of the devil. For we wrestle not against flesh and blood, but against principalities, against powers, against the rulers of the darkness of this world, against spiritual wickedness in high places."

The pursuit of *Trans-humanism* has reigned together with human aspiration, since the disobedient awareness of the first man. This disobedience ultimately bringing destruction to the first world only vaguely remembered. But the dream of *Trans-humanism* continues to survive. Even the great pyramids of Egypt are precisely calculated constructions designed as conduits to convey the earth-bound mummy of dead Pharaoh through some celestial transition. The careful embalming of the physical body, the elaborate preparation of a sealed sarcophagus, and the removal of vital organs separately preserved, all suggest an expectant resurrection more than biological. This is, and has always been, the deceiving promise of fallen Satan, the promise of immortality through mortal means. Not much has changed these many millenniums, except for the nature of godhood. Today we master technology like never before in remembered history, controlling mass and velocity daily, without considering the consequence of mechanical failure or human error. Slaughter on the roads, slaughter by too many weapons in the hands of increasingly fearful populations, slaughter inflicted upon the innocent trapped between opposing ideologies, and slaughter in the name of slaughter, until one day even metropolitan streets run red with human sacrifice.

Sooner or later all technology becomes a weapon against the living flesh of humanity. As man transcends the imperfection of his human nature, he becomes less in tune to the true potential of being. As the world becomes more digitized, the essence of imagination and creativity diminishes. Soon the perfect digital tone and the perfect digital pixel will represent the only concept that matters within definition of a politically-correct society conditioned by machines. A society spawned of mnemonic algorithms, where academia of mathematical modeling supersedes inspiration, and the consensus of many clones greater than the witness of spiritual revelation. Only a devil might wish to survive in an artificial world through the perception of an artificial soul. For the seethe of judgment is being prepared even now against the torment of those days to come; but in every generation the righteous before God called to salvation. For there is another code superseding thermodynamic design. A code conceived through the glorified element of a resurrected Christ no longer constrained to time and entropy. I wish to conclude this chapter with a sobering prediction found in the *Book of Revelation*, Chapter 16, verses 4-6 (KJV):

> *"And the third angel poured out his vial upon the rivers and fountains of waters; and they became blood. And I heard the angel of the waters say, Thou art righteous, O Lord, which art, and was, and shall be, because thou hast judged thus. For they have shed the blood of saints and prophets, and thou hast given them blood to drink; for they are worthy."*

Chapter 14
SYMPATHETIC VIBRATIONS HERE AND BEYOND

I experience a most interesting vision while under the influence of the hallucinogen Mescaline a few months before shipping off to Vietnam, Southeast Asia. I was so very young then, unfamiliar with spiritual ways. This will not be my last encounter with supernatural expansion of consciousness; but the first time I experience a distinct connectivity defining present diurnal existence and an elevation into timelessness.

Accompanying some friends to a local park on a Saturday afternoon, I sit alone under a tree and begin to chant the Buddhist **OM**, without even knowing the significance. After nearly an hour of this repetitious intonation, I consciously expand through an extraordinary *out-of-body* event, witnessing the perceived universe as a great mind. In this mind everyone that has ever lived, or would ever live, each exists as a singular cell repeating over and over again a consequential pattern of mortal choice. So acute the vision, I remember graphically passing above the treetops, then fading into a dimension without boundaries and spreading into infinity. The immensity of this consciousness is terrifying, imparting bitter wisdom to the smallness of my present position in a grader scheme. Then I find myself back under the tree again, an umbrella of stars winking as an eternal reminder of an unimaginable universe glittering between the swaying summer branches, yet finite in apprehension.

This vision of a mega-consciousness is not unique. A sense of oneness prevails in nearly every religion to rise out of Mesopotamia. As I have already explored through previous chapters, it is the true us, the very essence of our soul trapped in a temporal matrix. We are as much immortal as we are mortal, remaining grounded in present concept by interactive forces of rational and physicality constrained to the end of conventionality. But there is not a single soul among us, who is not tacitly aware that there is more to existence than contained in the sum of experience or what we think to know.

The pursuit of knowledge is an accumulative effect. It is like the wise old genie let out of the bottle with no way to put it back, each generation becoming more aware. Mankind has not changed much during the past six millenniums of documented civilization, except in technical achievement. Vessels have gotten bigger, military arsenals more destructive, and lighter than air supersonic travel, as common place as telecommunication from one distant town to another across a network of signals. Transmissions that once took days, hours, and minutes, reduced down to mere microseconds by highly compressed data packets propagated along wireless bandwidths. We have, indeed, become relativistic to the creation we inhabit. Which begs the question: *Are we evolving into Gods, as some mistakenly believe; or are we made from the beginning with an enormous potential not yet realized?*

No computer system in the world can shine so bright as one man's vision to bring something unknown into the light of the known. As when Albert Einstein gazed across the cosmos and perceived the relativistic importance of time as a calculable fourth dimension. He does not reason this from accumulated data only, but by a power of supreme insight born through revelation, perceiving the calculative potential of a fourth dimension to create new equations. In other words, Dr. Einstein, a man renowned for chronic absentmindedness, discovers in the applicable math a formulation to support his relativistic vision that the amount of energy contained in matter is equal to the mass times the speed of light squared. The existing math did not change, except in application. Just by adding an extra layer of perceptive definition to already familiar formulations, the hidden mechanics of the universe forever changes. Nor has there ever been a significant leap forward in understanding the topography of the real nature of surrounding space, before or since, except through inspiration to perceive the obvious.

While on the subject of genius, I wish to honor another man of contemporary astrophysics, whose theoretical gaze into the workings of the cosmos has inspired new dimensions of perception. Professor *Stephen Hawking*, stricken with Amyotrophic Lateral Sclerosis (ALS), a disease of the body affecting the way motor neurons transmit between brain function and synaptic relays of the nerve muscles, has inspired new definitions to the observation of relativistic application to the idea of perceived reality. The fact that this man has survived so long is a miracle. But even more miraculous the persistent challenge to accepted norms of entropic time. Perhaps because Doctor Hawking finds himself trapped in a shell of a slowly collapsing body in local time, he has gained some unique insight into the greater entropy observed in cosmic event. Even though his theories on black hole phenomenon have oscillated through the course of his career, I believe it consistent with subtle changes in his biological connection to a macro-scheme of abstract quantum. While most of us ignorant to time dilation, because of autonomic function without conscious perception, this man is acutely aware of progressive disassociation. It is my prayer that this unique individual (*not the legend*) may glimpse the face of spiritual salvation through the *Lord of Lords* before departure.

Up until the middle half of the last century, it was rationalized that the space beyond earth's atmosphere composed of gravimetric and electromagnetic fields generated through a transmission medium called *aether*. This tangible medium extended to the extremes of an infinite universe, supporting the theory of an undefined organic structure, invisible to detection, making valid the resonant connectedness of all matter and energy applied to practical scientific observation. *Aether* provided explanation to the laws of gravity in relation to velocity, mass, and relative distance. It further explained the behavior of orbital patterns, solar activity, and insight into local terrestrial events, such as the measurable flow of earth's jet streams through better comprehension of our planet's axis of rotation. The term *aether*, though defined with diminished importance to the idea of space-time theory, became incorporated into Einstein's gravitational explanation of General Relativity to describe the physical qualities of outer space. This definition of *aether* has become widely rejected by modern physicist, preferring a more Newtonian approach, which accurately describes practical models in local space.

Nevertheless, we are still left with more questions than answers when looking at stars and other galaxies far-far away. The phenomenon of a basic riddle still unsolved: *is light a wave or a particle?* If it is a resonant wave, this is suggestive of a physical medium of transmission. If it is a self-propagating photon packet, then it raises the question of sustainable velocity? There are those who believe that using evidence supported by scientific observation, the universe exhibits an organic consistency composed of an immeasurable medium of eddying forces, only evident through disturbance. Proof of this disturbance would further validate Einstein's theory of wave distortions in time and space. Plank's Constant is a correction denomination equation to justify the present mathematical formulae of energy output to frequency quantity used in the model of Quantum Mechanics. But like all models, its ultimate application is to provide a calculable unit of measure to formulate a real time event within context. It works locally, providing a mathematical tool to round off the edges. This ingenious equation serving as a corrective measure until a more precise measure divined. This also raises the question of which came first: math equations, or the phenomenon of space time event? Nevertheless, through present comprehension math is all that secular science has to better explain the observable mechanics of the universe. Indeed, light may be a particle passing through a physical medium, thus taking on the characteristics of wave eddies produced by an invisible wake; or it may be particle packets propagated and accelerated by gravimetric distortions relative to the point of origin. Or it may be both, or neither, or something altogether different.

The rational problem with science is that the same principle of logic relied on to make a deductive premise, also the logic that makes science inconclusive due to lack of comprehensive data. Present example of this contradiction can be found in modern interpretation of geology. In recent years a competing theory describing the nature and mechanics of planet has refuted hundreds of years of geological conclusions based on the idea of a living earth, or the Gaia principle. The well acclaimed geologist, James Lovelock, concludes that the earth we know is in fact a living organism designed to generate a living biosphere compatible to all other organisms within the contained system. As a result of this man's assertions the institutionalized science of modern geology has ostracized the *Gaianism* as a theoretical possibility simply because it lacks consensus through peer acceptance, simply because it contradicts more naive conclusions based on predictions supported by Uniformitarian time table. With the escalating advent of ecological change on our planet perceived an imminent concern, still science refuses to see this *geosphere* as a living organism made sick through abuse and neglect. For the past fifty years or more there have been many warnings that the world's strategically placed rainforests responsible for air recirculation. Yet no real effort advanced to stop the decimation of these critical lungs of respiration. The same goes for the blood flow of rivers and lakes. Even the mighty turbines of the ocean ignored, preferring an arrogant notion that perhaps man can one day inhabit the deep if things above become too toxic. As with most things in this world: just by understanding the mechanics of how things work does not insure the wisdom of the meaning.

There are many similar inconsistencies found in the scientific community. These contradictions analogist to the surface tension of a lake disturbed by the wave created by a single droplet of water; or to put it another way, the *butterfly affect* caused by the flapping wings of a single butterfly escalating into massive wind turbulence. Without the illusion of predictability science either becomes reduced to a tool of investigation, or elevated to the status of a religion necessitating an engagement of faith to leap over the void unknown quantum.

Even to ask the question of something that should be obvious to observation. Is sound simply a property of kinesis? Because it can travel through a medium of gas (air or liquid), it creates vibration decibels. Since sound can be converted digitally, it becomes redefined into radio transmission, which is a low spectrum of light energy. Naturally occurring radio emissions from space are propagations of distant Pulsars and Quasars, stars and star clusters which generate electromagnetic interference at regular intervals. These electromagnetic photon packets can travel great distances unimpeded by piggybacking on radiation streams along interstellar lanes. This transmission medium, though no longer referred to as aether, is referenced as dark energy with a neutral charge value making up nearly seventy percent of the universe. Another twenty five percent classified as dark matter, leaving only about five percent to account for all the detectable physical matter and energy that we are able to see and analyze. This is a pretty small figure compared to all that other invisible stuff!

An intriguing idea proposed by a brilliant contemporary evangelist is that the universe a giant simulation, and that nothing is real beyond the limits of local space. A great deal of evidence suggests a constructed reality validated by energy measurements consisting of cosmic particles that further indicates the presence of an underlying lattice of intelligent design. If I understand this gentleman correctly, then we all exist inside a bottle custom made to the complexity of life. This could explain why the cosmos looks uniformly the same from all perspectives, regardless of relative position.

Since time and distance only conventional measurements formulized to explain entropy; then why should we assume they are even valid beyond present locality? The singularity described as the Big Bang could have instantaneously expanded to proportionate value of present observation. This inflation period would explain the physics of mathematical modeling, including Plank's constant, and thus providing an illusion of age and directionality. Another puzzling aspect of the universal mechanical process is that all bodies--from the macro-gears of spinning galaxies to the subatomic structure of atoms--all have a compressed core of concentrated energy equivalent to the mass. Perhaps, this also indicates that the context of material interpretation analogist to relative conditions existing everywhere and at the same instance, like a telescopic inversion from the macro to the micro. The point being that the concept of time and velocity only valid in reference to the local observer, and that reality becomes what is expected. All mathematical models designed to fit the interpretation of the evidence. So we are back to the question: is light a wave or a particle? Or is it a phenomenon somehow dependent upon the anticipation of the experiment? It is amazing to find in the Book of Job (considered the oldest book of the Bible) these profound lines in verses 6-14 (KJV) concerning the nature of our pleasant jewel of existence, as viewed from a respectable astrophysical distance.

> "He stretches out the north over the empty place, and hangs the earth upon nothing. He binds up the waters in his thick clouds; and the cloud is not rent under them. He holds back the face of his throne, and spreads his cloud upon it. He hath compassed the waters with bounds, until the day and night come to an end. The pillars of heaven tremble and are astonished at his reproof. He divides the sea with his power, and by his understanding he smites through the proud. By his spirit he hath garnished the heavens; his hand hath formed the crooked serpent. Lo, these are parts of his ways: but how little a portion is heard of him? but the thunder of his power who can understand?"

I further wish to advocate a simple layman's perspective of cosmology, as it is presented in text books today. The main issue is, of course, how it all began. There are only two prevailing theories: either the universe has always existed in a steady state without explanation, or it begins with a Big Bang. Of course, neither theory is able to address the first cause, which is pointless to speculate on within context. So let us assume that the popular current scientific hypothesis is correct, and it happened with an undefined singularity exploding into being. What was the space time condition a trillionth of a trillionth of a trillionth of a second after the Big Bang? This seems to be the focus of much concentrated research, giving rise to the concept of String Theory laced with *quarks* and *flavors* to describe what might have happened.

All that is known for sure is that the event would have triggered an unimaginable release of energy hurling into motion the super mechanics of a relativistic model many times faster than the speed of light and eventual coalescence into spectrums of conventional definitions of matter and energy. This so called Star Dust principle has been proven mathematically by the famous French Canadian astrophysicist, Herbert Reeves, in his many years of research on heavy hydrogen atoms to describe the coalescence of star dust (or primordial matter) from a singularity event. Reeves, and his colleagues, do not venture to say what caused this event, only that the event happened. The main premise being that matter and energy forms simultaneously, achieving molecular cohesion through a cooling-off process. At the precise moment of this singularity event there is no such thing as time or velocity. Both measurements created instantaneously, representing infinite value, and existing without quantum association. This means that no one really knows how to apply physical deterministic model construction beyond present observation. It is just as possible that the age of the universe could be less than one cosmic day or the prevailing theory of 13.8 billion years, as already discussed. And since energy and matter born simultaneously from this singular mass expulsion, then why not assume that a homogenous connectivity prevails, much like the retentive quality of an elastic band spreading in all directions creating an inaccurate perception of time dilation.

When we see the twinkle of a star, we are observing the arrival of a light source from a great cosmic distance. Presuming this is not the reflected light from one of our neighboring solar planets, this light radiates at a mean distance in outer space of at least 4.2 light years from the closest star to our sun, appropriately named *Proxima Centauri* (that is approximately 24,673,277,682,000 miles). We have been conditioned to think in compressed values, rather than in terms of real space. A jet airliner can sprint around the world in less than 50 hours travelling 800 km per hour; whereas, it takes a luxury ocean liner approximately 45 days at an average speed of 20 knots. The distance remains the same, only the accelerated transportation medium relatively different. Also, something to think about: light travels in all directions at 360 degree angles. When we turn on a light source in a room, we term the resulting radiation a factor of illumination, not that photons are bouncing off the walls. If we contain this illumination within a sealed box, it ceases to travel beyond the boundaries of the enclosure. Einstein predicts that light does not travel in a straight line relative to the point of observation, but is influenced by gravity fields such as massive stars or other space anomaly. Later quantum theorist, such as Stephen Hawkins, predict that there are tiny singularities called black holes capable of altogether swallowing light, or any other mass or energy unfortunate enough to become caught within its gravity well. So it seems that light has some physical property capable of being captured or diverted.

Until recently, light speed considered an irrefutable quantum, making it the only reliable measure in the universe. But revised experiments have presented disturbing new evidence that this is not the case. Through a rather complex process each photon might fluctuate with independent energy in relation to vacuum conditions of a given space-time quantum gravity level of faster or slower potential. The nearest star body to the earth is, of course, our solar center. This star is a mere 93,000,000 miles away. Following chemical reaction, termed nuclear fusion, energy expels across space as spectrums of electromagnetic radiation reaching our planet in just several minutes. This radiation reaches the earth in the measurable form of heat and spectrum array of charged photons. However, the farther one moves from the source, the less intense the radiation. Our neighboring planet Mars, only an astronomical 227,936,640 miles away, receives about half the solar radiation when compared to earth. This suggests that the more distant one moves from the source, the less intense the radiation. To my knowledge, no one has ever received a suntan by bathing beneath the myriad of a night sky filled with many distant suns. Light from even the most radiant stars and star clusters on record are presumed to follow this same odyssey through space, which raises the question: why only a diminished spectrographic array observable? In other words, does a photon begin kinetically endowed with intense radioactive force, only to wane through transmission? It seems from analysis that by the time this photon reaches a source destination, say for example planet earth, it is only a photographic composite of the source structure, stripped of quantitative attribute. So what starts out as kinetic energy, discharges into strong electromagnetic pulse radiation, then fades into spectral density with decreasing wavelength.

If one considers that all matter and energy began simultaneously from the same singularity, then it is more appropriate to analyze cosmic events as a constant recession from the past to the present. In other words, the observer is always seeing the past from a relative position in an ever expanding void. This is one of the reasons why the gigantic Hubble Telescope, positioned in space beyond the polarizing distortion of atmospheric and gravitational influence, is able to create a time lapsed composite of distant galaxies and stars, later enhanced by computer modeling. What we see and analyze is actually a ghost image that may not even presently exist in our neutral frame of observation. Within context of an instantly hyper inflated universe, even the most remote galaxies could very well be the same age. This means that simultaneous creation occurred, providing an illusion of measured expansion and further supporting the unsettling idea that time dilation a factor of relativistic acceleration. This assumption could change everything physicists think to know about the observable cosmos. But better to have faith in at least one possibility, than to consider the alternative that existence a conventional reality with a contrived purpose.

Another just as disturbing potential is the behavior of subatomic structures. Experiments have revealed that neutrinos do not always pass through a physical barrier, but have the capability of phasing out in one location and rematerializing in another locality. If events of this nature are observable on a subatomic level, then why should the assumption prevail that similar phenomenon does not occur on a grander scale when trying to interpret cosmology? Maybe a vibrating photon is able to phase in and out of regional space, giving the perception of a much older universe. Do not get me wrong, I am not attempting to prove the universe is only 5775 years old, according to the Hebrew calendar. Only that it is not impossible it could be this within context of many conflicting theories.

The intellectual mind immediately grasps at all the accumulated evidence suggesting that such an assertion absurd, but often closed to the possibility that all inconclusive evidence remains subject to interpretation. Logical rigidity often prevails, until enough pieces of hypothetical evidence categorized to sufficiently redefine the mystery of the ever changing puzzle. In other words, to find a pebble on the beach does not mean it has been there all along, or that it even belongs within context. Just because apparent order prevails based on metered observation in local time and space, there can only be a speculative assertion that these same laws of consistency apply elsewhere in the universe. The best example of this contradiction discovered in the theory of how black holes work. The gravity well of these enormous space fluctuation so great that not even light can escape, thus defying laws of the mechanics we understand in normal space time. Just try to imagine how much grander must have been the primal beginning of matter and energy at the instant of the Big Bang singularity.

Nevertheless, there is only one written text translated from ancient times describing in detail the beginning of modern cosmology in lucid terms of how matter and energy first came into existence. It goes even further by providing clear explanation of the deterministic nature of the first cause, which remains a mystery to secular thinking. In the first book of the New King James Bible, verses 1-10 records an eloquent quote that might have been acclaimed by any modern physicist using simple terminology.

> *"In the beginning God created the heavens and the earth. The earth was without form, and void; and darkness was on the face of the deep. And the Spirit of God was hovering over the face of the waters. Then God said, "Let there be light"; and there was light. And God saw the light, that it was good; and God divided the light from the darkness. God called the light Day, and the darkness He called Night. So the evening and the morning were the first day. Then God said, "Let there be a firmament in the midst of the waters, and let it divide the waters from the waters." Thus God made the firmament, and divided the waters which were under the firmament from the waters which were above the firmament; and it was so. And God called the firmament Heaven. So the evening and the morning were the second day. Then God said, "Let the waters under*

the heavens be gathered together into one place, and let the dry land appear"; and it was so. And God called the dry land Earth, and the gathering together of the waters He called Seas. And God saw that it was good."

It should be noted that God declares order from the beginning. The proclamation *"let there be light"* is not a vague suggestion describing a condition of chaotic evolution, but is a clear statement of directed design. Nor does it suggest the presence of matter and energy before this singularity event. Nevertheless, there is more to the interstellar dimension than just matter and energy. The idea of universal resonance is as old as consciousness. It is this consciousness that first touched the ponderous distant stars or delved into the mystery of being. The idea that grander forces produce resonant association that reaches even to the subatomic level.

The ancient Greeks are credited with identifying and naming the wandering planets in our local Solar System. They were also aware of a resonant relationship between the orbiting planets, calling this cosmic harmony the music of the spheres. It turns out that they were especially right about the music. Centuries of solar observation has detected a corresponding relationship between the orbit and rotation patterns of local heavenly bodies in the immediate Solar System. The harmonic vibration, not unlike musical intervals, establishes a relationship of one to one impendence embedded in sonic fluctuations (a pattern of 2:1, 3:2, etc.) found in the Pythagorean diatonic model of tonality and later capitalized in the Fibonacci theorem of pattern association originating from Sanskrit associative dialectical interpretation of sound and meaning. Further to this harmonic correspondence is that an established link synchronizes between the gravimetric balance of seemingly random planetary spins and solar revolutions. Although this phenomenon not fully understood, it seems to indicate the invisible cogs and wheels of a giant precisely assembled cosmic clock. Even the counter directional spin of earth's sister planet Venus, suggest some adjustment to this clock with astonishing implications. Which begs the question, *who or what made the clock?*

Instead of humble questioning, there prevails an arrogant mentality, which stubbornly quantifies all physical evidence describing precisely balanced existence as a lottery of random chance. This mind prefers an elevated seat in the depths of entropy, rather than consider servitude to the creator of the magnificent universe perceived: *which is but a shadow of things to come!* Because mathematical organization is an imperfect temporal model based upon entropic observation, it is also in continuous revision. Laden with correction theories to reconcile discrepancy due to ever changing locality and time differential, it must constantly find ways to make the math balance. A classic example of this is the value of Pi, a transcendental equation to define the ratio of a circle regardless of size. Pi is not an exact figure, except in material application, particularly in terms of geometric construction. Even Plank's Constant, not so constant, except when rationalized through a deterministic model to justify an irrational dilemma. Therefore, Math is a calculation tool to predict a desired outcome specific to an entropic condition. Since there is little doubt that resonance exist in nature, it must be rationalized with complex formulation involving sub-space emulations described as weak energy patterns termed strings. String Theory begins to take on characteristics strongly similar to descriptions in the Bible of angelic presences sent from the throne of God and dimensions of outer darkness. This also implies the attribute of revelation, or glimpses into supernatural occlusion irrational to temporal condition. Although methodical equations can accurately predict the collapse of a star with statistical quantification within context of present observation, it cannot reconcile the obvious conclusion of the event, except by rational aspect. Only through spiritual elevation by a power termed faith can reconciling of both the cause and the affect be observed through concentric patterns of global destiny. So speak the prophets of God across time and ephemeral shadows of civilization predicting what must be with unfailing accuracy. .

An earlier assertion made that consciousness is a derivative of many communications discerned through cognitive sorting of data processing termed the mind. This mind must stubbornly substantiate a relativistic condition of quantum existence, therefore excluding the sum of any greater whole. Persistent to the idea that biological existence a vast complex of many organisms designed to a conventional end, why not presume this condition includes an even more complex energy field called a living soul made in the image of eternal God? This infallible assertion supported by the very nature of our kind. We do not cease tilling and harvesting the earth once our bellies are full, but devise ways to store and preserve our fruit for future posterity. We do not sit idle just because a warm breeze blows, but busily prepare against colder days to come. When we observe the heavens we do not sigh in despair because the stars are too far away from our touch, but rather imagine them more near. Our insatiable appetite for the unknown remaining not fulfilled because of a greater emptiness in our souls. This all suggest there is more to the geometry of being than rationalized through present value.

The idea of shape power is not a new science: an idea which proposes a common sense interpretation of energy matrixes within context of geometric atomic structure existing in *aether*. It supposes that the universe is composed of polarized energy conduits spreading in all directions like tangles of strings with directional *aetheric* particle flow, each capable of producing a vortex with magnetic poles. In terms of vibratory physics, this inspires the speculative idea that the electromagnetic activity, independently observed, is evidence of a *Toroidal* structure. This naturally occurring energy field either prevails over entropy, or is a result of the entropic process. An example of this could be that when light energy leaves the source, it is first a molecular particle composed of several composite properties of radiation, including heat and spectrographic excitement. Upon colliding with one of these electromagnetic conduits, it then propagates into a wave, thus losing its original classified signature, and becoming a wave- particle piggy-backing on a massive electromagnetic surge, much like a surfer catching a Tsunami. This photonic energy is now part of a greater whole, magnified through a *torus- shaped* matrix with an electromagnetic energy field and with a zero dimensional center called a *Vertex*. The radiating forces from this epic center become evidence of a plasma medium defined with organic structure. Each point of photonic excitement is like seeing the image of an individual tree within context of an invisible forest.

Let us assume for a moment that modern Quantum Mechanics only partially interprets the nature of local space, and that there actually is *aether* (composed of unionized plasma termed dark energy and dark matter) with resonating properties governed by directional polarity flow as earlier described. Then open field geometry becomes more important than ever to interpret time and scale. It also explains why time is unidirectional, locked into a rigid entropic pattern with variable compression value. Since time and entropy congenial to an ultimate countdown, then it presupposes that perhaps there is a purpose to existence not measurably defined within the physical universe. For all things physical have an end, as stated in 2 Peter, chapter 3, verses 9-13, concerning the inevitable course of entropy.

> *"The Lord is not slack concerning his promise, as some men count slackness; but is longsuffering to us-ward, not willing that any should perish, but that all should come to repentance. But the day of the Lord will come as a thief in the night; in the which the heavens shall pass away with a great noise, and the elements shall melt with fervent heat, the earth also and the works that are therein shall be burned up. Seeing then that all these things shall be dissolved, what manner of persons ought ye to be in all holy conversation and godliness, Looking for and hasting unto the coming of the day of God, wherein the heavens being on fire shall be dissolved, and the elements shall melt with fervent heat? Nevertheless we, according to his promise, look for new heavens and a new earth, wherein dwells righteousness."*

For resonant behavior to have acoustic meaning, it must be accompanied by the conceptualized design of a physical vessel. The idea of *Shape Power* assumes the existence of a universal blueprint with schematic references. It theorizes a tangible relationship between gravitational alignment and planetary resonance. It also theorizes that a rational energy matrix represents perfect existence, further believing that human consciousness has a geometry with a *torus* configuration like that found everywhere in the universe. In other words, shape power clings to the premise that we human beings are all star children seeking to bring harmony to the universe by finding harmony within ourselves.

Nor is it alone in this hypothesis. Tibetan gongs, also called *singing bowls,* usually made of bronze, are geometrical constructions to intonate the five global scaling harmonics believed to induce a deep meditative state. The purpose is to open gateways of consciousness in the brain, which in turn communicates with the soul. Buddhism believes that through unhampered meditative chanting one can reach *"samsara"*, a state of cyclic oneness with the universe, as I experienced in the beginning of this chapter. Here one begins the journey through the six realms of existence divided into three higher existences of gods, demigods, and human; and the three lower realms of animals, hungry ghost, and hell beings. This path, once embarked upon, leads to Nirvana (meaning to become everything) without individual distinctiveness; or to put it another way, to become everything by fading into nothingness.

I personally experienced another encounter with this spiritual force two years later, after returning back from U.S. military action in Vietnam. One of my subordinates was a young Japanese man with parents living outside San Diego California, several minutes from my Camp Pendleton base. One weekend I am invited to accompany my colleague to his family's home, where we are engaged with others in a ritual of chanting before a *Gohonzon*. The idea is to kneel in front of this Buddhist shrine and chant over and over *"Nam Myoho Renge Kyo."* Again, without knowing why, I follow suit, chanting over and over again the melodic phrase *Nam Myoho Renge Kyo*. Then, unexpectedly, brightness surrounds everything and I can sense the presence of spiritual forces: the minds of immense beings. This another vivid encounter with universal consciousness after the Mescaline trip many months earlier; but fortunately not my last.

The devotion of *Nichiren Buddhism* found in the Japanese *Lotus Sutra,* achieved through the repetitive chanting of the sacred Mantra. Presented as the supreme consciousness of universal good will and devotion to humanity, Nichiren Buddhism promises ascension through the ten spiritual realms: six being of carnal inception, three being the aspiration of enlightenment, and the last being altogether pure through submission to absolute knowledge. As in all Buddhist and Krishna observances, the ultimate goal is for the practitioner to lower conscious defenses and submit to an elevated consciousness of higher intellect. In other words, to allow one's thoughts to become part of a greater mind inhabiting an estate perceived as non-temporal value. I cannot stress enough that all such activity is perilous, since the participant is willingly led into the fortress of entities possessed with powers of great deception. *In second Corinthians, Chapter 11, verse 14-15 (KJV)* Paul warns:

> "And no marvel; for Satan himself is transformed into an angel of light. Therefore it is no great thing if his ministers also be transformed as the ministers of righteousness; whose end shall be according to their works."

The measure of resonance is based on a factor of magnitude. The phenomenon of wave energy induced by shape power evidenced everywhere in the world, even without the technical appreciation of resonant behavior. Physical locality, mental susceptibility, as well as cultural interpretation are determining factors of significant tone frequency. Examples are the specialized musical instruments originating from the Byzantium period, then spreading through Western and Eastern Europe. African drum beats, pipes and harps, all containing unique resonant patterns specific to a geo-sphere communication with spiritual influences. Nor must we exclude the biblical story of Jericho, whose walls tumble down with the blast of horns and a final shout, demonstrating that timing is everything. Resonance is a two way corridor with messages going out and messages coming in. The universe is filled with a *babble* of communication so common place that we hear only in part, as the sounds harmonize with heavenly bodies and our souls: this soul energy, as the apex of conjunction between real space and quantum space, a battleground manifesting the abode of Satan and his fallen angels against the spiritual force of God.

Returning to my own supernatural encounters, more than once I came into direct contact with acute force resonating beyond the spectrum of diurnal existence. The brightness of these presences undeniable, their communication clearly announced from a source coexisting in another dimensional layer on the fringe of present time-space continuum. I was already bound within a dark snare, only did not know it. This would have been my eternal habitation were it not for incursion of an even greater revelation after this encounter with this Buddha Mantra. The Lord of Lords as the magnitude of the rising sun compared to the illumination of a light bulb left on through the night. This miracle of salvation that overwhelms me then and now has no bases in science, nor can it be explained logically. Only I was dead, and now I live! I was lost and now I am found!

By the exuberant power of the Holy Spirit, I write this now. And as extraordinary as it sounds, I share this testimony of salvation, without wavering and without judgment. To every soul that hears this testimony, know that Jesus Christ has died on a cross of destiny for my sins and for your sins. Know that God by immutable power has raised this man from the grave of disassociation to be the perfect code of reconciliation for all creation in every corner of heaven. This is evidence of indivisible love flowing richly through a medium termed grace intentionally manifested from the progenitor of all lights visible and invisible. This enduring promise found in The Book of Revelation, Chapter 3, verse 20 (KJV), Jesus says to all:

> *"Behold, I stand at the door, and knock: if any man hear my voice, and open the door, I will come in to him, and will sup with him, and he with me."*

As you can appreciate from this personal testament, I am convinced that there exist many magnitudes of force, not altogether established within temporal value.

The problem with all models is that they are just reconstructions based on limited knowledge of what can be verified through many contradicting assumptions. Maybe dark matter and dark energy do not exist at all, and there are other cosmological explanations to the nature of spiral galaxies and *"gravitational lensing"* to describe how and why the universe works. The danger of any intellectual reconstruction is the foundation of logic: *logic being the interpretation of immense proportion from a minute limited perspective.*

Presently, we know only in part; and the part we do know subject to error of interpretation. At the end of the sixteenth century, a man by the name of Giovanni Bruno causes a wave of contention among those who held a fervent belief in a Ptolemaic interpretation of cosmology. Giovanni, a catholic Monk, proclaims to have had a vision that the sun only one star among many and that around this heliocentric center orbits the earth and other planets. He calls his visions revelations from God. Much controversy surrounds the life of this man, but also challenges the historical oppression imposed by the *"righteous inquisitions"*. Ironically, Giovanni would be the last martyr to this fallacious doctrinal interpretation. Although the church diocese eventually orders him burned at the stake on a variety of charges for heresy, it will also offend, causing centuries of dissention in many practical minds against the holy word of God.

The unfortunate fact is that the Catholic Church interpretation of cosmic order at the time did not reflect the true content found in scripture. But rather it became influenced by an agreement of temporal understanding predominant at the time. I am not haling Giovanni as a saint, nor as a child of Satan. He was a man born with reasonable comprehension of observable reality. A man respected to dare declare conviction of an inalienable truth existing beyond the veil of blinded institutional thinking. If his profound observations by divine revelation or by cosmological insight, I cannot say: only that there is a lesson to be learned from this man's life, as sharp as any two edged sword. Just as there are many stars of different magnitudes, so are there many conflicting wisdoms based upon personal interpretations: all which fall short of the truth. This emphasized in 1 Corinthians, Chapter 3, verses 18-20 (KJV).

> *"Let no man deceive himself. If any man among you seems to be wise in this world, let him become a fool, that he*

may be wise. For the wisdom of this world is foolishness with God. For it is written, He takes the wise in their own craftiness. And again, The Lord knows the thoughts of the wise, that they are vain."

Since relativity remains an undeniable factor complex to our perspective existence, then this also implies the possible existence of mega consciousness. Since we cannot know what this mega consciousness is with intellectual certainty, then maybe the more prudent course is to set aside prejudice and inconclusive assumptions. A lesson might be learned from a recent news event concerning the disappearance of a commercial jetliner flying from Malaysia to China.

Within a few weeks many diverse theories of international proportion spawned, ranging from terrorist high jacking, pilot suicide, to various scenarios of crash locations and reasons for the crash. All based on suppositions spun from insufficient evidence. It seems that what we do not know inspires greater controversy than the things we do know with a degree of certainty. So perhaps we should learn to remain humble daily, realizing there are things we simply must accept by faith, and decisions which must be made by choice: our choice, not the choice of someone else. The advocate that will accuse each and every one of us in the final day will accept no other testimony, except our own. Our only witness of defense will be the sacrificial blood of Jesus Christ. And only those written in the *Book of Life* exempted from the judgment of the law, as prescribed in the book of Revelation, Chapter 20, verses 11 - 15. (KJV)

> *"And I saw a great white throne, and him that sat on it, from whose face the earth and the heaven fled away; and there was found no place for them. And I saw the dead, small and great, stand before God; and the books were opened: and another book was opened, which is the book of life: and the dead were judged out of those things which were written in the books, according to their works. And the sea gave up the dead which were in it; and death and*

hell delivered up the dead which were in them: and they were judged every man according to their works. And death and hell were cast into the lake of fire. This is the second death. And whosoever was not found written in the book of life was cast into the lake of fire."

Perhaps, too, we should pause just for a moment beneath the canopy of a starry night and simply behold the wonder that stretches into the zenith of time and space, forgetting in the now all thoughts of what we will eat, or where we should lay our heads, or of great things we have yet to accomplish. But rather reside in the ever changing present, less certain of the things we think to see with our eyes, less trusting of whispers that confound our minds. Yes, and perhaps we should allow that faint voice of faith, a possibility as the small grain of a mustard seed to spring from the well of our soul. And, yes, rest our minds in the knowledge that God has manifested to the sons of men all the mysteries of the universe to be clearly understood in season. For even the wonder of this heaven and this earth shall roll away as a scroll into prevailing entropy. But from these ashes a better code embedded into every atom from the beginning: the perfect matrix of new heaven and new earth reborn into everlasting. For even the greatest of things made from the smallest of things.

In conclusion, I would like to leave you with this appropriate Bible verse. In the first book of Corinthians, Chapter 1, verses 27-30 (KJV), the Apostle Paul again writes:

"But God hath chosen the foolish things of the world to confound the wise; and God hath chosen the weak things of the world to confound the things which are mighty; And base things of the world, and things which are despised, hath God chosen, yea, and things which are not, to bring to naught things that are: That no flesh should glory in his presence. But of him are ye in Christ Jesus, who of God is made unto us wisdom, and righteousness, and sanctification, and redemption:"

Chapter 15
STUFF OF ANGELS

As a young child I always hoped there were angels, but never really sure. Now as an adult I am certain angels do exist, as clearly presented in text of the Holy Bible. I am even more certain that these celestial agents surpass all reason through imagination. In the course of life I have met other people inspired by unwaveringly conviction that seraphic beings surround us continually, providing protection to the innocent and resisting raging forces invisible. I have heard deathbed testimonies that proclaim appearance of an angel to escort their souls from the flesh. The hour of my salvation I am translated in the spirit and see angels prepared for a final battle. I am among them, as I am also here. This is a mystery I have yet to fully understand. I have also witnessed fallen angels, those spirits that are earthbound, no longer part of the heavenly hosts. I do not claim any authority on this very sensitive and surreal subject. Nevertheless, I feel compelled to address the complexity of this issue in the hope of some better comprehension to better discern the nature and purpose of these celestial creations.

In many world cultures, there exists in folklore a nether region transitional to the human soul after the cessation of anatomical function. This is a spiritually dark principality (a sort of quantum-holding cell) manifesting the seven evil estates of temporal existence. The Holy Bible makes reference to a place called Hades, described as being as far below the earth of men, as hell is below the heavens of angels. This is the place Christ descends after crying *"Abba, Abba,* (meaning Father, Father) *why have you forsaken me?"* --before surrendering his mortal ghost. This living son of man, although conceived in perfect faith, is condemned to the bowels of *purgatory* for the purpose of unlocking the chains of darkness that constrain those righteous souls trapped in limbo. They wait patiently for the restoration of all things by God's chosen Messiah, as proclaimed in the first book of Peter, Chapter 3, verses 18-22 (KJV).

> *"For Christ also hath once suffered for sins, the just for the unjust, that he might bring us to God, being put to death in the flesh, but quickened by the Spirit: By which also he went and preached unto the spirits in prison; Which sometime were disobedient, when once the longsuffering of God waited in the days of Noah, while the ark was a preparing, wherein few, that is, eight souls were saved by water. The like figure where unto even baptism doth also now save us (not the putting away of the filth of the flesh, but the answer of a good conscience toward God,) by the resurrection of Jesus Christ: Who is gone into heaven, and is on the right hand of God; angels and authorities and powers being made subject unto him."*

This is the first purgatory located in *"the lower parts of the earth"*, as stated in Ephesians, Chapter 4, where Christ must engage the enemy and free those captive, becoming victory of the *first resurrection*. Nevertheless, even this place still part of God's living consciousness, meaning that Satan and all those, who follow after disobedience, remain suspended in a dimensional passage until sin and death has run a course to the end of entropy. But this place of separation is not the hell of final judgment recorded in The Book of Revelation, Chapter 20, verses 10-15 (NIV):

> *"And the devil, who deceived them, was thrown into the lake of burning sulfur, where the beast and the false prophet had been thrown. They will be tormented day and night forever and ever. Then I saw a great white throne and him who was seated on it. The earth and the heavens fled from his presence, and there was no place for them. And I saw the dead, great and small, standing before the throne, and*

> *books were opened. Another book was opened, which is the book of life. The dead were judged according to what they had done as recorded in the books. The sea gave up the dead that were in it, and death and Hades gave up the dead that were in them, and each person was judged according to what they had done. Then death and Hades were thrown into the lake of fire. The lake of fire is the second death. Anyone whose name was not found written in the book of life was thrown into the lake of fire."*

The original Hebrew meaning of the word *Gehenna* describes a permanent condition. This is a place where the matrix of flesh, soul, and spirit exiled eternally by willful determination into the fiery depths of everlasting flames. I believe this to be the essence of God's eternal spirit. The creation returns to the creator: some to eternal existence, and others to eternal oblivion. For nothing created can be uncreated, only some remembered, some forgotten. This is especially true for the heavenly hosts that were formed first. For energy preceded matter in the creation, as the heavens shined upon the newly formed earth.

The evidence for this is not contained to the Bible alone, but can be absorbed from many other texts passed down through the ages of human civilization. The lost Book of Enoch, though often dismissed by many theologians, speaks in much detail concerning the political and spiritual condition of *pre-diluvium* civilization. Enoch is traditionally ascribed as being a patriarch of Noah, a great grandfather, described genealogically as *"the seventh from Adam"*, and Genesis, Chapter 5, verse 24 (KJV) says,

> *"And Enoch walked with God: and he was not; for God took him."*

Although the actual age of the written text disputed by scholars, the source material portrays the world, as it might have been before Noah and his close of kin sealed inside the Ark just prior to the floods of the deep that wipe out the pre-diluvia civilization. Its significance cannot be ignored. The persistent survival of this very old account is perplexing reminder that knowledge remains a tangled ball not so easily unraveled by tools of deductive reason.

The Book of Enoch is composed of at least five fragmented sections, each addressing a subject of investigative appeal, as well as containing spiritual value. For this reason the early educated Greek philosophers--*not the Hebrews*-- embrace these concepts of heavenly geography, meteorology, medicine, and particularly astronomy. To these thinkers, the "apocrypha" (*hidden or enigmatic*) passages contained in the ancient text, unveil a universe with intriguing possibility. The Book of Enoch inadvertently enriches the discourse of Hellenic culture that inspired the legends of fallen Gods. They are more easily able to relate to the idea of a superhuman offspring produced through some unknown science of hybrid mating, and appreciate their continuing influence in civilized culture. Despite its lack of acceptance by present day theology, there is little denying The Book of Enoch alluded to more than once in the New Testament concerning final judgment and the meaning of Messiah. The intention here is not to open a theological debate, but only to suggest that this cryptic book bears more than casual meaning when it comes to war in heaven. Perhaps to the wise of this world, the Book of Enoch preserved, as further testament to the plans made by agents of evil conspiracy begun even before God breathes life into Adam making him the first living soul. At present I will only submit to a statement made by Jesus in The Gospel of Mark, Chapter 9, verses 38-40 (KJV).

> *"And John answered him, saying, Master, we saw one casting out devils in thy name, and he followeth not us: and we forbad him, because he followeth not us. But Jesus said, Forbid him not: for there is no man which shall do a miracle in my name, that can lightly speak evil of me. For he that is not against us is on our part."*

There is no authority of greater testament, than Jesus' submission to death on a cross in Calgary. No voice of man or angel can deny the power and the glory of this meaning. So what are angels; the condition of their creation; and where is the residence of their abode? Since there is no qualified reference to address these questions, and since the purpose of this chapter is not to discern God's ultimate intent from the end of creation to the beginning, I purpose a speculative analysis based on scripted evidence only.

Within grander context, angels are forces of the cosmos designated by God, as conduits of incomprehensible power embodying the macro and micro universe. These tensions described by modern quantum science as *the strong and weak nuclear forces* that bind together elemental reality. The gravimetric relationship of mass and energy contained within these exploding singularities establishes the basics of *the theory of universal gravitation* in an attempt to describe the relativistic geometry of thermodynamic reactions observed throughout the universe. Tensions between intersecting event horizons represent energy helixes of symbiotic existences, transcending convergent dimensions; thus releasing measured force through fusion events, as notably observed in Quasars and all nuclear fission processes. Though defined locally as milliards of distant galaxies expanding in all directions, there exists a relativistic influence altering the structure of spatial and temporal mechanics rippling through the cosmos. In layman terms Angels are grounded potentials channeling vast energy from the immense to the minute of subatomic excitation. Hence, the saying *"an Archangel can straddle continents; whereas, a thousand angels can stand on the point of a pin"*.

Just as invisible electromagnetic energy generated in earth's atmosphere reaches full potential by the grounding forces of the elemental state, angels acquire manifestation through spiritually charged relay junctions in dimensional space. Like lighting striking a grounded source, these spirit beings appear within temporal context as values of multidimensional potentials without temporal value.

The best analogy to describe this dynamic process is to think of an electrical power plant and how energy is distributed within a closed system. First, there is a mass mechanical energy source: mega watts of raw energy produced by rotating turbines channeled into large collectors containing magnets wound in copper that spin to create electrons. As the electrons conducted through these generators, they are compressed and multiplied by hundreds of thousands of volts. This concentrated aligned electricity is then distributed along a network grid of high tension wires and gathered into substation transformers designed to decrease the voltage to more manageable quantum. By the time this electricity reaches the consumer, it is further reduced by smaller transformers to a safe feed of 220 / 110 volts in conformity to usage specifications. By incorporating even smaller transformers into a schematic of resistors and capacitors, this electrical flow pattern further manipulated into DC micro voltages, so small that they can safely power the quantum computer processors incorporated into almost every modern household device.

In this analogy, God's creative energy is the source. The angels, created first, become the heavenly principalities of light above and below the firmaments. These grand potentials serve to glorify God's new universe spreading into infinity, but lacking the grounded composite characteristic of the human soul constrained through mortality, and also lacking independence of moral discernment defining good and evil. They are either light or darkness, unable to repent; either with God, or allied with Satan, the chief lieutenant. Angels of God have no locality in time, space, or being. They are one presence; and one can become many. They can span the breath of galaxies, or manifest on a quantum level in dimensional time. But most importantly, angels derive their potential through God's abiding consciousness. They are the individual flaming spirits of omnipotent presence, created first with an ultimate design of symbiotic purpose. It is the mystery of this purpose, which brings heaven upon earth, as a messenger of benevolence to herald comfort and hope to mortal being. It is the Lord's angel announcing the "*good news*" of salvation when Messiah born in Luke's Gospel, Chapter 2, verses 7-14 (NKJV).

> *"And she brought forth her firstborn Son, and wrapped Him in swaddling cloths, and laid Him in a manger, because there was no room for them in the inn. Now there were in the same country shepherds living out in the fields,*

keeping watch over their flock by night. And behold, an angel of the Lord stood before them, and the glory of the Lord shone around them, and they were greatly afraid. Then the angel said to them, "Do not be afraid, for behold, I bring you good tidings of great joy which will be to all people. For there is born to you this day in the city of David a Savior, who is Christ the Lord. And this will be the sign to you: You will find a Babe wrapped in swaddling cloths, lying in a manger. And suddenly there was with the angel a multitude of the heavenly host praising God and saying: "Glory to God in the highest, And on earth peace, goodwill toward men!"

Because angels are the stuff of quantum mechanics, they occupy an esoteric dimension contained through models of accelerated potentials on a much grander scale than the firefly awareness of lineal human history. But not all angels serve the prescription of eternal salvation. Fallen angels are agents of entropy inside the clock. These occupy hyper dimensional plains based on models of probability, and thus becoming algorithms of polarized energy potential forming the matrix of invisible tensions contained in every atom of elemental existence defined through earth, air, water, and fire. There have been many mortal attempts to harness and utilize this raw code of entropic consequence to the end of personal and global perdition. Sorcery, witchery, and wizardry are all attempts of communicating with these beings of this higher dimension through incantation, through cryptic decipher codes using the medium of a pentagram, and experimentations of alchemy.

Even scientific meddling threatens to open a rift in space time, potentially allowing these destructive forces to cross over. Like the protagonist in Christopher Marlow's play Dr. Faustus, man's higher potential blinded to the miracle of present existence by the prideful quest for knowledge and physical immortality. In an attempt to live forever, mankind will believe a lie fabricated since before the days of Noah. A lie that brought swift judgment upon the earth that was then.

The unleashing of these entropic powers will generate the final rehearsal of Armageddon, as prophesied in the Book of Revelation.

Because Jesus Christ conceived directly by God's Holy Spirit mixed with human DNA, he becomes a new source code incorporating spirit, soul, and flesh. This makes possible for the spirits of God's angels to migrate into flesh and blood existence through indwelling of the Holy Spirit. They become us; we become them. A new creature born from corruption, reviving the old man of the earth committed to sin and death conceived through the disobedience of the first Adam. This is the miracle of salvation and the greater meaning of being born again! This mystery revealed in part by Paul's first letter to the Corinthians, Chapter 15, verses 45-47 (KJV).

> *"And so it is written, The first man Adam was made a living soul; the last Adam was made a quickening spirit. Howbeit that was not first which is spiritual, but that which is natural; and afterward that which is spiritual. The first man is of the earth, earthy: the second man is the Lord from heaven. As is the earthy, such are they also that are earthy: and as is the heavenly, such are they also that are heavenly. And as we have borne the image of the earthy, we shall also bear the image of the heavenly. Now this I say, brethren, that flesh and blood cannot inherit the kingdom of God; neither doth corruption inherit incorruption. Behold, I shew you a mystery; We shall not all sleep, but we shall all be changed, In a moment, in the twinkling of an eye, at the last trump: for the trumpet shall sound, and the dead shall be raised incorruptible, and we shall be changed. For this corruptible must put on incorruption, and this mortal must put on immortality. So when this corruptible shall have put on incorruption, and this mortal shall have put on immortality, then shall be brought to pass the saying that is written, Death is swallowed up in victory. O death, where is thy sting? O grave, where is thy victory? The sting of death is sin; and the strength of sin is the law.*

> *But thanks be to God, which giveth us the victory through our Lord Jesus Christ."*

It therefore becomes clear that God has kept the original blueprint of this perfect code from the very beginning. Before creating man, God first creates the inter-dimensional beings we know as angels. Then after the molecular cohesion of matter and a hydrostatic atmosphere congealing into the jewel of mother earth. From the pools of this new world flourishes the plants and the animals, all things after a kind. Finally, the first man made from mineral and water, formed in the likeness of the almighty, a creature like no other, made whole at inception. This man receiving breath of life from almighty God to become eternal living soul. But for man to be God, he needs to know the difference between what is truly good and what is truly evil. The same potential that gives the angels force becomes also a polarity of allegiance. When Satan, the most supreme heavenly creation, realizes vanity, he changes into vanity; and those that follow him changed into eternal violence of rebellion. The first Adam falls under the shadow of sin because his innocence overshadowed by deceptive reason. This sin remaining until *John the Baptist* preaches the gospel of repentance, preparing the way for Messiah. As confirmed by Jesus in the Book of Mathew, Chapter 11, verses 12-15 (KJV).

> *"And from the days of John the Baptist until now the kingdom of heaven suffers violence, and the violent take it by force. For all the prophets and the law prophesied until John. And if ye will receive it, this is Elias, which was for to come. He that hath ears to hear, let him hear."*

The Bible and many supporting records suggest a dramatic difference between angelic force and angelic being. There are at least three distinct categories of angels described in the Bible, further supported by passages found in the Book of Enoch. The main categories seem to be Cherubim, Seraphs, and Archangels. We often think of Cherubim as cute little Cupids sent on romantic missions to inspire chocolate laden love between individuals. They are anything but cute and cuddly. The two Cherubim stationed at the entrance of the Garden of Eden described as frightening creatures prepared to slay any man or beast that might approach. The Cherubs of the Bible are always depicted as powerful entities, often more like machines, than anthropomorphic, serving as instruments of dispassionate motive force decisively executing righteous decree. They appear as multidimensional beings, having many eyes and more than one face, each representative of regional hierarchy (human, lion, oxen, and eagle, etc). They serve as guardians, as well as executioners, being the nearest potential to God's unapproachable glory. These are the first magnitude of angelic existence, designed according to a transcendent order.

The second magnitude of angel is the order of Seraphs. These *"fiery ones"* are often the subject of controversy, bringing warning, or bearing the consequence of impending judgment. They often represent the ministry and the authority of appointed rulers, such as worldly princes and kings. Though vague resemblance to human beings, they are usually depicted as having more than one pair of appendages similar to wings, and radiating the proximity of God's consuming glory. In the Book of Enoch, these creations are referred to as *"drakones"*, dragon-like creatures serving as intercessors of the creator's direct intervention into human affairs. These are not *"good news"* messengers, as we will see in the next position of angelic potential, but are consequential enforcers, meaning that they are the clockwork instruments of the timeline. Just as the cogs and gears of a timepiece calibrated to the passage of change, Seraphs are the statues of righteous judgment: the elemental substance of global destiny precipitated through temporal directional choices of principalities, of kingdoms, and of nations leading inevitably to the day of *Armageddon*. In The Book of Revelation, Chapter 4, verse 8 (KJV), they are described as four all-seeing beast with six wings proclaiming continuously the uncontestable deity of God and his appointed messiah as one.

> *"And the four beasts had each of them six wings about him; and they were full of eyes within: and they rest not day and*

night, saying, Holy, holy, holy, Lord God Almighty, which was, and is, and is to come."

Before exploring the third, and most familiar, angelic potential, I would like to take a moment to discern the relative purpose of their creation within context. The Book of Genesis refers to angelic beings as *"the sons of God"*, meaning that they are direct offspring of the Holy Spirit. They are also called *"the Watchers"* in the Book of Enoch, an association supported in many religions by placing effigies of gargoyles on the corners of church steeples to ward-off evil spirits, as found at the top of Notre Dame Cathedral in Paris. Those angels fallen by choosing to abandon their estate are reserved in confinement of darkness becoming the end of entropy. Those angels that choose to remain serve God's design are the enigmatic energy of a living universe comprised of worlds without end. Both these angelic host emanate from another space termed Heaven, manifesting into temporal space as reflective energy that can be observed, but not quantifiable.

The difficulty for us humans is that we are linearly confined to the slowest track of an ever expanding revolving disc, trying to make sense of events perceived through local observation. As mortal beings, we think in terms of how many, how far, and how long? The past five thousand or so years of recorded civilized history is analogist to seeing a changing landscape from an altitude of 5000 feet and ascribing logical value to the topography of an entire planet. In this analogy, angels reside at an altitude of 500,000 feet, aware not only of the planet below, but of vast distances between many celestial planes. Although these creations not omniscient, their wisdom of the universe more comprehensive than all the accumulated knowledge of mankind. Although not omnipotent, they are beings endowed with a force of unimaginable potential. And even though lacking omnipresence, these super intelligences have no locality, and therefore appear as gods to the spiritually unenlightened. Nevertheless, it is important to stress that these spirit beings created with the absence of a living soul breathed by God into flesh and blood formed from clay of the earth. This makes them subordinate to human kind, as referenced in Psalm 8 verses 3-6 (KJV).

> "When I consider thy heavens, the work of thy fingers, the moon and the stars, which thou hast ordained; What is man, that thou art mindful of him? and the son of man, that thou visit him? For thou hast made him a little lower than the angels, and hast crowned him with glory and honor. Thou made him to have dominion over the works of thy hands; thou hast put all things under his feet:"

Returning to the description provided in the Book of Enoch, there is a further classification of angels called Archangels designated as ruling positions over the cardinal points of classified star systems observed in the four quadrants. The Archangel Michael to the north called *Formalhaut*, marks the position in ancient times of the winter solstice; the Archangel Gabriel in the west, called *Antares*, considered the beginning of the autumn equinox; the Archangel Ariel in the east referred to as *Albebaran* for the spring equinox; and finally the Archangel Raphael in the south, described simply as the *Visible Star* for the summer solstice. It is interesting to note that these royal heavenly principalities also represent astrological positions found on maps of the zodiac, believed by some even to this day to shape the permafrost destinies of individual lives here on earth. In Yiddish the word *"mazel tov"* means good luck based on the chance influence of the stars. This comes from the term *"mazalot"*, a word in ancient Hebrew closely associated with *Kabbalistic* astrological mapping, as referenced in the 38th chapter of the Book of Job, verses 31-38 (NIV).

> "Can you bind the chains of the Pleiades? Can you loosen Orion's belt? Can you bring forth the constellations in their seasons or lead out the Bear d with its cubs? Do you know the laws of the heavens? Can you set up God's e dominion over the earth? "Can you raise your voice to the clouds and cover yourself with a flood of water? Do you send the lightning bolts on their way? Do they report to you, 'Here we are'? Who gives the ibis wisdom or gives the rooster understanding? Who has the wisdom to count the clouds?

Who can tip over the water jars of the heavens when the dust becomes hard and the clods of earth stick together?"

It seems there is a finite value to the actual number of these quantum designated beings. Only a few are named in the Holy Bible or in the Book of Enoch. It is immaterial if there are only the four forces mentioned above, or if there are seven (as many Judaic based religious texts suggest) or if there are thousands, or hundreds of thousands. What is important is that these seraphic creations represent supreme hierarchal positions endowed with a polar charge of allotted energy defining the contained universe within thermodynamic potential. To modern science, this process is called the state of *enthalpy*, which describes the physicality of energy transference within a thermodynamic system, irrespective of how that energy derived. It should be noted that this is different from the concept of *entropy*, which is random decline into disorder and eventual thermodynamic collapse. These inspired heavenly principalities, or *Watchers*, sent by God, transcendent of time and space. Being the messengers of God's spirit, they come to inspire human awareness, as to their importance in the matrix of a resurrected creation, destined to rise from the ashes of present entropic design. They are the light and power of the *Holy Ghost* to make creation complete in the resurrection of souls.

Angelic positions are not static, but engaged in progressive action and reaction. This is a condition often overlooked through intellectualization. These phenomenal beings appear within grander context frozen in time, as though painted on a mural in ages past. They are actually occupied in mounting defenses and counter offenses: angelic dominions first conceived, becoming timeless principalities during the first micro seconds of described infinite velocity. Divisions between them arose immediately instigated by an angel of highest potential. Lucifer perceives himself the brightest of all values radiating a countenance equal to the creator. Because of the unrepentant nature of the transgression, this supreme archangel cast out of heaven, along with those spirits that align the magnitude of their assigned forces with him. But this is not a historical permeation, but rather an instantaneous reaction of cause and effect. The temporal interpretation of these distant observations characterized by the birth of galaxies and the event horizons of collapsing black holes in the fabric of inconceivable vastness. Perhaps from our mortal perspective, we are actually witnessing the war in heaven, as described in The Book of Revelation, Chapter 12, verses 7-8 (KJV).

> *"And there was war in heaven: Michael and his angels fought against the dragon; and the dragon fought and his angels, And prevailed not; neither was their place found any more in heaven."*

In other words, because of mortal condition, man observes the universe in linear slow- motion, unable to grasp the full meaning of actual events. It would be like perceiving the months of summer through fleeting generations of dayflies, born and dead during the passage of hours, unaware of the changing seasons. This war has only now begun, a battle for the most precious commodity in this present universe: a rich harvest of human souls weighed in the balance. But the children of God have already prevailed through a perfect code conceived in the fullness of time.

When an angel assumes anthropomorphic form, it becomes a medium element between chronological and non-chronological being. Hence, it acquires human characteristic, neither spirit, nor the living matrix of biology, but an imprint of both. This *seventh heaven* existence becomes subject to material and sensory temptation grounded in earthly conditions. As I have already stated, a phenomenon of indwelling occurs when mortal and immortal elements intertwine, translating both elements into the consciousness of God's Holy Spirit outside of sequential time and space. Through this condition men become embodiment of angels, and angels as men: manifesting as emissaries delivering divine messages through segments of temporal agency. Such were the *men*, who physically grabbed lot and his family and led them out of the condemned city of Sodom. And again in The Books of Acts, Chapter

12, verses 7-11 (NIV), the Apostle Peter is led out of prison by an angel, left momentarily confused by the experience.

> *"Suddenly an angel of the Lord appeared and a light shone in the cell. He struck Peter on the side and woke him up. "Quick, get up!" he said, and the chains fell off Peter's wrists. Then the angel said to him, "Put on your clothes and sandals." And Peter did so. "Wrap your cloak around you and follow me," the angel told him. Peter followed him out of the prison, but he had no idea that what the angel was doing was really happening; he thought he was seeing a vision. They passed the first and second guards and came to the iron gate leading to the city. It opened for them by itself, and they went through it. When they had walked the length of one street, suddenly the angel left him. Then Peter came to himself and said, "Now I know without a doubt that the Lord has sent his angel and rescued me from Herod's clutches and from everything the Jewish people were hoping would happen."*

In this instant, mortal reason becomes overshadowed by a powerful supernatural apparition. At another time an angel appears again to Peter, instructing him to accompany the men seeking him from Caesarea, a more direct communication, conveying message to this stubborn Apostle that salvation has come even to the *Gentiles*. Something similar happens to Paul and Silas, as recorded in The Book of Acts, Chapter 16, verses, 25-34 (NIV), but without physical manifestation. However, this deliverance results in the miraculous salvation of the prison guard and all in his household.

> *"About midnight Paul and Silas were praying and singing hymns to God, and the other prisoners were listening to them. Suddenly there was such a violent earthquake that the foundations of the prison were shaken. At once all the prison doors flew open, and everyone's chains came loose.*

The jailer woke up, and when he saw the prison doors open, he drew his sword and was about to kill himself because he thought the prisoners had escaped. But Paul shouted, "Don't harm yourself! We are all here!" The jailer called for lights, rushed in and fell trembling before Paul and Silas. He then brought them out and asked, "Sirs, what must I do to be saved?" They replied, "Believe in the Lord Jesus, and you will be saved—you and your household." Then they spoke the word of the Lord to him and to all the others in his house. At that hour of the night the jailer took them and washed their wounds; then immediately he and all his household were baptized. The jailer brought them into his house and set a meal before them; he was filled with joy because he had come to believe in God—he and his whole household."

This jailer probably knew nothing about angels and perhaps even less about the customs of Jews. But he understood the great power witnessed with his own eyes and submitted to the abiding witness of those prisoners given to his charge, as did those in his household. In another instance, the Apostle Phillip is instructed by an angel to go near the chariot of the questioning Ethiopian referred only as a eunuch under the Ethiopian Queen Candace. Upon hearing the words of salvation, this aristocrat of position believes and is baptized. After the message delivered, the apostle unceremoniously swept up in the spirit and physically translated to another place. This even recounted for our benefit in Book of the Acts, Chapter 8, verses 39-40 (KJV).

"And when they came up out of the water, the Spirit of the Lord carried Philip away, and the eunuch saw him no more, and went on his way rejoicing. But Philip was found at Azotus: and passing through he preached in all the cities, till he came to Caesarea."

As we might conclude from these examples, Angels are sometimes external emotive presences endowed with grand energy. Sometimes they are manifestations of meditative prayer with clear instruction. Always these celestial agents instruments of greater purpose. I personally picked up a hitcher on a lonely stretch of highway between Arizona and New Mexico. The stranger's appearance is that of an old man; yet possessed with a spiritual presence undeniable. Silence remains between us for over twenty miles. Then the man turns his head and says,

"I need to go to Tulsa. I have a daughter in a hospital there that needs me."

Tulsa is nearly a hundred miles out of my projected route. But for some inexplicable reason I feel convicted in the spirit to help this total stranger. I drive out of my way and offer him some money. With a twinkle of gratitude in his eyes, this strange acquaintance whisked away in a crowd. This moment I feel overshadowed by a peace beyond understanding. In later reflection, I know in my soul that I entertained an *angel unaware*.

Another event of similar bearing happens to me earlier in my life driving back to my Marine Corps base from South Carolina to Camp Pendleton located in southern California. I pick up a young couple on the Texas border hitchhiking their way to San Francisco. They are altogether broke, so I pay their food and lodging. Taking the Hollywood exit, I locate a Greyhound Bus Station and buy tickets to their final destination. At this time I did not yet know God's mercy in my life, but felt a sense of compassion not in my nature since returning from the Vietnam conflict. Yet, in clear retrospect I can see the hand of a God I did not know preparing my salvation even then. I had become an unsuspecting agent to the needs of this young couple stranded in a world made by consequence. But power did not reside in my own goodness. Rather the spiritual manifestation of sin being remitted, and an even greater grace prepared to my awakening soul. For there is no righteous behavior in the human heart, except it be ministered through the spirits of God's holy messengers. In 2 Corinthians, Chapter 12, verses 1-7 (KJV), Paul humbly makes statement concerning spiritual translation and warfare of self pride.

"It is not expedient for me doubtless to glory. I will come to visions and revelations of the Lord. I knew a man in Christ above fourteen years ago, (whether in the body, I cannot tell; or whether out of the body, I cannot tell: God knows;) such an one caught up to the third heaven. And I knew such a man, (whether in the body, or out of the body, I cannot tell: God knows;) How that he was caught up into paradise, and heard unspeakable words, which it is not lawful for a man to utter. Of such an one will I glory: yet of myself I will not glory, but in mine infirmities. For though I would desire to glory, I shall not be a fool; for I will say the truth: but now I forbear, lest any man should think of me above that which he sees me to be, or that he hears of me. And lest I should be exalted above measure through the abundance of the revelations, there was given to me a thorn in the flesh, the messenger of Satan to buffet me, lest I should be exalted above measure."

The symbiotic relationship that exists between the human soul and these celestial quickened spirits can only be appreciated within context of a purpose as yet unfulfilled: a meaning that will be made clear at the last trump of victory in a final battle that rages even now. This bonding of supernatural indwelling should not be confused with demon possession. These evil spirits, separated from God's glory, utilize deception through carnal apatite to possess and corrupt the human soul to the end of death. This spiritual inception is a dark alliance doomed to a destructive conclusion. Instead of life, this kind of indwelling results in eternal chains of darkness.

Because angels are the composition of collective energy, and manifest as agents of a source directive, they can only materialize in local time and space as a potential. Thus, when they transcend their heavenly abode, it is a deterministic permutation with polar directive. To those mortal they appear, either as immaterial reflections, or as flesh and blood beings. This is an important distinction. We are led to believe that human replication is as easy as having a strand of *DNA* and a Petri dish. This magnitude of being is far more complex and unique than organized within our shell existence reveals. But even with all their great knowledge, those angels of rebellion descended from their heavenly abode have failed in many attempts spanning millenniums here on earth to construct a human being with an elevated soul. The *Nephilim* were as close as they got in prehistory, an achievement made possible through constructed technologies modern man is only beginning to glimpse through the science of gene manipulation and chemically induced cross breeding. These original offspring of the fallen *sons of God* became vicious predators, unruly and cannibalistic, lacking any awareness given to even the baser instincts of human complexity. The end of their mortal existence, a host of demonic beings trapped in an interspatial dimension. Since this historical race of monsters and their imminent return discussed earlier, I believe further reference unnecessary.

Scriptures make clear that angels do not marry or engage in relationships unique to the convention of flesh and blood beings. I think it safe to assume that the motive of those fallen spirits far more sinister than desire based on carnal appetite. I suspect, rather, that these exiled beings are aftermath evidence of quantum thermodynamic action confined within the mechanical universe of entropic collapse. This is the true condition of their dark realm! Once light, these beings are descended into an estate of utter darkness, bitterly envying the human soul of eternal potential that could have made them complete. This is the ugly reality they wish to conceal from human kind. They are the many false gods found in antiquity made of gold, bronze, and stone. These lifeless effigies fashioned from the elements in the likeness of evil, but remaining powerless, without the willingness of a human heart or the activity of human hands corrupted to evil imaginings. Presently contained, these rebellious entities seek an aperture of escape into conscious time to fulfill their final destruction.

The Bible refers to Satan and his angels as *'deceiving spirits';* whereas, God's glorified messengers an extension of the holy trinity designed from the beginning of creation. The book of Daniel describes angelic warfare in heaven and upon the earth. Twice before, Daniel recounts how angels intercede to spare the lives of men devoted to the worship of God. The record of Shadrach, Meshach, and Abednego, men thrown into a fiery furnace for refusing to bow down to King Nebuchadnezzar's golden idol, but are spared certain death by the direct intervention of an angel. Daniel himself also left alive because an angel shut the mouths of hungry lions after being cast into their liar for the crime of making prayer to the God of Israel, instead of praying to that same king of Babylon. An unnamed messenger, who many mistakenly presume is just any angel, appears to Daniel with an important message to the prophet. After being much delayed by *'the Prince of Persia'*, until reinforced by the Archangel Michael, this angel provides insight on what is to come. He speaks of the coming of Cyrus the Great, a mighty Prince for Persia. This king of kings will subdue the Babylonian Empire, releasing the Jews from their seventy year captivity in that great walled city. By force, he instructs the freed generation of Israel to reluctantly return to their homeland and rebuild Jerusalem and the second Temple, as predicted by the Prophet Jeremiah. This glorified messenger to Daniel further speaks of his future struggle with the King of Greece, which Cyrus' grandson, Xerxes, will unsuccessfully invade many years later with the greatest army the world had ever seen. This son of Darius driven by pride and arrogance believes it his destiny to rule the earth. Instead he only infuriates the residents of Macedonia, thus forcing the Greek Polis to unite into a consolidated victorious empire lead by Alexander the Great. This begins the Golden Age.

These are the world empires that were, and are yet to come. This spiritually alive entity that appears unto Daniel is not representative of a condition in temporal time and space, but a quantum presence waging a transcendent war against a strong enemy spanning many generations of men. This is evident through the manifestation of angelic presence (*many theologians believe to be Christ*) giving a spiritual report on how the war is raging. In the book recorded by this notable prophet, Daniel, Chapter 10, verses 10-19 (NIV), we are given a glimpse into the nature of this celestial battlefield:

> *"A hand touched me and set me trembling on my hands and knees. He said, "Daniel, you who are highly esteemed,*

consider carefully the words I am about to speak to you, and stand up, for I have now been sent to you." And when he said this to me, I stood up trembling. Then he continued, "Do not be afraid, Daniel. Since the first day that you set your mind to gain understanding and to humble yourself before your God, your words were heard, and I have come in response to them. But the prince of the Persian kingdom resisted me twenty-one days. Then Michael, one of the chief princes, came to help me, because I was detained there with the king of Persia. Now I have come to explain to you what will happen to your people in the future, for the vision concerns a time yet to come." While he was saying this to me, I bowed with my face toward the ground and was speechless. Then one who looked like a man touched my lips, and I opened my mouth and began to speak. I said to the one standing before me, "I am overcome with anguish because of the vision, my lord, and I feel very weak. How can I, your servant, talk with you, my lord? My strength is gone and I can hardly breathe." Again the one who looked like a man touched me and gave me strength. "Do not be afraid, you who are highly esteemed," he said. "Peace! Be strong now; be strong."

This celestial war begun at the instance of man's creation: a war that has lasted from the end to the beginning, a multidimensional conflict taking place even now. After providing Daniel the prophetic vision of future events concerning the Jewish people and world nations, this personage born of flesh and spirit returns to the front lines of an ongoing battle. It is this same Christ that stands on the glory of a cloud leading a prepared arm of sanctified Angels and Saints into battle to vanquish Satan's rule over the earth. as given witness in the Gospel of Mathew, Chapter 24, verse 30-31(NIV).

"Then will appear the sign of the Son of Man in heaven. And then all the peoples of the earth will mourn when they

see the Son of Man coming on the clouds of heaven, with power and great glory. And he will send his angels with a loud trumpet call, and they will gather his elect from the four winds, from one end of the heavens to the other."

In regards to earth's violent history, it is not difficult to imagine a perpetual struggle with a predictable outcome raging unseen throughout time and history. Michael, considered one of the chief heavenly princes, and Gabriel, whose name means *'man of God'* or the *'strength of God'*, along with their host are always referred to as *glorified beings*, meaning they are the motive force of God's Christ. Those angels allied with Lucifer's rebellion forces of evil, their light changed to darkness, spirits absent of the illumination of creative instruction.

I have a glimpse of this decisive conflict the night I receive the *Holy Spirit* and am *born again*. I think these opposing forces not just battalions of angels, but the indwelling union of saints against demonic opposition, poised on a precipice separated by a timeless abyss. For an instant, I am there, prepared to battle; but also restrain here in time to remain for reasons of faith designed beyond my comprehension. The only evidence I can provide, not revealed in the weaker element of flesh and blood, but as one who has received a message of deliverance. My witness of these events sent to those blinded through worldly wisdom, not just to those who believe already. The rest I submit into the hands of the Lord to be revealed in season.

The Book of Enoch emphasizes the supreme importance of God's Messiah to restore order and peace to the living jewel of creation and to heavenly principalities. This Messiah entering into temporal condition, born of flesh and of the Holy Spirit, in a time divided by time, and to the end of life everlasting. Enoch also born in the midst of division, translated into a heaven prepared by faith, all the while beholding clearly the future promise of God's salvation to all creatures above and below. The Messiah clearly portrayed in this written text, lost to the conscious world of men, very similar to the returning *King of Kings* in the Book of Revelation. Remember that these visions presumably recorded many hundreds of *earth-time* years before Noah and his family stepped into the belly of the Ark and the world that was then destroyed. In the Book of Enoch, Chapter 46, we read:

> *"There I beheld the Ancient of days whose head was like white wool, and with him another, whose countenance resembled that of a man. His countenance was full of grace, like that of one of the holy angels. Then I inquired of one of the angels, who went with me, and who showed me every secret thing, concerning this Son of man; who he was; whence he was; and why he accompanied the Ancient of days. He answered and said to me, This is the Son of man, to whom righteousness belongs; with whom righteousness has dwelt; and who will reveal all the treasures of that which is concealed: for the Lord of spirits has chosen him; and his portion has surpassed all before the Lord of spirits in everlasting uprightness."*

Since it is suggested that angels are by definition more than singular existence, they often manifest in transcendent appearance. Meaning they seem to have the ability to translate from potential to actual being. As already pointed out there are many occasions throughout the Bible where a supernatural personage appears to men bringing messages of good tiding or a forewarning. These messengers are always sober, translating commandments of eternal promise within temporal context. In other words, they are decelerated to chronological association, bearing comfort and guiding influence to souls obedient to faith. These stand continually with the Messiah, whose manifestation intercedes all generations and all principalities. They are also the guardian angels we hear so much about: heavenly potentials assigned to the protective guidance of individual destiny through the course of temporal passage. *They are us reborn.*

These *non-temporal* agents possess the capacity to be much more. Not only are they the power of righteousness upon the earth, but grand forces of judgment from heaven. Not only are they the opposite of present entropy, but the instrumentation of causality. In short angels are soldiers armed sent to combat evil in the world, capable of indwelling a human host, as when Samson picks up the jaw bone of an ass and slays a thousand men of warring Philistines; or the arm of a boy, who brings down the giant with a sling and a small stone. There were raised up many judges in Israel, all inspired with power of heavenly retribution, but none by the will or strength of a mortal hand. Their stories are unlike the accolades of classical societies glorifying the self-willed actions of heroes and great warriors. History observes that the mighty less excellent, than the submission of a chosen vessel.

There have been times in my life when God has used me as an instrument of judgment to battle positions of worldly defiance. At these intervals I am overshadowed by a peace surpassing understanding, my purpose no longer restrained to visible elements. During these episodes my soul shouts Hallelujah with the angels in heaven. At such moments I am cognitive of potent forces that surround us continually, spirits in the air raging war in heaven. This is power of the Holy Spirit grounded through mortal presence. Flesh and blood but a garment soon to be discarded for a robe more elegant. The man Jesus knew by faith the hour of his persecution and also by faith trusted the will of his Father in heaven. Surely he is aware that within him resides the power to summon legions of angels in his defense. But also by faith knows the only way to insure victory over Satan and restoration of men's souls is to submit to a death already prepared. Jesus makes it clear that there is a vast difference between the ambitions of this world and the pending judgment to come in the Gospel of Mathew, Chapter 24, verses 1-14 (NIV).

> *"Jesus left the temple and was walking away when his disciples came up to him to call his attention to its buildings. "Do you see all these things?" he asked. "Truly I tell you, not one stone here will be left on another; every one will be thrown down." As Jesus was sitting on the Mount of Olives, the disciples came to him privately. "Tell us," they said, "when will this happen, and what will be the sign of your coming and of the end of the age?" Jesus answered: "Watch out that no one deceives you. For many will come*

in my name, claiming, 'I am the Messiah,' and will deceive many. You will hear of wars and rumors of wars, but see to it that you are not alarmed. Such things must happen, but the end is still to come. Nation will rise against nation, and kingdom against kingdom. There will be famines and earthquakes in various places. All these are the beginning of birth pains. "Then you will be handed over to be persecuted and put to death, and you will be hated by all nations because of me. At that time many will turn away from the faith and will betray and hate each other, and many false prophets will appear and deceive many people. Because of the increase of wickedness, the love of most will grow cold, but the one who stands firm to the end will be saved. And this gospel of the kingdom will be preached in the whole world as a testimony to all nations, and then the end will come."

The angels of God are more than just bodyguards. Nor are they anything like the creatures that rebelled and have fallen already with their Lieutenant. These holy beings are perfected through the flesh and spirit conception of the resurrected Christ, non-quantum potentials transcending time and space, thus becoming the third axis of the Holy Trinity. They are the abiding testament to the souls of saints, existing as lighted candles through a dark passage. This once again raises the question: *What is the stuff of angels?* The answer to this is that angels exist everywhere and nowhere to be found, except by faith. To this end victory secure through obstacle of every trial and against every enemy seen and unseen. In 2 Kings, Chapter 6, verses 15-17 (NIV), Elisha, the prophet of God, reveals to his servant the invisible world of angelic forces surrounding all of us continually: holy armed battalions standing upon the precipice of eternity in protection of every soul that trusts in the Lord of salvation

"When the servant of the man of God got up and went out early the next morning, an army with horses and chariots

> had surrounded the city. "Oh no, my lord! What shall we do?" the servant asked. "Don't be afraid," the prophet answered. "Those who are with us are more than those who are with them." And Elisha prayed, "Open his eyes, LORD, so that he may see." Then the LORD opened the servant's eyes, and he looked and saw the hills full of horses and chariots of fire all around Elisha."

Unknowingly all creation runs a course of time, events that have already happened and been predetermined by the domino effect on global scale. But though the lens of faith all things possible to the sons of God; those that live by faith and not the lust of the eyes are the will of the flesh. This is no secret thing to all reborn the Holy Spirit, as Paul states in a letter to the Romans in Chapter 8, verses 14-31 (NIV).

> "For those who are led by the Spirit of God are the children of God. The Spirit you received does not make you slaves, so that you live in fear again; rather, the Spirit you received brought about your adoption to sonship. And by him we cry, "Abba, Father." The Spirit himself testifies with our spirit that we are God's children. Now if we are children, then we are heirs—heirs of God and co-heirs with Christ, if indeed we share in his sufferings in order that we may also share in his glory. I consider that our present sufferings are not worth comparing with the glory that will be revealed in us. For the creation waits in eager expectation for the children of God to be revealed. For the creation was subjected to frustration, not by its own choice, but by the will of the one who subjected it, in hope that the creation itself will be liberated from its bondage to decay and brought into the freedom and glory of the children of God. We know that the whole creation has been groaning as in the pains of childbirth right up to the present time. Not only so, but we ourselves, who have the firstfruits of the Spirit, groan inwardly as we wait eagerly for our

adoption to sonship, the redemption of our bodies. For in this hope we were saved. But hope that is seen is no hope at all. Who hopes for what they already have? But if we hope for what we do not yet have, we wait for it patiently. In the same way, the Spirit helps us in our weakness. We do not know what we ought to pray for, but the Spirit himself intercedes for us through wordless groans. And he who searches our hearts knows the mind of the Spirit, because the Spirit intercedes for God's people in accordance with the will of God.

And we know that in all things God works for the good of those who love him, who have been called according to his purpose. For those God foreknew he also predestined to be conformed to the image of his Son, that he might be the firstborn among many brothers and sisters. And those he predestined, he also called; those he called, he also justified; those he justified, he also glorified. What, then, shall we say in response to these things? If God is for us, who can be against us?"

To this my soul says amen!

Chapter 16
A HUMAN EQUATION

No man in history is accredited with greater wisdom than Solomon, a royal *King of Kings* sitting upon the throne of a grand palace in Jerusalem, a city whose name means the *foundation of peace*. But not only is this man wise and prosperous, but a sovereign exceedingly capricious. Before the *Pleasure Dome of Kublai Kan* succumbed to legend, this wealthy sovereign indulges in every delight of eyes and imagination. He pursues the depth of every worldly measure, only to learn the truest meaning of vanity and worldly futility. He explores pleasures of the flesh, only to realize nothing satisfies. He dines on the finest feast, only to know hunger another day. He gathers dazzling riches from exotic ends of the earth, only to be disappointed through dreams tarnished by imagination. But most tragic of all revelation to the human condition, he learns that no matter how one proportions quantity in this world through natural reason, a pint can only hold a pint. From the height of his exalted throne, King Solomon becomes a man most miserable by the inescapable clarity of wise apprehension, as he states in Ecclesiastes chapter 1, verses 9-18 (NKJV).

> *"That which has been is what will be, That which is done is what will be done, And there is nothing new under the sun. Is there anything of which it may be said, "See, this is new"? It has already been in ancient times before us. There is no remembrance of former things, Nor will there be any remembrance of things that are to come By those who will come after. I, the Preacher, was king over Israel in Jerusalem. And I set my heart to seek and search out by wisdom concerning all that is done under heaven;*

this burdensome task God has given to the sons of man, by which they may be exercised. I have seen all the works that are done under the sun; and indeed, all is vanity and grasping for the wind. What is crooked cannot be made straight, And what is lacking cannot be numbered. I communed with my heart, saying, "Look, I have attained greatness, and have gained more wisdom than all who were before me in Jerusalem. My heart has understood great wisdom and knowledge." And I set my heart to know wisdom and to know madness and folly. I perceived that this also is grasping for the wind. For in much wisdom is much grief, And he who increases knowledge increases sorrow."

As a young boy Solomon is crowned the third king of all of Israel. Saul, the first anointed king, a man desired by the people, disappoints through cruelty, self-serving ambition, and deceitfulness. David, the shepherd boy, who slew the Philistine giant Goliath with a stone released from his sling, ascends to the throne a most remarkable and passionate leader. As a man he is less than perfect, yet remains faithful in the eyes of God. In many ways David's life follows a course as tragic as his predecessor. He betrays to death one of his captains, a Hittite named Uriah, so that he might marry the other man's wife, Bathsheba, following an adulterous relationship. David's favored son named Absalom arranges the murder of his brother because the latter rapes their sister. Absalom flees from the wrath of his father north, finding refuge among sympathetic rebels, where he is eventually killed in battle fighting against David's forces. King David manages to reunite the kingdom before the end of his forty year reign but at a great personal loss. However this man is most remembered by his unfeigned faith in God, humbly accepting judgment and dishonor, as well as honor. He knows in his heart that it is God's hand that has raised him to this worldly position. Unlike most men, David trusts more in the future promise of his Lord's Lord, than in the strength of present mortal decree. Regardless of personal regret, the contrite nature of this man makes him most remarkable through the parade of biblical history. David witnesses salvation to his sinful soul through vision of grace assured by the coming of a Messiah his mortal eyes will not see. Through the loins of this fearless general in the battlefield will flourish the prophetic seed of God's Christ, the chosen one of Israel.

Bathsheba is impregnated twice by her husband, but only Solomon survives. Through her persistent urging, David appoints this last son heir to the throne. After a long and turbulent reign, King David dies without ever knowing the peace his son famously enjoys. At the end of Solomon's prosperous seat upon the throne sharp division will splinter the southern tribe of Judah from Israel to the north, becoming two separate kingdoms. In time disagreement between the two factions will escalate into bloody conflict of brother against brother destined to continue until the days of Nebuchadnezzar and the Babylonian captivity lasting seventy years. So it is with the chronicle of kings ruling over kingdoms everywhere.

However, God has a plan for this earthly kingdom historically known has Israel. Since the mercy seat of Moses, matters of law allocated to responsible individuals; and those appointed priest from the house of Aaron serving as mediators between the ten tribes and the Holy Ark of the Covenant. At particular times God sends judges and prophets anointed with a spiritual directive to instruct and correct the people to keep them distinct from the sins of other nations. Nevertheless in the days of the prophet Samuel, the houses of Israel demand a king like the nations surrounding their borders. The prophet warns that this will only bring distress to the people, because they have already begun to trust more in worldly denomination, than in the God that delivered them from captivity in Egypt. But still they insist. Finally God gives in to their demands with this prophetic promise in 1 Samuel, Chapter 8, verses 10-22 (NKJV).

> *"So Samuel told all the words of the LORD to the people who asked him for a king. And he said, "This will be the behavior of the king who will reign over you: He will take your sons and appoint them for his own chariots and to*

be his horsemen, and some will run before his chariots. He will appoint captains over his thousands and captains over his fifties, will set some to plow his ground and reap his harvest, and some to make his weapons of war and equipment for his chariots. He will take your daughters to be perfumers, cooks, and bakers. And he will take the best of your fields, your vineyards, and your olive groves, and give them to his servants. He will take a tenth of your grain and your vintage, and give it to his officers and servants. And he will take your male servants, your female servants, your finest young men, and your donkeys, and put them to his work. He will take a tenth of your sheep. And you will be his servants. And you will cry out in that day because of your king whom you have chosen for yourselves, and the LORD will not hear you in that day." Nevertheless the people refused to obey the voice of Samuel; and they said, "No, but we will have a king over us, that we also may be like all the nations, and that our king may judge us and go out before us and fight our battles." And Samuel heard all the words of the people, and he repeated them in the hearing of the LORD. So the LORD said to Samuel, "Heed their voice, and make them a king. And Samuel said to the men of Israel, "Every man go to his city.""

This prophecy concerning kings has proven true throughout the history of kingdoms, with Israel being only a specimen under a microscope. Already this people had forgotten the strength of their existence. So what is it about mortal nature that desires a physical leader? Someone born in like-manner, made of the same flesh, only braver, stronger, and wiser: this *better man* representing a better code of what it means to be human, and therefore worthy to follow?

It is a natural affection to prefer things that are unblemished and appealing to the eyes; but more importantly, to seek out the exceptional among the common, to find a single pearl of great value hidden in the ever-changing tide of unpredictability. Through mortal reflection, the discovery of one man of pure linage, endowed with shared values, willingly able to take up the sword of justice and lead victorious. A man of the people, the desire of every band of happy men and den of thieves, raised up to encourage and to protect against any would be aggressor. A man such as this portrayed by Israel's first chosen king described in 1 Samuel chapter 9, verse 1 (KJV).

> *"There was a man of Benjamin whose name was Kish the son of Abiel, the son of Zeror, the son of Bechorath, the son of Aphiah, a Benjamite, a mighty man of power. And he had a choice and handsome son whose name was Saul. There was not a more handsome person than he among the children of Israel. From his shoulders upward he was taller than any of the people."*

But a king is only a vessel, empty, until filled with an interpretation of ideology. It is not just his vision, but the vision of the collective. He is the instrument of an earthly confederation, becoming an agenda of mega consciousness. This mega consciousness can be defined in terms of the better good or to the end of evil tyranny. This should not be confused with wars of attrition or wars of independence. Although the Punic Wars between Rome and Carthage last nearly twenty five years, there is no major change in the ultimate decline of the fragmented empire. And even though the American Civil War forces brother against brother, the end sees reunion of a nation united before. These are only skirmishes in the greater scheme: battles of alignments between supernatural generals with a unified agenda. Whereas, wars raged by empires and nations against nations decides alliances of a global directive, ultimately drawing rigid battle lines. Even the violent turbulence between Sunni and Shiite extremism in the Middle East little more than a family quarrel to rid the world of chafe before the real storm of affliction strikes.

The first great world war of the last century brings to an end colonial expansion, while at the same time unifying ideological regions preserved through silent agenda. The second world conflict, twenty-one years later, sets the stage for present power demographics of globalization. If we look back through the lens of history, we see a clear pattern of organization, like concentric patterns drawn in the sands of time. The giant of Persia, during the days of Xerxes, not the vision of just one man, but is a continuation of a monarch lineage with a collective vision of world domination. Hitler did not motivate the German people without their consent; rather, they march against their European neighbors with the inspired belief in a pure Aryan race. As we have already observed, the kings of the earth destined already to join forces together under Satan's command, which is the mind of this world against God's Messiah. It is interesting to note that the armies of this world struggle always for territory, ever wanting to expand and to subdue. But the expectations of tiny Israel have always been the same: to receive the vineyard of God's promise made to Abraham more than four thousand years ago. No matter the decisive efforts of secular Israel, spiritual Israel will turn suppliant to God's Messiah to the end of salvation.

There is more than just military aggression shaping nations. Propaganda is now the preferred weapon. Win the hearts and souls of a population; the rest is all too easy. Through the influence of media control lased with half truths, the infusion of accepted views with emotional humanism, and the 'dark web' of personal access begins to take form. There exists a paradox in human equation overshadowing the clarity of individual conscience. Our souls wither into an ocean of consensus, as we rely more on the arm of earthly power, than upon greater witness manifest through unseen principalities of faith. We actually begin to believe in a lie that we are part of some defined unified collective. At the same time forgetting that legality does not always mean right, and to win by any means is only acknowledgement to the fear of defeat. We easily adopt the tactics of our enemy forgetting that this is what makes us different from our enemy. This raises the question: *what does it truly means to be human within human context?*

A key element in social psychology is the idea that individuals and populations can be conditioned under favorable circumstances to conform to a prescribed system of values. The first thought that comes to mind is Pavlov's experiment of salivating dogs by utilizing reinforcement behavior modification techniques. Although psyche interaction more complex than those of other animals, human reaction to external stimuli can be altered to conform to a given structure, as long as that structure identifiable to some logical objective. But human beings possess something else that our fellow creatures lack: *a free will* based not only on environmental conditions. The factored element of this *will* cannot be underestimated, but often ignored, except by those in positions of power wishing to control the masses. Since *free will* separates higher cognition from basic instincts, it also is the potential of good and evil. Because of this elevated ability to choose, there exists a delicate barrier between conscious interaction deduced through accepted evidence of a perceived reality and basic morality prescribed by emotive response. For this same reason it is also subject to corruption. Like any human attribute, a conscience must first be realized and then instructed.

Physical affection or threat of painful consequence is a familiar type of reinforcement behavior modification traditionally applied to raising children. Another is organised training facilities engaged in teaching individuals how to function as a team. An example of this is my experience in the late 1960s undergoing Marine Corps Boot Camp training, deemed as a lesson in mental and physical discipline. *"We are here to break down the weak elements to build a stronger and better Marine," states* the motto of my Drill Sergeants. Out of more than a hundred men who enter the program, only 70 graduate with the proud title of a U.S. Marine. This can be termed a positive enforcement technique to build strength of character and to instill a sense of communal responsibility. But it contributes something else even more important, a quality of determination that has never failed me in all these years. The challenge of this early experience reinforces strength in my will of character, making my mind stronger than limits imposed by sensory input. However, this will power is not the same as faith.

What is termed human will is an attribute of ideological orientation toward patriotic values and associations based on complex alliances and associations. It is the essence of character, an earthly conviction, usually associated with an affiliation of shared comradely, sometimes more powerful than fear of death. Faith is the peaceful submission to present conditions; while at the same time acutely aware of a promise not evident through natural observation or present experience. The first is a component of the mind, the second a gift of the Holy Spirit. In the Apostle Paul's correspondence to the well versed *letter-of-the-law* Hebrews, Chapter 11, verses 1-16, (KJV) an excellent description given concerning the certain attributes of faith.

> *"Now faith is the substance of things hoped for, the evidence of things not seen. For by it the elders obtained a good report. Through faith we understand that the worlds were framed by the word of God, so that things which are seen were not made of things which do appear. By faith Abel offered unto God a more excellent sacrifice than Cain, by which he obtained witness that he was righteous, God testifying of his gifts: and by it he being dead yet speaketh By faith Enoch was translated that he should not see death; and was not found, because God had translated him: for before his translation he had this testimony, that he pleased God. But without faith it is impossible to please him: for he that cometh to God must believe that he is, and that he is a rewarder of them that diligently seek him. By faith Noah, being warned of God of things not seen as yet, moved with fear, prepared an ark to the saving of his house; by the which he condemned the world, and became heir of the righteousness which is by faith. By faith Abraham, when he was called to go out into a place which he should after receive for an inheritance, obeyed; and he went out, not knowing whither he went. By faith he sojourned in the land of promise, as in a strange country, dwelling in tabernacles with Isaac and Jacob, the heirs with him of the same promise: For he looked for a city which hath foundations, whose builder and maker is God. Through faith also Sara herself received strength to conceive seed, and was delivered of a child when she was past age, because she*

judged him faithful who had promised. Therefore sprang there even of one, and him as good as dead, so many as the stars of the sky in multitude, and as the sand which is by the sea shore innumerable. These all died in faith, not having received the promises, but having seen them afar off, and were persuaded of them, and embraced them, and confessed that they were strangers and pilgrims on the earth. For they that say such things declare plainly that they seek a country. And truly, if they had been mindful of that country from whence they came out, they might have had opportunity to have returned. But now they desire a better country, that is, an heavenly: wherefore God is not ashamed to be called their God: for he hath prepared for them a city."

However not all behavior conditioning programs have a design toward positive enforcement, but an agenda to annihilate--not just the flesh, but also the spirit. Victor Frankl, a renowned 20th Century psychologist, survives the physical trauma of being a prisoner in a concentration camp during the Nazi *Final Solution Program,* beginning with its own civilians consisting mostly of Jews. In Frankl's book written after the fall of this evil regime, titled Man's Search for Meaning, he employs a famous quote by Niche that states *"He who has a will to live can bear with almost any how."* This man, along with millions of other individuals, men, women and children, suffer inhuman treatment by an authority dedicated to genocide extermination of a race. Although the Jewish people become the original target of Germany's radicalized hatred machine, it is only the beginning of an Aryan philosophy to cleanse the world of perceived imperfection. This shadow of tyranny spread over Europe, sparking a devastating Second World War, threatening every shore around the globe. Two deadly forces engaged in a battle to the end. The future democracy of civilized humanity weighed in the balance. But who won, and what was won?

The outcome of this horrific conflict not won just because God stands on the side of the righteous, but further sets the stage for the war of wars *Armageddon.* You might ask what I mean by this. Surly this Second Great War on this planet at the dawn of modern times represents the defeat of evil as demonstrative example of the ultimate victory of the unified good of mankind. Magnificent cities destroyed and rebuilt better and more material than before. Europe becomes unified as never in history, becoming a model vision of future commerce and economic prosperity. The new United States of America now a dominate world power patrolling every international neighborhood continuously scrutinizing the nefarious activities of bad players. Why suspect an elephant in the room when capitalistic prosperity within reach of all?

An analogy to this foreboding is when a sperm impregnates an ovulated egg. The two individual parts cease to exist, becoming a new whole. This born entity now a collective of something different than contained in the separate components. A fact of history, the Roman Empire never came to an end, but rather is assimilated. The soul of Rome remains two thousand years later the foundation of law and commerce. Likewise, the Nazi Reich ended, but not the essence of spiritual influence. Because of unspeakable medical experiments conducted on living hosts, a new direction in medicine realized. Because of techniques to split the subatomic structure of elements, weapons so horribly destructive that no one in their right mind should ever feel safe again. Just as history confirms that once Pandora's Box opened, the evils released cannot be put back in, but morph into new meaning.

Looking across the span of time we call history as source of instruction, the last five millenniums have witnessed the rise and fall of many empires. Each of these worldly principalities spread as cancer into unmapped territories in search of new lands with rich resources and populations to absorb. Such do not seek peace or peaceful alliance, except when confronted with equal force. Perhaps, one of the greatest military Armadas ever unleashed into the world was the formidable Persian army of more than a million soldiers led by King Xerxes. It is said that this horde lapped lakes dry and decimated the land like locust. However, it is important to note that this impressive campaign's eventual demise a consequence of its mass. The retreating Greeks burn their homes, their fields, and even poison their drinking wells. During its humiliating return to Asia, this army-nation finds few resources to sustain itself. Only a remnant makes it back home alive. History has repeated itself since with similar consequence. As when Napoleon retreats out of Russia; and the same fatal error repeated by Germany's invasion of Moscow, forced to retreat in winter-- *but none on the scale of Xerxes.*

One would think that habitation within a society as simple and rehearsed as organized coordination. But empirical evidence demonstrates that beneath surface appearance this less true. It has been well documented that kinetic resonance a natural phenomenon demonstrated by crowds of pedestrians crossing a suspension bridge, unconsciously coordinating a cadence with potentially destructive consequence. Motivated by fatal experience engineers have since devised stress designs to compensate for this mass herd event. Another example is how women's biological menstrual cycles coincide naturally when living within close proximity over a period of time. This socialized event unrelated to any other condition except biochemistry. Men who share extreme hardships together generally form a bond so strong that they are willing to actually die for one another. Recent research has concluded that the human posterior pituitary gland releases a secretion of little known hormones called *oxytocin* and *vasopressin*. The *oxytocin* neurons make other peptides (*neuroendocrine*), which by excitation generate action potential to the *neuro-modulator* of the brain. What this means is a modulation in behavior occurs, involved through anatomical intimacy. An association of pair-bonding, particularly between partners, triggers ethnocentric behavior involving feelings of loyalty through intimate identification. This chemical reaction further evokes an incorporation extended to others in a perceived family creating a foundation of mutual trust and empathy. These mirror neurons are at the base of how we feel about others and how far we are willing to go to protect the integral ideology of association. This is perhaps the primary reason why people get married and why persecuted groups make mass exodus' to establish new colonies in distant savage frontiers. It is also how armies of destructive force bond with a singular objective to win or go down fighting; and the primary reason for mass suicides.

There is a saying, *"Unless you learn to think for yourself, there is always someone else who will do the thinking for you."* It is important to note that this *someone* is not a person, but is a devil, like a hungry lion searching for whom he may devour. The phenomenon of being human cannot be accessed through logic or reason only, but by created forces invisible, innately present, yet disguised as to their true nature. In Ephesians, Chapter 6, verses 11-12 (KJV) Paul gives this warning concerning our spiritual struggle against powerful unseen forces:

> *"Put on the whole armor of God, that ye may be able to stand against the wiles of the devil. For we wrestle not against flesh and blood, but against principalities, against powers, against the rulers of the darkness of this world, against spiritual wickedness in high places."*

We are all victims of these collective agents, increasingly aware of our nakedness amid forces of uncontainable possibilities; yet grasp at feeble straws of intellect to cover the shame of our ever-escalating sin. The world admits to religion, but refutes the unique character of God, as revealed through the historical transformation of sound doctrine of instruction on how to live with one another. Invented institutions of outward appearance pretend repentant reflection, while deceiving many to follow their false teachings and stumble into a labyrinth of mystic interpretations. The mind of intellect seeks answers in the firmament above and in the firmament below, while embracing the thimble of combined wisdom spawned in an ocean of shared arrogance. Honest values purposely corrupted by a mind of limited vision, based on logic of consumable value only. Common acceptance of any idea or interpretive value a poison to kill the souls of good men blinded to the brief wonder of existence, as morning mist in the wake of the rising sun. Well does the Apostle Paul speak in Romans, Chapter 14, verses 21-23 (KJV), concerning the true nature of sin.

> *"It is good neither to eat flesh, nor to drink wine, nor any thing whereby thy brother stumbles or is offended, or is*

made weak. Hast thou faith? have it to thyself before God. Happy is he that condemns not himself in that thing which he allows. And he that doubts is damned if he eat, because he eats not by faith: for whatsoever is not of faith is sin."

Is sin a condition of the herd or just an individual? The idea of *Collective Consciousness* as an innate characteristic of humanity is nothing new. There are on record many test studies that successfully proves this purely instinctive mechanism has valid agreement. A concept first introduced by the late eighteenth century French Sociologist, Émile Durkheim, to describe the mechanical solidarity of individuality to create a social consciousness of shared values and prejudices. This is similar to member affiliations and those with shared ideologies. Indoctrinated idealism, such as Darwinism, theological reasoning, or any other belief system requiring an intellectual embrace of a theory based on a cooperative agreement of interpretation deemed as a collective embrace. It is also similar to motivations that impose prejudice of alienation leading to racism, anti-Semitism, and allied resistance to multiculturalism. This term *Collective Consciousness* represents a more innate phenomenon, becoming a formalized social norm of acceptable behavior within context, which ultimately influences architecture and communal interaction. It is even responsible for molding idealized standards of social correctness. Although these principals may vary from one generation to another, and are defined differently by different world cultures, the basic regiment of dominate cohesion remains universally intact. The ancient Ethiopian civilization was no less fashion-conscious than the later Greeks or Romans. Egyptian women in the days of Ramses as diligent about applying makeup and coloring their hair as women are in modern society. Even the savage Scythian warriors on the Russian Steppes spent hours grooming their beards and proudly sported ornate tattoos. Little has changed in the vanity of mankind over many recorded centuries. But it is misleading to conjecture that vanity alone constructs the skeleton of a collective social consciousness.

I have an aunt in her eighties, who earnestly believes that all women ought to wear only dresses to church on Sunday, and that all men should be strong and silent without any outward display of emotion. This may be considered extreme in light of today's many social revolutions. But remember this is the defined world my aunt grew-up in. Even today's devoted sports fans to particular activities might fall into the category of being collectively extreme. In the last decade the new addition to computer games falls into this category of obsessive behavior. Though bordering on psychosis, these examples rarely infectious to an entire society, but are limited to a few like-minded individuals. So by limited definition maybe collective conciseness is as much about conditioned conformity within the confined vision of a generation, as it is about personal recognition. In other words, as long as greater society dictates the rules, then we need not think for ourselves, and just cruise along on automatic without taking any person responsibility. This can be particularly conflictive to those who do not exactly fit the mold of any particular collective.

Although similar in nature, collective consciousness is not the same as Mass Hysteria. Mass Hysteria is a condition whereby large numbers of people share a phenomenon of belief or experience often resulting in obsessive group behavior. This collective swept away by an irrational urge inspired through conviction of core values. This social manifestation usually initiated by fear or anger, negating legal or more argument. More recent historical examples might be when people accused of witchcraft in late seventeenth century Salem, Massachusetts. Citizens routinely rounded-up, tried, and publicly condemned to be burned at the stake or drowned. But true mass hysteria is far more insidious constructed upon the framework of a sociological integration. It provokes a type of temporary insanity that motivates masses to irrational action: a dark spiritual rebellion suddenly coursing through a human collective based on perceived threat. This carnal hysteria born of xenophobic idealism easily indwells and spreads through a human collective. The collective body becomes a mob orchestrated by zealous demand. A conditional situation, when sin is unmasked, allowing the soul no place of refuge, and escalating into concerted animal rage of a mob orchestrated by zealous inspiration. A graphic example found in the Book of Acts of the Bible describing the murder of a young spirit-filled convert named

Stephan. Another young man by the name of Saul, a Sanhedrin Jew sent with a commission to arrest and charge all who profess the name of this new religion. He will later be known as Paul, a Lion of God, proclaiming salvation to both Jew and Gentile in the name of Jesus Christ after an astounding experience through the Holy Spirit. This first martyr recorded in Acts, Chapter 7, verses 54-60 (KJV).

> *"When they heard these things, they were cut to the heart, and they gnashed on him with their teeth. But he, being full of the Holy Ghost, looked up steadfastly into heaven, and saw the glory of God, and Jesus standing on the right hand of God, And said, Behold, I see the heavens opened, and the Son of man standing on the right hand of God. Then they cried out with a loud voice, and stopped their ears, and ran upon him with one accord, And cast him out of the city, and stoned him: and the witnesses laid down their clothes at a young man's feet, whose name was Saul. And they stoned Stephen, calling upon God, and saying, Lord Jesus, receive my spirit. And he kneeled down, and cried with a loud voice, Lord, lay not this sin to their charge. And when he had said this, he fell asleep."*

The most classic case in point is when Jesus brought before Pontius Pilate, falsely accused of heresy against his fellow Jews and their shared religion. The legitimacy of the accusations has little legal bearing on perceived guilt or innocence of the man. Jesus is presented a scapegoat because of mounting oppression Israel experiences under Roman rule. The religious leaders of the time have decided it better one man should die than the Jewish history be clouded with interpretation esteemed illogical to sectarian agreement. They collectively agree to elevate their position of authority by punishing the man they believe to be a heretic. I doubt that many in the crowd knew who this Jesus was or the many miraculous acts he performed. Nor do they know much about Barabbas, a felon they hysterically demand to be released. The cry *"Crucify him, crucify him"* rings out as the voice of the mob, not of the individual.

Voices so overwhelming that not even the appeal for leniency from this prefect of mighty Rome able to sway the tide of popular consensus. In the Gospel of Luke, Chapter 23, verses 20-25 (KJV):

> *"Pilate therefore, willing to release Jesus, spoke again to them. But they cried, saying, Crucify him, crucify him. And he said unto them the third time, Why, what evil hath he done? I have found no cause of death in him: I will therefore chastise him, and let him go. And they were instant with loud voices, requiring that he might be crucified. And the voices of them and of the chief priests prevailed. And Pilate gave sentence that it should be as they required. And he released unto them him that for sedition and murder was cast into prison, whom they had desired; but he delivered Jesus to their will."*

But we need not look only at the Biblical record from two thousand years ago to see the aftermath of social hysteria which can grip a population. This happens in Nazi Germany, an entire nation devoted to world domination, inspired by the charismatic fervor of one man possessed of a devil. It happens again in the aftermath of Russia's revolution, after the creation of the Communist Manifesto by Jewish intellectuals. Men like Carl Marx, Engels, and Trotsky inspired by elevated idealism of better social justice. But from this genius rises a butcher named Stalin responsible for slaughtering millions. A thirty year reign of terror that changes a dream of equitable utopia into a nightmare of Communist dictatorship. There is no demographic exempt from Satan's agenda; all nations of the earth destined to bend knee to the tyranny of his short earthy reign. This includes the nation of modern day Israel and the United States of America once promising a better vision of personal freedom enjoyed in the Iles of democracy. Present world institutions are teetering on financial brink, soon to be swallowed whole into the belly of Mammon.

Even as I write this a dynamic shift is taking place in western society that will ultimately redefine the concepts of liberty and principals of faith. A war between the greedy of this world and those displaced, both wanting the same prize of glittering pyrite. When even democratic governments begin considering militant response to legitimate concerns of its citizenry in the guise of public safety, then the iron fist of oppression wears the same gloves of authoritarian control. In the name of a global economy and homogenized values of social media defined humanism, Babylon is being prepared to receive the approaching day of Antichrist as clearly described in the bible. And as always Satan stands upon the precipice of intellectual rationalism speaking lies to unbelieving societies that there is no God and that contained in a laboratory test tube is a medical miracle to make man live forever. This is the magician's hand trick used by self-glorified Lucifer since the beginning. And still the lie is believed. Nevertheless, grave consequence will prevail once this false council of a New World Order runs its course as prophesied in the Book of Revelation, Chapter 18, verses 9-20 (NIV).

> *"When the kings of the earth who committed adultery with her and shared her luxury see the smoke of her burning, they will weep and mourn over her. Terrified at her torment, they will stand far off and cry:" 'Woe! Woe to you, great city, you mighty city of Babylon! In one hour your doom has come!' "The merchants of the earth will weep and mourn over her because no one buys their cargoes anymore—cargoes of gold, silver, precious stones and pearls; fine linen, purple, silk and scarlet cloth; every sort of citron wood, and articles of every kind made of ivory, costly wood, bronze, iron and marble; cargoes of cinnamon and spice, of incense, myrrh and frankincense, of wine and olive oil, of fine flour and wheat; cattle and sheep; horses and carriages; and human beings sold as slaves. "They will say, 'The fruit you longed for is gone from you. All your luxury and splendor have vanished, never to be recovered.' The merchants who sold these things and gained their wealth from her will stand far off, terrified at her torment. They will weep and mourn and cry out:" 'Woe! Woe to you, great city, dressed*

> *in fine linen, purple and scarlet, and glittering with gold, precious stones and pearls! In one hour such great wealth has been brought to ruin!' "Every sea captain, and all who travel by ship, the sailors, and all who earn their living from the sea, will stand far off. When they see the smoke of her burning, they will exclaim, 'Was there ever a city like this great city?' They will throw dust on their heads, and with weeping and mourning cry out:" 'Woe! Woe to you, great city, where all who had ships on the sea became rich through her wealth! In one hour she has been brought to ruin!' "Rejoice over her, you heavens! Rejoice, you people of God! Rejoice, apostles and prophets! For God has judged her with the judgment she imposed on you."*

Paul's many letters to the churches are not just religious documents prescribing how to live within greater society; but how to be a community separate and with values not based on weaker elements of vanity, material strife, and life at any cost. They are reminder that we as human beings are made after a pattern, not sewn into the world alone. That above every mind is the mind of Christ to make mediation of peaceful restitution. Those engaged in social media today ought to reflect that we are all a community made up of *us and them*. By forgetting this simple fact *an all about me* society becomes the normative standard. In the name of broader acceptance, modern society is becoming a quantum gateway into xenophobic ideologies where *selfie* pictures become the only definition of who we are, and where only those that share the same following worthy of our attention. Again this is nothing new in the world classic idioms. A not so distant historical example is the Brown Shirts during the Nazi regime. Comprised mostly of young people, these local enforcers armed with authority carry out fascist dictates of a society defined by an Aryan vision turned evil. This should be sobering reflection to those on both sides of political extremism. Such becomes fertile ground to worldly minds hungering for power. It is through carnal reasoning that differences made palatable. A warning summed up in 1 Corinthians, Chapter 15, verses 33-38 (KJV).

> *"Be not deceived: evil communications corrupt good manners. Awake to righteousness, and sin not; for some have not the knowledge of God: I speak this to your shame. But some man will say, How are the dead raised up? and with what body do they come? Thou fool, that which thou sowest is not quickened, except it die: And that which thou sowest, thou sowest not that body that shall be, but bare grain, it may chance of wheat, or of some other grain: But God giveth it a body as it hath pleased him, and to every seed his own body."*

Even sociologists make notes of observation that peer pressure and the need to conform powerful influencers, particularly among young people. In most cases failure is not an option, as the constructed reality of consensus outweighs the alternative perception of the few. In contemporary society, conformity is an irresistible vice controlling nearly every aspect of our lives. What we wear according to our gender, our social position, and our inculcated values. Thinking ourselves free, we are actually a normative definition imposed since the moment of birth. We tweet and hash tag daily the same unconstructive rhetoric, as though we have something relevant to say so long as it does not violate the acceptance of the whole. If we fit in, no one notices. And if we are out, then the punishment becomes isolation. Even our role models are the role models of others linked to a chain going back to the roots of every civilization inventing earthly legacies of what it means to be human. Each creating iconic examples to keep its populations grounded in the vain perception of being. After all, if there are no gladiators, then we are all as folder fed to hungry lions. And if all mere mortal biological men and women burdened with the physical and social responsibility of producing future generations, then where the dream of glamour queens to grace the isles of tabloid society, or leading barons of wealth and sophistication. It is preferable to be blinded by the material of unsatisfying excess, than to accept the inescapable temporal reality of our present condition within historical context.

However, to do so also means grander reflection into the definition of life in the moment. There exists in each of us an inescapable truth: *we are all of the same flesh to the core.* This reflection so frighteningly beheld--more revealing and more liberating than ever we might imagine! What prevents us most from our true humanity is the invisible mind of this world made visible through rebellion formed in the likeness of sin before ever we are conceived. A mind that continues in every generation to whisper the grandest of lies: *All is as it has always been.* One might legitimately ask, if this is the way of men, then who can be saved? The Apostle Paul addresses this specific question in his first letter to the Corinthians, Chapter 13, verses 11-12 (KJV).

> *"When I was a child, I spake as a child, I understood as a child, I thought as a child: but when I became a man, I put away childish things. For now we see through a glass, darkly; but then face to face: now I know in part; but then shall I know even as also I am known."*

On the day of Armageddon all people of every nation will be convinced of a righteous war, but will be deceived into slaughtering mankind in the name of mankind by declaring war against God's chosen Messiah. This should be a sobering reality. When we march off on a patriotic campaign, it is important to consider the ultimate objective. Not for vague ideas of patriotism, or because of fear of some future potential; but because there really is no other alternative. Even to kill in the name of God and country does not remove the stains in our conscience--even for the rest of our mortal time here on earth! It is no light matter to become an instrument of death and destruction.

After receiving the Holy Spirit, I remain still in the Marine Corps, uncertain if I should extend my enlistment or to take my discharge. The decision not easy then, but I realized upon reflection that I had little choice but to leave my position as a Sergeant E-5 and to abandon a earthbound future already prepared. Within the military context, you are only a cog in the wheels of a greater machine. The life of a soldier is not to think, but to take orders and do. This philosophy works most of the time. However, to be under the command of any organized world power can be a morally unsettling apprehension. When the Christian Crusaders marched off to Jerusalem to fight against the Muslim hordes, many are filled with zealousness to serve the official decree of the church. Yet, history records these campaigns horrendous, as both sides carry out indiscriminate slaughter of Jews and the local populations. Images of this time depict piled-up heads of desecrated victims and screaming babies at the end of bloody spears. Few left alive today remember the horrors of the trench battles during War World I, as men butcher each other for years, beginning as a political decision by aristocratic warmongers. Years of stalemate as men's lives shuffled on a board table in war rooms of commanding generals. Nor let us forget the famous lines from German soldiers guarding the extermination camps in Eastern Europe, stating that they *"only followed orders"* in service to their country. It seems the only thing that really ever stops war is when mankind sickens if the carnage.

I am not saying that one should not stand firm with conviction. Only that conviction should be tempered with respect for life and the knowledge that we all share the same human bond of brotherhood. But above everything else mindful that we are all born under the same yoke and prisoners to the mind of this world, until released by witness of the Holy Spirit. Remembering, too, that without benevolence, there can be no victory. When young David stands before the Philistine giant, he does so as an instrument of God, not as a proud warrior of Israel. When Moses stands before mighty Pharaoh and leads the children of Israel out of Egypt, he does so reluctantly, knowing that the power in his hand the hand of God. Even after Jesus' resurrection, his apostles submit to the hour of their calling in willing consent as sheep to the slaughter. But never do any of these men of God take upon themselves the countenance of this world. They condemned sin because it appears sin, but relinquish all judgment to the Lord of host. They refrain from condemnation and from setting up tribunals of execution, knowing all under the same grace. For whom among any of us able to instruct the blindness of our neighbor or judge a more righteous comprehension of present conduct? To those that stand most righteous, I remind that all stand as living testament to unmerited salvation in Jesus Christ, our Lord. We are not sent as elite righteous representatives or as a body of armed crusaders to change the conditions of the times. The ancient city of Nineveh spared became a reluctant prophet named Jonah sent to them with the message of repentance, which they hear and obey. None come to repentance, except first they are called; and that the voice of God spoken to the hearts of all men in season. There is never pleasure in killing one's enemy, remembering we are also our enemy's enemy. I submit to you constant reminder of what it means to be a Christian in a sinful generation found in Paul's letter to the Ephesians, Chapter 2, verses 8-10 (KJV).

> *"For by grace are ye saved through faith; and that not of yourselves: it is the gift of God. Not of works, lest any man should boast. For we are his workmanship, created in Christ Jesus unto good works, which God hath before ordained that we should walk in them."*

The world is violently opposed to lasting peace. The secular skeptic will say that things today are as they have always been. There is much truth to this idiom, only that the convergences of concentric patterns found in history continue to repeat in an ever tightening noose. After more than half a century, militarized North Korea still breathing threatening provocation against its sister border country to the south and against the United States. And perhaps the most contentious region in the world today is the Middle East, a hornet's nest of radicalized forces, many supported by the ancient kingdom of Persia. Fanatical groups such as the Palestinian Liberation Army, the sworn blood-enemy of neighboring Israel, voted into power by the Palestinian population, as a suicidal voice of rebellion to the last man, woman, and child. Unrepentant war mongering of Hezbollah in neighboring Lebanon remains hell-bent on ever increasing violence and carnage. To such there can be no rational solution. These forces stand deterministic defiant of all logic, promising only destruction in the wake of destruction. It is as a lover willing to murder his beloved so that no one else may ever have possession. Such is the ultimate end of directional forces set into motion. For those that think God ignorant of the times, consider the announcement of this chilling prophecy voiced by Ezekiel concerning the destiny of spiritual Israel and the judgment against rebellious forces collectively surrounding her borders. This forewarning announced over six hundred years before the birth of Christ found in the Book of the Prophet, Chapter 28, verses 25-26 (NIV).

> 'This is what the Sovereign Lord says: When I gather the people of Israel from the nations where they have been scattered, I will be proved holy through them in the sight of the nations. Then they will live in their own land, which I gave to my servant Jacob. They will live there in safety and will build houses and plant vineyards; they will live in safety when I inflict punishment on all their neighbors who maligned them. Then they will know that I am the Lord their God.' "

Chapter 17
THE SEVEN MOUNTAINS

Genesis chapter 8 verses 3-4 (KJV) reads:

> *"And the waters returned from off the earth continually: and after the end of the hundred and fifty days the waters were abated. And the ark rested in the seventh month, on the seventeenth day of the month, upon the mountains of Ararat."*

Noah is described as the eighth soul: a preacher of righteousness, a living testament to the old world that was; and the progenitor of the new world after the ark rests on theses mountain slopes mentioned by name. Throughout the Bible the numbers seven and eight become often interchangeable, meaning perfection and the end or beginning. Both are prime numbers representing resurrection and new beginning from entropic collapse. According to Jewish custom an eighth candle is added to the Menorah on Hanukkah to commemorate the oil supply of one day that miraculously lasts for eight days after the plunder of the temple by the Romans, as recorded by a Jewish historian named Josephus. In layman terms it seems that the number seven represents perfect completion. The number eight is the end of something, but also the resurrection or continuation of something else better than obtained in the first state. One might infer this last condition an eighth estate providing concept of measure and meaning to the idea of perfection.

I think it no coincidence that there are seven pillars of traceable religion roots upon the earth today; and that from these seven roots sprout the many sects and doctrines appealing to so many. People are often born into a religion; others convert through marriage or personal conviction. Since religion represents a value system based on more than carnal concerns, it appeals to the hunger of our soul for something that cannot be realized through material existence. However, as we have seen in recent years, it can also be a deadly weapon loaded with politicized interpretation of ideology. In the Book of Revelation, Chapter 1, verses 10-11 (NKJV) reads:

> *"I was in the Spirit on the Lord's Day, and I heard behind me a loud voice, as of a trumpet, saying, "I am the Alpha and the Omega, the First and the Last," and, "What you see, write in a book and send it to the seven churches which are in Asia: to Ephesus, to Smyrna, to Pergamos, to Thyatira, to Sardis, to Philadelphia, and to Laodicea."*

These seven churches represent seven earthly estates, each having a common thread of genesis and trajectory of future destiny. The testimony of the resurrected Christ (*not the religion*), infused with the authority to revive living souls, and thus freeing multitudes from the snare of religious, political, and spiritual restraints. But more importantly this returning Messiah has the power to change entropic destiny. This includes those complacent to the confusion of a worldly defined Christianity. Because these seven churches spiritual grounded through physical locality, they are evident positions of a warfare happening on a grand scale. They exist upon the seven continents of earth, and are the manifestation of peoples, and tongues, and philosophies. From these seven principalities, rise kingdoms willingly instructed by angelic hosts. Four of these angelic positions are fallen, according to the witness of the prophet Daniel, a fifth that rises from the four, one that continues today, and one that will shortly appear. From the fall of these seven will rise-up the eighth, which is the incarnation of Lucifer in temporal time, born a mortal man, referred to as the Antichrist. The Christ John sees in his vision is the visage of a victorious warrior coming on a cloud of glory to end the reign of the dragon that was since before Adam's condemnation through sin: *this Day of Judgment even now at hand.* This is the eighth and final principality to come, a day commemorated by a great battle referred in the Bible as *Armageddon*.

Perhaps, the first question of address should be: *What is Armageddon?* Figuratively speaking, the word is translated from the Hebrew "*Har Megiddo*", a term meaning mountains. In present world geography the nations of the world are arranged on seven continents protruding out of the streams of global oceans. It seems likely from this definition that Armageddon is a focal point bringing together into one place all the nations of the seven continents. I have read many commentaries and interpretations of world kingdoms found in the annals of history and mentioned often in the Bible. Past and present, there are kingdoms many, and principalities ruled by cruel tyrants, as myriad as the pages of history. So what are the seven world dominions spoken of in the Book of Revelation?

Before this can be answered, I think we must first ask: what constitutes a nation? The dictionary defines nation as a group of people made distinct by a common language, ethnic identity, and religious acceptance. Traditionally, this has always been the norm when different cultures collide. There are many theories of how language originated, most based on evolutionary processes that even linguist cannot adequately agree upon. Then there is the highly contested *block association theory*, where language is a distinctive element from other patterns of association, an innate characteristic specific to a group.

Returning again to the Tower of Babel, this is perhaps the best historical reference to how language begins and the potential of consequence. The true nature of this unified project is anyone's guess. Were the descendants of Noah just building a tower, or some more sinister construction engaged through their unified efforts? Perhaps, they were trying to resurrect a formulae passed down from ancient knowledge that existed before the flood to make possible Lucifer's physical return upon the earth. Or even some kind of broadcast beacon to communicate a signal to reunify the several unseen principalities that exist around us through an illusion of time, space, and distance. At least the shattered pieces of the puzzle pertaining to this ancient technology would have survived embedded in the DNA memory of the surviving population. I think this confusion the only way to allow these children of Adam a second chance so that Messiah might appear.

From the generations of these early migrants rises the divided city-states of the Sumerian kingdoms of Mesopotamia, builders of the enigmatic Ziggurats, designated the dwelling place of their many gods. Egypt of the Nile, architects of the great pyramids and irrigation systems, producing enough crops to one day feed drought-stricken populations. And the founders of the early dynastic territories of Far East China, inventors of precise navigation systems, printing, and dynamite. But those remaining in the near vicinity of original Babel will retain the greater advantage, eventually morphing into a great empire with an obsession of reunification.

Legend establishes Cush, the eldest son of Noah, as the first Babylonian founder, further echoed in the disjointed tales of Gilgamesh. It is even suggested that Nimrod, an offspring of Cush, the one responsible for the initial project to build the great astrological tower to reach into heaven, declares vengeance because of the destruction upon the earth that wiped-out the many accomplishments of his forefathers. A persistent culture of law and mathematical advancement ensues from these crumbling reminders of a failed project to become the basic principles of Hammurabi Code. From this dragon's tooth will mobilize the first military aggression of world domination.

So what happens when a nation or groups of nations mature into a powerful empire? In the book bearing his name, Daniel a prophet chosen of God sees in a vision four kingdoms like beast rising out of the sea. These terrible chimeras sufficiently describe the four great world empires before the temporal birth of God's Messiah in the Judean city of Bethlehem. Although the geographical borders have gone through shuffles over time, nevertheless the language roots of national identity sprout that forges a dialectical lattice for human history to climb.

The first is like a lion with the wings of an eagle. Most scholars agree this is the Semitic Chaldean Empire brought to its height by Daniel's captor, King Nebuchadnezzar. It is described as a beast given the heart of a man and standing on two legs. History has revealed that this beginning source established the base of present day Semitic languages, which flourished from civilizations woven into the fertile basin lands of Egypt, into Africa, mingling into cultures of the future Middle East, thus establishing the root languages from Syria to the borders of Arabian Peninsula.

The second beast resembles a vicious bear consuming other animals. This is thought to be the expansion of the Achaemenid Empire (*Media and Persia*), catalyzed by Cyrus the Great, founder of legal principalities in Far East Mongolia, eventually sweeping into the great region known today as China to fan glowing embers of the many Asian dialects.

Daniel looks up and sees yet another beast, resembling the body of a leopard with four feathered wings, like those of a bird, and with four heads. This is most notably the Hellenic Empire, forged into existence by Alexander the Great. From this significant empire born the Cyrillic alphabet and becomes the base of Proto-Indo-European dialects, used throughout Greece and Macedon, spreading later into Thrace and Asia Minor. Its influence will be felt into Middle East Asia, Egypt-Palestine, and onto the Northern Scythian Steppes. The four heads are the pillars of support being amalgamated into present day Europe and the Russian Soviet Union of the Baltic region.

The fourth beast witnessed by Daniel is more terrible and powerful than all the former. With teeth of iron, this chimera lays waste to all before it, crushing under its feet all resistance. It is different from all the rest in that it has ten horns on its head. Three of the ten horns are uprooted by the sprouting of another horn with human features. Many believe this to be the crushing Roman Empire ruled by a linage of judiciously cruel Czars, inspiring an order of law and execution not seen since the Hammurabi Code. By assimilating the culture of the Hellenistic Greeks, and other cultural elements it found desirable, Rome becomes the longest surviving empire in recorded history, covering three continents, historically declared master of the world because of a judicial policy of systematic conquest and assimilation as the mechanism of expansion.

In fact many historians agree that Roman influence never actually vanished, but melds into the seven worldly pillars of present civilization. Spreading like a cancer, Rome metamorphoses into a conglomeration of assimilated philosophies, materialistic in nature, but lacking the condition of an enlightened soul. After division of the empire during the rule of Emperor Diocletian, the regions to the east became known as Byzantine, while the west remained the assets of traditional Roman government. By the time Emperor Constantine converts to Christianity, Rome seeks new birth becoming the Vatican center of world Christianity. Eventually a power shift from the seat of Emperor to the holy office of Pope, altogether redefining the western image. This revived principality inspirational to the idea of God's physical church on earth. With a history as dark and bloody as the Caesars that precede them, the office of the papacy ushers in a political interpretation of letters and correspondences left behind by the first Apostles of Christ. Men--who in contradiction--did not choose their habitation to the glory of worldly temples; nor were they tempted by material acquisition. What is once the witness of a living new testimony of the resurrected Christ, now a material fortress of Old Testament interpretations, as dead and spiritually empty as the Temple and the law it proposes to replace.

Religion declares war on religion, saving some, while slaughtering multitudes. Despite the carnage of the bloody crusades and the greed of political expansion, some men of personal sacrifice continue in humble submission, the wheat sewn with the tares. These continue to proclaim the good news of salvation against powers of dark force disguised in undiscovered realms of Satan's stronghold. The exploits of the next several hundred years inadvertently fulfilled a necessary spreading of the gospel, which the Bible refers to as the *Age of the Gentiles*. Because of this advent of colonial exportation, there are today effigies of hope proclaiming the spiritual meaning of resurrection dotting nearly every skyline of every worldly metropolis.

Although these vacant church steeples represent an empty symbol to many today, jaded by hypocrisy of institutional fortification, religious value still retains a potential to personal awakening. More Bibles populate this planet than there are people, translated into every tongue and every dialect (*spoken or unspoken*). There are few who have not heard the testament of Jesus Christ; fewer still unaware of the persecuted history of the Jews. Even as I write this, there is mounting tension throughout the Middle East and the world, with Israel, as always, bulls-eyed in the center. Against all odds, God's abiding promise remains to every empire, great or small, and a seed of promise to every generation.

This age of religion brings to mankind a sense of human value and respect for different cultures unpracticed in the annals of history. However, when Hitler declares aggressive actions against Germany's neighbors, he assaults the values of western society recently given up on ideas of colonial expansion. It soon becomes clear that this is a duel to the death, requiring the blood of all nations. Only toward the end of this desperate conflict does civilization realize the true evil of this mind that so completely captured the imagination of a country. Not only does Hitler declare war against all of Europe, but against the God of heaven by intentionally and systematically slaughtering innocent Jews and all other groups he considers inferior. It should be noted that this is the fervor of every tyrant since earliest record. But why does it so often come down to persecution of the Jews?

The answer is always the same. The Jews are a people chosen to be a testament of hope for all mankind through a linage to ultimately sire God's appointed Messiah. Satan knows this, thus using the power given him upon the earth in an attempt to corrupt the promise of this goodwill offering to the souls of all mankind. After the fall of the German Third Reich much of the west lays wasted, including land of the Fuhrer. The United States, now an industrial giant, provides the material and American ingenuity to help rebuild Europe, while at the same time replenishing its own economic prosperity. With the threat of the Russian Cold War and mounting new tensions rippling throughout Asia, forcing international communities to enter into an era of greater cooperation. Since the formation of the United Nations and the fall of the Berlin Wall, globalization has become the new norm.

Even distant China has awakened from its dynastic slumber, now a Genie of commercial production supplying businesses of distribution around the globe. This interdependency has consistently raised the standard of living throughout most of the west, while at the same time creating a climate of unprecedented inflation. It is this inflation presently most challenging to the world nations. So great the flow that international stock markets fluctuate daily with alarming consequence, providing opportunity for Jihadist groups, like Isis and al-Qaeda, to make clandestine advancements into powerful economic machines providing them the means and material to wage terrorist wars as easily as make a daily trade. As with all money markets, it is greed and self indulgence providing the flow of resources. Modern society is networked today in a way not thought possible even when I was child born in the middle half of the last century. The challenges facing world governments are unprecedented in recorded history. The new demographic is truly global in proportion, unimaginable even in science fiction. So what comes next? In the Book of Relation, Chapter 12, verses 7-12 (NKJV) is a glimpse of what is happening on a celestial battlefield even now.

> *"And war broke out in heaven: Michael and his angels fought with the dragon; and the dragon and his angels fought, but they [a]did not prevail, nor was a place found for them in heaven any longer. So the great dragon was cast out, that serpent of old, called the Devil and Satan, who deceives the whole world; he was cast to the earth, and his angels were cast out with him. Then I heard a loud voice saying in heaven, "Now salvation, and strength, and the kingdom of our God, and the power of His Christ have come, for the accuser of our brethren, who accused them before our God day and night, has been cast down. And they overcame him by the blood of the Lamb and by the word of their testimony, and they did not love their lives to the death. Therefore rejoice, O heavens, and you who dwell in them! Woe to the inhabitants of the earth and the sea! For the devil has come down to you, having great wrath, because he knows that he has a short time."*

Battle lines are drawn when Adam and Eve expulsed from God's Eden, raging into the destruction of the old world, until the days of Noah. Through migration it has continued to wage ever since through the continuous rise and fall of world empires. The birth, death, and resurrection of Messiah represents final victory to this war in heaven. But those fallen principalities now trapped here in a non-linear dimensional spaces devising a way of escape. These darkened angelic minds, being soulless, not born of human reason. They are the lie that creation the image of the created. Even they do not comprehend that their fallen estate directional forces determined to entropy. Satan's interest in humanity is jealousy only. The brightness of first creation made to shine so bright, now dimmed by a greater potential. Lucifer's beauty changed to darkness because of envy, declares himself enemy of mankind. A rebellion forged in defiance and committed to destruction, rather than share. An arrogance born of hatred, believing that reflected glory the source of created light. This lie he transfers to others like him seated in high places. And the lie whispered to the souls of mankind through deception of reason. Just as the angels of God rejoice for the salvation of one soul lost, so does this angry Seraph glory in one soul deceived. Now that he in fallen, this once beautiful morning star changed to a dragon with hunger to consume mankind into his own perdition, as witnessed in the Book of Revelation, Chapter 12, verses 13-17 (NKJV).

> *"Now when the dragon saw that he had been cast to the earth, he persecuted the woman who gave birth to the male Child. But the woman was given two wings of a great eagle, that she might fly into the wilderness to her place, where she is nourished for a time and times and half a time, from the presence of the serpent. So the serpent spewed water out of his mouth like a flood after the woman, that he might cause her to be carried away by the flood. But the earth helped the woman, and the earth opened its mouth and swallowed up the flood which the dragon had spewed out of his mouth. And the dragon was enraged with the woman, and he went to make war with the rest of her offspring, who keep the commandments of God and have the testimony of Jesus Christ."*

Historians might argue that the only reason Christianity as a religion survives is because of the conversion of Emperor Constantine of Rome over three hundred years after Christ's ascension. All reborn in the Holy Spirit will disagree knowing that true Christianity is a seed watered in the world by miracle, brought to fruition by the hands of many husbandmen, and harvested by angels, But what did happen is another deceptive maneuver by the chief advocate that condemns us continually before the throne of God. His is the mouth of worldly reason conceived through perceived materialism and fear of the unknown.

Considering that the continental shelves drastically altered at the instance of the flood by the gushing *fountains of the deep*, geological evidence suggests there are a total of seven tectonic land masses observed upon earth today. Upon these seven moving tectonic plates inhabit distinct groups of populations sorted by ethnicity, dialect, customs, and beliefs. The Bible implies there are seven worldly conditions that will inhabit the earth from the time of the flood to the day of Armageddon. Of course, this is a contested position, when viewed through the microscope of evolutionary science or the accepted history of continually shifting borders and human migrations. But raw data can be interpreted in more ways than one, depending on the premise of accepted norms. Consider that models of reality only as reliable as the insertion or deletion of supporting data. All that is known with any certainty about ancient past events begin with hard evidence left behind by earliest civilization dating back between 6000 to 8000 years ago.

John states that from seven earthly positions the eighth will appear. A principality restored which is not, but once was, and will be. I believe this to be the resurrection of the old world dominion that existed before the flood of Noah, when fallen angels visibly walk the earth among mankind. The power of all these worldly kingdoms given to Satan in illusion of light and shadow, vaguely perceived during temporal sojourn. All this so that man might know the difference between good and evil through measure of God's greater creation.

Upon these seven mountains are the seven constructed principalities of Satan and his army of rebellious angels. All destined to judgment in the irresistible flow of temporal conclusion. Being of the seven, the manifestation of the eighth represents the carnal end born by the sin of the first Adam through deception. For this Adam must first die that the new Adam may be reconciled unto God, the creator, through transfiguration. Both Daniel and John agree on the powers that be and on the powers to come. Both prophets record angels as being cardinal elements of nature, which radically disturbs mortal events.

Even though the fallen angels no longer part of God's celestial body, they remain elements of consequence. That is they fulfill a prescription of being within the clockwork web of entropic design. The closest analogy would be the chemical reactions observed in a dying star undergoing radical gravimetric changes. In other words, the seven collapsing estates of Satan's kingdom are not static, but dynamic conditions. The war in heaven begins the moment Adam cast out of Eden; the victory at Armageddon achieved the moment Jesus dies and Christ resurrected. But this war is going on even in the now. Only that local time and space is moving perceptually too slow for us to comprehend it through the natural senses.

Because we reason through sequential concept, we remain partly ignorant of a designed chronological model consistently winding from past to present. Remembering that there are forces on scales far more immense, our short existence should be humbling within context. If one accepts colonialism as the fifth kingdom referred to as one of seven in John's Book of Revelation, then we cannot ignore the enormous impact this has had upon populations around the globe in a relatively short span of time. Built upon the collapsed ruins of the once great Roman Empire, begins the seeding of cultures and different races that otherwise would have remained alien to one another. Whether in the name of spreading the gospel or the pursuit of treasures, colonization makes the world self-aware. The awakening of the Renaissance revives the latent memories of immortal beings and demigods that once ruled the earth.

Symmetry and reason reduces the grand creation of heaven and earth to a logical quantum, while embellishing the idea of the noble human spirit. This gives rise to the industrial revolution, as mankind seeks ways to control the elements in an attempt to make planet earth more domestic. But it is Nazi Germany that really kicks starts civilization into technological advancement of unprecedented possibilities. The war to end all wars also sires globalization, the sixth kingdom. This is where we find ourselves today. A world condensed to seconds and microseconds of communication. A world conceived in the realization of multiculturalism, and where masses of populations travel to and fro with consuming appetite. Even though man has better insulated himself from the thermodynamic harshness of nature; and although he has escaped the hungry jaws of wild animals, he still faces perils just as deadly in the form of cancer-causing agents, hordes of mechanical devices, and a sense of hopelessness in the face of the perils conjured through insurmountable evils. Yet, paradoxically, modern man denies the existence of both evil and creation, grasping at straws of psychology and parapsychology in a feeble attempt to ascribe meaning to the escalating epidemic of human avarice and violence. And this is the optimistic report as presented in the daily news.

In the second half of the 20th century, the United States of America becomes one of the greatest military powers in the world, engendering special agencies devoted to research and development of weapons designated mass destructive. Russia excels with equal arsenals, turned aggressively antagonistic to the west, promising nuclear retaliation as a deterrent to protect its own perceived territories. This deadly standoff between the east and the west has lasted more than fifty years, with Europe caught in the middle. With the symbolic fall of the Berlin Wall, Russia has taken more of a backseat position (not altogether out of the picture, but less vocal). While in the same span of history the United States and other countries have escalated its weapons development programs. Some of the technologies leaked to the public seem almost like science fiction; others that have proven terrifyingly real.

Since the detonation of the first Atomic bomb in the deserts of New Mexico, code name Trinity, as part of the Manhattan Project, lethal weapons technologies have mushroomed into ever more destructive devices. Hydrogen bombs, many more times devastating than the two bombs dropped on the populations of Japan at the end of the Second World War, have proliferated in alarming numbers. Nuclear fission proficiency discovered in uranium and plutonium was only the first steps toward even more deadly arsenals. Next generation Neutron bombs limit destructive potential, thus sparing reclaimable infrastructure, while effectively exterminating personnel. In combination with better long range delivery systems, more refined yield production, and decreased public concern, these weapons of mass destruction have become part of the landscape of far too many developing nations. There is a statement made famous by the late physicist J. Robert Oppenheimer, also known as father of the Atomic bomb, *"Now I have become death, the destroyer of worlds."* Oppenheimer was paraphrasing a passage from the Hindu *Bhagavad Gita* after witnessing the destructive capacity of the first test results conducted by the Manhattan Project.

I believe this man's regrets well founded when one really pauses to reflect on the potential of hidden arsenals around the world. Even conventional weapons are upgraded daily, with improved killing efficiency. Bullets made to shatter upon entry, landmines designed with undetectable elements, often left abandoned even years after the conflict has ended; and laser- guided projectiles with an extended killing radius, yet configured precisely with computer chip technology for maximum effectiveness. The modern face of war is to try and surgically spare the divers habitations, while killing the biological populations.

Bio-weapons, though banned by every nation in the world, continue to hold special interest for many researchers. Poison gases and anthrax are only the tip of the iceberg, as extinct contagions are routinely literally resurrected from the grave: horrible plagues such as a modified version of the infamous Bubonic Plague that decimated 14th century Europe, a more resistant strain of Smallpox, and the resurfacing of Ebola spreading out of Africa. I personally met one of these scientists while visiting a friend in Maryland during the late seventies. He lived and worked in the District of Colombia, commuting daily to a secret government research laboratory. One evening over a drink, he shares with me that he was presently working on a secret project that terrifies him so much that he is no longer able to sleep at night. "I can't tell you the nature of the bio-agent. Only that if even one specimen should escape our controlled environment, it will mean the end of civilization as we know it, and the beginning of apocalypse." There is a chilling deadness in his eyes, and I could tell that this relatively peaceful young man hates his chosen profession. And this was over forty years ago.

A recent acronym circulating among conspiracy advocates is *"Angels don't play HAARP!"* HAARP (*High-frequency Active Auroral Research Program*) represents more than fifty years of atmospheric study by the United States Air force based on technology enhancements achieved by Nikola Tesla. Officially, its purpose is to analyze the properties of the ionosphere with the intent of propagating better radio emissions and surveillance by studying the magnetic charges trapped at high altitudes by the doughnut shaped Van Allen radiation belt located between the equator and the poles. Many think the lengthy research more than passive, and perhaps may play some role in the shifting of jet streams and radical weather patterns observed in recent years. Considered part of the Star Wars program, HARRP serves an active role in magnetic disturbances and frequency amplification models by targeting specific ranges of radiation curves to channel energy to a desired potential. It may also be responsible for much of the global warming concerns expressed with growing anxiety by the scientific community. Considered by some instructed with Biblical understanding, this to be one of the apocalyptic horsemen described in the Book of Revelation. This 21st Century meddling may precipitate irreversible damage to earth's delicate stratosphere. HAARP still in an infant stage of development anticipates Tesla's vision of controlling the enormous geophysical and atmospheric potential of mother earth. Irresponsible melding into nature's delicate balance could trigger an irreversible ecological disaster by damaging the plentiful productive viability of food and energy resources causing a cascade of global economic systems. This quantum change in the earth's ability to reproduce will spell disaster, as described in the sixth chapter of the Book of Revelation, verses 5-8 (NIV).

> *"When the Lamb opened the third seal, I heard the third living creature say, "Come!" I looked, and there before me was a black horse! Its rider was holding a pair of scales in his hand. Then I heard what sounded like a voice among the four living creatures, saying, "Two pounds of wheat for*

a day's wages, and six pounds of barley for a day's wages, and do not damage the oil and the wine!" When the Lamb opened the fourth seal, I heard the voice of the fourth living creature say, "Come!" I looked, and there before me was a pale horse! Its rider was named Death, and Hades was following close behind him. They were given power over a fourth of the earth to kill by sword, famine and plague, and by the wild beasts of the earth."

The clandestine existence of Area 51 is perhaps the most disputed location in North America. It first comes to public attention after the mysterious Roswell Incident in 1947, when it officially reported that a weather balloon crashed outside of Roswell, New Mexico. This sparks the beginning of UFO enthusiast claims that the crash was in fact a flying saucer of unknown origin. Credible witnesses describe the remains of the wreck relocated to a nearby air force base underground facility called Area 51 as something from a science fiction movie. There have been volumes of speculation written about this event to either prove or disprove the validity of extraterrestrial potential. Nor does it stand alone, as an unsolved mystery involving an alien craft unlike any on earth falling from the sky. Another supposed crash occurs less than a year later in Aztec, New Mexico, meticulously presented in a book authored by Frank Scully. As with the Roswell incident, alien bodies are recovered, as well as many intact technologies. I will refrain from any further details of these two very public events, since they can be easily researched on the net by anyone with a computer. However, if there is any truth to the rumors of recovered technologies from these spacecrafts of other worldly design, then it is likely there would be some evidence of at least one component of revolutionary application.

Interestingly, within less than ten years of these speculative events, the invention and successful application of a transistor embedded into a semi-conductive material. The semiconductor represents the greatest singular scientific breakthrough in the twentieth century. Based more on quantum theory than real science, this simple switch can organize the directed free flow of electrons through a maze of other switches, or act as an amplifier to increase activity for some desired gain capacity. Some believe this phenomenal breakthrough to be the result of years of supervised *reverse-engineering* with the secret aid of military funding. It is worthy to mention that the United States Air Force becomes the primary recipient of this new age of semiconductors. A few short years later, the construction of a fast supercomputer called the SDC 6600, first delivered to Geneva, Switzerland officially designed to analyze photos of bubble chamber packs. There have been many supercomputers built around the world since, providing substance to conspiracy theories of global control, such as the nefarious 1974 fictional legend of the *"beast"*, a three-story supercomputer believed to exist in Belgium, as a data resource of the European Common Market. But what is not science fiction is the UPC code stamped upon nearly every product we buy or retail. This bar code is based on a numeric value used by international money systems. At the risk of sounding redundant, I would like to remind the reader that this use of three Bar Guards, which to a programmer visually resembles an even parity of the number 666, is a numeric value of a flexible binary formulation. This *bar-space-bar* configuration is identified with 1-0-1 for the computer language. To a programmer this *right code* is interpreted as six, and nothing else. If this is a coincidence, then it is a fascinating one within context.

There are few not apprehensive about this age of data collection by impersonal machines, whose design is to reduce the human experience down to an algorithmic statistic categorized by carnal habit. RFID technology is the next generation bar code with the purpose of identifying individuals. Microscopic devices designed to be implanted under the skin, invisible to all except a computer scanner. It is envisioned that these tiny transmitters will change the way we shop, the way we do business, and the way we live. Every living moment recorded and uploaded to a main server somewhere in the world of cyberspace. Even had the prophetic machine from more than half a century ago been real, it would be obsolete compared to more advanced data gathering devices much smaller in size. In fact it maybe did exist, shrouded in denial, and has since evolved into something far more menacing. Today an average cell phone has greater capacity to invade our privacy through any available Wi-Fi network. The point being that locality and compartment no longer a factor. Now human beings willingly surrender their individuality and identity to faceless international servers through an insatiable desire to feel connected with a predefined abstraction of a politically censored whole.

We read in the Book of Revelation Chapter 13, verses 15-18 (KJV):

> *"And he had power to give life unto the image of the beast, that the image of the beast should both speak, and cause that as many as would not worship the image of the beast should be killed. And he causes all, both small and great, rich and poor, free and bond, to receive a mark in their right hand, or in their foreheads: And that no man might buy or sell, save he that had the mark, or the name of the beast, or the number of his name. Here is wisdom. Let him that hath understanding count the number of the beast: for it is the number of a man; and his number is Six hundred threescore and six."*

As a personal observation, I believe the real beast of apocalyptic concern is servers of massive data storage facilities such as Oracle and the Cloud. Since before the time of the post World War I aid-program, known as the *New Deal*, evangelicals have been struggling with the interpretation of the *"beast"* and the mark of his name found in this chapter of the Book of Revelation. Looking for an economical link, they rightly perceive a connection between commodity distribution and the basic needs for individual survival. Nevertheless, just as in the days of martyrdom, when true believers forfeited their lives to a living undeniable testimonial, so I ascertain the choice will be made clear to those who willing receive the mark of worldly perdition. Nor do I think it will be slipped into the fine print, requiring many levels of cryptic understanding of embedded secret codes, but will be a bold declaration of clarity impossible to deny. The decision based upon what one truly believes or does not believe. Such is the example found in Abraham's faith within context of pagan society. There is no refuting the technologies that flood our awareness of the world daily. The future and the present slipping into alignment, as artificial intelligence become the conscious mind of a corporate mentality created in the image of soulless financial institutions. All made possible by the humble transistor.

Since the implementation of the Marshall Plan to rebuild war-ravaged Europe, the global community has expanded trade relations exponentially. Equally paced is the telecommunication industry. With improved efficiency of signal compression and a greater number of technologically advanced satellites orbiting the planet, the world has become a click away, even in remote areas. Since energy markets are the primary driving force, mostly supplied by the OPEC oil producing nations of the Middle East, the former empires of the old world have reemerged. Particularly threatening are Iran, formerly Persia, Iraq, formerly Babylon, and Syria. Israel was declared a nation again in 1948, guaranteeing the continuation of a micro-conflict that has lasted over 3500 years. However, the greatest threat facing the world today is uncontrollable inflation. No longer just global communities of trade agreements, the present world leaders desperately need a standardized monetary system. The League of Nations known as the EU is perhaps the beginning of a new world government. Although imperfect in implementation, the existence of the united planet of nations is a dream first conceived by the Freemasons more than 600 years ago. Early in the 1770s, the powerful Rothschild family draws up the first plans for a global government controlled by a unified monetary system. Less than ten years later, a member of the Free Masons, Adam Weishaupt, founds an offshoot organization called The Illuminati. The two groups form an alliance, both recognizing that real power necessary for global influence requires economic and religious control by a wise few.

Today the G20 represents finance ministers and central bank governors of nineteen countries devoted to economic stability. However, behind the scenes are the puppet masters of this membership, estimated to be no more than 300 of an elite secret society devoted to the vision of a New World Government. All that is needed another world depression to complete the final stage of this ambitious plan. The new monetary system is the beginning of the seventh kingdom, a financial beast straddling the seven continents of the world in preparation for the eighth and final worldly kingdom within entropic design.

As witness to an unholy union between spiritual Rome and spiritual Babylon, the last book of preserved Bible text makes startling perdition from outside entropic space and time. This revelation provides a reference point within fleeting context of a conditional meaning embedded in the history of unfolding events. Since time is a contained system that flows in one direction only, God orchestrates the future from the end to the beginning.

This approaching seventh kingdom grander than any preceding principality; in other words: *it was, it is, and is to come.* Even the prophet John is dazzled, as he marvels at the material excess, describing it as a sumptuous woman riding upon the back of a scarlet beast straddling many waters. This is the spiritual Babylon reincarnated, becoming the bride of spiritual Rome. In Chapter 17, verses 3-18 (NIV) of the Book of Revelation, the prophet writes:

> *"Then the angel carried me away in the Spirit into a wilderness. There I saw a woman sitting on a scarlet beast that was covered with blasphemous names and had seven heads and ten horns. The woman was dressed in purple and scarlet, and was glittering with gold, precious stones and pearls. She held a golden cup in her hand, filled with abominable things and the filth of her adulteries. The name written on her forehead was a mystery: BABYLON THE GREAT THE MOTHER OF PROSTITUTES AND OF THE ABOMINATIONS OF THE EARTH. I saw that the woman was drunk with the blood of God's holy people, the blood of those who bore testimony to Jesus. When I saw her, I was greatly astonished. Then the angel said to me: "Why are you astonished? I will explain to you the mystery of the woman and of the beast she rides, which has the seven heads and ten horns. The beast, which you saw, once was, now is not, and yet will come up out of the Abyss and go to its destruction. The inhabitants of the*

earth whose names have not been written in the book of life from the creation of the world will be astonished when they see the beast, because it once was, now is not, and yet will come. "This calls for a mind with wisdom. The seven heads are seven hills on which the woman sits. They are also seven kings. Five have fallen, one is, the other has not yet come; but when he does come, he must remain for only a little while. The beast who once was, and now is not, is an eighth king. He belongs to the seven and is going to his destruction. "The ten horns you saw are ten kings who have not yet received a kingdom, but who for one hour will receive authority as kings along with the beast. They have one purpose and will give their power and authority to the beast. They will wage war against the Lamb, but the Lamb will triumph over them because he is Lord of lords and King of kings—and with him will be his called, chosen and faithful followers." Then the angel said to me, "The waters you saw, where the prostitute sits, are peoples, multitudes, nations and languages. The beast and the ten horns you saw will hate the prostitute. They will bring her to ruin and leave her naked; they will eat her flesh and burn her with fire. For God has put it into their hearts to accomplish his purpose by agreeing to hand over to the beast their royal authority, until God's words are fulfilled. The woman you saw is the great city that rules over the kings of the earth."

This seventh kingdom will reign but for a short span of time. Then will be the days of the Antichrist spirit, the kingdom *"that was, and is not, even he is the eighth."* Evil was not defeated at the end of World War II, but given sinew and flesh, born inconspicuous into physical being. This is the same kingdom that was before the geological cataclysm, predating the flood that ensues in Noah's lifetime. But what is this kingdom that was, is not, and will be again? To best give a reasonable answer to this question, we must return once again to the latter first half of the twentieth century, four years after Chancellor Hitler voted into power.

This frail, under-educated man born of a family without influence, becomes one of the most dominate presences the world has ever known. Although his life story intriguing, it provides shuddering evidence of how many unseen forces conspire toward an inevitable conclusion. A major proponent in the formation of the infamous Nazi Party, Adolf Hitler rises to charismatic dictator worshipped by a zealous population dazzled by the vision of a new world order with Aryan purity at his core. More than political consensus, more than military strategy, the fascist awakening of the *Third Reich* opened the door to potentials of insurmountable evil. There has been much written about the occult, Hitler, and the Nazi Party. Historians often refuse to take such research into serious consideration for fear of being labeled as hysteric. Also there is the uncomfortable acceptance that if inspired evil exist in such a public arena, then this implies the existence of a divine God of creation. Many modern scholars, nurtured at the feet of renowned atheist such as Comte and Nietzsche, laying the foundation of modern intellectualism, create paradigms of constructed preferences for more pragmatic conclusions. Nevertheless, there is a great deal of documentation that suggests the Nazi Party conformed to every description of a satanic cult. Nazism has its roots in the self-proclaimed occultist Thule Society, a membership devoted to German antiquity and the belief that the Aryan race genetically superior, a bloodline originating from the lost continent of Atlantis. Although Hitler not a registered member of the Thule Society, he had close association with Dietrich Eckart, who completely embraces the core beliefs and mysticism presented by the society. Eckart sees Hitler as the prophesized redeemer of Germany and recognizes that a great power of darkness manifested through this willing host. No one had greater influence on Hitler and the philosophical direction of the Nazi Party than Eckart. He once refers to Germany's Fuhrer, as a puppet to immortal forces; and that he, Eckart, serves as the string-master of manipulation. *Was Adolf Hitler possessed of a powerful evil spirit?*

Many theologians think he was: a possession that takes place sometime in childhood. Even his suicide coincides on Walpurgis Night,

April 30, an ancient occult feast when demons reverend Satan as their supreme leader. But there is more than just ritualistic demonic control that forever changes the world. Secret documents later reveal that in 1937 the Germans recovered what appears to be a crashed UFO outside of Berlin. This singular event spurs renewed determination to locate certain occult artifacts scattered throughout the world. Nazi agents sent to Egypt, South America, India, and even as far as Tibetan China in search of these mystic treasures. Since there were so few defectors, then I think it reasonable to assume the participants motivated by more than nationalistic ideology. Military advancements quickly follow. The world's first jet plane, Messerschmitt 262, plus many secret projects like the stealth wing fighter and V series missiles quickly pass from the drawing board to actual test vehicles. Hitler personally envisions an intercontinental ballistic devise named the V-3 to attack major cities in the United States. Fortunately, time was not on his side. Although appalling, the systematic human carnage enacted by this evil regime remains a grim reminder of how xenophobic idealism can morph into justification for mass murder. But even more terrifying, is the confiscated stockpile of technology, either incomplete, or not yet fully activated. Remember, it was Nazi Germany that provided the world with the blueprints for a functioning Atomic bomb. They manage to develop mechanical cranes that dwarf any machines ever conceived, medical advancements years ahead of all other nations, and war mechanisms of superior design. Secret files, not released to public scrutiny, reveal unworldly technologies as well. Photographed vehicles, definitely saucer-like in design, as well as recovered performance reports in different stages of development. Most intriguing is the enigmatic Bell saucer, which is believed to have been a device capable of creating interdimensional rifts in space-time. There is speculation that the United States Air Force recovered such an object and conducted extensive test after the war ended. It is an undisputed fact that America's race to the stars during the successful Saturn project largely due to the genius of the SS German physicist and mathematician, *Wernher Von Braun*, developer of the V-3 solid fuel rocket, who travels to the United States after the war and joins NASA.

Although regarded with much skepticism, this tiny nation of east Europe dramatically altered world vision of the future. This Pandora cannot be closed again, regardless of how much we might wish to return to naive innocence. Hitler was just a man; Germany only a nation. But the demon that influenced this dreadful history continues, and has a plan with predetermined purpose. Armageddon, the war of seven mountains, will surely pounce upon the world as suddenly as terrorist attacks in a busy metropolis. No, this present world is not a safe place, nor is it made to last forever. Nevertheless, we have surety in one, who has gone before, providing comfort and peace to all that will receive him, as a little child unconcerned of the danger. I personally need no further witness of clarity than the prophecy spoken by Jesus Christ to his apostles in the Gospel of Mark, Chapter 13, verses 5-33 (NIV).

> *"Jesus said to them: "Watch out that no one deceives you. Many will come in my name, claiming, 'I am he,' and will deceive many. When you hear of wars and rumors of wars, do not be alarmed. Such things must happen, but the end is still to come. Nation will rise against nation, and kingdom against kingdom. There will be earthquakes in various places, and famines. These are the beginning of birth pains. "You must be on your guard. You will be handed over to the local councils and flogged in the synagogues. On account of me you will stand before governors and kings as witnesses to them. And the gospel must first be preached to all nations. Whenever you are arrested and brought to trial, do not worry beforehand about what to say. Just say whatever is given you at the time, for it is not you speaking, but the Holy Spirit. "Brother will betray brother to death, and a father his child. Children will rebel against their parents and have them put to death. Everyone will hate you because of me, but the one who stands firm to the end will be saved. "When you see 'the abomination that causes desolation' standing where it does not belong—let the reader understand—then let those who are in Judea*

flee to the mountains. Let no one on the housetop go down or enter the house to take anything out. Let no one in the field go back to get their cloak. How dreadful it will be in those days for pregnant women and nursing mothers! Pray that this will not take place in winter, because those will be days of distress unequaled from the beginning, when God created the world, until now—and never to be equaled again. "If the Lord had not cut short those days, no one would survive. But for the sake of the elect, whom he has chosen, he has shortened them. At that time if anyone says to you, 'Look, here is the Messiah!' or, 'Look, there he is!' do not believe it. For false messiahs and false prophets will appear and perform signs and wonders to deceive, if possible, even the elect. So be on your guard; I have told you everything ahead of time. "But in those days, following that distress," 'the sun will be darkened, and the moon will not give its light; the stars will fall from the sky, and the heavenly bodies will be shaken.' "At that time people will see the Son of Man coming in clouds with great power and glory. And he will send his angels and gather his elect from the four winds, from the ends of the earth to the ends of the heavens. "Now learn this lesson from the fig tree: As soon as its twigs get tender and its leaves come out, you know that summer is near. Even so, when you see these things happening, you know that it is near, right at the door. Truly I tell you, this generation will certainly not pass away until all these things have happened. Heaven and earth will pass away, but my words will never pass away. "But about that day or hour no one knows, not even the angels in heaven, nor the Son, but only the Father. Be on guard! Be alert! You do not know when that time will come."

We search the world for proof, scriptural interpretation for meaning, and rely on a temporal understanding to discern the signs of the times. Prophecies we read and think to understand are spiritually inspired, a reflection of events on an enormous scale in high places, our existence here only a figment of more profound being. I recently listened to a debate between two Rabbis: one an Orthodox Jew, the other a Jew for Christ, both invoking the same scripture from the Book of Isaiah to prove their positions. These two men held the same position concerning the survival of modern day Israel, and both agreed that only a miracle capable of bringing peace to the Holy Land. Except that the Orthodox Rabbi spoke from a position of learning with clarified interest in the juxtaposition of previously defined words and meanings, all suggesting that Israel solely responsible for its own survival. Whereas, the other Rabbi shared his experience from a position of spiritual faith, proclaiming that Israel's survival contained within the scriptures clearly painted an unmistakable portrait of the Messiah Ben Joseph, found in both the Old and the New Testament Bible.

This Jesus was not a gentile. Nor were the twelve chosen apostles who followed him. The majority of the world outside of Jewry worshipped idols of wood and stone, readily debating the meaning of every philosophy. This man Jesus taught no other interpretation of meaning not contained in the Book of Moses and the Prophets. Toward the end of his ministry in the Gospel of Luke, Chapter 19, verses 37-44 (KJV), Jesus weeps over Jerusalem because of the hardness he sees and the future consequence reserved to God's people.

> *"And when he was come nigh, even now at the descent of the mount of Olives, the whole multitude of the disciples began to rejoice and praise God with a loud voice for all the mighty works that they had seen; Saying, Blessed be the King that cometh in the name of the Lord: peace in heaven, and glory in the highest. And some of the Pharisees from among the multitude said unto him, Master, rebuke thy disciples. And he answered and said unto them, I tell you that, if these should hold their peace, the stones would immediately cry out. As He approached and saw the city, He wept over it, Saying, If thou had known, even thou, at least in this thy day, the things which belong unto thy*

peace! but now they are hid from thine eyes. For the days shall come upon thee, that thine enemies shall cast a trench about thee, and compass thee round, and keep thee in on every side, And shall lay thee even with the ground, and thy children within thee; and they shall not leave in thee one stone upon another; because thou knew not the time of thy visitation."

As already mentioned this part of the prophecy comes true less than seventy years later when the second temple burned by a Roman commander named Titus, during the Jewish rebellion. After the fire, he orders the temple dismantled stone by stone to recover the gold that has melted into the cracks. This Roman has no idea of his role in fulfilling the prophecy of Jesus; nor even knew who this Jesus was. One precept abundantly clear, God has chosen Israel as a lightening rod of diurnally prescribed history.

If it were even possible for one to go back in time and kill the baby Hitler, would the Holocaust never have happened? Would such an act make a historical difference in the present escalation of violence? Even if Iran were to deploy nuclear weapons and use these instruments of mass destruction against any of its neighbors or perceived foes, it would only make itself a target of annihilation. Already this Islamic republic has enough material to create dirty bombs, but the signature of the fallout would inevitably lead back to them. And it is not impossible that they do not already possess such a devise after so many decades of uncensored research and development.

The greatest problem in the Middle East today is the absence of accountability. Fear of proliferation is perhaps the greatest concern. The more nuclear armed nations there are, the greater the likelihood of sparking a global holocaust. Considering that it takes a lot of resources and professional coordination to develop long range lethal systems, the more plausible scenario would be purchases of smaller nuclear devices by wealthy consortiums such as Saudi Arabia from uncensored exchanges. Nuclear weapons have been around since a long time, with threatening potential. Remembering the nuclear arms race of the middle half of the previous century, the threat just as real then, as it is today. The greater danger being in the hands that possess this deadly technology, than proliferation only.

The Russian Bear to the north never hibernated to extinction, and is even now beginning to awake. Leopard spotted China and those principalities to the east have not abandoned a design of world domination, only wears a disarming face. The sobering reality is that if ever these death-headed rockets reach into the sky, it will mean the devastating end to civilization-- *possibly even life on planet earth!* It is more likely that the possession of these weapons will ensure a counterbalance for land aggressions: in other words, the steady march of land armadas toward the prophesized battlefield of Armageddon. This is the real elephant in the room that everyone wishes to ignore.

Should the present day Israeli military launch a preempted strike against Iran in an attempt to prevent that sovereign country from acquiring nuclear weapons? Is mass murder of men, women, and children justification enough to insure the survival of a restored nation on the steps of the Golan Heights? I say plainly that Hitler was allowed access to a worldly position, as surely as God raised up the Pharaoh of Egypt against the Hebrews, to prove that the God of Abraham still abided in the days of Moses. Iran will have its nuclear bomb, and there will be terror in the Holy land. As dispassionate as it may sound, history cannot be changed in the past or in the future. These prophecies are not just shades of things that might be, but things that are. The true enemy is not the pawns of flesh and blood that appear from season to season, but the manifest strategies of Satan and his plans to deceive mankind.

The nation Israel was, was not, and is now. Nor is it the geography of secular dispensation only. There is the secular nation called Israel today, and there is the spiritual, which will rise from ashes as a phoenix reborn. Not by might of military response, not by imposed international peace agreements, but by oblation to the heir of their salvation, as it is written. In that notable day the appendage of deliverance will be the mighty finger of God. Nevertheless, all these things must come to pass in fulfillment of prophecy before the Messiah appears on a cloud of power and glory. For it is through the promise of this spiritual Israel that

Messiah is come: the seed of eternal salvation to every man, woman, and child, who call upon the name of the Lord, not forsaking those who remain faithful in Israel to this day. As recorded in the Book of Judges, the two books of Kings, the books of the Prophets, an overview of Hebrew society within historical context. Judges are sent as instruments of correction when the children of Abraham stray from the teaching of Moses and begin worshipping the material images of other gods. When the people demand a king to follow, they are often led astray until the coronation of another king, whose heart turns to God's will and correction made with the determination of a strong hand. Once again the people turn from the way of sin and death to the statues of the one God of heaven and earth. The prophets appear as chimeras of warning, predicting a consequential certainty of a directional future. In every generation God raises up men and women, who refuse to bow to these false principalities, who remember the ways of God in their heart, and who walk in the power of faith provided through promise. Upon this hill God has reserved to the end of days as a continuing testament to men and angels that look for the second coming of *Messiah Ben David*. The resurrection of spiritual Jerusalem is certain--a history written since the foundations of the world.

This is an astonishing promise delivered to mankind by the creator of all the immensity perceived from mortal perspective. The human experience is to the benefit of our immortal soul, an opportunity to awaken spiritually and be born again. The forces of logical intellect, material desire, and temptation of power-- all designed to keep us dormant in the prideful belief that what we see is all that is, and that only a fool believes in things intangible. This has been Satan's lie all along: *You will know good and evil as God.* For the sake of all humanity, the earthly Israel that presently appears must endure the greater affliction, as well as the greatest revelation of salvation in the resurrected *Christ*, the rejected cornerstone of an unshakable foundation. In season all will be made clear, as spoken by the prophet Joel in Chapter 2, verses 27-32 (NIV).

"Then you will know that I am in Israel, that I am the LORD your God, and that there is no other; never again will my people be shamed. And afterward, I will pour out my Spirit on all people. Your sons and daughters will prophesy, your old men will dream dreams, your young men will see visions. Even on my servants, both men and women, I will pour out my Spirit in those days. will show wonders in the heavens and on the earth, blood and fire and billows of smoke. The sun will be turned to darkness and the moon to blood before the coming of the great and dreadful day of the LORD. And everyone who calls on the name of the LORD will be saved; for on Mount Zion and in Jerusalem there will be deliverance, as the LORD has said, even among the survivors whom the LORD calls."

Satan's final defeat properly begins with a man named Jesus, who at thirty years old is baptized by another man named John and journeys 40 days into the wilderness of Judea. It is here that Satan confronts the spiritually conceived Son of God with earthly temptation; and it is here that Jesus defeats the master of this world. Utilizing all the usurped powers given into his hands, Satan offers these in exchange for worship. He knows the weakness of flesh in the first Adam and believes that this second Adam no different. During the temptation, Jesus is momentarily removed from temporal condition, and literally offered all the glory of earthly existence in exchange for worship. Past, present, and future pass before his eyes, with the promise of becoming a great *King of Kings* of this failing principality just by submitting allegiance to the self-appointed god of this world. But Jesus sees through the eyes of Messiah, knowing all this grandeur illusion. In the book of Luke, Chapter 4, verses 5-8 (KJV) we read:

"And the devil, taking him up into a high mountain, showed unto him all the kingdoms of the world in a moment of time. And the devil said unto him, All this power will I give thee, and the glory of them: for that is

delivered unto me; and to whomsoever I will I give it. If thou therefore wilt worship me, all shall be thine. And Jesus answered and said unto him, Get thee behind me, Satan: for it is written, Thou shall worship the Lord thy God, and him only shall thou serve."

This victory marks the beginning of the four Gospels of the New Testament Bible testifying of the last few years in the life of a living breathing man known by friends, family, and acquaintances as the son of a carpenter. These eyewitness accounts tell about a man that exhibits extraordinary abilities to heal those infirmed, to cast out demons from those afflicted, raises the dead, feeds multitudes with limited resources, and defies the immutable laws of nature. But more importantly they detail a public execution and how this man raised back to life by spiritual determination and transformed in a way that defies all logic of understanding as the Messiah witnessed by prophets and angels. This only the beginning, as all except one of these men also filled with the Holy Spirit on the day of Pentecost, themselves becoming living new testaments of an unfailing principality yet to come.

I add my personal testimony to this abiding witness as further reference. I am only one born imperfect in my generation saved by grace; Israel a nation also saved by grace. Nevertheless, I believe that actions define us as individuals, as well as a collective; and the choices we make make all the difference. To condone mass murder out of worldly fear we become no different than the mortal enemy we wrestle against. To think in terms of quantum value is to abandon the essence of moral authority. If Israel stands as an example of God's earthly presence, then it must rise above all nations as a standard of exemplified faith. This is a spiritual manifestation, not accomplished by carnal design. This hymn of David written by Israel's most notable king says plainly all that we can know found in Psalm 23, verse 1-6 (NIV).

"The Lord is my shepherd, I lack nothing. He makes me lie down in green pastures, he leads me beside quiet waters, he refreshes my soul. He guides me along the right paths for

his name's sake. Even though I walk through the darkest valley, a̱ I will fear no evil, for you are with me; your rod and your staff, they comfort me. You prepare a table before me in the presence of my enemies. You anoint my head with oil; my cup overflows. Surely your goodness and love will follow me all the days of my life, and I will dwell in the house of the Lord forever."

This is the only certain hope provided to our understanding in mortal passing. For I am convinced that knowledge is to the end of edification by faith *(and that being from the Lord for a predestined purpose)*. Just as the great constellations made in heaven constrained to a clock- work pattern irresistible; so, too, the destiny of nations, the entropic end to principalities visible and invisible, and the passage of all that is designed from the beginning.

Chapter 18
KNOWLEDGE OF EVERYTHING

As intriguing as the unknown possibilities of past history, the prevailing hope is that only myopia of present understanding holds keys to unlock the door for a more promising future. The most holy grail of knowledge is to divine the perfect code of everything. It is believed that one day the discovery of one primordial element will become a keystone to universal comprehension of mechanical process. Or to put it another way: *to find that most elusive God particle.*

Does such a particle exist in the present universe? Since the cosmological model of everything we observe a progression of entopic process, then how can a perfect code emerge from the present program of thermodynamic decline? It is analogist to suggesting that, given enough time, a better model vehicle will spontaneously evolve from the dissolving elements of global junkyards. Not only is this an absurd assumption, it defies the defining rules of logical discourse. Nevertheless this is the prevailing reason embraced by progressive intellectualism. It is more likely that the architecture of such an enigmatic code can only exist in a design conceived outside of directional time and space. It is this hyper-reality potential I wish to address in these few pages within context of relevant significance.

Modern scientific research has devoted much energy and resources to solving this riddle of contained in thermodynamic process. From the subatomic structure of molecular cohesion, to the radiant energy of distant collapsing stars, there is no end to the imaginative potential of mankind's gaze toward even the most remote end of the universe. From a purely objective perspective, this is the most admirable quality of human curiosity. However to make relative assumptions the definitive model of reality is proportional to claiming to know the composition of a galaxy from a handful of star dust.

Intellectual reasoning is based on five primary principals: observation of a phenomenon, the interpretation of data using comparatives to form a hypothesis, testing that hypothesis within context of other hypothesis, and the bias of assumption. These first four are self evident; but the fifth, raises many contentious issues. From the accumulated data, or lack thereof, a conclusion of meaning formed to describe a phenomenon within context. Thus the fulcrum of belief engenders a dividing line of opposing faith: *deterministic existentialism or the recognition of creative design*. It is the basic platform of this intellectual controversy I wish to address. Not as a debate, for I am in the middle. But as one, who bears witness that God is true and the Holy Bible physical evidence of spiritually inspired communication manifested into the conscious history of mankind. These collected scriptures are not just elemental doctrine to construct wise theologies, but revelations of spirit and truth, each word with independent potential within context of the whole. For I am convinced that salvation comes through an understanding transcendent to natural reason, becoming the conception of a two way communication between the living soul of a man and the revitalizing power of the Holy Spirit embodied through the resurrected Christ.

Philosophy teaches that we are each the sum of our thoughts. Beneath the austere gaze of a Biologist's microscope, we are a collection of warring microbes and electrical impulses. The Physicist concludes all creation a grand cosmic accident begun by the undefined mystery of a fortuitous singularity. The atheist convinced life meaningless, void of faith, with a deterministic future. And the religious cleric proclaims we are the physical manifestation of an omnipotent will beyond our understanding. Perhaps we are a little of all these things; and definitely so much more.

Consensus among Theoretical Physicist is the persistent idea that perceived reality is the surface tension of string theory connectivity, whereby, all matter and energy in the physical universe only evidence of a much vaster potential. Just another layer of existence, tangibly real, originating in a subspace dimension of multi-universes interpreted through the unconscious mind. In part this theory correct, except that the corridor of temporal existence within context of present observation equivalent to seeing through the peephole of a nebulous passage conditions separating eternal heaven from eternal hell, habited of spiritual agents engaged in strategic grand entropic conflict.

The knowledge that spirits abound is as old as the earliest recorded cave drawings found at Lascaux, in southern France, left behind by the inhabitants known as *Magdalenian*. These magnificent, and often sophisticated drawings of animals captured in action, inspire a wonder of creation witnessed in the natural world. Present day dating techniques establish a chronology between 12000 to 15000 years ago. Even if this time scale should prove inaccurate, it establishes that these early hunter gathers were acutely aware that something else existed beyond the physical beings captured in the shadows of these cave walls. Captured within these palaeolithic drawings are entities, embodied with metaphysical presence, insidiously more disturbing than the surrealism of mythological inspirations drawn by torchlight.

In fact, there is not a culture in world history that does not have some embrace of the supernatural. The awareness that all matter and energy emerged from a singular creative consciousness permeates the human genesis with an awe of inspiration. Even more frighteningly real, the knowledge that all matter and energy in a progressive state of disassociation or *"entropy"*. In modern scientific terms, this observation of physical existence described as three thermodynamic exchange processes, which ultimately must fail. The first of these laws states that energy cannot be created or destroyed. The second law states that organization of reaction must inevitably decay into chaos. And the third law states that all contained values will eventually reach absolute zero. In other words, all processes begun at the instance of the Big Bang will eventually run out of fuel and dissipate. However by reason of an abstraction called the human soul, there exists an innate awareness that we are more than the sum of all that we know, founded on greater elements than just the construction of many complex parts organized through subatomic excitation. This innate part of our being aware it is eternal, contrary to all the accumulated evidence. In short it sees that which cannot be seen or touched in natural existence.

A collective consciousness, described in philosophy as the Zeitgeist, or *"spirit in time"*, ascribes a condition of social integration on the level of abstract potential exceeding the value of a quantifiable sum. What this means is that we are in some vague way connected to a generational context during the transition of corporeal life cycle, while retaining an identity unique to individual meaning and freedom of choice. But what is this mega-conscious energy that connects us? And what significance does it hold after the expiration of the physical body?

All organic life is a collection of molecular cohesion stimulated by chemical reaction. There thrives a cosmos of interstellar life forms composing every cell of the human body. These complex chains of nuclei infusion stimulate protein production, thus encoding groups of enzymes into a gene sequence of DNA strands and RNA copies to formalize an accommodation of chemical reaction. Through this collusion forms the building blocks of bacteria, further escalating into higher organization of cell production. *To say that the human body is alive is an understatement!* Each individual is a contained universe with far more billions of populations, born and perished in a single day, than all the generations of human beings that have collectively inhabited the earth. And yet despite the carnage of a perpetual condition of warring factions, order prevails with balanced precision, unless interfered with by a foreign agent. This is not to imply that the present design eternal, only that the potential of perfected being possible beyond the model of present thermodynamic reaction: a condition ultimately restrained to physical boundaries wisely imposed by laws designed into composite temporal state.

Nevertheless, mechanical existence, although remarkable, is only a fading garment compared to the animating life-force, which is far more astounding in complexity! To suggest we are the product of creative cognition is cliché within reference. Yes, science and philosophy may ponder wisely the dilemma of which came first: the chicken or the egg. However, until someone can produce a blueprint for the construction of a single free atom, then all the posturing seems little more constructive than children playing with prefabricated Lego blocks sold at a *Toys-R-Us* store, while bragging their many reconstructions.

A working analogy of world reason today can be equated with the paradoxical question: *what is an egg?* The kitchen chef responds it is a culinary food source with delicious accent. The artist responds it is a remarkable design richly contoured to provide symmetry within a universal context. The spiritualist responds it is the irrefutable evidence of divine handiwork. The analytical scientist responds it is a genetic product of a specific genius originating from hybrid evolution. Despite the formal agreement contained within these observations, none approach to the vaster meaning inscribing the subatomic structure of all physical matter. Therefore, if what we perceive is so profound, then much more that which we do not see!

The inescapable conclusion of all observation must, therefore, be based on limited perspective relative to position. We may not be aware of a body in space through our senses, yet are able to determine *(not only its presence)* but many relevant factors, such as mass and motion, just by the invisible gravitational influence accompanied through spectral light curvature. If we are willing to make such assumptions in real space based on model interpretation, then why not consider the organization of an unseen quantum coexisting as a manifestation within the fabric of living matrix?

Many questions arise when considering what exist-- *if anything*-- beyond the animation of living matter. Are spirits disembodied souls wandering the earth capable of haunting dark corridors of imagination? Are they immortal? And what is an *"old soul"* we hear so much about in writings of the new age occult? The Holy Spirit has revealed to me that there is a tangible realm inhabited by creatures inspired with a different quantum influence than the elements of light and shadow consciously perceived. Through my spiritual journey in the Lord, I have encountered these entities on occasion, made aware of their dangerous potential to ensnare a human soul into their dark habitation. I knew them once before in a more familiar way, only then unaware of their deceptive power. I am in personal agreement with the Apostle Paul, when he writes in a letter to the Ephesians, Chapter 6, verse 12, (KJV), concerning the spirits of the air:

> *"For we wrestle not against flesh and blood, but against principalities, against powers, against the rulers of the darkness of this world, against spiritual wickedness in high places."*

Many philosophies consider that a *half-life* condition continues for a time after death of the body, this being physical evidence of a separate entity called the soul. As supportive proof they point to the well-documented technique of *Kirlian* photography, an imaging process that captures the electromagnetic field created by a living organism, producing a recordable aura of presence. The autonomic cessation of the biological host liberates this energy; whereby, it remains integral for a time, until absorbed into a grander matrix. It is thought that this life energy remains trapped for a period in a maze of fluctuation analogist to the filament of a light bulb at the instance of separation. Since this transition phase lacks cognition of physical connection to thermodynamic reaction engaged by the living, souls of the departed lose the awareness of temporal association. The best equivalent would be to exit a throttled jet plane in mid flight. Sudden transition from one relative condition to a different resistance of acceleration would be traumatic.

But there do seem to be strings of coherence that remain in lineal time progression after physical cessation. Perhaps, this is how clairvoyants are able to communicate to a disembodied shade by the use of sympathetic vibrations and artifacts, such as requested by *King Saul* to a woman of unique ability known as the *Witch of Endor*. This sensitive summons a presence identified as the prophet Samuel. The Bible, however, warns that such communication is dangerous to all those involved, as it opens the door into principalities of darkness inhabited by demonic force. In this example it is uncertain if the actual soul of the departed person appears, or a figment of energy residue that once symbiotically existed between the polar connections of Saul and Samuel, and thus creating a resistance of tangible influence compelled to speak in the prophet's voice. Meaning that King Saul knew already his judgment, and judges himself in accordance with the prophet's mouth, which he accepts to be just and true. By all accounts this *Witch of Endor* escapes immediate retribution, contrary to the King's own decree. Nevertheless, this event does suggest that all flesh grounded to temporal value of the present universe, until liberated through the transcendent manifestation of the Holy Spirit. For even those spirits that first rebelled know and fear the God of creation and his chosen Messiah, who has also descended into hell to free those righteous souls restrained.

It is interesting to note within context that before the Prophet Samuel those with the power of divinity were referred to as Seers. In every culture Seers are described as individuals with a special connection to unseen spirits endowed with often vague abilities to construct the shades of future events. The most famous example would be the Seers of Delphi in later classical Greece, who regularly consult the oracles for advice from polytheistic entities. What makes Samuel different is that his visions come directly from the Holy Spirit. He, and the many prophets after him, lifted up as God's mouthpieces of correction to insure fulfillment of a promise made to Abraham that persevered through his seed would be birth of Messiah.

Also, this Samuel is also last of the Judges sent to Israel by God, making this man's life a pivotal fulcrum between flesh existence and spiritual direction. After Samuel God provides clear guidelines on how to discern the message of a true prophet sent by the Holy Spirit from the deceptive communications of soothsayers inspired by familiar spirits. It is possible that Samuel's soul remains in a temporal holding cell, until freed by the Messiah descending into the depths of hell to release those trapped there. This why the *Witch of Endor* able to communicate with his grounded entity using her gift of sensitivity. All we know is that a soul described as Samuel relates the true words of final judgment to this first King of Israel on the eve before Saul's death. It also suggests a divine provision to liberate souls of the dead from the depths of purgatory by prescription of a spiritual directive.

Even Christ warns Mary after the resurrection not to touch him, until he first undergoes a *"trans*figuration" that must be accomplished through transition from mortal being. This implies a time lapse from moment of death to eternal translation, as stated in the Gospel of John, Chapter 20, verse 17 (KJV).

> *"Jesus said unto her, Touch me not; for I am not yet ascended to my Father: but go to my brethren, and say unto them, I ascend unto my Father, and your Father; and to my God, and your God."*

Fallen angels and demons are not the same. It is my comprehension that demons are the combined elements of a once human soul possessed and infected by an earthbound influence. These demons are able to migrate from one living host to another, sharing memories and abilities through many incarnations. These are the *"old souls"* often sensationalized by media coverage, suggestive of the quasi proof validating reincarnation. Lacking true being, these demonic entities are more like spiritual parasites enjoying a symbiotic relationship, thus allowing them to cross over into present existence as corrupt seeds finding root in fertile ground. They know something that we have forgotten through mortal conditioning: *human stature made lower than the angels, but in the image of Almighty God.* This means that each of us provided the gift of a living soul with the capacity of being born again in a revitalized kingdom through the Holy Spirit. Although created from the elements, becoming flesh and blood after the similitude of sin and death, we have something that the heavenly principalities unable to obtain on their own. We have the potential to become resurrected from sin and ascend in the similitude of God through the likeness of Jesus Christ. What better place to conceal the riddle of immortality, than in the potential of mortal incarnation? In 1 Corinthians, Chapter 15, verses 49-55 (KJV), the Apostle Paul writes concerning the resurrection:

> *"And as we have borne the image of the earthy, we shall also bear the image of the heavenly. Now this I say, brethren, that flesh and blood cannot inherit the kingdom of God; neither does corruption inherit incorruption. Behold, I*

show you a mystery; We shall not all sleep, but we shall all be changed. In a moment, in the twinkling of an eye, at the last trump: for the trumpet shall sound, and the dead shall be raised incorruptible, and we shall be changed. For this corruptible must put on incorruption, and this mortal must put on immortality. So when this corruptible shall have put on incorruption, and this mortal shall have put on immortality, then shall be brought to pass the saying that is written, Death is swallowed up in victory. O death, where is your sting? O grave, where is your victory?"

Suppose the living body analogous to a composite machine generating an electromagnetic field. Then this field generator, as so defined, is capable of both sending and receiving message frequencies. Just as certain sound potentials or spectrums of higher resonance are perceived innately; so are these communications perceived through subconscious interpretation. There have been numerous studies conducted to define the cognitive state that determines the definition of consciousness and the buffer zone of reality termed the subconscious. Young babies show signs of awareness, yet lack the experience of association. It has been postulated that a child, before the age of three, possesses a more acute sense of displacement, thus seeing between the layers of reality taken for granted as we develop into adulthood. Just as dogs and other animals are able to discern sounds and light waves beyond the range of normal adjustment (such as an approaching earthquake, or a threat by an unseen attacker), young children become quickly attuned to sympathetic vibrations to which an adult remains altogether blind. In fact an infant under the age of one has a visual focus range of only a few inches, yet can easily discern the presence of a mother from that of a stranger. The unconscious emits a sensory net of attuned oscillation, not dissimilar to the way bats navigate in a pack, slightly alternating their frequencies to eliminate confusion. Instead of using acoustic telemetry, the unconscious is a composite of soul energy. This means that another proponent, other than grounded biological field generation, becomes instrumental to our perceptual cognition and basic survival instincts.

You have all heard the adage: *the first impression is usually the best impression.* This suggests further validity to the persistent idea that some individuals have a highly developed sixth sense. The first five we know as taste, touch, smell, hearing, and (most deceptive of all the senses) *sight!* This sixth sense is based on intuition, which altogether bypasses the conscious interpretation of light and shadow.

Even at the university level, higher learning becomes a competition of scores based on unquestionable assumptions. It is a proven fact that some people learn better how to take test than others with the acuity to navigate through a maze within established parameters. It is questionable if this is a sign of intelligence, or the byproduct of reinforcement behavior. The achievement of graduate and PHD becomes a specialized devotion to a particular focus within context. The nature of life and the universe then becomes the narrative language of an organized program with predetermined expectations, while dismissing all other potentials not consistent with a given hypothesis of interpretation. Professionalism becomes a myopic priesthood of collective existence empowered with sure doctrine of all that was, all that is, and all that will be. However, if this is the new definition of what it means to be human, then why be endowed with an unconscious at all? Which raises an even more perplexing consideration: *since it is the balanced destiny of all organic structures to perish in the irresistible flow of time, then why the human spirit made to greater comprehension of time and space and existence?*

There is some abstract component in human nature capable of a connection, not based solely on physicality, but upon a powerful link forged through the unconscious. Strip away the veneer of the conscious conductor and subconscious interpreter of the mind, the ensuing babble would drive us surely mad! The unconscious sees all things and believes all things. It is the primal receptor organizing input data, thus relaying that data to the subconscious, where it is provisionally sorted before reaching the analytical threshold of the conscious mind. Very often the subconscious becomes a willing deceiver, allowing only partial cognition to manifest, working in tangent with the more rigid barriers of expectation of what the conscious mind will accept through a construct of rational. Dreams are a classic example of this presorting. The sleeper rarely remembers more than vague images with any cognitive clarity, as the subconscious struggles with the unconscious over consensus and meaning. This apparently is not always the case, as evidenced in the translated visions of prophets accumulated in the Old and New Testament Bible. In these rare glimpses through the veil of temporality, an agreement reached between the three states of consciousness. This documented phenomenon inspiring a more comprehensive view of time and space, not limited to the clockwork order of chronology.

But as we have already witnessed, not all spiritual communication from the same source. As one might assume there are other minds that whisper thoughts to our unconscious that are not altogether fixed in present state. Here past, present, and future intersect on a mega-consciousness level that defies analysis, altogether surpassing natural reason. This indiscernible mediation is evidence of a direct link of rapport established between spirits of external origin and the spirit of man communicating tacit awareness to the understanding.

This raises the question: *is what we think of as reality even real?* There are bold new theories suggesting that we live within context of a digitized cosmic program providing the illusion of infinite time and space. That everything observed in the detectable universe delivered to our comprehension through quantized packets generated in a simulated model, with matter and energy reflecting in upon itself through a process described as gravitational *"lensing"*. In other words, presently defined existence may be only a Beta test; the simulation of an imperfect code designed to work out all the bugs before the final release. This is a profoundly intriguing idea, implying that a perfected code already possible, which can only be realized through an essence called faith. In the letter written by the Apostle Paul to the Hebrews, Chapter 11, verses 1-3 (KJV), we find a startling proclamation concerning the mysterious construction of the observable universe.

> *"Now faith is the substance of things hoped for, the evidence of things not seen. For by it the elders obtained a good report. Through faith we understand that the worlds were*

framed by the word of God, so that things which are seen were not made of things which do appear."

With this in mind, I have attempted to examine some of the many inconsistencies so apparent in nature, and particularly the flaws inherent to interpretation potential. I therefore admonish the reader not to pray just for peaceful shelters in the present, subject to the elements; but for an estate unshakable where neither rust, neither the corruption of time, nor any other element prevail. Pray that we see with eyes wide open, and not through the dark reflections of a worldly mind. This project I submit to you in faith, knowing that no truth remains in obscurity and no lie a beacon of light. There is, indeed, a God particle of perfect design and perfect organization. This code manifest in the resurrection of the Messiah, a mediator between man and Almighty God, the living New Testament of what creation designed to be. This spiritual revision provided to the old man of the flesh in the promise of a glorified heaven and earth and worlds without end. To this end the Holy Spirit bears witness that eternal salvation of men's souls a personal revelation given to every individual in season; not the encryption of a treasured prize reserved to any collective.

Chapter 19
COUNTING AMONG THE SHEEP

You can never know a wolf
Until you have counted among the wolves
Sat at the council rock of the moon
Made laughter lost of reason soon
Stepped silent while shepherds sleep
As shadows counting among the sheep

You can never know a sheep
Until you have counted among the sheep
Surrendered love to the peace of night
Seen visions without the eye of light
Unafraid to the sound of approaching feet
As wolves are counting among the sheep

This poem composed by myself some years ago serves well to begin this final chapter. Regardless of the bios of interpretation, the human population on this planet represents a collective of tribes streaming from the pool of a single genesis. And even though there are differing archetypes, yet each of us as unique as snowflakes seen under an electron microscope: *those differences only chromosome deep.* Because of tribal nature mankind appears fragmented, subdivided by age, gender, race, culture, societal integration, and --*most vehement of all*-- by ideology. Little wonder that human history is a saga of violent aggressions interrupted by brief intermissions of peace.

The analogy of wolves and sheep should be self evident. Within surface context, the wolves are willful agents running in packs seeking to infiltrate and exploit cohesive society; whereas, the sheep represent faithful existence through the harmonious integrity of the whole. The shepherd is institutional guardianship to insure order and judicial process. There will always be wolves, and always sheep, mingled together in the shadows of time and progress: the intangible integrity of the human condition. Nor are wolves always wolves, or sheep always sheep. For this reason, we must remain diligent that there are *always wolves counting among the sheep.*

I begin as a sheep, a quiet child content to be in the world through the wondrous apprehension of innocence; but in time learn to be a wolf through the assault of worldly forces that afflict my inexperienced soul. In time I change into what the world wants me to be. I learn violence, how to hate, embrace prejudice against a perceived enemy, and accept to serve as an instrument to the necessity of worldly power. I refuse to become part of any pact, and therefore, a lone wolf given power to execute judgment. I begin to imagine myself greater than the myopic being born of flesh and blood, born under a cloud of sin and death. I think the sheep of this world a weaker element in need of the protection of my proud benevolence. Then in a time divided by time, the shepherd of my soul reveals grace and forgiveness to my hardened heart. Instantly, I am born again! This moment I know the measure of true strength and the wonderful joy of being a lost sheep found in the arms of my Lord and Savior Jesus Christ.

As modern science peers ever deeper into the subatomic reality of existence, revelation that beyond each surface layer are complex networks of construction held together by tentacles of unknown energy signatures. These strings evidence of an undetectable matrix emanating from other spaces of sub-dimensional source. This is an astounding contradiction to conclusions of present observations with a deterministic goal to place everything into a neat predictable academic package. If one looks at history objectively, a clear pattern begins to emerge. In each generation human reason becomes more defined through quantum value. Although analogist to a dayfly trying to comprehend the span of a hundred years during its several hours of existence, still insistence that myopic models tell the whole story. Because Satan and his fallen legions are trapped in a quantum universe collapsing into entropy, they know nothing else. This makes the quantum lies commanded through natural reason seem all the more real.

As already stated, humankind is reaching the stage where it is collectively being conditioned to think and process information like the created artificial intelligence infiltrated into every aspect of modern living. Moore's 1975 perdition that computer chips would double every two years is a theory less accurate than believed a decade earlier. Nevertheless, it still has merit pertaining to chip-size in relation to calculation possibilities. Now we are on the horizon of chips so small that they can be inserted into a host via a hypodermic needle syringe. This will fulfill the quantum condition of censorship necessary for the reign of Antichrist.

As with all technologies this age of computer flourishes from hidden agenda: *a breadcrumb trail that ultimately leads to hill of the Seven Mountains as foretold in Biblical prophecy.* But make no mistake, there is a war going on here; raging battles that surround us daily on a level of grand proportion incomprehensible to human reason. The substance of our eternal souls in the balance. Spirit is not just a conditional position comprehended through present value. It is the greater value of all things, impossible to comprehend or provide context through mortal vision. Those reborn of the spirit see through eyes of the spirit and speak spiritual things. They proclaim testament of the resurrected Messiah as powerfully stated in a letter to the Hebrews, Chapter 11, verses 1-16 (NIV).

> *"Now faith is confidence in what we hope for and assurance about what we do not see. This is what the ancients were commended for. By faith we understand that the universe was formed at God's command, so that what is seen was not made out of what was visible. By faith Abel brought God a better offering than Cain did. By faith he was commended as righteous, when God spoke well of his offerings. And by faith Abel still speaks, even though he is dead. By faith Enoch was taken from this life, so that he*

did not experience death: "He could not be found, because God had taken him away." For before he was taken, he was commended as one who pleased God. And without faith it is impossible to please God, because anyone who comes to him must believe that he exists and that he rewards those who earnestly seek him. By faith Noah, when warned about things not yet seen, in holy fear built an ark to save his family. By his faith he condemned the world and became heir of the righteousness that is in keeping with faith. By faith Abraham, when called to go to a place he would later receive as his inheritance, obeyed and went, even though he did not know where he was going. By faith he made his home in the promised land like a stranger in a foreign country; he lived in tents, as did Isaac and Jacob, who were heirs with him of the same promise. For he was looking forward to the city with foundations, whose architect and builder is God. And by faith even Sarah, who was past childbearing age, was enabled to bear children because she considered him faithful who had made the promise. And so from this one man, and he as good as dead, came descendants as numerous as the stars in the sky and as countless as the sand on the seashore. All these people were still living by faith when they died. They did not receive the things promised; they only saw them and welcomed them from a distance, admitting that they were foreigners and strangers on earth. People who say such things show that they are looking for a country of their own. If they had been thinking of the country they had left, they would have had opportunity to return. Instead, they were longing for a better country—a heavenly one. Therefore God is not ashamed to be called their God, for he has prepared a city for them."

Label the present human condition as you will. Born into a world of sin or born from the stars, we are all traversing together this brief passage called life. As an objective observer conceived in the pool of my own genealogical value, I can only assert what I think and believe through the lens of local experience. We are all dominos in the middle: positioned by what went before and subject to a series of events inevitable. Yes, I suppose it is an easy thing to say the sea of present existence would be better off were it not polluted. Nevertheless, it is polluted and the pollution is only getting worse. I am not making a cry of despair, nor am I proclaiming a prophetic warning. I merely point out that to see through the eyes and experience of even one brother or sister (*whom God loves*), then we glimpse the hope and resurrection of all humanity. In other words, we begin to understand what it means to give our minds and our hearts to higher purpose, and choose willingly to *count among the sheep*. Some might call this humanism, but to these I submit that such is the mind and actions of Jesus Christ during his sojourn here on earth. Are we better than our Lord? Is his cross so difficult to bear?

How easily we accept that there are differences in normative physiology, yet appalled by the sight of deformity. Within context of every generation and in every culture are sown the seeds of "dappled things"--recalling the words of the poet Gerald Manley Hopkins in his poem *Pied Beauty*. Who can ignore the historical visage of a hunchbacked king; a famous sixteenth century painting of two women born conjoined; and collected historical volumes chronicling the birth of monsters? Such conceptions, once considered evidence of bestiality and of evil communication, paint the frightened portrait of xenophobic society ignorant of causation, and thus subject to fears of superstition. Thanks to the dedicated efforts of many humanitarians, at least some of us now accept that these are fellow human beings, genetically the same as any other. Their physical afflictions often the result of horrible mistakes in the DNA code from a number of potential causes. Nevertheless, some exceed their limitations, giving much more than they take, making the world a better place to live. I am humbled by the thought that by the grace of God, I am as they.

I recently read an inspiring article about a young man born without eyes and bound to a wheelchair because of a curvature in the spine. Yet, since early childhood this unique individual discovered that he possesses the impeccable ability to hear cadence and play music with flawless appreciation like a modern day Beethoven. Another born without legs wins a number of running competition against strong competitors with the aid of artificial appendages. And so many others conceived into this world less than perfect, far from whole, and yet overcome adversities, overcome the consensus of self-pity, and overcome the judgments of a world in righteous pursuit to produce a perfected society.

Having the good fortune to touch the lives of several children passing from innocence and into adulthood, I remain humble to the fortuitous condition that each received a burden custom to their natures. We rarely consider the plight of those beyond the orbit of our local awareness. Nor do we consider the plight of those trapped within physical bodies damaged from birth, maimed by war, or by a condition of being in the wrong place at the wrong time. We know only the anthill of our local existence, preferring to remain oblivious to the greater significance of being. I am further reminded of what Jesus says to his apostles concerning the moral condition of a blind man, whom he just healed, in The Gospel of John, Chapter 9, verses 2-3 (KJV).

> *"And his disciples asked him, saying, Master, who did sin, this man, or his parents, that he was born blind? Jesus answered, Neither hath this man sinned, nor his parents: but that the works of God should be made manifest in him."*

I know a woman prescribed the drug *Countergan* in 1957, as an over-the-counter prescription to relieve symptoms of morning sickness during her second pregnancy. She remembers distinctly standing in front of the mirror and holding the bottle of medication in her hand. Just when she is about to take a pill, an urgent voice within warns her not to. My friend, not particularly religious or superstitious, yet unable to ignore the apprehensiveness she feels. Without further consideration, she pours the contents down the toilet. Several months later news surfaces about many catastrophic births of infants with severe handicaps. Some with stumps for limbs, some with no limbs at all, many blind and deaf, complications of a variety of urinary diseases and even deformities of the heart. Over fifty percent of these babies die immediately worldwide. The survivors later labeled as *"thalidomide children"* (so named after the genetic disruptive component in this new generation wonder drug) horrible living reminders of the dangers concealed in chemical intervention, even when meant for a good purpose. Nor should we forget the many thousands of Agent Orange soldiers, whose chromosomes damaged from prolonged exposure to a highly toxic herbicide while stationed in the jungles of the Republic of Vietnam, leading to cancers and birth defects in their future offspring. This author is one so exposed while serving my tour of duty in this remote corner of the world.

Recent history is a collage of one contaminant disaster site after another. Further compounding the problem is the overwhelming quantity of urban pollution from cost-cutting waste management to improper disposal of discarded medications, which represents one the greatest ecological social challenges of the 21st century. And even the drugs we think safe, laced with chemical agents contaminating to the carcass, as well as to the mind. Besides being chemically disruptive to biological coding sequence, some certified medications cause greatest harm through addition. One drug in particular that comes to mind is the pain inhibitor *Oxycodone*. Labeled dangerous by the Drug Enforcement Administration, this drug is considered a controlled substance because of its potential for abuse. Meaning that the more you take the stronger the effects. The effectiveness stimulated by bonding to certain *opioid* receptors in the brain and throughout the nervous system, becoming an effective manager of even chronic conditions of pain. The most obvious drawback is the addictiveness. A friend's husband started taking this prescribed opiate after suffering whiplash in a car accident. Within a year, he is hopelessly addicted. In less than three years he loses his job, his wife, and his home. When he can no longer find a doctor to write his prescription, he turns to street drugs and simply disappears into a nefarious fold of society. His story is by no means unique. I personally knew a lovely, highly intelligent woman that became addicted to Demerol after an accident resulting in the amputation of her large toe. Because of her profession as a medical practitioner at the time, this trained physician continues to self-prescribe herself this powerful opiate, until the addiction becomes obvious to her family and colleagues. She spends a year of forced medical absence on a Methadone withdrawal regiment. But when the program concludes, this lady befriends a local pusher, eventually overdosing on street heroin. Before her fatal incident, I try to reason with her in the spirit--and as a friend--only her heart by now too hardened. I feel to this day a sense of guilt that I could not reach this woman's soul with a testimony of hope; nor am I qualified to judge what happens to her soul. I only pray that she found the Lord of peace in the end. There are other pharmaceuticals just as debilitating: some for physical trauma, others to alter the delicate chemical balance in the brain. All reported as having devastating social and health consequences.

Through context of a lie people often place their faith easily in competing advertisements about some miracle drug or in government sanctioned advice given by a panel of doctors sharing an agenda of consensus. They do this partly out of ignorance, but mostly because of fear in the unknown. Believe in a quantum reality provides parameters of certainty to a condition of infinite possibility. This creates a bias of perception through logical assumption that what we see in the magician's hand all that is, thus becoming the foundational grid-work of all constructed ideas. As a world community, we have become comfortable with the idea that someone higher up knows more and is more qualified to call the shots. It is easier to believe in models of half truth, than in the truth of present being. Conditioned to look upon professionals for guidance to discern values of complex construction, we simply stop taking responsibility and stop thinking independently. Through cohesion of social pressure, it is easier to feel justified to just go along with the program and hope that the information correct, without truly applying our own cognitive tools of independent reason.

We are able to graphically observe this mechanism at work in the way drug companies and medical institutions prescribe medicines and mandates in futile attempts to address biological malfunction and eventual failure. These impressive data models represented by quantified statistics designed to create a representation of reality through theoretical manipulation using arbitrary baseline comparisons. What does it mean really when a combined chemical formulae advertised proven to be effective in a certain percentages of the cases? What about those cases that show no benefit, or those that react counter to the intended results? Always the small print disclaimer by the manufacturer that some of the ingredients of these powerful laboratory produced toxins laced with potentially fatal side effects deemed clinically dangerous. In other words take at your own risk and hope you fall upon the stone of higher statistic.

But the unfortunate reality is that many look for a genie in a bottle to compensate for bad life choices. We need no medical practitioner to save organ failure often attributable to other sanctified chemical abuse such as cigarette smoking, party drugs, and excess alcohol consumption. Even the foods we ingest flavored with salt that is not salt, sweetened with high- fructose, and often processed with code sequences unrecognizable by the metabolic engine responsible to distribute important nutrients for optimal body function. I once knew a man named Jim prescribed as many as 13 medications to compensate for numerous medical conditions ranging from heart arrhythmia, liver processing, and kidney function. After several operations to implant a pacemaker and defibrillator, he is afterwards placed on a rigid pill regiment until eventually succumbing after nearly three years of agony.

"I just want to die," he once confided to me. "I can't sleep, no longer can taste, and I can never get comfortable."

He finally did die after a fatal heart attack. But then the defibrillator kicks his heart back into a beat, even though he is already considered clinically brain dead. Jim's body is rushed to a hospital and maintained in a coma. Mistakenly the care professionals administer a blood thickener. His constant companion at the time is given a choice of amputation of both his legs or unplugging the body from machines keeping it alive. Out of mercy this lady chooses the latter. It is my personal belief that this man's soul already departed by then.

Something similar happened to my younger brother Rudy. At sixty years old he nearly dies from impaired liver function. Miraculously he is saved and stabilized. Two years later his health begins to improve; given an optimistic prognosis that if he stays away from alcohol, then he might live eight years or even longer. But on the third year he secretly begins drinking again. Like Jim my brother ends up on a barrage of different drugs to compensate for the lack of normal bodily functions. Rudy spends his last days in my mother's condo cared for by my two sisters. Fortunately he died relatively peaceful. And I believe that the Lord Jesus appeared in a vision to give peace to him and to me in the last hours of Rudy's life on earth.

These two men have a few things in common. One they both fell into projected numbers on a data sheet of demographic probability and both share a history of irresponsible drug and alcohol use. And even after their perspective diagnosis', neither able or willing to commit to a change in direction. I say this without judgment. I loved both these people deeply, only disappointed in their choices and the consequence of those choices. And there is no prescription in this world that can directionally change a willing belief, even if that belief fueled by addition, reminding me of verse 12 found in The Book of Proverbs, Chapter 14 (NKJV).

"There is a way that seems right to a man, But its end is the way of death."

But I also sincerely believe that it is better to lose one's life here on this earth and to find salvation of the soul, than to endure for a millennium in healthy security without ever knowing Christ. I can only say that I believe there something good in both these men and I am thankful to have had opportunity to share deeply with them. I think no communication wasted when two hearts and minds sincere in pursuit of true wisdom. The rest I leave in the hands of my Lord.

Modern medicine and pharmaceuticals arguably preferable to blood leeches and the days of blindly drilling holes into patience's skulls. We may no longer consult oracles or throw lots to the stars. But we do trust in the lords of brand name medicines, while praying blindly to a host of promised remedies. In other words, we surrender our faith to profit driven corporations entrusted with industrial benchmarks; yet lacking the constraints of moral responsibility. This is by definition a combination of the most evil of potentials. And it is because of fear in death that the world prepares the way for Antichrist to one day soon control every aspect of human existence by making each individual just another number in a model of statistics.

If the sorcery of controlled pharmacology is not enough frightening, then consider that tons of poisonous chemicals leeching into our water tables daily and mixed into the air that we breathe. In the late 1980's, while visiting Michigan, a friend and I witness nightly apparitions igniting in the dark waters of Lake Erie. This *eerie* (pun intended) phenomenon caused by chemical reactions from chance combination of two pollutants lurking in this massive inland sea. Along with the rapid decimation of the oxygen producing rainforests around the planet and the accumulating tonnage of smog spewing from the chimneys of industrialized nations, the global future looks increasingly grim. There are many serious studies suggesting that chromosome mutation evidence of evolution. Of course this is like saying that the rising statistics of young children diagnosed with type 2 diabetes, indicates the beginning of a new age of man with diminished pancreas function. Or the increased numbers of children with Autism evidence of acute mental evolution. Equally absurd, the notion of observable evolutionary throwbacks, such as the occasional birth of human offspring with tails. Precisely these globules have been proven, not to be tails at all (at least not as formed along the vertebrae of certain animals); but a fatty mass caused by a genetic mistake, similar to the coding sequence of replicating cancers. Also organs once thought superfluous to the genotype of modern Homo sapiens, such as the tonsils and the appendix, are regarded with new respect as immune filters and potential reservoirs of bacterial fighting agents necessary to resist against certain biological aggressions. In fact the universally accepted philosophy of evolutionary science falls prey to its own skepticism in light of present human adaptation to altered environmental conditions, providing little or no evidence that a new and better species lingers within the genetic depths of the collective genus.

Despite all of the professional posturing regarding the evolutionary ladder connecting us to a distant primordial past spanning millions and millions of years, the present availability of evidence does not support the orchestrated conclusions of this evolutionary theory. If you were to take one hundred persons out of a thousand from every nation, from every tribe, and from every subculture, you would accumulate DNA one hundred percent human down to the last chromosome: no hybrid species with intelligent factors more or less evolved, no humans with monkey genes, and no monkeys developing into *Homo-erectus*. We are, however, led to believe that this stark absence of evidence is because we have not lived long enough as a species. Or that there is evidence, only that we fail to recognize the process because it coincides with cellar damage caused by external exposure to adverse elements, such as insecticides and other potentially lethal agents.

I doubt even *Darwin*, the proclaimed *father of evolution*, might agree that present day accumulative affects of chemical pollution (even those widely distributed through the foods we consume in the form of flavor enhancers and unpronounceable preservatives irresponsibly approved by barons of profit) evidence of species evolution. No objective observer would conclude that chronic obesity a platform of natural selection, forcing the emergence of a better, more improved kind of human; or that liver toxicity the beginning morphology of a new and improved species. As an enlightened society armed with an arsenal of improved empirical tools, we do know with absolute certainty that polluted conditions yield mutations over time; but once a critical level reached, total indigenous extinction. Disturbingly, we find reference to this kind of eventuality in the Book of Revelation, Chapter 8: verses 5-11 (NIV).

> *"Then the angel took the censer, filled it with fire from the altar, and hurled it on the earth; and there came peals of thunder, rumblings, flashes of lightning and an earthquake. Then the seven angels who had the seven trumpets prepared to sound them. The first angel sounded his trumpet, and there came hail and fire mixed with blood, and it was hurled down on the earth. A third of the earth was burned up, a third of the trees were burned up, and all the green grass was burned up. The second angel sounded his trumpet, and something like a huge*

mountain, all ablaze, was thrown into the sea. A third of the sea turned into blood, a third of the living creatures in the sea died, and a third of the ships were destroyed. The third angel sounded his trumpet, and a great star, blazing like a torch, fell from the sky on a third of the rivers and on the springs of water— the name of the star is Wormwood. A third of the waters turned bitter, and many people died from the waters that had become bitter."

I remember as a child visiting my grandfather's farm in lower Alabama. The last week of my visit, he slaughters two pigs for winter meat. I had grown fond of these animals during my stay, appalled at this unexpected murder. I later better understand the nature of being here on earth, and eventually find place in my heart to forgive my grandfather for this horrible transgression. But I also learned something on that day about the foods we eat and the sacrifices made daily for our continued survival. From a farmer's perspective, animal husbandry is a practical undertaking with considerable investment. He does not need to be an endocrinologist to recognize a good studding animal; nor will he waste much time and resources to force a non- breeding animal. But will, rather, sell it quickly or butcher it for meat. To this dedicated producer in the food chain, it all comes down to profit and resource management. The law on a farm dictates that an animal born maimed, or otherwise infirmed, quickly dispatched for the betterment of the whole. A controlled decisive condition of natural selection judiciously executed. This kind of practical decision-making prevails in societies with limited resources and survival conditions harsh. As these conditions improve, a more tolerant attitude of moral leniency supersedes pragmatism. Fortunately, today we live in a society where the young not exposed to the elements because of a birth defect. Or because someone born a midget, another severely handicapped, some blind, and others deformed. Some destined to reproduce; and some perish before puberty. And some, as Jesus himself, ordained to pass through this moment of flesh solitary and without a physical foundation to call home or a future of genetic offspring. It is not so difficult for those of us born whole and fulfilled to have *Aryan* imaginations of perfected society. I shudder to think of all the extermination camps necessary to accomplish such a dream. Let us not forget that at least one man in his generation attempted such a conquest to rid the world of perceived imperfection-- a mere mortal born in a small country of Western Europe. This man inadequate to the standards of a perfect vision is responsible for the murder of millions. But was his this the doctrine of a man or of a devil? What man or human collective capable of perceiving a better code of organization through present entropy of the human condition to make a superior man or a monster? Perhaps it is better if some are forfeited the natural linage of producing offspring. In Mathew, Chapter 19, verse 12 (KJV) Jesus states:

> *"For there are some eunuchs, which were so born from their mother's womb: and there are some eunuchs, which were made eunuchs of men: and there be eunuchs, which have made themselves eunuchs for the kingdom of heaven's sake. He that is able to receive it, let him receive it."*

Just for a moment let us consider the meaning in this statement. In previous statements Jesus makes clear the meaning of a revitalized creature in the resurrection. He says there will be neither male nor female, emphasizing that mortal beings of this present incarnation exist in a conventional state. This implies that the new body unlike the old body, becoming symbiotic to all other bodies through the process of regeneration by extension of God's Holy Spirit exemplified in the translated Christ. As we have already observed the seeding of one's progeny is perhaps the most primeval human instinct. This drive embellishes almost every aspect of our life from the first activation of the sex drive at puberty and sustains well into later years. It is an overriding mandate in our fleshly existence, a commandment genetically coded into every kind from the beginning. It is the very definition of *"vital"* ascribed to all living things.

Nevertheless, this is not the ultimate purpose with all men, as evidenced through historical observation. We must consider within perspective that Jesus, the son of man, did not procreate after the manner of men. Surly this man capable, but considers the prescription of his visitation of greater mandate than continuation of earthly linage. There have been many intellectual attempts to refute this fact through fictitious accounts, such as the elaborate histology of The Da Vinci Codes, as well as other text that purposes Christ somehow survived the cross, marries, and bears offspring. If this should be true within any stretch of the imagination, then Christianity reduced to just another religion of deception and faith in resurrection foolishness. I know this proposed tale of genealogy to be the enemy's greatest deception of secular reasoning. *My immortal soul bears true witness that Jesus Christ is indeed alive even in this doubting generation!* In fact, as we peer back into the history of God's chosen vessels, not all produce offspring for reasons we can only speculate. Even the end-day prophet Daniel, scribe of the inspired book given his name, in all likelihood was an eunuch, made so by the conquering King of Babylon, as prophesied in the book of Isaiah, Chapter 39, verses 5-8 (KJV).

> *"Then said Isaiah to Hezekiah, Hear the word of the LORD of hosts: Behold, the days come, that all that is in your house, and that which thy fathers have laid up in store until this day, shall be carried to Babylon: nothing shall be left, says the LORD. And of thy sons that shall issue from thee, which thou shall beget, shall they take away; and they shall be eunuchs in the palace of the king of Babylon. Then said Hezekiah to Isaiah, Good is the word of the LORD which thou hast spoken. He said moreover, For there shall be peace and truth in my days."*

It is also interesting that despite the several long genealogies mentioned in the Old Testament, none aspire to an incorruptible sovereign linage of men and women righteous by nature. Rather these many genetic portraits of human beings born within context of a collective, inspired toward a spiritual destiny, exclusive to any earthly family tree. Their eyes opened by faith to a promise not contained in the works of worldly participation. The Jesus that we know, and the Christ that we worship is conceived of the Holy Spirit of God, joined in flesh, and made a new creature both flesh and of spirit. This is a holy thing, elevated far above the scripted linage of mortal ancestry. In Paul's letter to the Hebrews we are provided with an elevated idea of who and what really is the Messiah found in Chapter 1, verses 1-14 (NIV).

> *"In the past God spoke to our ancestors through the prophets at many times and in various ways, but in these last days he has spoken to us by his Son, whom he appointed heir of all things, and through whom also he made the universe. The Son is the radiance of God's glory and the exact representation of his being, sustaining all things by his powerful word. After he had provided purification for sins, he sat down at the right hand of the Majesty in heaven. So he became as much superior to the angels as the name he has inherited is superior to theirs. For to which of the angels did God ever say, "You are my Son; today I have become your Father"? Or again, "I will be his Father, and he will be my Son"? And again, when God brings his firstborn into the world, he says, "Let all God's angels worship him." In speaking of the angels he says, "He makes his angels spirits, and his servants flames of fire." But about the Son he says, "Your throne, O God, will last forever and ever; a scepter of justice will be the scepter of your kingdom. You have loved righteousness and hated wickedness; therefore God, your God, has set you above your companions by anointing you with the oil of joy." He also says, "In the beginning, Lord, you laid the foundations of the earth, and the heavens are the work of your hands. They will perish, but you remain; they will all wear out like a garment. You will roll them up like a robe; like a garment they will be changed. But you remain the same, and your years will never end." To which of the angels did God ever say, "Sit at my right hand until I make your enemies a footstool for*

your feet"? Are not all angels ministering spirits sent to serve those who will inherit salvation?"

The obsession with tracing one's genealogy has become an absorbing passion by many since recent years. As skeletons and heroes rise out of the ashes from the past, as irrefutable evidence that no mortal timeline perfect. All have poisons *"lurking in the mud to hatch out",* as stated by the portrayed characterization of the late Roman Emperor Claudius in the captivating 1976 CBC series *I Claudius.* Yet, we persist to believe that the past somehow justifying the present and that a genotype will emerge better than has ever lived before sired from a gene pool corrupted. Each generation hoping to become the proud mother and father of a remarkable progenitor of a better society. We are reminded that such a man will arrive in an hour already predicted: a *false Christ* to usher the world to the end of destruction! This physical manifestation will be sired with great worldly wisdom and present timely answers to humanities social and economic dilemmas. A mouth speaking many noble words, so seductively righteous that even the elite risk being deceived. This man of perdition, which the world will receive with great honor and blind adoration, found in The Book of Revelation, Chapter 13, verses 3-9 (NIV).

> *"One of the heads of the beast seemed to have had a fatal wound, but the fatal wound had been healed. The whole world was filled with wonder and followed the beast. People worshiped the dragon because he had given authority to the beast, and they also worshiped the beast and asked, "Who is like the beast? Who can wage war against it?" The beast was given a mouth to utter proud words and blasphemies and to exercise its authority for forty-two months. It opened its mouth to blaspheme God, and to slander his name and his dwelling place and those who live in heaven. It was given power to wage war against God's holy people and to conquer them. And it was given authority over every tribe, people, language and nation. All inhabitants of the*

earth will worship the beast—all whose names have not been written in the Lamb's book of life, the Lamb who was slain from the creation of the world. Whoever has ears, let them hear."

Even as I write this there are sinister forces eating at he core of fruitful society. The world of contemporary residence is being reconfigured daily like an upgraded circuit board encoded with new directive. Right and wrong redefined, consensus the new morality, and existentialism being all there is. For this reason mental health has become the new global crisis with puppet masters in high places pulling the strings. There is no analytical guidance through the maze of unseen labyrinths, and no statue of religious interpretation of greater enforcement than mortal submission to the architect of our being. To the end it is God by communion of the Holy Spirit that guides our individual destinies. Only template of the chosen Messiah able to resurrect our souls from the wages of sin and death. Make no mistake. The blame game has always been the Devil's playground. And we all play in it for a season as prescribed.

Yes, all communications are spiritually divined, and therefore relevant to spiritual discernment. The mystery of constructed source, not always integral to logical meaning, but contains a meaning elevated above the reason of logic. Since all doctrine designed through instruction of the Holy Spirit, then the interpretation also spiritual, made clear through a unique revelation within unique context. These communications are not intended as global statues of a renewed religious participation. God's laws inscribed by a finger of unquenchable fire into stone made equally immutable. The Ten Commandments written upon parchment of DNA before the first man formed from clay. Through rebellion of sin these perfect statues corrupted, becoming shackles of condemnation in the hands of the chief advocate of the law standing daily before God to condemn the weakness in mankind.

The Messiah born in mortal time to forever break bonds of corruption and to bestow upon the sons and daughters of men a clear conscience before the Father, spotless and without sin. Jesus came not to forge another contract of bondage in the process. He did not come to first save men, so that women might also be saved. Nor are women made sinless through submission. Some men are not made superior by genetic purity; nor some women purified in the flesh to bear righteousness into the world. This only Son of God has come to save the potential of all humanity, within the context of each sinful condition. The Son of Man made in the likeness of flesh and blood to fulfill the numerous divinely inspired passages found in scripture, proclaiming our righteousness as filthy rags before God's holiness. The just mind of God's holy righteousness timeless from the end to the beginning, which is as far above carnal thinking, as heaven is from hell.

The unprovoked nature of wolves in the fold of peaceful submission is a xenophobic restlessness, making them as predatory agents inspired by the same spirits of violence that once drove the *Nephilim* to global destruction. Such hide discreetly among flocks of good intentions. It is in humble praise that the good shepherd knows the number of his own. Humbler still the revelation that there is only one straight way designed through the maze of spiritual passage, which Jesus makes clear in John's Gospel, Chapter 14, verse 6 (KJV):

"Jesus saith unto him, I am the way, the truth, and the life: no man cometh unto the Father, but by me."

This is a certain promise made by the guarantor of our forfeited souls before righteous God. A sure witness manifested in every generation and to the end of foolishness in every philosophy. It is not a voice given to an elite few. It is not a call only to the genetically whole, to the intellectually aware, or to the morally pure. It is not the voice of religion or a zealous battle cry to arms. It is the distant voice of our Good Sheppard calling to lost sheep in a wilderness, inspiring peace to those that hear and understanding in the season called. It is Jesus Christ born in mortal body, crucified by worldly sin, and resurrected the archetype of a new creature. This perfect code designed above all others made to life everlasting and worlds without end!

I felt compelled to write this record in my generation, as a living testament to the many mercies revealed to me in my lifetime. I am not an individual of perfect understanding, nor is my life exemplary to any other. I struggle with a nature potentially violent, daily surrendering that nature to the Lord of my salvation. I speak here only the things I know, and of possibilities far greater than ear has heard, eye has seen, or has entered into the imagination. My spirit bears witness that the simple text known as the Holy Bible inspired by revelation of a hyper reality existing in parallel to the world of light and shadow we experience through sensory perception. I am convinced by this same witness that Messiah is come; and is even now with God, the father. Through this promise we are born again and saved from the course of perdition. I rejoice that I am able to share this good news in the time allotted. I am thankful for my present sufficiency, desiring no more or no less to the necessity of my present needs.

The institutional scientist will label this work as pseudoscience, falling short of academic acceptance based on modeled interpretation. To these I say that all things conditional to a source; and all faiths subject to continued scrutiny. The trained clergy will say that without the guiding hand of a Sheppard, then the sheep of this world will go astray. To these I say feed the sheep given you in season and allow your hearts be led by the Sheppard of us all so that none stumble along the way.

This earth we think to know has a certain trajectory through time and space that none may prevent. Written here are only the things made through observation, meant neither to judge, nor to condemn. The purpose of this book is not to guide personal or political destiny, but as a message of hope and clarity in the midst of confusion. I pray that it speaks a message of edification to even one soul in search of salvation. In this present hour, I count among the sheep, and wish to count among none other. I wait patiently the second coming of Messiah through continual remission to the end of purification. I wish to conclude this difficult and challenging examination with these beautiful words of consolation and promise taken from the King James 2000 translation of the Apostle Paul's first letter to the Corinthians, Chapter 13, verses 1-13.

"Though I speak with the tongues of men and of angels, and have not love, I am become as sounding brass, or a

clanging cymbal. And though I have the gift of prophecy, and understand all mysteries, and all knowledge; and though I have all faith, so that I could remove mountains, and have not love, I am nothing. And though I bestow all my goods to feed the poor, and though I give my body to be burned, and have not love, it profits me nothing. Love suffers long, and is kind; love envies not; love vaunts not itself, is not puffed up, Does not behave itself rudely, seeks not her own, is not easily provoked, keeps no record of evil; Rejoices not in iniquity, but rejoices in the truth; Bears all things, believes all things, hopes all things, endures all things. Love never fails: but whether there be prophecies, they shall fail; whether there be tongues, they shall cease; whether there be knowledge, it shall vanish away. For we know in part, and we prophesy in part. But when that which is perfect is come, then that which is in part shall be done away. When I was a child, I spoke as a child, I understood as a child, I thought as a child: but when I became a man, I put away childish things. For now we see in a mirror dimly; but then face to face: now I know in part; but then shall I know even as also I am known. And now abides faith, hope, love, these three; but the greatest of these is love."

God's ultimate design witnessed through coming of Messiah, *Jesus Christ*, the first, and the last, manifested through division of infinite velocity to ultimately transfigure a universe already condemned to prevailing entropy. This event profound beyond measure, transcending every science and every religion, and is the truest definition of abiding love. To the glory of my God, and your God, rejoice all with the angels: *Peace on earth and goodwill--Amen!*

www.ingramcontent.com/pod-product-compliance
Lightning Source LLC
Chambersburg PA
CBHW021422070526
44577CB00001B/16